The Apocalyptic Angel

by

W.B. Godbey

First Fruits Press
Wilmore,
Kentucky c2017

The apocalyptic angel. By W.B. Godbey.

First Fruits Press, © 2017

ISBN: 9781621717355 (print), 9781621717379 (digital), 9781621717386 (kindle)

Digital version at http://place.asburyseminary.edu/godbey/8/

First Fruits Press is a digital imprint of the Asbury Theological Seminary, B.L. Fisher Library. Asbury Theological Seminary is the legal owner of the material previously published by the Pentecostal Publishing Co. and reserves the right to release new editions of this material as well as new material produced by Asbury Theological Seminary. Its publications are available for noncommercial and educational uses, such as research, teaching and private study. First Fruits Press has licensed the digital version of this work under the Creative Commons Attribution Noncommercial 3.0 United States License. To view a copy of this license, visit http://creativecommons.org/licenses/by-nc/3.0/us/.

For all other uses, contact:

First Fruits Press
B.L. Fisher Library
Asbury Theological Seminary
204 N. Lexington Ave.
Wilmore, KY 40390
http://place.asburyseminary.edu/firstfruits

Godbey, W. B. (William Baxter), 1833-1920.
  The apocalyptic angel / by W.B. Godbey. – Wilmore, KY : First Fruits Press, ©2017.
  513 pages ; cm.
  Reprint. Previously published: Cincinnati, Ohio : God's Revivalist Press, ©1914.
  ISBN: 9781621717355 (pbk.)
  1. Palestine--Description and travel. I. Title.
     BX7990.H6 G62 2017

Cover design by Jon Ramsey

asburyseminary.edu
800.2ASBURY
204 North Lexington Avenue
Wilmore, Kentucky 40390

First Fruits Press
The Academic Open Press of Asbury Theological Seminary
204 N. Lexington Ave., Wilmore, KY 40390
859-858-2236
first.fruits@asburyseminary.edu
asbury.to/firstfruits

The Apocalyptic Angel

BY

REV. W. B. GODBEY, A. M.

AUTHOR OF

"Commentaries on the New Testament," and Numerous Books and Booklets on Holiness and Travels.

GOD'S REVIVALIST PRESS
RINGGOLD, YOUNG AND CHANNING STREETS
CINCINNATI, OHIO, U. S. A.

Copyrighted, 1914, God's Revivalist Office.

CONTENTS

CHAPTER I.
Outward Bound.............................. 7
CHAPTER II.
The Holy Land.............................. 89
CHAPTER III.
Sacred Mountains 122
CHAPTER IV.
Land of Uz, and Syria....................... 198
CHAPTER V.
Heavenly Ages............................... 234
CHAPTER VI.
Satanic Ages................................ 248
CHAPTER VII.
Mediatorial Kingdom......................... 254
CHAPTER VIII.
Post-Edenic, Ante-diluvian Dispensation........ 263
CHAPTER IX.
Post-diluvian Patriarchy...................... 271
CHAPTER X.
Egyptian Dominion........................... 279
CHAPTER XI.
Mosaic Mediatorship.......................... 284
CHAPTER XII.
Phœnician Dominion.......................... 299
CHAPTER XIII.
Hebrew Dominion............................. 304
CHAPTER XIV.
Chaldean Dominion........................... 309

CONTENTS

CHAPTER XV.
Medo-Persian Dominion........................ 313

CHAPTER XVI.
Grecian Dominion............................. 319

CHAPTER XVII.
Roman Dominion.............................. 325

CHAPTER XVIII.
Johannic Precursorship........................ 334

CHAPTER XIX.
Messianic Dispensation........................ 362

CHAPTER XX.
Pentecostal Dispensation...................... 374

CHAPTER XXI.
Moslem Dominion............................. 405

CHAPTER XXII.
Mogul Dominion.............................. 416

CHAPTER XXIII.
German Dominion............................. 428

CHAPTER XXIV.
Swedish Dominion............................ 442

CHAPTER XXV.
French Dominion............................. 447

CHAPTER XXVI.
Anglo-Saxon Dominion........................ 460

CHAPTER XXVII.
Millennial Kingdom........................... 466

CHAPTER XXVIII.
The Jews.................................... 490

CHAPTER XXIX.
Homeward Bound............................. 501

PREFATORY NOTE

This book is one of the many written by Dr. Godbey on his travels. Versed in the history, both sacred and secular, of the lands of the Old World, he is, Dr. Godbey has travelled with eyes that see and a mind that understands. We send it forth to you, its readers, believing that it will prove as instructive and interesting as any of its predecessors. Trusting that it will also help mightily in the purpose for which Dr. Godbey both travels and writes—namely, the upbuilding of God's kingdom in all the earth, we are

Faithfully yours,
THE PUBLISHERS.

The Apocalyptic Angels

CHAPTER I.

Outward Bound.

We sailed to Glasgow, Scotland, on the steamer "California." We had some inclement weather, superinducing much seasickness. I never have it, although the Lord has permitted me to make these four tours, and to travel by sea about seventy-five thousand miles, as in 1905-'06, we traveled entirely around the world. I believe the secret of my glorious freedom from all seasickness is the fact that always, embarking, I ask Jesus, by faith, to keep it off. "As your faith is, so be it unto you." (Matt. 9:29.) This was the Lord's current maxim throughout His entire ministry, as pertinent to the body as to the soul. Throughout the voyage, I exhorted my comrades, and did my best to fortify them against seasickness, but they all suffered more or less, and one brother almost crossed the ocean on his back.

We repeated a couple of days, and were turned out of our course by immense reefs of floating ice dislodged from the coasts of Newfoundland. We entered Glasgow through the Gulf of Clyde River, the ship moving very slowly into her moorings, thereby fortuitously giving us a grand opportunity to inspect the dockyards, in conspicuous view on either side. They are pronounced the greatest and best in the world, thus giving dear old Scotland the banner of the nations in ship-building.

Peter the Great, the civilizer, champion and Christianizer of great Russia, an obscure, uncultured youth, tramped away to these dockyards and labored for wages till he learned how to build ships. Then, going home, he taught his people this great and valuable mechanism, as well as all the arts and sciences of Christian civilization. Thus he led those rude, barbaric nations—Goths, Huns, Vandals and Heruli—into the liberal arts and sciences, and united them into the great Russian nation, with her 325,000,000 of Russianized subjects, the greatest nationality on the globe.

Glasgow, with her 100,000 enterprising citizens, is one of the most beautiful cities in the world.

As we traveled through that lovely land of Scotland, we were charmed with the horticultural and agricultural perfection on all sides, adorning the beautiful, green hills and prolific vales. My heart praised the Lord for dear old Scotia's lovely island, and the Knoxes, Burnses, Bruces, Wallaces, and their noble comrades, whose names are in the Book of Life. Their monuments of heroism, patriotism, arts, sciences, and Christianity now flash the luster of their achievements around the world, girdling the globe with the just encomiums of lovely Scotland.

When Bloody Mary, the Roman Catholic queen, sat on the throne, and was burning the Covenanters (the Holiness people of Scotland), as fast as her soldiers and bloodhounds could catch them, John Knox, their redoubtable leader, walked into the royal palace and issued the thunderbolt of prophecy which God had given him. He, like a messenger from Heaven, denounced her wicked administration, and told her he was going to pray her down from that throne. Then he walked out with the heroic tread of Elijah from the presence of Jezebel and Ahab.

When she recovered from the shock, she charged her soldiers to go into Scotland and hunt that man with bloodhounds till they found him. She observed that she feared his prayers more than all the armies of Europe. Well she might, for he prayed her down from the throne till she dropped dead, and Elizabeth, the friend of Protestants, free grace and a free Bible, took her place, and, in the providence of God, laid the foundation of the British Empire, this day at the front of the world.

The reason we have missionaries in every land and wide-open doors for millions more, is because British gunboats thunder from every shore, and the Union

Jack floats beneath every sky, the auspicious precursor of King Jesus coming in a cloud to arrest the devil, take him out of the world, and fill the whole earth with the glory of God.

John Knox, with his Holiness band, in his sequestered garden, was holding an all-night prayer-meeting, then in the dead of night, rising from his knees with a shout, he assured his comrades, "Deliverance has come!" No electrical appliances, no telephones then; news came with tardy pace. But what was it? As nearly as they could tell later, it was at that very hour that Bloody Mary dropped dead. The solution is easy—John Knox had prayed the prevailing prayer which the Holy Ghost gave him (James 5), and the answer came. There was but one way, and that was to take Queen Mary out of the world.

The iron horse, after a race of fifty miles an hour, dumped us all in the world's metropolis, founded by Julius Cæsar, the great Roman. It was called Londinium, now felicitously abbreviated London. She now has seven and a half millions of people, and an annual increase of a hundred thousand, pouring hither from the ends of the earth, as her great ocean steamers peregrinate the globe, gathering from 1,700,000,000 of all nationalities. London is not only almost double the size of any other city, but is the most rapidly growing in all the earth. The mind grows dizzy contemplating the possibilities of her coming magnitude.

As this was my fourth visit to the city in sixteen years, I immediatly favored my comrades with a trip to the most important sights.

While in the metropolis, the Third Centennial Anniversary of the King James' translation of the Bible was held. God has wonderfully made this translation a sunburst on the world. It was the best in its day, three hundred years ago, when there was so little light on the Bible compared with the present age. Superstition has always been used by Satan to hold people in bondage to error, simply because of its antiquity. N. B. We can only be justified by walking in all the light God gives us. (1 John 1:7.) The present generation has light superior to all our predecessors. We cannot be saved in the light of our fathers and mothers, from the simple fact that God requires us to walk in our own light. My preaching father and shouting Methodist mother both used tobacco and ordered me to use it, pursuant to the foolish advice of our neighbors, who said: "Make that little runt chew tobacco and it will start him to growing."

My happy conversion, under the preaching of my sainted mother, in her lap before she had taken off my baby costume, and my early Bible reading had given me a very tender heart, which I nearly broke when I disobeyed my parents. But this time I simply concluded to receive the flogging for disobedience, rather than to chew the disgustingly filthy weed. I am so glad I never used the narcotic nervines, which are so hard on the brain and mental faculties. If I were to use tobacco now, I would sin against light and knowledge, and Satan would get me. I know my father and mother are in Heaven, and I soon expect to meet them there. They walked in all the light they had, which is all any person on the globe has to do to be saved, as people only lose their souls by rejecting light.

We have a magnitudinous responsibility, for the most copious and brightest light that has ever shone on the earth is now shed abroad. Therefore we should not only, like the Bereans, search the Scriptures diligently and walk in every ray of light we have, but do our best to carry the light to all others, as we will be responsible for our delinquency. If we do not, in the Judgment Day, millions of heathens, Mohammedans, Jews, Catholics and ignorant Protestants may go up to Heaven with a shout, and we be left out. Not that anybody will pass the pearly portals with sin in him or in her, but those walking in all the light they have will get cleansed from all sin (1 John 1: 7.), while those who have the brighter light, but fail to walk in it, will go down under condemnation.

N. B. The omnipotent grace of God in Christ is not only free for all, but sufficient for every emergency. So there is no apology for the damnation of a solitary soul, as they are only lost because of light rejected.

We now hastened away to the British Museum, covering a great square of the city. There we saw the etymological and artistic world, i. e., all nations in their statuary, costumes, arts, inventions, and all sorts of implements of all by-gone ages. In that Museum you have access to the whole world, and receive the valuable information of a life time of study and world-wide traveling. Though those monuments, specimens and souvenirs have cost many millions of dollars, yet these wonderfully instructive sights are all free. This is due to the paradoxical benefaction of the British Government, the greatest colonizer, educator, civilizer, and evangelizer in all the world. You can go there and study gratuitously ad libitum.

We then hastened away to the great Zoological and Botanical Museum, in which you see all the animals that have ever lived on the earth, both terrestrial and oceanic in all ages and nations, including all the feathered tribes. You will also see there specimens of the entire botanical world, from the smallest to the greatest. It is exceedingly instructive to see every creature God has ever made to inhabit the whole earth by land and sea. This vast and edifying Museum is like that of all the nations' arts and inventions, free to all the world; the great benefaction of the British Government, now standing at the front of the world. If the Lord lets you go to London, do not forget to visit these and other sights of valuable erudition.

Next we went to the Art Gallery, where we saw the master spirits of the British Empire as depicted in the most beautiful paintings, very large and conspicuous. We saw John and Charles Wesley, Dr. Clarke, Fletcher, Whitefield, and many others whose books we have read.

Then we all mounted a great electric omnibus, and dashed seven miles to City Road Church, built in years long gone by. I climbed up in the old-style stairway pulpit, and, standing in the footprints of Father Wesley, preached the everlasting. Gospel. We all retired to his tomb, and that of Dr. Clarke and their comrade saints now in glory. We united in prayer and felt that we were truly treading on holy ground.

During my three preceding visits I had much enjoyed Westminster Abbey, the sepulchre of the great among the Anglo-Saxon people. There are buried the magnates of church and state, kings, queens, heroes, poets, orators, philosophers, saints and martyrs. There lies Bloody Mary, the Roman Catholic queen who burnt the Protestants till John Knox, of Scotland, prayed her from the throne, and she suddenly died and was succeeded by her sister Elizabeth, the friend and protector of the Protestants. Thus, by the change of administration, God radically and permanently revolutionized the government. This is manifested by the interment of Mary and Elizabeth in the same sepulchre, the latter above the former.

Oliver Cromwell, the Holiness man (Puritan), who had revolutionized the kingdom, superseding the monarchy by the Protectorate, had been buried in royal splendor. After the Restoration they disinterred him, tried and condemned him as a criminal. They hung his body, cut his head off, and cast the rest of the body into a yawning abyss.

When going around looking at all the tombs, we saw busts of John and Charles Wesley there among the kings, queens and magnates of the British Empire.

David Livingstone, the great apostle of Africa, who lived in the heart of Africa alone and preached to the savages for a third of a century, died among them. His body was then carried two thousand miles to Zanzibar, where a British ship took it and its sable porters and carried them all the way to London. There the people spent quite awhile carrying them through the streets, and finally buried Livingstone's body among the kings in Westminster Abbey. You will find his tomb near the center of the nave. It is said that the world's metropolis made greater adoo over this humble pilgrim of the Lord than over any of the crowned heads lying all around him. I was sorry the place was closed while we were there, and my comrades were deprived of the many interesting souvenirs there to be seen.

We visited the Tower of London, where the city was founded. It now covers thirteen acres of ground which are crowded with places of profound historical interest. Here William the Conqueror founded the British nationality 850 years ago. He was a Norman, i. e., a North man, a Scandinavian.

About nine hundred years ago, those Northmen were the greatest navigators in the world. Without compass or chart, they crossed the Atlantic Ocean, and are believed by the best authorities to have discovered America and made many visits to it, calling it "Vineland." If that is a fact, however, the Indians must have exterminated them all, as the site of the place was lost, and for many centuries no one had crossed the ocean till Columbus came in 1492. It is certain that those Northmen excelled all others in nautical skill and heroism.

> "Fierce, hardy, proud,
> In conspicuous freedom bold;
> Those stormy seats
> The warrior Druses' home.
> From Norman blood
> Their lofty line they trace.
> Their lion courage
> Proves their generous race."

The Tower of London was long the seat of government and the residence of the king. It has great notoriety as a prison, in which martyrs and many others were incarcerated. We were on the spot occupied by the scaffold on which so many good and noble people were beheaded; e. g., the wives of Henry the Eighth, Lady Jane Grey, and other historic notables. Rev. John Fisher had his Greek Testament, his precious companion, in the prison with him, when they suddenly opened the door, led him out and cut his head off. He fortuitously opened the Book with these words: "O Lord, give me a Scripture that shall comfort me in this trying hour." Then his eyes rested on 1 John 4:18: "Perfect love casteth out fear." Closing the Book, he said: "Quite enough, O Lord, for time and eternity," then the cruel ax severed his head from his body.

Again, we were in the prison where the pilgrims and martyrs were kept till their execution, the time of which was never known to them till the executioner opened the door. The first notification Lady Jane Grey received of her own immediate destiny was the presentation of the headless body of Lord Dudley, her noble husband.

In this Tower we saw the warriors of by-gone centuries, invested from top to toe in shining steel and mounted on their horses, which were protected in a similar manner. As they had no firearms, the cavalier thus panoplied, defensively and offensively, could ride into an army, cutting them down on all sides with comparative impunity.

From London we crossed the English Channel to France. Fortunately we went by New Haven and Dieppe instead of Dover and Callais, as we had hitherto gone the latter way with terrible storms and awful seasickness. I recommended the other route, as it was calm and delightful.

Paris, with her three millions of population, built stellate, i. e., in the shape of a star, radiating out from the center, has been pronounced the beauty of the whole earth. We peregrinated the city spellbound by her beauty, and with great interest visited Napoleon's tomb. In 1899 I visited his Panorama, with much edification. We saw his battles moving around us in impressive reality, actually seeing the fire of the guns and imagining that we could hear their roar and smell the powder, and men and horses were falling in piles all around. As the Panorama has been moved out of the city, we did not have time to go to it.

Reaching France the first of April, we found the season far in advance of the same latitude in America. This is owing to the Gulf Stream, a river in the Atlantic Ocean two hundred miles wide, flowing out of the Gulf of Mexico, between Cuba and Florida, then turning north to Newfoundland, thence east across the ocean, and impinging against the coast of France. It so moderates the temperature there as to make the winters exceedingly mild, and to cause the vine and semi-tropical fruits to abound throughout that delightful country.

On the long run of 960 miles from Paris to Rome, we were all much edified. As we approached the great Alpine range, we passed through many tunnels, the one under the center of the Alps, twelve miles long, said to be the longest in the world. Napoleon, Cæsar, and other great warriors, left the world most romantic histories by crossing those great mountains. The change between then and now is wonderful, as now the iron horse gallops through at fifty miles an hour.

Thus we passed that long tunnel, and suddenly found ourselves on the sunny side, in the lovely land of Italy, so long the seat of the great iron empire of prophecy.

The great Alpine range on the north border of Italy all the way so protects it from the north winds as to superinduce spring and autumn the year round. The sea breezes on fifteen hundred miles of Mediterranean coast so mitigate the summer heat as to verify the song which the happy inhabitants sing: "Oh, happy land! where flowers never fade and fruits never fail, winter never comes and summer ever lasts."

Just before we reached Rome, we ran through an exceedingly fertile, delightful and fruitful plain, by the ancient poets denominated "Elysian fields." Suddenly the glittering dome of St. Peter's Cathedral and other lofty towers burst upon our vision, and the iron horse soon halted for rest and recuperation in great Rome, the illustrious capital of the renowned iron kingdom of prophecy.

As in my former visits, we stopped at the Capitol Hotel, under the immediate shadow of the state capitol and in full view of the Victor Emmanuel monument, erected at the cost of eleven millions of dollars. They were working on it when I was there sixteen years ago, and it is not yet complete. It commemorates the man who shook the Pope down from his temporal throne, A. D. 1866. While this is towering in full view of the Vatican palace, when the "Holy Father" (as the Pope is called), mortified by the sight, seeks relief in looking the other way, his tearful eye can but behold the monument of Garibaldi, who defeated the French army sent to reinstate the Pope.

When I was in Rome sixteen years ago, we had no street-cars. Now she is pretty well supplied. During the Papal reign, this city, longer than any other in all by-gone ages, remained the capital and metropolis of the whole world. She had a population of four millions in her palmy days, but dropped down to a hundred and fifty thousand. However, she has been constantly growing since the Pope's dethronement, and now has five hundred thousand of a population.

We first ran away to St. Peter's Cathedral. It is built on what was the Campus Martius, where the apostle was crucified with his head downward, at his own request, because he had denied his Lord.

In the center of this wonderful superstructure— which is 835 feet long, 330 feet wide, and 448 feet high, and built of the finest marble, much of it transported from Africa at the cost of $200,000,000 and two hundred years of constant labor—you find what is said to be Peter's sepulchre. It is illuminated night and day, and contains his remains in a golden coffin. His bronze statue stands nearby, for the convenience of all the pilgrims who come to kiss the feet. In this way the toes of the statue have been almost worn off.

Within the Cathedral, the finest statuary everywhere abounds. It is a universally recognized fact that the Catholic Church is the greatest conservator of the fine arts on the globe to-day, and all the apostles and many other saints of that church are shown up in this cathedral in gigantic statuary.

One there sees St. Dominique, the founder of the Inquisition, exhibited, and a mad dog standing by him with a bundle of flaming fagots in his mouth. This manifests his awful rage against the people called heretics, he being ready to hunt them with mad dogs and burn them with fire.

The "Holy Door" of the cathedral is only used by the Pope once in twenty-five years. Then he breaks it open with a silver hammer, walks out, and standing on the veranda, prays for all the people in the world, and claims to forgive their sins. So if you are twenty-five years old, the Pope has forgiven you once.

On the veranda you see the great bronze statue of Charlemagne, the king of France who, in the ninth century, founded the Holy Roman Empire, i. e., the dominion of the Pope over the whole world. This the Pope will audaciously assert when the Great Tribulation sets in, and he will be the antichrist of prophecy. As Charlemagne was a great warrior, his statue exhibits him mounted on his war horse.

High up in the interior corridors, we see, in letters nine feet long, Matthew 16:18, in Latin: "Thou art Peter, and upon this rock I will build My Church, and the gates of Hell shall not prevail against it. I give unto thee the keys of the kingdom of Heaven, and whatsoever thou shalt bind on earth shall be bound in Heaven, and whatsoever thou shalt loose on earth shall be loosed in Heaven."

This Scripture is the pillar of popery, prelacy and priestcraft, assuming that Peter was the first pope, which is utterly untrue, as there never was a pope in all the world till A. D. 607, when Procas, king of Italy, crowned Boniface III., bishop of Rome, supreme pontiff of all the churches, and he became the first pope. Peter had played on his golden harp five hundred years before there ever was a pope. They grossly misconstrue the above Scripture.

"Petros" (Peter), as Jesus cognomened him, calling him "rock" on account of his firmness, means a broken rock, such as you everywhere see in buildings, whereas "petree," this rock, is feminine gender, and means the great, unbroken stratum underlying the continents and oceans and constituting the foundation of the world. Throughout the Bible God calls Himself the Rock (Sermon on the Mount). The simple meaning of this Scripture is the fact that the Lord gave Peter and his comrades the keys of the Kingdom, i. e., the precious Word by which they and their successors to this day unlock the door and throw it wide for all who will leave their sins to come in and enjoy bona fide citizenship forever. Meanwhile, against the contemptuous rejecter the key is turned, excluding him eternally from the kingdom of grace and glory.

(a) We left the cathedral and went away to the Coliseum, the largest theater the world ever saw—1,800 feet in circumference, 160 feet high of solid walls up to the eaves, and with a seating capacity for 100,000 spectators. It was built by captive Jews, led thither by Titus after the destruction of Jerusalem. The order was to sell into slavery all the Jews who survived the sword, pestilence and famine. During the seven years' siege, a million perished, and at the conclusion of the devastation ninety thousand were sold into slavery. There was left on hand a vast host they could not sell, as the market was supplied, thus verifying the awful prophecies of Ezekiel and Isaiah: "They will sell you and no one will buy."

This vast captive train was led to Rome and turned over as the crown slaves of the emperor. The Coliseum was one of the first public works they performed. This day in America it would cost fifty million dollars. It cost the Romans nothing, as the work was all done by the captives, among whom the greatest mechanics and most skilful artificers did abound.

In A. D. 68 came the great conflagration of Rome, for six days and seven nights wrapping the city in an ocean of flame. At that time Nero, the demonized emperor, sat upon a lofty tower (it is still standing—I have seen it), played his fiddle, and sang of the destruction of Troy. Thus he treated that awful calamity so levitously as to superinduce the popular conclusion that he had ordered the conflagration. To rid himself of this appalling criminality, he laid it on the Christians, condemning them all to die for high treason. Thus he lifted the floodgates and inundated the world with martyrs' blood, which thereafter flowed unobstructed for 253 years, or until the conversion of the Emperor Constantine, A. D. 321. As Rome was an absolute monarchy, the Christianization of the emperor produced a universal reaction in behalf of our Lord's disciples.

But the emperors, during the long period preceding this, had done their best to exterminate Christianity from the globe, under the double crimination of high treason against the government and heresy against all the gods, which they thought had given them the whole world. During this long, bloody age, the most lucrative entertainment in the Coliseum was feeding the Christians to the wild beasts, for which they had made lairs in the mountains upon which the city is built. I have often gazed on the old, subterranean tunnels through which they brought in the beasts to the Coliseum, purposely so starved that they would come roaring for their prey.

They called the north gate of the Coliseum the "Gate of Life," because people were brought in to the arena through it alive; and the south gate the "Gate of Death," because through it their bones were carried out.

In the last sixteen years, God has permitted me

four times to visit Rome and stand in the arena of the Coliseum, central in the building for the convenience of all; this is simultudinous to the vast edifice having two foci, giving the building the properties of a whispering gallery, so that the ordinary voice was distinctly audible throughout that assembly of 100,000. Walking over that sacred dust, I always felt that I was treading on holy ground.

Paul, in his Roman letter, sends greetings to Cæsar's household. While Cæsar is the cognomen of Roman kings, Julia is that of the queens. A beautiful damsel, through whose veins coursed the royal blood, was brought into the Coliseum to feed the wild beasts. A heathen priest walked in by her side with a censer in his hand, on which he claimed holy fire was burning, and said to her: "Now, Julia, just drop incense on this censer one time, and you are free, for we love you and do not want to hurt you, but must be true to the Roman gods who have given us the whole world." To her prompt refusal, he says: "Do you not hear the lions roaring? They will be on you in a minute." She responds: "I do, but I hear the angels calling and see the chariot lowering. I shall soon mount aboard and fly away to Jesus, who is now bidding me come."

The Coliseum was pronounced one of the seven wonders of the ancient world. I trow you want to know the other six. Here they are: (1) The Temple of Jupiter Olympus, at Athens. It was 400 feet long, 125 feet wide, and 90 feet high up to the eaves, supported by fluted, cylindrical marble columns. (2)

The walls of Babylon, 350 feet high, 87 feet broad, and fifteen miles square, encompassing the city—with its gardens, a million acres. (3) The Colossus at Rhodes. This was the wonderful work of Phineas the sculptor, and exhibited a human giant so altitudinous that the ships passed in and out between its feet. (4) The Temple of Diana, at Ephesus. It was two hundred years in building, and was finally burned down by Erostratus, who confessed under the gallows that he did it for sheer notoriety, that his name might go into history. (5) The Pyramids of Egypt, those stupendous wonders of ante-diluvian enterprise; and the Sphinx in their midst, the figure with the body of a lion 120 feet long and 60 feet high, the head of a man and the face of a virgin. This showed up to all the world that the Egyptians worshiped a god having the strength and courage of a lion, the intelligence of a man, and the purity of a virgin. And (6) the wonderfully beautiful monolithic red marble temple in which the pyramid builders worshiped the Sphinx.

(b) Now we all mounted a cab and went away four miles to the Catacombs, where the Christians, during the persecutionary ages, excavated houses for themselves under the earth, in which they lived, and where as many as escaped martyrdom died and were buried. It is the city of the dead beneath the ground.

Escorted by a monk, with burning tapers in our hands, we peregrinated this city with much edification from the things revealed in statuary, engravings and pictures on the sepulchres. I was much impressed with the superscriptions, "Jesus is Everything," "Christ is All," etc. There I saw John baptizing our Savior, pouring the water on His head as He stood. I saw the same in other places while exploring the antiquities of the city. These Catacombs were made A. D. 100 to 600, and give us an indubitable revelation of the apostolic age.

As we drew out of the city along the Appian Way (in Rome they say "way" instead of street; in London they say "road"), over which Paul entered the city, I saw a beautiful, white stone edifice on the left superscribed, "Domine, quo vadis?" (Lord, whither goest thou?) History says that when the persecutions broke out in 68, and they had already beheaded Paul, the Christians pressed hard on Peter to leave the city, as they knew he would be killed if he stayed. They alleged that it would be too afflictive to the Church to do without them both. Peter had reluctantly acquiesced and was hurrying away making his escape, when suddenly he saw Jesus coming to meet him, walking rapidly. Looking on Him, Peter said (in the Latin language), "Lord, whither goest thou?" He turned on him with the response, "Peter, I am going to Rome to be crucified again"—that moment vanishing out of his sight. Peter took the hint, concluding that the Lord took that method to reveal to him that he was to be crucified in Rome. Therefore, turning back, he reported to the Christians that Jesus had met him and revealed to him his crucifixion in Rome. A church to his name this day occupies the spot where they certify he sealed his faith with his blood. You will be much edified by visiting both it and his sepulchre.

(c) We next visited the old Forum, down in a valley surrounded by three of those famous seven mountains on which the city was built—the Palatine, the Capitoline and the Avaline, crowded all round by magnificent temples to the Roman gods. During the long ages of desolation, the debris from the surrounding highlands had so accumulated in it and so filled it up as to make even its identity a matter of research. When I saw it sixteen years ago, they were beginning the great work of excavation, which is now pretty well consummated.

There we stood on that notable historic spot where the greatest men in the world in their day—Cicero, Cato, Brutus and the mighty Cæsars—delivered those orations which shook all nations. There Julius Cæsar, at the moment he had, with life's toil and peril, conquered the world, fell and bled his life away, pierced with twenty-three wounds inflicted by those he regarded his best friends. Oh, how unstable and capricious our poor humanity! Verily there is nothing true but God.

We also visited Cæsar's palace, two thousand years ago radiant with gold and silver, as if a thousand noonday suns were flashing their light from that wonderful mountain whose ipse dixit shook the world and evoked the acquiescence of all nations.

We stood in Cæsar's judgment hall, where Paul was tried by Nero, and condemned to die, but not by crucifixion, as the law did not permit them to inflict this death upon a Roman citizen. But, leading him away out of the city, they granted him a private execution by decapitation.

We stood on the spot where projected the great royal porticoes, in which reclined the kings and queens of the earth, looking out on the chariot races in the Circus Maximus, while in the rear the athletes were displaying their championship in foot races and pugilistic contests.

We stood in the great royal festal hall, where the magnates of the earth reveled in Bacchanalian banquets. I saw the vomitorium, whither they went to relieve their stomachs of the voracious contents by eructation, that they might enjoy the pleasure of eating again, after the quickening influence of appetizers.

We visited the spot on the banks of the Tiber where Romulus and Remus, the twin boys, were exposed by the King of Alba to be devoured by wild beasts, lest they might some day get in the way of his dynasty, as they, too, had royal blood. We visited the cave where the wolf had her warm bed, and sauntering out for food found the babes, took them in her strong mouth, carried them to her cavern, and warmed them, externally by her long hair and internally by her vitalizing, nutritious milk. So they grew rapidly, and became the progenitors of the greatest nation the world ever saw, by Daniel so brilliantly written up as the "Iron Kingdom," subduing the whole earth. This mythical history is to-day corroborated by the presence of the memorial wolves constantly kept on the Capitol mountain. We repeatedly saw them in this journey.

We next visited the Mamertine prison in which

Paul and Peter were incarcerated till they got ready to execute them. It is at the base of the Capitoline mountain, and within full view of the old Forum. It was formed by clearing off the debris from a great stratum, drilling down till an ample door was chiselled out. Then they excavated laterally in all directions as well as perpendicularly, till they opened a great room, surrounded on all sides by the native strata, and with no entrance except the circular aperture at the top. This prison was used for the worst imperial criminals, as jail-breaking and escape were utterly out of the question.

They say that the jailer and his family were converted by Paul's preaching, and they show a fountain of nice, living water flowing from a crevice in the rock certifying that it spontaneously broke out when Paul needed water to baptize them. They show the active administration of the baptism, Paul pouring it on their heads, thus corroborating every other testimony in all Bible lands relative to this matter, which has become a theme of popular controversy, and, sad to say, an awful source of idolatry in the modern Church.

(d) A short distance, then we again entered the Pantheon, as the name reveals, from "pan," all, and "theos," god. It was built by the Roman emperors two thousand years ago, and is a magnificent temple. It is a perfect circle, 200 feet in diameter and 200 feet high, with two great doors on opposite sides, and no windows except a circular aperture at the top in the center, 32 feet in diameter, over which there is no roof, consequently rains and snows without obstruction fall down on the stone floor. Of course the shrines of the gods are all next to the wall, and are protected from all inclement weather.

The Pantheon is now used as a Christian church. I believe I have seen people worshiping in it every time I paid it a visit.

Paul's hired house, where he conducted his city mission those memorable two years after his arrival in Rome, is now St. Mary's Church. Of course pilgrims delight to walk in the footprints of the Great Apostle.

We then took the car for St. Paul's Church. The car carries you out of the city, through St. Paul's Gate in the old wall, named for him when they led him out through it for execution. When I was at this church in 1905, they had been building it fifty years and had expended $50,000,000 on it. When I went back in five years, they had just finished it, at the cost of $55,000,000 and fifty-five years of constant toil. Among the specimens of the fine arts, it stands at the front of the world. For elegance, beauty and artistic splendor, it is pre-eminent. Of course Paul is the most conspicuous character shown up in the beautiful gigantic, marble statuary which adorns this edifice on all sides.

The words of Jesus to Paul, when He met him on the Damascus road: "Thou art a vessel of election unto Me," are conspicuously displayed in large, marble letters; meanwhile all the apostles are exceedingly prominent in the statuary. In the interior corridors, all the popes (about 300), from Peter down to the present incumbent, are shown up in gigantic and most impressive statuary.

All the inscriptions in this church are in the Latin language, which I read, consequently it was exceedingly impressive to me. I was astonished that this building was not erected on the site of the Apostle's martyrdom, which is about two miles northwest. I suppose they thought that the cathedral would there be too inconvenient for the city.

The street-cars (all of which have been introduced since my first visit sixteen years ago) terminated at this cathedral. Therefore we walked on to the place of the Apostle's decapitation, now the Convent of St. Clement, erected as a memorial. They certify that when the soldiers cut Paul's head off it bounded about twenty feet and struck the ground, which is there inclined about twenty degrees from the horizon, and there a fountain of living water leaped out of the earth and has been flowing ever since. Then it bounded again, striking about the same distance further down the hill, where, striking the ground, another living fountain sprang up, and it has been flowing ever since. It bounded the third time, and the third fountain leaped out of the earth. The fountains are all there, as I have seen them several times and drank out of them all. You say, "Brother Godbey, I do not believe it"? That is none of my business; it does not cost you anything.

We walked back to St. Paul's Cathedral to take the cars, and ran a half a dozen miles to St. John's

Cathedral. It is really a wonder of wonders. In it are all the apostles in gigantic statuary, most brilliant and imposing. As all the apostles sealed their faith with their blood, these statues show up how they all died. Oh, how edifying to study them! There also they show up the apostolic baptism, as in all other places, by simple affusion.

As we came out of this church, on the right hand side, we, by having a door opened, could see the "Holy Stairway," up which they certify Jesus climbed when He stood at Pilate's bar and was tried for His life. They say this stairway was carried from Jerusalem to Rome during the Crusades, and they certify that the angels did it.

When Martin Luther walked all the way from Germany to Rome, that he might enjoy the wonderful means of grace and receive the full salvation for which his heart did sigh and his soul cry night and day, then, when he saw the towering spires of Rome from the summit of a distant mountain, he fell down crying out: "Sancta Roma, salvo te!" (Holy Rome, I salute thee!) He thought that Rome was the emporium of all grace, and the Pope the dispenser of it, through his innumerable priests.

On arrival, those priests put him in pursuit of all sorts of penances, that he might receive that for which his soul longed. While fasting till he was almost starving to death, and wearing himself out running after these excruciating penances, a day came when he was climbing up this "Holy Stairway" on his bare knees, marking every step with blood, as the skin on his knees was worn through. Then he heard a voice from Heaven: "The just shall live by faith." Rising, he walked down the stairway, and told the people that they could not get saved by any of those penances, but that salvation is by faith alone, without works. (Eph. 2:8.)

He returned to Germany a flame of fire, preaching to everybody salvation full and free, the gift of God in Christ, received and appropriated by faith alone.

When this news reached Rome, the Vatican thundered, the hierarchy raged, and the Pope anathematized, laying under contribution all their wits to suppress the alarming heresy. But Luther rapidly grew in grace and religious activities, and was utterly incorrigible to all their threats. The Pope wrote to the bishop of Wittenberg by all means to stop that man's mouth with gold, he believing the popular maxim that "every man has his price." Making a total failure on that line, the bishop wrote back to Rome the melancholy letter: "Holy Father, I am sorry to say the German beast does not love gold, consequently I can do nothing."

Then the Pope sent his bull of excommunication, pronouncing Luther an outlaw, liable at any time to be burnt, like John Huss of Bohemia, or the bones of Wicliffe, which, after an interment of forty years, had been dug up and burnt, because his writings had sown so-called "heresy."

On reception of the papal bull, Luther observed to the by-standers: "As this is a burning business, we will begin at this end of the line." Then, going out on the public square and building a fire, he burnt the Pope's bull. This "threw all the fat into the fire," and the Pope at once summoned Luther to meet him and his cardinals in the city of Worms, Germany, there to give an account of himself. As all knew that the Pope and cardinals aimed to burn him, they did their best to keep him from going. But mounting his mule and riding away, he said to his friends: "I will enter Worms if I there meet as many devils as there are tiles on the roofs."

Sure enough, the grave council convened and Luther stood before them all with his open Bible, fearless of men and devils. The controversy waxed hotter and hotter, till the volcano exploded in a general carousal, uprising and skedaddlement. In the stampede, Luther was captured and carried away into a great, lonely mountain, to a venerable castle on the summit, where he was put down into a deep dungeon and kept a whole year. Meanwhile his enemies at Rome celebrated his death by bonfires and illuminations.

During this year of rest and quiet, he translated the Greek Testament into German, so that it became accessible to the rank and file of the people, instead of to only a few priests.

In the run of the year, the seeds of truth, which Luther had so copiously sown, sprang up and brought forth a grand harvest. This the friends of truth and righteousness gloriously reaped in the Augsburg Conference, where the princes of Germany met and repudiated the authority of the Pope. Thus they felicitously laid the foundation of the Protestant Church and turned a sunburst on Christendom, which, for a thousand years, had been deluded by priestcraft and hallucinated by Satan's trinity (sin, ignorance and superstition), when not one man in a thousand nor one woman in twenty thousand could read or write.

During that memorable year of his imprisonment, Luther thought his enemies had him, while all the time he was in the hands of his friends, who were afraid to make themselves known unto him lest he would get away from them and his enemies would kill him. Therefore they held him in blissful ignorance of their identity the whole year, while the truth he had preached was spreading among the people and his enemies were weakening all the time, till at last the cause of a free Bible and omnipotent grace had developed into a giant panoplied and ready to fight its own battles.

(e) In the providence of God, we were in Italy early in April, when the whole country was overgrown with blooming flowers and growing fruits, and gardens, groaning under their copious crops, were everywhere superabounding in that lovely land, where chilling winter and burning summer mutually retreat before blooming spring-time and fruitful autumn. Though the land has been cultivated continuously for twenty-five hundred years, yet it is this day an exhibition of continuous gardens and fruitful fields.

The run to Naples was delightful through that charming country. We passed the Appian Way, the Forum, and the Three Taverns, whither a delegation of the brethren walked out forty miles to meet Paul, and saluted, welcomed and escorted him into the city.

No wonder he thanked God and took courage, to find zeal so ardent and Christian affection so stirring.

While Rome is the capital, Naples is the metropolis of Italy, with a population of seven hundred thousand, and rapidly increasing. If you want beauty, grandeur and sublimity combined into harmonious symmetry, go to Naples. It is all built on those majestic mountains encircling the bay, a delectable arm of the great Mediterranean. Our ship sailed at nightfall for New York, 4300 miles away. The beauty of the scene not even the inspired pen of eloquent old Homer, the father of poets, could ever portray. The lights of the city reminded me of a great chandelier, forming a gorgeous circle like the rainbow, bespangled with all the various tints and hues of the prismatic spectrum.

Drop your eyes back and climb the rolling ages of by-gone eternity, "before the mountains were brought forth," when the great sea spread over that vast region and the site of this beautiful city was all buried beneath the thundering billows of the great bay, now restricted in her territory since mighty Vesuvius uttered the stentorian thunders of his tremendous volcanic upheavals. A stream of lava shot up in the middle of the sea, and continued the stupendous current of its mighty river leaping out of the deep maw, thus relieving terra firma of the contents of her superabounding abysses, till these voluminous ejectments piled up four thousand feet above the sea level; at the same time rolling out in all directions until the demiurgic hand has built him a throne on which he might sit in judgment, dispensing to the inhabitants of earth their condign rewards and retributions.

Mount Vesuvius is all volcanic, having leaped up out of the sea long before Adam was created, as you must remember "one day with God is a thousand years." (2 Pet. 3:8.) These were God's days, not man's fleeting span of twenty-four hours. Lava is the richest soil in all the world. Vesuvius has one hundred thousand acres of this rich and productive soil, and enjoys all the climates of the earth, i. e., tropical, semi-tropical, and temperate, determined by the altitude. It produces almost every luxury growing on the face of the earth. The chestnuts growing on that mountain are several times the size of any others I ever saw, and the trees are exceedingly prolific, so they ship them throughout the world. Oranges, lemons, olives, figs, grapes, and a variety of unmentioned fruits, nuts and vegetables superabound.

This mountain is so rich, and sea and land are so combined, as to make the beauty of the situation, as well as the geniality of the climate, paradoxically magnetic. Thus the great mountain has become the magnet of that great country, which stood at the front of the world longer than any other. But oh! how it holds over the people the castigatory rod, sometimes turning in with Judgment Day retributions, as in A. D. 79, when, at noonday, it disgorged such a mighty river of burning lava, pouring its fiery floods in all directions. In a moment it buried Herculaneum and Pompeii in a magnitudinous, fiery sepulchre, snuggly wrapping those beautiful and flourishing cities in fiery winding-sheets, which were so awfully terrifying that the people who escaped fled far away and never did go back.

Those cities remained buried seventeen hundred years, till a man out chasing a rabbit with his dog, thinking he had run it into a cave, entered in pursuit and found himself in a house under the earth. The city had been buried so long that soil had accumulated on it, great trees had grown up, and they had built a city over it and were cultivating the rich garden lands. Then they began to excavate, and have been at it ever since, having uncovered twenty-six acres of Pompeii. I have traversed it, seeing all of those fine houses peculiar to prosperous cities. When they exhumed them, they found people at their work in all sorts of attitudes. They had been suddenly suffocated and petrified.

Herculaneum is still under the city of Naples, the people living in their houses and cultivating their gardens directly over it. If you should visit the city, you must go to Pompeii, climb Vesuvius to the summit, and look down into the burning crater to see the great wonders. You should also visit the Museum, where you will be much edified, as it is very large and well supplied. In it you will find the Pompeii division, of much interest as a diagnosis of the times in which the city existed—up to A. D. 79.

You will open your eyes with horror to see that the very wickedness for which God destroyed Sodom and Gomorrah was indulged in in Pompeii to its awful destruction. While Naples is this day so beautiful and prosperous, yet, like in other cities, the wickedness is so great that all luminous souls abide in constant alarm for the doom of the city. Several times has the volcano buried cities in their own fiery sepulchres so suddenly that escape was impossible. He gives his warnings all the time, sending up volumes of smoke and often pouring devouring flames out of his crater.

The truth of the whole matter is that this earth is a ball of fire with a thin crust formed on the exterior, and with four hundred volcanoes giving their alarms in lightnings, thunders and earthquakes. Thus God is warning all the people to be constantly ready for the fiery deluges foretold in the Bible, and liable to transpire at any moment, superinducing that fiery baptism which will expurgate the earth not only of all sin but of the effect of sin, really sanctifying it wholly. This is after the manner of the human soul, which is destined to be fully expurgated of all unrighteousness, and thus eternally identified with the Lord of glory, soul and body, and reunited never again to be separated, our Lord's temple world without end.

(f) Again we mounted the iron horse, and galloped away through the lovely and charming sunny south of Italy, dashing through tunnels and over deep chasms all the time, the romance of this great Appenine range proving utterly indescribable. I have traveled around the world, climbing the great mountain ranges on the rack and pinion railroad system running by cogwheels, and have climbed mountains beneath every sky, and I believe the Appenines along the southern coast of Italy are the most romantic I ever saw. On you rush, leaping out of a dark tunnel, across a deep chasm—one moment midnight, the next noonday—and looking down on the tree-tops beneath your feet; and again you dash through a tunnel, the majestic mountains kissing the skies above your head.

At Brindisi we took the sea again, for two nights and a day. It was the beautiful Adriatic, the terror of all sailors, notorious as a storm-breeder. However, the Storm-king heard prayer, and blessed us with a calm sea and a delightful voyage. On this sea we sailed by the rocky island of Scio, small, poor and insignificant, and yet celebrated in all the earth; because, in God's providence, it was the nativity and residence of Homer, the father of poets and the greatest of them all. Poetry draws on imagination for its resources, while philosophy must have knowledge. Therefore the increase of knowledge means intrenchment on imagination, which, in the absence of history, science and erudition, has nothing to do but spread her pinions and fly to the ultimathule of the universe, tossing worlds from the tips of her fingers, responsively to the caprices of her own creation.

Homer lived before the age of science, literature, philosophy and erudition, hence he had the universe at his option. Oh, how he revels ad libitum in the creation of worlds upon worlds, inhabited by heroes and demigods, the obsequious creatures of his own phantasmagorial imagination. He wrote the twenty-four books of the "Odyssey," which took the palm for poetry then and have retained it ever since, felicitously

> "Achilles' wrath,
> To Greeks the direful spring
> Of woes unnumbered,
> Heavenly goddess, sing;
> That wrath which hurled
> To Pluto's gloomy reign
> The souls of mighty chiefs,
> Untimely slain.
> Declare, O muse,
> In what ill-fated hour
> Sprang the fierce wrath,
> From what offended power.
> Latona's son
> A dire contagion spread,
> And heaped the camp
> With mountains of the dead.
> Since great Achilles
> And Atrides strove,
> Such was the soverign power,
> And such the will of Jove."

(g) Our ship ran by the island of Ithaca, the celebrated kingdom of Ulysses, the greatest of all the heroes at the siege of Troy, which siege lasted ten years and was finally ended by the stratagem of the wooden horse invented by the crafty Ulysses. Hector, the greatest Trojan hero, had fallen in a hand-to-hand battle with Achilles. The latter attached his body to his chariot and dragged it three times around the city, till old King Priam, Hector's father, came out and begged him for it. Conquered by his tears and moved by his pathos, Achilles gave it up.

The ten years having flown, the Greeks feigned desperation, raised the siege, embarked on their ships and sailed away, to the infinite relief of the Trojans, who had borne the siege those awful ten years. They allotted a place on the earth 900 B. C. Hear him sing:

landed on an island and went into an ambuscade. The Trojans, weary, went to bed and slept soundly.

Then Simon, a Greek, feigned himself a deserter from the Grecian ranks, came to the Trojans with a tale of woe against the Greeks, and asked them to receive him as a citizen. They asked him what that great monster in the shape of a horse, left by the Greeks on their camp-grounds, meant. He told them it was an offering to Minerva, the tutelary goddess of their city, made by the Greeks to appease her wrath for besieging her favorite those ten years. He succeeded in persuading them to take it into their city. It was so large they could not take it in through the gates, but had to take down a section of the wall. That night after they got it in the city, Simon opened the piney doors of the horse, and the Grecian heroes, Ulysses himself and all the magnates of the army, poured out, set Troy on fire, and gave the signal to the ambuscaded host of Greeks, who soon rallied and captured the city. So that awful night the ancient kingdom of Priam fell to rise no more.

Now that their work was done, the Greeks all sailed for home, after an absence of ten long years. Minerva, exasperated over the fall of Troy, sent an awful storm to meet the fleet. Storms are to this day the terror of sailors, despite our wonderful advantages over our predecessors in having the mariner's compass and the steam engine, and owing to the paradoxical magnitude of our ships. In that day storms at sea meant watery winding-sheets instead of life-preservers, which now abound on every ship.

In this storm the fleet of Ulysses got entirely separated from that of the rest of the Greek army, so they saw no more of it and took it for granted that they were all buried in the dark, deep sea. In this the Greeks were mistaken. Ulysses and his men were driven away upon unknown seas, wrecked on wild shores inhabited by barbarians and giants, and exposed to terrible perils. They passed through most thrilling adventures, written up by Homer in the twenty-four books of the "Odyssey."

The remainder of the Grecian army, however, passed the storm perils and arrived safe at home, proclaiming the awful news appertaining to their great leader Ulysses, that he was lost with his ships and followers. Soon the young princes of Greece began to pay their addresses to Penelope, the beautiful and accomplished wife of Ulysses and queen of Ithaca, royal regent in the absence of her husband. She at once notified them all that her husband was alive and coming home. They disputed it, unanimously assuring her that he, with all his ships, was sunk into the sea. They gave her great annoyance, lounging in the palace day and night, and eating up the substance of the kingdom, she being afraid to withhold royal courtesies lest they make war on her and take the kingdom from her in the absence of her noble husband. They insisted that she make a selection from among them, assuring her that the rest would all acquiesce and go away satisfied. She resorted to various excuses, finally telling them that she was weaving a great web for a funeral shroud for Laertes, the super annuated king of the island, so old that he would soon go to his grave. At that time there were no factories in the world, and weaving could only be done by hand, and was looked upon as a great honor, worthy the encomium of a queen.

The job ran on so long that the suitors became suspicious of a stratagem somewhere, so proceeded to watch Penelope, finding that she raveled out at night what she had woven in the day, in order to prolong the job and postpone the answer to the suitors. Finally ten years had flown away, making twenty since the departure of Ulysses, when behold! he came home. Having heard of the trouble in the court, he appeared in the disguise of an old beggar, lest the suitors kill him outright and take his queen and kingdom. Thus disguised, no one recognized him but Penelope, who identified him on the glance. He gave her the wink to maneuver the stratagem, which she did to perfection, overtly treating him simply as a beggar. Homer says his old dog, which had not seen him in twenty years, also recognized him, fawned on him, and dropped dead at his feet, so overjoyed with the return of his master that he would live no longer.

Things moved on and Ulysses drew the suitors into a shooting match, defeated and slew them all; then, throwing off his disguise, he declared publicly his own identity, and ascended the long vacated throne of his kingdom.

Those ancient Greeks had no Bible, but here you see the beautiful Bible truth appertaining to the bridehood of the bride of Christ gloriously radiated.

Ulysses is symbolical of our absent Lord; Penelope of His faithful, waiting bride; and the suitors of the princes of the earth who are doing their best to capture her in wedlock with the world, which has sadly been the case with the rank and file of the Church, no longer true to her absent Spouse, but gone off and married to antichrist. Some of these days our Ulysses will come back; in the Great Tribulation slay the worldly lovers who have so much annoyed His faithful bride, and, amid the shouts of the angels, archangels and redeemed spirits, enter upon His glorious millennial reign.

(h) We then disembarked at Petras, Greece, boarded the train for Athens, and ran along on the banks of the beautiful Ionian Sea two hundred miles to Corinth, through a delightful country crowded full of vineyards and olive orchards, figs and a diversity of semi-tropical fruits abounding on all sides.

We ran through southern Greece, the Achaia of Acts 18, of which Gallio was at that time governor, when the unbelieving Jews led Paul to his tribunal, to answer charges for teaching people to worship God contrary to law. The governor simply non-suited them. As the Greeks, when they conquered all the world under Alexander the Great, had adopted all the gods worshiped by all nations, therefore it was lawful for Paul (and everybody else) to preach any God and any religion he pleased. Therefore the proconsul threw the case out of court.

As the Jews were but a handful in that great city of one hundred thousand, the Paris of the ancient world, and as they always are shrewder in speculations than the Gentiles, getting rich where the latter stay poor, they were, as this day, universally envied and hated. Consequently they lit on Sosthenes, the chief ruler of the synagogue, in the succession of Crispus, who had been converted to Christ by the preaching of Paul, and gave him a regular flogging. Gallio did nothing to prevent it, he having already told them that, if Paul was guilty of any misdemeanor or transgression of the civil law, he would bear with them patiently and adjudicate the matter, but if it was simply a question appertaining to their own religion, he would have nothing to do with it. It seems that that thrashing did Sosthenes good, because the next time we hear of him (1 Cor. 1:1), it says, "Paul . . . an apostle . . . and Sosthenes our brother, to the saints in Corinth." Hence you see he had been converted, turned preacher and missionary, and gone away with Paul to Ephesus in Asia to preach, and Paul honors him with recognition as his associate evangelist.

In the Baltimore Conference a hundred years ago, a circuit in the Alleghany Mountains was awfully troubled with a big blacksmith, who whipped every circuit rider sent into that country and ran him off. The case became so alarming that no preacher was willing to go, consequently the bishop had to call for a volunteer. Peter Cartwright responded and went to the circuit. At his first meeting in that neighborhood the blacksmith was on hand; he told him what he had been doing, and said that he was going to do the same for him, as he believed a preacher to be a nuisance, humbugging the people. Peter asked him to wait till he had preached, then they would go out in the yard and he would have the chance to run him off, if he could. In that age firearms were not generally used, and any man resorting to them would forfeit his claim to the championship.

Sure enough, when Peter wound up his sermon and announced his appointments, he stated the matter with the man and said that he had reluctantly consented to go into a pugilistic encounter as his only chance to maintain his liberty to preach the Gospel in that country. Therefore the people stood by and saw that each had fair play. All arrangements were made and at it they went, but Peter proved too much for the blacksmith. He got him down flat on his back and sat astride him, thumping his ribs, but at the same time praying for him with all his might and preaching the Gospel to him, despite his contempt and antagonism. At the same time he told him he was never going to let him up till he promised to let him alone, come to meeting and behave like a gentleman. The blacksmith finally accepted the situation. To make a long story short, suffice it to say that before the year had half gone the blacksmith was wonderfully converted, and became a flaming shouter, and Peter's best friend and right-hand man in all that country.

Of course the next Conference could not pass Peter's character, but had to prosecute him for fighting, which no preacher was allowed to do. Peter stood before the Conference and plead his cause, making his humble confession: "Brethren, I did for Jesus' sake endeavor to beat religion into the man." The case of Sosthenes at Corinth is surely a parallel.

Now all cities are founded in the most accessible places. In the olden times, when all nations were belligerent, they selected the most inaccessible sites, i. e., a precipitous mountain, up which they could all climb and get out of danger when besieged by armies. Therefore, while Corinth stood on a beautiful, rich plain bordering on the Ægean Sea on the east and the Ionian Sea on the west, yet it was hard by a precipitous mountain, on which they could erect their citadel and fortify themselves against their enemies very successfully, as firearms were then unknown.

Long before we reached Corinth, we saw this mountain, the Acro-Corinthus (citadel of Corinth) and the city was built on the beautiful plain at its base. It was in its day, like Paris to-day, the leader of styles, fashions and the fine arts. Paul there held his longest protracted meeting and built up his largest church. As he had made a failure at Athens, rejected by the philosophers, he came to Corinth much discouraged, and went to his trade of tent-making. It was then the most profitable trade in all the world, as the Bedouin Arabs, rigidy walking in the footprints of Father Abraham, who never lived in a house, always live in tents; consequently Paul could sell to them, and earn enough by tent-making to support him and his Gospel helpers. Therefore, with Aquila and Priscilla, practitioners of the same trade, and by the grace of God, his converts and associate evangelists, he went to work till the arrival of Timothy and Silas, whom he had left at Berea with the understanding that they would return to Thessalonica and preach there, in due time to join him at Corinth. In the meantime while Paul was making tents and his young men were preaching in the north country, God gave him a mighty vision. Standing over him, He exhorted him: "Fear not, for I am with thee, and no one shall set on thee to hurt thee, because I have much people in this city." Those people were not saved at that time, but God knew they would be and counted them.

During those times Paul got into serious trouble, and they resolved to kill him, so laid him on the block to cut his head off. Then Aquila and Priscilla both ran in and laid down their necks and begged them to take them both as a substitute for him and let him live. The scene so wrought on the people that they released them all. You see an allusion to this in Romans 16.

During the ages of desolation, the beautiful city of Corinth suffered awfully. It abounded in specimens of the fine arts in its palmy days. When Mummius, the Roman proconsul, conquered it, he loaded up this splendid statuary and sent it to Rome, telling the captain to be sure he didn't lose it in the sea, and if he did he must furnish just as good in return. This was impossible, since there was no artist on the earth competent to make such, as the glory of Greece had departed. While Greece had been beautified by the fine arts during her palmy days, amid the long night of a thousand years, when not one man in a thousand nor one woman in twenty thousand could read or write, this light of the world suffered terrible spoliation.

(i) When the whole civilized world, a hundred years ago, yielded to a philanthropic wave in behalf of celebrated, glorious and immortal Greece, for long ages spoliated by different nations and especially the Turks who ruled over them with awful rigor, responsive to this philanthropic reminiscence of her by-gone glory, the nations united and gave her her freedom again.

At that time (A. D. 1832) Corinth only had about six thousand inhabitants. When, forty years ago, they built the railroad along the bank of the Ionian Sea, they led it thither, and Corinth has been growing ever since. The railroad crosses the Isthmus of Corinth, connecting Achaia (southern Greece) with Hellas (central Greece), and running over the canal which has been cut through that Isthmus, it connects the Ionian Sea on the west with the Ægean Sea on the east.

Off toward the south and east of the Ionian Sea was ancient Sparta, so celebrated for her heroism, making the penalty death to retreat on the battlefield. Lycurgus was her celebrated lawgiver, and his laws remained in force fourteen hundred years. This was because finally, when he was old, he told the people he wanted to go on a journey, and obligated them to obey his laws till he returned; then he went away and did not go back, preferring to die in exile to hold the people to their obligation to obey his laws.

In that country is celebrated Mt. Parnasus, on whose summit is the fabulous Pyerian fountain, which is said to have the power to inspire the one drinking therefrom with the true genius of poetry, oratory and the fine arts. Pindar, Sappho, and other aspirants climbed that mountain to enjoy those inspiratory waters.

As we dashed on along the bank of the Ægean Sea, ere long we disembarked in the literary emporium of the ancient world (Athens), named for the goddess Minerva, or Athena, the patron of literature, science, philosophy and the fine arts.

(j) We went at once to the Acropolis, the citadel of Athens, a precipitous mountain overlooking the beautiful plain on the seashore. Like the Acro-Corinthus, the citadel of Corinth, the Acropolis is the fortification of Athens.

When Paul arrived in Athens (Acts 17), he found it all given up to idolatry. He spent a fortnight preaching in the synagogue on Sunday and on the streets to all the passers-by during the week. Eventually he attracted the attention of the Epicurean and Stoic philosophers, who escorted him away to the Areopagus (Mars Hill), separated from the Acropolis by a deep valley. On it stood the great auditorium where the philosophers held their meetings and adjudicated every matter of interest, calling the popular attention. So they led Paul up thither and gave him a chance to speak to the wisest audience in the world, to whose feet the kings of the earth sent their sons to learn wisdom.

The English version of the Bible here has it that Paul said: "I perceive that in all things you are too superstitious." That would have repelled and insulted them at the outset. What he did say to them was: "I perceive that in all things you are very religious," complimenting them and drawing them to him.

When the Greeks conquered the world, under the leadership of Alexander the Great, they had adopted all the gods worshipped by all the nations of the earth and erected for them temples and shrines there at Athens, their capital and metropolis. During Paul's peregrinations in the city, he had been looking at all their religious edifices and reading the superscriptions on them to the different gods. Among them he had seen a shrine superscribed, "To the Unknown God." They were so anxious to enjoy the favor of all the gods that they had built temples and shrines for them, but after all this, lest here might be somewhere in the universe a god whom they did not know, that he might not be offended, they erected a shrine and superscribed it to him.

Here Paul gets at them, certifying that though they did not know this God, yet he did. Thus he elicited their attention and electrified them with interest to learn all they could about that God for whom they had built a shrine and whom they were already worshiping.

So in this way he got an attentive hearing by the

most learned audience in the world. They all listened spellbound and electrified, till he spoke of the resurrection of the dead, which is a truth utterly out of reach of human ratiocination and can only be received by faith. Here they broke down on him, dropping him like a hot potato till they had time to study out the matter, when they proposed to hear him again. Then he left them, having made but two converts, **Dionysius, the sexton, and Sister Damaris.**

(k) Standing on the Areopagus, we had a conspicuous view of the temple of Theseum, twenty-five hundred years old, and built of marble supported by colonnades of fluted marble. It is said to be the first house in Europe used as a Christian church.

Over on the Hill of the Muses we saw the prison of Socrates, pronounced by the Delphian oracle the wisest man in the world. He was imprisoned and executed for teaching the communion of the Holy Spirit, which by them was condemned as introducing new gods. When the weeping executioner brought him the hemlock to drink, he blessed and comforted him telling him that he was going above the clouds to live forever. I also saw his house where he lived and taught his sublime philosophy.

We also stood in the bema of Demosthenes, the greatest orator the world has ever known, where, with his trumpet voice, he held spellbound the listening thousands. At first he had an impediment in his speech, which he cured by speaking with pebbles in his mouth, so that he actually came to the front of the oratorical world, receiving the crown of championship.

We had a conspicuous view of the Hill of the Nymphs, supposed to be little divinities which help people in all situations of practical life. It is commemorated by an observatory built on it. They taught the nine muses, which evidently were simply the nine gifts of the Holy Spirit shining out in the light of nature, unassisted by the written Word, as they had none.

We then climbed the Acropolis, passing the temple of Nike, erected to the Goddess of Victory when the Grecians so wonderfully triumphed over the Persians in that notable invasion of Xerxes. He came against them with an army of two and a half millions, said to be the largest ever mustered on the earth; and besides, he had the largest and best equipped fleet of ships in the world. He felt sure that he would sweep the Grecians from the face of the earth, as they were the only people on the earth who had not submitted to his universal sceptre, and he was determined to sweep all possible defalcation from the field.

As we stood on the portico of the Acropolis, we had a beautiful view of the imperial mountain, on whose summit Xerxes had his throne erected; in order to enjoy a conspicuous view of the naval battle coming up between his magnificent fleet and the few little ships of the Greeks, he being perfectly sanguine that the former would speedily and utterly demolish the latter. To his unutterable surprise and consternation, he saw the Greeks, with their little barks, attack his magnificent fleet, board his ships, set them on fire, sink them in the sea, and his last hope take its flight.

Meanwhile news came from the plains of Marathon, where Themistocles had met Xerxes' two millions of land forces, after Leonidas, with his three hundred Spartan braves had held them all at bay three days before they succeeded in passing the Pass of Thermopylæ, which they never could have entered if they had not discovered another route through the mountains. What was the news from Marathon? Why, the Greeks were triumphant on all sides. Consequently this grand army of two and a half millions was everywhere on the skedaddle, defeated on all sides, by land and sea.

The haughty Xerxes had them lay forty lashes on the sea for wrecking his ships in a storm. This great and decisive victory was a brilliant sunburst prophesying the oncoming conquest of the whole world under Alexander the Great.

The temple of Nike, which you pass on your right as you ascend the Acropolis, is still standing in a perfect state of preservation.

The Propylæa, i. e., the portico supported by marble columns, we now passed through, and found ourselves on the Acropolis. The temple of Hercules was on the right, that of Diana on the left, and the great temple of Minerva, the tutelary goddess of the city (for whom it was named "Athens" from the Greek Athena), stood on the summit, supported by sixty-four great, cylindrical, marble columns. The city was really illuminated with marble temples, the marble for which was abundantly supplied by the quarries of Mt. Pentelicus, overshadowing the city on the east.

As we moved on toward the south, we soon entered the museum of Grecian antiquities, in which we were much edified. From the Acropolis we had a splendid view of the city, one of the most beautiful in the world. During the long roll of the Dark Ages, it was spoliated and many valuable monuments carried away. At the time of Greece's emancipation from the Turkish yoke (1832), the city only contained seven thousand people; now, including the environments, it has a population of two hundred thousand, and is rapidly growing.

(1) Descending from the Acropolis, we passed the Odeon Theater on the left, capacious, and elegantly supplied with marble pews. It was used for all sorts of musical entertainments. Going on south, we came to the Theater Bacchus, the wine god; large, and seated with marble pews. It was devoted to wine festivals and all sorts of hilarities and jollifications. Passing on southwardly, we reached the temple of Jupiter Olympus, 400 feet long, 125 feet wide, and supported by great, cylindrical columns of fluted marble, 90 feet high, and the roofing mounting up to a dizzy altitude. This temple was pronounced one of the seven wonders of the world, along with the Colossus of Rhodes, the walls of Babylon, the temple of Diana at Ephesus, the Egyptian pyramids, the Sphinx and the temple of the Sphinx, and the Coliseum at Rome.

Out on the campus to our left, we recognized the

beautiful monument of Lord Byron, erected to his memory because, leaving his seat in the House of Lords, of England, he went away to help the Greeks in their war for independence. With others, responsively to the stirring appeals of his own pen, he tried to arouse the civilized world to reciprocate the blessings it had received from the poets, orators, philosophers and heroes who brought ancient Greece to the front of the world, leaving her footprints forever ineffacable on the sands of time. Hear his appeal:

> "Great shades of chiefs and sages,
> Behold the coming strife.
> Hellenes of past ages,
> Oh, spring again to life!"

He, responsively to his own trumpet-call for volunteers, leaving his delightful home, and the world's metropolis, and his seat in the House of Lords, went away to desolated and downtrodden Greece, and there heroically laid down his life for their emancipation from the galling yoke of Turkish tyranny, under which Greece had groaned for generations and centuries. His monument exhibits the Goddess of Liberty placing the wreath of victory on his brow.

We next crossed over the classical river Ilissus, immortalized by the poets, and entered the Stadium, so celebrated twenty-five hundred years ago, when the victor in the quadrennial games here held was actually honored with the calendar, i. e., the time from that epoch to the next was given the name of the world's champion. Paul, in his Epistles, frequently makes brilliant and edifying allusions to these Olympic races.

Heb. 12:1, 2: "Therefore, . . . laying aside every weight and the sin which doth so easily beset us, let us run with patience the race set before us, looking unto Jesus, the beginner and the finisher of our faith."

None but the native Greeks were eligible to these contests. Born Greeks could all be runners, but only one could receive the crown. They carried weights on their bodies and underwent sundry gymnastic exercises to develop all their muscles and nerves; then, laying aside all weights, and living meanwhile very abstemiously, they spent four years getting ready for the contest, which magnified them in the eyes of the world. All nations came to witness the races, wrestling, boxing and diversified exercises, yet none but Greeks were eligible to participation.

Paul frequently refers to these Olympic games and races as illustrative of our race for glory. But there is this great difference. In the former, only one could receive the crown; in the latter, there is a crown for everyone who will make the run successfully. None can be runners but those born from above. The supernatural birth brings you into the stadium where you can be a runner. Then you must get rid of inbred sin by sanctification if you would win the prize.

Sixteen years ago, on my first tour, I found the ampitheater without a solitary seat. Everything had been carried away during the ages of desolation. Now it is elegantly seated with marble pews, accommodating 100,000 spectators. This was the benefaction of a noble Greek, who went away to Egypt, made a fortune, and with his own money restored the ancient

Stadium; thus restoring the ancient Olympic games after an interregnum of fifteen hundred years, much to the interest and edification of all students of the Pauline Scriptures.

(m) In our exodus from the lovely land of poetry, oratory, philosophy, heroism and the fine arts, we sailed for Alexandria, Egypt, having on our right the Grecian archipelago, in which is the Isle of Patmos, commemorated by the exilement of the Apostle John, and the real, glorified presence of our Savior, throwing light from the door of Heaven and revealing to John the transcendent wonders recorded in the Apocalypse. It rose before us in gorgeous panorama, verifying the scene of the greatest and most electrifying theater ever opened this side the pearly portals.

Before John's exilement, Patmos was the synonym for death, as it was used by the Roman emperors for the perpetual exilement of the worst criminals. The atmosphere was so malarious that all in-comers soon died. In A. D. 95, the Emperor Domitian got so mad at John for preaching the truth that he had him cast into the soap cauldron, the normal effect of that cauldron being to melt all the animals cast into it, separating the oil from the bones, hair, horn and hoof, antecedently to their saponification. To the unutterable bewilderment of his persecutors, he does not saponify. As he proves invulnerable to the boiling oil, shouting glory to God and being delighted with the hot battle, they change their minds, take him out and banish him to Patmos. Arriving at nightfall

Saturday, he enjoys the whole night in prayer. With the day-dawn, the glorified Savior stands before him, in the glorious manifestation of Prophet, Priest and King, opening to his enraptured soul the panorama of time, judgment and eternity.

Proving invulnerable to the malaria as hitherto to the boiling oil, they release John from his exilement, permitting him to return to Ephesus to spend the remnant of his days dictating those wonderful books, his Gospel, Epistles and Apocalypse. Then, at the age of a hundred and one years, he was honored with the translation. Like Enoch, unseen by mortal eyes, and Elijah, who did his best to hide, and succeeded with the exception of Elisha, John's translation was invisible to mortal eyes, i. e., he was missing and could not be found. This pursuant to the words of our Savior relative to his abiding until His glorious appearing. However, Justin Martyr and Irenæus, who lived and wrote in the second century, in which John lived twenty-one years, certify that he was translated, not claiming, though, that they themselves were personal witnesses. John Wesley solidly believed it. Why does not the Bible mention it? Good reason: John himself was the last writer. We have no mail line hither from the Glory-land. He could not drop down a postal card certifying his translation. But we have an excellent mail route from earth to Heaven, i. e., the dying saints constantly flying up thither and bearing good news to gladden the hearts of our friends in Glory.

(n) Crete, the largest Greek island, we looked

upon not only on the evening of our embarkation, but on the ensuing day, and while we did so, we read and contemplated in memory the Epistle to Titus, whom Paul appointed bishop of the island. He exhorted Titus to deal candidly with the Cretans, making no compromise, but rebuking them, sharply observing, "The Cretans are all liars, evil beasts and slow stomachs." In the language of one of their own prophets (Aratus), "evil beasts" were the sinners and "slow stomachs" the unsanctified Christians. The stomach is the great laboratory of the system, transforming the food into blood essential to the nourishment of the 208 bones, 500 muscles, 1,000 nerves, and all the sinews, ligaments and cartilages constituting this "harp of a thousand strings," which, to our own astonishment, keeps in tune so long. Hereditary from the fall, all human bodies are encumbered more or less with physical ailments impeding the vigor of digestion and defeating the normal assimilation pertinent to healthy organism. Jesus is not only the Resurrection of the dead (John 11th chapter), but the Healer of all ailments, spiritual and physical. In the regeneration He imparts spiritual life to the dead soul, thus transforming the evil beasts, i. e., the venomous serpent, into the innocent lamb; while in sanctification He administers the infallible elixir of His own blood, expurgatory of all soul ailments, giving us perfect health. Though this is true, we are still left encumbered with multitudinous infirmities, exposing us to the constant liability of committing unknown sin and of falling into all sorts of mistakes and blunders, from which we will never be delivered till this mortal puts on immortality and we triumphantly participate in the third great work of the Holy Ghost, i. e., glorification. This confers on us angelic perfection, simultudinously to His great second work of grace, in which He sanctifies us wholly, thus superinducing the normal fruit of regeneration, which is resurrection from the dead. (Rom. 6:22.)

(o) Egypt is down on the sea level, with no mountain heights kissing the blue skies and attracting the longing eye a great way off, as is the case in other countries. Oh, how cheering to catch a view of the blue pinnacles of American mountains penetrating the azure skies, when approaching my lovely native land after a long tour in foreign climes! For example, when I had traveled around the world on a ticket from New York to San Francisco, by way of the East, how my heart did leap for joy when the towering pinnacles of the Sierra Nevada and the Cascades burst upon my enraptured vision! How my heart did sing:

>"Lives there a man with soul so dead,
>Who never to himself hath said,
>'This is my own, my native land!'?
>If such there be, go mark him well,
>For him no minstrel raptures swell.
>High though his titles, power and pelf,
>The wretch, concentered all in self,
>Living, shall forfeit fair renown;
>And doubly dying, shall go down
>To the vile dust from when he sprung,
>Unwept, unhonored and unsung."

While approaching Egypt, we first recognized the lighthouse, Pompey's Pillar and other high towers. Pompey's Pillar is a thing of beauty and a world's wonder. It was erected in honor of that great man who once stood at the head of Daniel's iron kingdom and who conquered Egypt about 70 B. C. It is a monolithic shaft, i. e., one solid piece, sculptored out of the beautiful red granite at the Nile Cataracts, ninety-four feet long and eight feet in diameter, standing on a pedestal ten feet high and wearing a caption five feet high, giving an altitude of 109 feet. Oh! what a wonder it is, beggaring the ratiocination of the spectator and truly taking rank among the wonders of the world.

As Alexandria was founded by Alexander the Great 2,200 years ago, compared with other places in Egypt, that mother of nations, it is hardly recognizable as an ancient city, and consequently, compared with Memphis and Cairo, has but few curiosities. Besides Pompey's Pillar, which deserves the special attention of every traveler, you should visit the tombs of Alexander the Great, in the Prophet Daniel Mosque, and of the Apostle Mark in the Church of St. Mark (Anglican). The reason why these two tombs are so interesting is because they represent two characters of world-wide fame, diametrically antithetical each to the other, representing the two poles of the world's battery. The one sought all the world and got it all; the other rejected it all, gave all up for Christ, and eminently succeeded in his aspirations. When Alexander had conquered it all, yet in his youth (only thirty-three), he wept that there was not another world to conquer. When he died, they buried him in a gold coffin in Greece, but as robbers would surely have gotten it, they took him out and put him in a beautiful sarcophagus hewn out of marble.

Mark was not one of the original Twelve, but at that time was a youth in the home of Mary, his mother, in Jerusalem. When the Church sent Barnabas and Paul on the first missionary tour, they took Mark with them as an assistant evangelist. Having preached through the island of Cyprus, the nativity of Silas, and reached Pamphylia, on the continent, Mark deserted them, and returned to Jerusalem. The critics believe that the robbers scared him off, as they are, even to this day, fearful in the mountainous range intervening between the sea plain and the interior tablelands. For this reason you see (Acts, 13th chapter) Paul refused to take him on his second tour, alluding to his former desertion as his reason for leaving him behind, as he could not afford to be bothered with a coward. As Barnabas was anxious to make something out of his cousin, he held on to him, even to the forfeiture of his former companionship with Paul.

The solution is easy: Paul having started out as the junior, had progressed so rapidly that he was about to eclipse Barnabas, and had already shown his competency to lead an evangelistic band. As two bands would reach more people and do more good than one, it was to the interest of God's kingdom for them to separate. The English version "sharp controversy" is here misleading; good people have concluded that temper was shown; e. g., a Holiness writer said in his exposition that Barnabas was to blame because he was not then sanctified, thus giving himself away, because Barnabas was a senior preacher, and had the Blessing before Paul. The Greek word is "paroxysm," which means the separating of the earth in its quaking. Now what causes an earthquake? God puts down His foot and breaks up the earth, producing the alarming phenomenon of the earthquake. In this case, God put His hand on the duumvirate and shook them asunder, and Barnabas took Mark and went away, and Paul took Luke and Silas, and in a short time added to them Timothy, and went another way, and the result was more preaching and more souls reached than was possible with a single cohort. Paul had no depreciation of Mark, as we see in his Epistles he called him to come and help him and said he would be useful in his work.

God blessed Barnabas in his noble efforts to make a man out of his cousin. Though not one of the original Twelve, Mark afterward got sanctified and became an apostle. In the final distribution of the whole world among the apostles, Mark received Egypt as his field of labor. Going thither, he faithfully preached till bloody martyrdom set him free, a howling mob dragging him through the streets of Alexandria by his feet till he expired.

Matthew received Ethiopia, so, going thither, he preached heroically till he sealed his faith with his blood.

Matthias, who was elected by the Eleven in the succession of Judas, received Abyssinia as his field of labor, where he also faithfully pushed the battle till bloody martyrdom gave him his heavenly passport. Thus three apostles found graves in Africa.

(p) We next ran away up that charming Nile valley, through the rich delta, planted with superabounding fields and gardens far as the eye can penetrate on either side. The tall and beautiful palm-trees, which feed the world on sweet dates, everywhere magnetize the wondering eye by their great, leafy and limbless umbrella tops. I have often read, while studying the classics in college: "Aiguptos anlioudoron est" (Egypt is a gift of the Nile). I also read the maxim: "Caput Nilon reperire" (to find the head of the Nile) as the symbol of impossibility. This arose from the fact that it flows through the great Sahara Desert, 1300 miles of burning sand right under the equator, where nobody lives except a few nomadic tribes, and it is also infested with lions, tigers, and great boa-constrictors, i. e., serpents many feet long and the size of a large ox around the body, and so carniverous that they devour people as fast as they can get hold of them. Consequently the head of the Nile was never discovered till 1891. It rises far south of the equator in the Mountains of the Moon, flows north 4,300 miles, and empties into the Mediterranean, the largest sea in the world.

The Nile is the only river in Egypt, all the country being desert interspersed with oases here and there. The annual inundations of the Nile, when the great snow-fields on the Mountains of the Moon melt, deposit a stratum of rich soil throughout the great valley, on either side, thus forming a soil of inexhaustible fertility, from the simple fact that there is a new deposit every year.

The climate of Egypt is intermediate between the tropical and temperate, the intense summer heat being mitigated by the sea breezes, and as they have no clouds, rains or snows, there is no winter. They grow four crops a year on those wonderfully fertile lands, therefore in all ages it has been the granary of the world.

On arriving in Cairo, the capital and metropolis of Egypt, with a population of 800,000, and growing rapidly since Britain captured it in 1882, we went at once to Eden Palace Hotel and took our rooms, then proceeded to explore that oldest country in the world, the mother of nations and the cradle of civilization. The great pyramids, those wonders of ante-diluvian enterprise, are so conspicuous from the city that travelers always dash off on arrival to explore them. Sixteen years ago they had no street-cars, and we had our choice of going in a carriage or riding donkeys about twelve miles across the charming Nile valley.

When I first went, I was in the vigor of my manhood, though sixty-two years old, and so went for everything in the way of exploration, investigation and curiosity. So I climbed the highest pyramid to the apex (it is 550 feet high and said to cover thirteen acres of ground). Though I had a big Arab holding my right arm, another my left, and a third pushing my back, even with all this help, it was the hardest work of my life, and made me so sore that I was a long time convalescing.

I also went into the interior. I have just now made my fourth tour, and never wanted to repeat those arduous labors. I believe in every case one time satisfies.

We next viewed the Sphinx, having the body of a lion, 120 feet long and 60 feet high; the head of a man and the face of a virgin; thus forcefully exhibiting the god worshiped by the pyramid builders, having the strength and courage of the lion, the intelligence of man, and the purity of a virgin. Within a few paces of the Sphinx stands its temple, in which the pyramid builders worshiped. It was justly catalogued with the seven wonders of the world. This temple is built exclusively of the beautiful red marble quarried at the Cataracts of the Nile, and every piece, whether door-post, arch, or whatver it is, is a monolith, i. e., just one piece. Hence it is a wonder of wonders and a beauty of beauties.

(q) We then visited the Museum of Egyptian Antiquities. As Egypt is the oldest country in the world, the alma mater (cherishing mother) of the nations, and led off in all the arts and sciences, her antiquities eclipse those of all nations in the way of interest, magnitude and multiplicity. If you ever visit that country, do not expedite through this museum.

The ancient Egyptians knew, and practiced with great success, the art of embalmment, which has been lost. No tongue can tell the toiling efforts which have been made to recover that lost art. Any person discovering it, would be a millionaire that moment. The impression everywhere prevailed among the Egyptians that man was immortal so long as his body endured; that his soul would survive just that long.

Go into that museum and you will look into the faces of people who walked upon the earth, commanded armies and did mighty works, four thousand years ago. The labors expended on the sarcophagi (stone coffins) was simply incalculable. In these tombs they put everything that humanity finds necessary to happiness. They are constantly finding these catacombs, over which the sands of the desert (in which they always bury) have blown and so accumulated that the very spot has been unknown for centuries and ages.

Since I have been visiting that country, during the last sixteen years, many tombs have been discovered and the mummies taken out of the coffins. I visited one which had recently been discovered by some Frenchmen. It was about one hundred feet deep, elegantly walled, and they found in it three mummies, supposed to be a king, queen and their son. They found in the sepulchre, among other things, two hundred thousand dollars in gold. Of course they at once appropriated the gold, but, not satisfied to let those people rest in peace, they took them out and sold them for more money, as the mummies are much in demand to supply the museums in all nations and command a high price. There was a case of where they toiled hard and long to immortalize their bodies and to supply them with ample resources, but those cunning adventurers found them despite all, and exhumed them, not only robbing them, but even selling them for filthy lucre.

In the museum, I saw Rameses II., the Pharaoh who sat upon the throne and rejected the Gospel at the hands of Moses and Aaron. I also saw Rameses I., Rameses III. and Rameses V., Rameses IV. being missing; presumptively, the embalmment had failed on him.

They also embalmed little children, and quite a diversity of animals, as they worshiped so many, believing that they were diversified manifestations of God. Especially did they worship the sacred ox, the symbol of strength and patience; and the lion, the symbol of strength and courage; also the eagle, symbolic of swiftness.

We again visited Memphis, the ancient capital and metropolis, whither Abraham, Isaac, Jacob, Joseph and his brothers went.

As the Nile, by its annual inundations, deposits a stratum of earth every year, its bed is constantly filling up, superinducing a constant elevation to a higher plane. Consequently the time came when the waters so flooded the cellars and even the houses of Memphis, as to superinduce the necessity of migrating to higher ground. Therefore they moved the city to the site of Cairo, across the river and twenty miles down stream, there finding nice, elevated grounds, where the great and flourishing city stands this day.

In the ruins of Memphis, your attention will be arrested by the gigantic statues of Rameses I. and II.; the former, forty-five feet high, twelve feet across the shoulders, and ten feet across the loins; the whole body perfectly symmetrical, beautiful, and exceedingly elegantly executed. The reason they did not move them is because they are so heavy. I expect they will move them to the museum in Cairo eventually, as I saw them moving sarcophagi weighing a million pounds, drawing them by a capstan over an extemporized movable railroad. In this way, they avail themselves of paradoxical power, so as to draw up ships sunk to the bottom of the sea.

The statue of Rameses I. is white marble and that of Rameses II. beautiful, bright red marble, gotten at the cataracts of the Nile.

They are now constantly excavating in many localities all over the site of old Memphis, the whole earth really abounding in beautiful and valuable souvenirs. I saw two great marble statues of lions which had been exhumed, but not yet carried away to the museum.

The great site of that capital and metropolis of the whole world in the days of Moses is now vast fields of wheat, barley, cucumbers, onions, and immense varieties of valuable vegetables and fruits, as the soil is wonderfully rich. The palm-tree superabounds on all sides.

In my visits to that country, the Lord has let me see it in the different seasons of the year. At first I wondered how they gathered the fruits, because the palm-trees have no limbs. The leaves of the trees are so great and strong that they use them for timber, the poor people building their houses and corraling their stock with them. In 1905 my puzzle was elucidated, as it happened to be the date harvest. I saw them just walk right up those trees, a hundred feet in height, almost as rapidly as they walked on the ground, then, pulling up a great basket with a string, they filled it with fruit and let it down. They begin with the trees when first set out, trimming off the leaves, every stub sticking fast in the bark becoming a pedestal for the foot. As the trees grow, they keep them trimmed, then they just throw a belt around a tree and around their body, and walk up on those leafy stubs, lifting up the belt as they step, and it is really wonderful the way they climb. The trees are very fruitful and bear from the beginning, so of course several years elapse before they have to climb them. The fruit is always at the top, and the wonderful power of the tropical sun so paradoxically sweetens it that it needs no sugar. It grows there in such vast quantities that they ship it to all the ends of the earth.

(r) Into Memphis the Ishmaelites carried Joseph and sold him. He is the most beautiful type of Christ, because there was not a solitary stain on his character from his infancy, he being perfectly irreproachable. As he was the eldest son by his favorite wife, Jacob recognized his birthright by giving him a coat of many colors, thus dressing him like a king, in beautiful harmony with his symbolization of Christ, King of kings and Lord of lords.

When the little fellow dreamed that they were out binding a field of wheat, and that all their sheaves stood up and fell down before his; and again, that the sun and moon and eleven stars fell down and paid obeisance to him, the dreams were so brilliant, and lingered so in his mind, that he could not forbear telling them, though he did not know what they meant. But the maturer minds of his father and mother and elder brothers readily saw the point, that he was to be king and that they would all obey him. These dreams so aroused the jealousy of his brothers that they not only envied him, but hated him on account of them.

While Jacob was living in the valley of Succoth, between Mts. Gerizim and Ebal, he sent Joseph to bear word and love tokens to his brothers herding the stock. As they had changed their location, he failed to find them till he encountered a man who told him that they had gone to Dothan, a dozen miles away, quite a distance for a little child of twelve years in that wild, mountainous country. But he followed, and came in sight of them while they were sitting down eating their dinners. They looked out, saw him coming, and said, "Yonder comes the dreamer. Let us kill him and see what will become of his dreams." But Reuben, the eldest, sought to save him, and said, "Don't kill him; how awful for his blood to be on our hands. Let us put him into that dry cistern." As he would starve to death there, they all acquiesced, despite his cries and tears.

Reuben aimed to let Joseph stay in the pit until his brethren went away, then get him out and send him home to his father. But while he was off after the herds, a caravan of Ishmaelites, on their way down into

Egypt with merchandise, came along. Then his brothers took Joseph out of the pit and sold him to the Ishmaelites for ten dollars, the price of a young slave. How brilliantly symbolic of selling Jesus for fifteen dollars, the price of a grown slave!

So the caravan passed on, with Joseph on a camel. Then Reuben came back and found him not in the pit and was deeply troubled, fearing that they had killed him. They slaughtered a kid of the goats and besmeared Joseph's coat with blood, then carried it to his father. Jacob looked at it, identified it, and wept aloud, "Oh! my son Joseph is dead, an evil beast hath devoured him." He wept night and day, refusing to be comforted, meanwhile loudly wailing, "I will go down to my grave weeping over my son!"

The Ishmaelites, pursuing the plain old caravan road, went on into the venerable capital of Egypt, and sold the promising youth to Potiphar, the captain of Pharaoh's guards. He found him so good, truthful, industrious, patient and smart that he turned over his business into Joseph's hands, and as the years came and went, he confided in him the more, until the time came when his domestic affairs were entirely committed to this noble young Hebrew.

Eventually Potiphar's wife yielded to the carnality in her own heart, and made an awful assault on the beautiful, lovely and bright stripling, in whom her husband had unbounded confidence. When she had exhausted all her devices in the way of temptation, and signally failed, in desperation, her love turned to wrath, and she brought to her husband an evil report against Joseph. She had his confidence, her version of the story being unimpeached. Therefore he had Joseph cast into the imperial prison, where the offenders in the royal court were incarcerated. There seven dreary years rolled away, Joseph being tortured by vermin in the loathsome prison. Then two new prisoners were cast in, the chief butler and the chief baker of the king.

Ere long the former told Joseph he had dreamed a dream which was giving him deep trouble. Said he: "I saw in my slumber three vines grow up and bear fruit, luscious, bright, and exceedingly delicious. I had Pharaoh's golden cup in my hand, gathered the grapes, pressed out the wine, carried it to him, and he took it from my hand and drank it with avidity." Joseph responded: "The three vines are three days, on whose expiration Pharaoh will send and take you out of this prison, and restore to you your butlership again, so you will minister to him again as in former days."

The chief baker was encouraged by the felicity of the interpretation, so he proceeded to tell his dream. "I had on my head three willow baskets, containing the diversified sweet cakes I prepare for Pharaoh's table. The fowls of the air swept down and ate the bread out of the baskets on my head." Joseph proceeded with the interpretation: "The three baskets are three days, on whose expiration Pharaoh will send, take you out of this prison, hang you on a tree, and the vultures will eat your flesh off your bones."

Sure enough, when three days had elapsed, Pharaoh

sent, took out the chief baker, and hung him. At the same time taking out the chief butler, he restored him to his butlership again. On hearing the good news of his release and restoration, Joseph said to the chief butler, "When it goes well with you, remember me." But frail humanity, when all things go well, is prone to forget others in trouble. So Pharaoh had to dream dreams before Joseph could get out of that prison. He dreamed, and sent for the magicians, astrologers and soothsayers to interpret the dreams, but all of them got bewildered and signally broke down. The chief butler then spoke out and said, "O king, I confess my sins; please forgive my delinquency. There is a young Hebrew in the prison who is wonderfully shrewd in the interpretation of dreams, visions, and perplexing problems of every kind." Pharaoh said to his servants, "Bring him straight to me." They rushed to the prison, and washed, trimmed and dressed Joseph to stand before the king. Oh, the brilliant symbolism of our Savior's humiliation manifested in the case of Joseph's long and loathsome imprisonment!

Then arriving in the royal palace, Joseph stood before the king, who proceeded to tell him his dreams. "I stood on the bank of the Nile and saw seven wheatstalks grow up, rank and strong, and bear the biggest and heaviest heads I ever saw, ponderously drooping toward the earth. Then I saw seven more grow up, stunted, weak, dwarfed, blasted by the east wind, and their heads were nothing but chaff. They attacked the seven well-filled heads; ate them all up, and showed no change. Then I saw seven of the finest cattle on which my eyes ever rested come up out of the river and graze on the bank of the Nile, and seven stunted, dwarfed, staggering, ill-favored kine came up out of the river and ate up the seven fat, elephantine cattle, and showed no difference.''

Then said Joseph: ''The dream is double because it is certain. The seven fine cattle and the seven copious wheat-heads are seven years of bounty, in which the earth will teem with her fruits as never before known. These will be followed by seven years of famine, in which the crops will all fail and starvation will look man and beast in the face, and if we do not now take warning, and provide, we, with our herds and flocks, will pass from the earth. Now, Pharaoh, the thing to do is to proceed at once to garner the fruits of the earth, because the seven years of plenty are now on us, beginning this day. Therefore the king should appoint some wise man to look after this matter, and store the fruits, that none go to waste, and keep them, that we may have sustenance through the seven years of famine which will follow the seven years of plenty.''

Then said Pharaoh: ''Who is so wise as thyself, to whom the God of Heaven has given wisdom? Therefore I take you for this great work. All the land is before you. I alone will outrank you on the throne.'' Then he put a golden chain around Joseph's neck, a golden sceptre in his hand, had him ride in a golden chariot second only to his own, and had fifty men run before him shouting to all he met, ''Bow the knee, for the king cometh!'' Oh, what a brilliant symbolism of our Savior's second coming in His glory, to conquer and to reign forever!

Sure enough, the earth groaned beneath the exuberant crops. In Egypt they have four crops a year, therefore in the seven years there were twenty-eight crops. Joseph peregrinated the whole country, had capacious storehouses built, and gathered in the fruits of the earth, storing away the wheat and barley for the people in the panic, and sesame and millet for the animals, and also accumulating for the latter hay and forage inexhaustible.

The seven years have flown, and never did the ages know such a supply of sustenance on the earth for man and beast. Then the dearth set in; the crops blighted, withered and failed, but the Egyptians had an abundant supply on hand. The famine was in all the earth. The second year was moving along and the famine was sore in the land of Canaan, but the report had reached there that there was corn in Egypt. (This "corn" was wheat and barley, as they had none of our corn, which never was known until the discovery of America, when the discoverers found it here with the Indians.)

Then Jacob had his sons take the plain, old caravan road and go down into Egypt to buy food, each one taking the money to pay for his load. On arrival, Joseph recognized them at once, knowing every one of them though twenty-two years had elapsed since he had seen them. As he was a little boy of twelve years when they last saw him, and was now thirty-four and covered up with the royal robes, they had no dream of his identity, but just thought he was the king of Egypt. Though he knew their language, he did not use it, but spoke to them through an interpreter, asking them who they were, the name of their father, and how many sons he had; at the same time imputing to them evil intentions in coming to spy out the land and to make war on the Egyptians. Then he arrested Simeon, to hold him as a hostage in pledge of their fidelity till they would bring their little brother down to Egypt, as a confirmation of the introduction they had given him and of their veracity and integrity. They were awfully scared and talked among themselves, thinking he did not understand them, but he did. They had already told him they had a dead brother, and in their talk they trembled and cried and said to one another, "This is a righteous judgment God has sent on us for our maltreatment of our little brother, when we pulled off his coat and sold him to the Ishmaelites, and he cried so." Then Joseph had to turn his back, and finally he was crying so that he had to go away and wash the tears off his face. They wondered what was the matter with the king of Egypt that he was crying so.

He had his steward fill up their sacks and put the money in the mouth of the sacks. When they discovered this, it alarmed them and gave them much trouble, they thinking he was trying to raise a fuss with them. When they got home and the father found Simeon had been kept by the king as a hostage, he wept, and wailed: "Joseph is dead and gone, and now they have taken Simeon and I will never see him again. Thus I am deprived of my children."

Eventually they had eaten up the bread brought from Egypt, and starvation was staring them in the face. Then the father said, "You must go again to Egypt and buy bread for us." But they said, "It is not worth while for us to go unless we take Benjamin, for the king says we shall not see his face again without him." To this the father said, "You cannot take him. His brother is dead, and if you take him away he will never get back." Then Judah took the case, and proposed to give Jacob his two sons as a substitute for Benjamin. Finally the old man surrendered, and said, "Take him along, for we must have some bread."

When they arrived in Egypt, the king brought out Simeon with him, looking better than they had ever seen him before. He took Benjamin in his arms, and it astonished them much to see the king of Egypt cry over their little brother. When he gave them their dinners, he set them down in the order of their ages, which astonished them much, for they could not think the king of Egypt knew their ages and wondered how he was guessing so well. When he dished out their dinners, he put on Benjamin's plate five messes. Hence the Christian's maxim, "A Benjamin's mess," meaning a glorious, rousing blessing.

(s) Then Joseph spoke out and told them the secret. Hitherto he had not spoken in Hebrew, but in Coptic, and an interpreter had given it to them in Hebrew. Now he came out and talked to them in their own language, saying, "I am Joseph, whom you sold to the Ishmaelites." It was like a thunderbolt from a cloudless sky, scaring them almost to death. But he went around and kissed every one of them, begging them not to grieve and telling them he had nothing against them; that they did not do it, but God sent him before them to provide bread to keep them all from starving to death. What glorious symbolism again! Jesus says (John, 6th chapter), "I am the Bread of Life, having came down from Heaven."

They wept and shouted so that Pharaoh in his palace made inquiry as to what was the matter, and they said to him that Joseph's brothers had come and that they were all shouting together. Then Pharaoh said to send wagons and bring them all down into Egypt where there was plenty to eat. Therefore they all went back to Canaan accompanied by the wagons. On arrival, they told their father the wonderful news that Joseph was alive and was ruler over all the land of Egypt. That was an awful thing for them to have to tell, for it was a confession that they had been lying to him all those years, and had told the tale so often that they believed it themselves.

When they told their father, he fainted away under the shock, and did not believe it until he saw the train of wagons that had come to carry them all into Egypt. Then he said, "My son Joseph is yet alive; I will go down and see him before I die." (There were in all seventy-five souls, not as the English version has it, seventy.)

Jacob lived in Egypt seventeen years and died. Then Joseph sent his body, with a great funeral train.

all the way back to the land of Canaan, and buried him in the cave of Machpelah, at Hebron, with the holy family—Abraham and Sarah, Isaac and Rebecca, and Jacob's wife Leah, the sepulchre of Rachel being near Bethel.

Joseph reigned over Egypt sixty-one years, and died at the age of 110. On his dying bed, he called for the elders of Israel, prophesied their return to the land of Canaan, and obligated them to carry his body with them and bury it there. They remained in Egypt 154 years after the death of Joseph, but they had embalmed him and put him in a marble sarcophagus, i. e., a stone coffin, so when they went out of Egypt they took him with them. It was a great procession, 200,000 people following the coffin. History says that Joseph, in his coffin, on a wagon drawn by twelve oxen (as that big stone coffin was so heavy, it took that many), led that procession, under cloud by day and fiery pillar by night, and through the sea, for forty years through the wilderness, and finally through the Jordan into the land of Canaan. There he was buried in the portion of his elder son Ephraim, and within five hundred yards of Jacob's well in the valley of Succoth, at the base of Mt. Ebal. I stood by his tomb in the present tour as well as repeatedly in my former journeys. I have seen many people who were embalmed in Egypt long before Joseph was and who are now in a perfect state of preservation, looking natural. If Joseph's coffin was opened, there is no doubt but that you would see him there mummyized and preserved to this day.

The reason for having so extensively written up this sketch of Joseph is because he is the paragon for us all, and especially the youth, as his whole life was without a blot, he having been happily converted in his childhood, which is God's time, before the forfeiture of infantile justification. This was the happy lot of your humble servant, gloriously converted in my mother's lap before she took the baby clothes off of me. I remember it as well as the events of yesterday. My grandfather, for whom I was named, had come to see us, bringing me a dress which my mother made girl fashion. I had it on when she took me on her lap and told me wonderful things about the kingdom of God, the resurrection of the dead and the Judgment Day. I was then and there converted and called to preach. That call never ceased to ring in my ears. I began to preach at the age of twenty, fifty-eight years ago. I expect soon to exchange the silver trumpet for the golden harp.

(t) Throughout the catacombs of Egypt we see a vast world of hieroglyphic writings, the first on the earth. If the ante-diluvians had anything after the order of literature, it must have perished in the flood. The Book of Job is the oldest in the world, having been written nine years before the departure of Israel out of Egypt. The Pentateuch of Moses was written by him 3,578 years ago. I have seen it a number of times and had it in my hands in the Samaritan convent in Shechem. But these hieroglyphics, which are not letters, but pictures, are the first writing in all the world. The ancient Egyptians certainly had indefatigable patience and perseverance. In all your travels in Egypt, especially in the catacombs and the museum of antiquities, you will be much interested by these hieroglyphics.

While Egypt was the first country to stand at the front of the world and lead the way in the arts and sciences, Phœnicia was her immediate successor, and, availing themselves of the Egyptian hieroglyphics, they proceeded to invent the alphabet, and thus launched the world-wide book learning, which is now, like the sands of the sea, enveloping every shore.

(u) We now visited the citadel, from whose heights we enjoyed a conspicuous view of the great city of Cairo with her 800,000 people, and of the Moslem minarets towering like a forest on all sides. (There are said to be four hundred of them.) The great mosque standing on the citadel, built by Saladin, the world's conqueror nine hundred years ago, is one of the finest buildings on the earth, being 400 feet high and constructed of marble, much of it alabaster.

The University in Cairo has ten thousand students preparing to go to the ends of the earth and preach the religion of the False Prophet and the Koran. They are exceedingly aggressive in the wilds of Africa, and have the greatest antagonism to the evangelization of the Dark Continent.

We saw the Mameluke's Leap, where the only survivor out of that illustrious cohort of 487 soldiers escaped by leaping his horse over the iron banister and down a precipice of 160 feet, the noble animal losing his life, but the Mameluke escaping. Originally the Mamelukes were simply the king's body-guard, but eventually they began to encroach upon the royal prerogative, manipulating the administration and really eclipsing the king. Then he decoyed them into the citadel, that he might compliment them with a royal festival, at the same time clandestinely making all arrangements to shut them up and kill them all. This took place one hundred years ago, so we happened to make our visit on the first anniversary of that notable catastrophe, in which that grand army that ruled the country all perished but a solitary survivor. So that was the last of the Mamelukes, who had ruled the country for generations and centuries.

While we were in London, they celebrated the third centennial of the King James' Translation of the Bible. While that translation was a sunburst on the world three hundred years ago, and has been wonderfully blessed in its world-wide circulation, we should beware of the superstition that looks upon it as the infallible word of God. For that we must go to the original Hebrew and Greek. As there was so little learning in the world three hundred years ago, many errors appear in the translation, which are now corrected. Therefore we should not let superstition and prejudice paralyze our efforts to ascertain the true word of God appertaining to everything. We often hear people say: "The King James' translation was good enough for our fathers and mothers, and it's good enough for us." N. B. We cannot be saved in the light of our fathers and mothers, from the simple fact that God has given us light which they did not have. For example my preacher father and shouting Methodist mother both used tobacco and ordered me to do the same, pursuant to the advice of our foolish neighbors, who said, "Make that little runt chew tobacco and it will start him to growing.". It broke my heart to disobey them, as my baby conversion and early competency to read the Bible, "Children, obey your parents," filled me with anxiety to obey them in everything. I am glad now I disobeyed them in that order. Suppose I would walk in the light of my sainted parents, I would use tobacco. Do you not know the devil would get me? Did he get them? No! They went to Heaven with a shout, because they walked in all the light they had. If I am ever to meet them there, I must do the same. God, in His mercy, put us all meek and lowly at His feet, where, like little Samuel, we say, "Speak, Lord; Thy servant heareth." God's trinity of graces—faith, hope and love—have their antithesis in Satan's kingdom, i. e., sin, ignorance and superstition. Be sure you are filled with the former and gloriously free from the latter, remembering that you cannot be justified unless you walk in all the light God gives you. We have brighter and more copious light than any preceding generation.

Nearly all the soul-destroying heresies in the world are founded on the errors of the King James' translation. Lord, make us like the Bereans, searching the Scriptures day and night, to see if these things are so.

(v) On the citadel we saw Joseph's well, which he dug for his father Jacob, who spent life's evening of seventeen years in Egypt. It is 280 feet deep, and

16 feet square at the top, gradually contracting so that it can never cave in. It is never dry.

From the citadel we went to old Cairo and again prayed in the Coptic church, where they certify that Mary and Joseph did abide with the infant Jesus, a month, till the angel notified them to return to Nazareth. It is now used as a church memorial of our Savior's infantile sojourn in Egypt.

Our guide also took us to the place on the river bank where they certify Moses was found by Pharaoh's daughter.

We then boarded the train for Port Said, where we took steamer for the Holy Land. We traveled along the old caravan route from Palestine down into Egypt, along which Abraham, Isaac, Jacob, Joseph and the patriarchs traveled on camels and donkeys, and as pedestrians, so frequently. At Ismailia, we encountered the Suez Canal, where our train turned north and ran on the bank to our destination. The iron horse has very largely superseded the camel caravans in that country, which through by-gone generations and ages were the constant and universal means of transportation through the great East.

The Suez Canal is the greatest enterprise of modern times. Begun forty-seven years ago and twenty-five years in building, it is 100 miles long, 100 yards wide, and 40 feet deep, elegantly walled up with solid masonry, and cost $100,000,000. It was built by the united nations of Europe, Britain leading the way and subsequently buying out most of the balance, till she now mainly owns it and fully controls it. It abbreviates the distance to India and the great Orient one-half. As they can have no competition, the tonnage of ship transportation through the Canal is very costly.

Port Said is the daughter of the Canal, born when it was begun, and it has grown one thousand in population every year, giving it to-day forth-seven thousand inhabitants. It is a young, beautiful and growing city, and has a vast amount of shipping

CHAPTER II.

THE HOLY LAND.

As Joppa has no harbor, and her landing is dangerous when the sea is rough, on arrival we had quite an ordeal, our ship sailing round and round in a great circle out where the water is deep, but in full view of the city, for thirty-six hours, waiting on the Lord to calm the sea so we could land. As we had on board 450 pilgrims for Jerusalem and much cargo, she could not afford to sail by, especially as she had already sailed by en route for Port Said, and returned, only to find the sea still too rough for that dangerous landing. Never can we forget those thirty-six hours, round and round in a circle waiting for the sea to calm; meanwhile almost every one on board suffering awfully with seasickness, including all of my party but myself.

On disembarkation, we went at once to the house of "Simon the tanner, by the seaside," where Peter was praying when the messengers sent from Cæsarea by Cornelius arrived. God had already felicitously prepared him by the descending sheet, containing an infinite diversity of animals, and a voice ringing out, "Arise, Peter; slay and eat." He responded, "Not so, Lord, as nothing unclean has ever gone into my mouth." God having repeated the vision three times, simultudinously to the trinity of races, red, black and white, supervenient in the house of Noah (accommodatory to the different climates of the earth—black for the tropical, red for semi-tropical and frigid, and white for the temperate zones), said to Peter, "What God hath cleansed, call thou not polluted nor unclean," finally taking them all up to Heaven again. Thus He knocked off Peter's hard shell and made him a glorious, free-grace Holiness evangelist.

When Peter heard Cornelius' servants knocking at the gate and calling his name, the Holy Ghost said to him, "Go down, doubting nothing, for I have sent them." Having lodged them, the next morning they all started off on foot, accompanied by six brethren from Joppa. Arriving the ensuing day, they found an appreciative audience waiting in the house of Cornelius. Peter preached and Jesus baptized this devout Gentile and his godly people with the Holy Ghost and fire, thus throwing open the Gospel church to the Gentile world, and administering to them water baptism, symbolizing the only baptism known in the plan of salvation, which they had already received.

As we were a little pressed for time, we did not visit the tomb of Dorcas, whom Peter raised from the dead, my comrades being satisfied with a grand view of the Russian church, conspicuous from the depot. However, I visited the tomb in 1905.

Joppa is down on the sea level, surrounded by the

rich plain of Sharon, and then, as well as all the Holy Land, was gloriously beautified by the roses of Sharon, which constantly saluted our vision during our entire sojourn of April and May. The gardens of Joppa are splendid; it just looks like a world of orange orchards, then red, ripe and beautiful, sweet, juicy and delicious. I never found an exception though we had oranges constantly on the table. Truly no country on earth has fruits equaling those of Canaan.

My dragoman pointed out for me a house in Joppa in which two American missionaries were murdered in 1852. He said that when the news reached America the Government at once sent a warship to Joppa. On arrival, casting anchor, the captain sent for the governor to come aboard, then he demanded of him the murderers of our missionaries. He unequivocally denied knowing anything about it. Then the captain said he would give him forty-eight hours to bring him those murderers, and in case of delinquency, he would bombard the city. Two hours before the expiration of the time, the governor came aboard the ship with the murderers. The captain hung them to the bars of the ship till they were dead, tied rocks to them, dropped them down into the sea, raised anchor and sailed away. There we have an illustration of the manner in which we have to deal with Mohammedans.

In our run to Jerusalem, we passed over the great plain of Sharon, the Philistine country. They were one of the strongest nations in all of the land of Canaan, so brave that Israel never did succeed in conquering them. They were not properly a kingdom, but five principalities united for mutual security, each one ruled by its own lord; Ekron, Askelon, Gath, Gaza and Ashdod being the metropolitan cities.

This gigantic, formidable nation survived until Nebuchadnezzar carried Israel into captivity, B. C. 587, when he also carried off the Philistines, and we never afterward hear of them. Of course they were dispersed throughout the world-wide Chaldean Empire. Whereas God raised up Cyrus, the Medo-Persian, to emancipate the Jews, restoring them to their own land, the Philistines met no such fortune, and consequently never got back to trouble Israel any more.

In our run, we soon passed, on the right, on an eminence to which our dragoman called our attention, the site of the House of Dagon, where Samson wrought his last miracle, throwing over the great palace with its thousands of travelers celebrating the honors of Dagon, and smashing it all into smithereens, thus suddenly sweeping them all into eternity, he himself suffering amid the crushing ruin, and thus slaying more in his death than in his life.

As these were the magnates of the Philistine kingdom, their overthrow by Samson illustrates the consolatory assurance which is given us by his name being in the faith roll in Hebrews, 11th chapter. Though, seduced by the charming Delilah, Samson grieved away the Holy Ghost, losing his experience, God, in great mercy, gave it back to him in the article of death.

On the right we also looked out over Yazoo, where Samson caught the three hundred foxes, attaching firebrands to their tails and turning them loose to seek their hiding in the dense, ripe harvest-fields, so setting them on fire till they burned like an ocean of flame, thus bankrupting the Philistines.

On the left we saw Lydda, where Peter healed Æneas of an eight years paralysis, so that he arose and carried away his bed. It was to Lydda that the saints of Joppa sent for Peter to come and raise Dorcas from the dead. We also, on the left, recognized the city of Zorah on a distant height. It was the birthplace, home and tomb of Samson. Our dragoman also pointed out to us the way down to Timnath, whither Samson went on his first expedition against the Philistines. It was on this road that the lion roared against him, and he taking him up crushed in his ribs as though he had been a kid, and slew him. On his return, recognizing the carcass of the monster, he found it full of the most delicious fresh honey, a swarm of bees having improvised it for their hive. Taking out the honey, he went on home eating it voraciously and carrying a fine lot to the family and friends. This is beautifully confirmatory of the consolatory fact that when we slay old Adam we will be happily surprised to find him full of honey to sweeten our own souls and lives, and to so supply us that we can sweeten our friends and loved ones to the astonishment of all.

On the left our guide also pointed out the valley of Sorek, so lovely and shining, where had dwelt the beautiful Delilah, whom the Philistines used to ruin Samson. O preachers, beware! When Satan loads his gun to shoot at you, far better were it that he fill it up with sixty-four-pound cannon balls and blow you into smithereens, than to load it with women.

We also recognized, off to the north, the battlefield of Beth-horon, where Joshua commanded the sun to stand still over Gibeon and the moon over the valley of Aijalon (also in full view), till he could wind up his battle against the thirty-one kings (representing all south Canaan) who all lost their heads. Also on the left we saw the geat cave Etam, high up on the precipitous mountain, where Samson fortified himself against the Philistines, and rested.

On the right, we then came to Lehi, Samson's battlefield where he slew a thousand Philistine giants, all armed with swords, spears and battle-axes, he himself having only the jaw-bone of a donkey, with which he beat them hip and thigh and heaped the plain with mountains of the dead.

We also had in full view the battlefield of Elah, where King Saul was waging war with the Philistines when Jesse sent David from Bethlehem to call on his brothers Eliab, and Abinadab, and Shammah, in Saul's army, to bear them some love tokens and to take their pledge, i. e., hold a class-meeting with them and see whether they were backslidden. David arrived about nine in the morning, just in time to see them all going out to put the battle in array. Then his attention was arrested by a huge giant covered all over with a steel panoply, which rendered him invulnerable to sword, spear and battle-axe, so that, as they had no firearms then, he could stand amid strokes and whizzing arrows, and with his great sword and spear just cut down his enemies on all sides. David saw the giant walk out with the tread of a conqueror, and cry aloud, "Why do you not send me a man to wind up this war in a hand-to-hand combat, without all this effusion of blood?" Meanwhile he defied them and lampooned their cowardice, cursing them in the name of the Philistine gods and blaspheming the God of Israel. No one moved a foot or said a word. David was astonished at their reticence and said to his brothers, "Why does not some one accept this challenge?" They responded, "A hand-to-hand combat with that giant means certain death. He is so large and stout we are but grasshoppers in his presence." David responded, "Brethren, some one must accept this challenge and take away the reproach of Israel. We cannot afford to let this uncircumcised Philistine run over us rough-shod and thus defy the army of the living God. If no one else takes him up, I will." Then his elder brothers scolded, "Go back to those few sheep you have left on the hills of Bethlehem. Surely you have just come out here from vanity to see the battle."

But a by-stander ran and told King Saul, "There is a lad out here ready to fight the giant for you." Saul responds, "Bring him at once; anything for a fight, to take away our reproach." Therefore they at once led David to him. The king says, "My little lad, they tell me you are willing to fight the giant." "Oh, yes, if you can do no better." Then Saul observes, "You are but a stripling, and he a mature man of war with a very ripe experience in all sorts of contests." Then David says, "The God of Israel, who delivered into my hands a great lion when he came to feed of my flock, and on anothtr occasion a monster bear, will also deliver to me this giant. Just as I caught up the lion and the bear and crushed them as I would a kid, so God will attend to this uncircumcised Philistine."

Then Saul, as David was unarmed, put his armor on him, as it was the best in Israel, but it was so large as to be unwieldy. Consequently David took it off and went unarmed to meet the giant. When the giant saw David had neither sword, spear nor battle-axe, he thought he had come out to mock him. Though David had his haversack, in which he carried out his dinner to eat while serving his flock, and a sling in which to throw rocks to protect his flock, the giant at his distance did not see them, and thought he was entirely unarmed. So he denounced him as a fool, saying, "I will feed you to the dogs this day."

As David crossed the brook, he picked up a few smooth stones and put them in his haversack. When a long way off, entirely out of reach of the giant's sword, spear or battle-axe, he took out a stone from his haversack, fit it in his sling and whirled it round his head with great rapidity, till it had accumulated lightning momentum; then he let it fly, aiming at the giant's eyebrow, where his helmet stopped in order to give him vision. Whiz! it went, struck him just below his helmet, entered the eye-socket, and darted up into his brain. Therefore he suddenly fell prostrate, with tremendous clangor of resounding arms, Then David ran, took his sword, cut off his head, put it on the spear, and came back waving it high. Meanwhile the Philistine army all skedaddled every one to his own home, dispersing among the five provinces of Philistia—Ekron, Ashdod, Gath, Gaza and Askelon —thus winding up the war with Israel victorious.

(w) We had passed over the plain of Sharon, and the iron horse was toiling hard, climbing great Mt. Zion, forty miles from base to summit, and now we were ascending the foothills. We passed Arimathea (Acts 28) where Joseph and Nicodemus, the buriers of our Savior, lived. This city, though during the ages of desolation it went to ruin, has been colonized by the Jews and is very flourishing, containing about 10,000 inhabitants.

We also, off to the right, passed Beth-shemesh in Judah, where the Philistines first sent the ark after they had captured it in battle at Mizpah and kept it several years. It had caused Dagon their god to fall down before it in the temple, and when they set him in his place the next morning he was found fallen down again and his hands cut off. The people also were terribly plagued with emerods, a most painful and loathsome disease, while the country was awfully infested with rats and mice, which ate up their substance and brought starvation on them. Therefore, having determined to take the ark away, they made a new cart to carry it, and hitched two unbroken, new cows to it, their calves being shut up during their absence. The sign was that if the cows spontaneously carried it back to Israel, they knew that they were right in sending it. So they hitched the cows to the cart, and immediately they set out, bellowing aloud, and carried it to Beth-shemesh, the nearest city of Israel. There many people dropped dead by inadvertently looking in the ark, so they soon took it away to Kirjath-jearim, in Benjamin, to the house of Abinadab, who consecrated one of his sons to take care of it. It stayed in his house twenty years, till David built the tabernacle on Mt. Zion in Jerusalem. Then he went down after it with his army, and appointed Uzzah and Ahio to take care of it. When the oxen stumbled and jostled it, Uzzah laid hold of it, and dropped dead. This so alarmed David that he gave up taking it to Jerusalem at that time, and turning aside, he put it into the house of Obed-edom, where it stayed three months, and meanwhile God wonderfully blessed that home. At the end of the three months, David went down with his army in grand parade, took it away and deposited it in his tabernacle, where it stayed until Solomon built the temple. There it was deposited in the sanctum sanctorum.

Kirjath-jearim was also off on the right as we made the run to Jerusalem.

While climbing great Mt. Zion, we came to a ruined city dell, which, in the palmy days of Israel, was a powerful fortification. Its name is Bethar. The Romans, when pushing their conquests over that country as well as all the world, besieged it three and a half years, and destroyed it, killing fourteen thousand men, whose blood flowed all the way to the sea, forty miles.

Now we ascended the great mountains of Judah and Benjamin, till the towers of Jerusalem burst upon our view. The highest of all these towers is the Russian, on Mt. Olivet, across the valley of Jehoshaphat, east of Jerusalem, and the highest mountain in all Palestine. This stone tower is 275 feet high, and, approaching Jerusalem from all directions, it can be seen a long way off. When one first arrives in Jerusalem, it is a good plan to climb some of these towers, from whose apex can be had a view not only of the city but of all the surrounding country. Many of the towers give a splendid view, but as the Russian is the highest of all, the better plan is to go thither at once, take your time and study the situation. Assisted by maps, as all travelers are, you get it located in your mind, which will prove a powerful auxiliary in your understanding the diversified locations. As Jerusalem is literally filled up with sights of great historic interest, if you are not careful, you will make the mistake of exploring it too superficially, in order to economize time. I have been there four times abiding ten, eleven and twelve days during every tour. There are many auxiliaries of which you can avail yourself after you get there, constantly remembering the admonition of James, "Let patience have her perfect work."

(x) Jerusalem means the "possession of peace," i. e., peace with God and all mankind. That name has been badly contradicted in all ages, as no other city on the earth has ever had so much war. This arises from the fact that it is evidently understood to be the city of God. Satan is the god of this age (not as the English version has it, "this world"). The time is coming when Satan's age will have expired; the Apocalyptic angel will descend and arrest him, and lock him up in Hell that he may deceive the nations no more. Then the glorious millennial age will set in.

As we are now living in Satan's age, he plays God on the people, deceiving them by millions so that they actually worship him for God. During these Satanic ages all nations have always fought Jerusalem. All the kings of the earth have done their best to blot it out, as it is the city of God and a constant rebuke to them. For this reason Jerusalem has been besieged seventeen times and destroyed seven times.

Now-a-days all cities are built in the most accessible places. Not so in the olden times, but the very opposite. As all nations were belligerent, they founded their cities hard by some great, precipitous mountain, which they could climb when the enemy came and defend themselves. As they had no firearms in those days, having the advantage in situation, they could roll down great rocks on the enemy and a few people could actually defend themselves against an army.

Jerusalem has the great valley of Hinnom on the west, impassable to an invading army. That of Jehoshaphat on the east, still more impassable, which coiling around Mt. Moriah and assuming a southwestwardly trend, moves on until it intersects the Valley of Hinnon at Enrogel, where Adonijah held his barbecues in order to capture the heart of the people when his father David was about to die, so they would crown him king.

People generally think the city of David and Jerusalem synonymous. This is a mistake; the city of David constitutes that promontory projecting out from the summit of Zion, between Hinnom and Jehoshaphat, in the shape of a smoothing-iron, its back toward the north. This point is fortified by nature, and they built a great wall on the summit of the mountains and also across the mountain in the rear; consequently Joshua never succeeded in taking it during all his seventeen years war. The Jebusites held it till the days of David—five hundred years—and believed it to be impregnable. But when, after Rechab and Baanah decapitated Ishbosheth, the son of Saul and king of Israel, the ten tribes met at Jerusalem and crowned David king, his first enterprise was the capture of this citadel. When he began to talk about it (as you will read in the Bible), the Jebusites made all manner of fun of him, as they did not believe it could be taken, defiantly remarking that he would have to take away the blind and the lame before he could ever capture it, thus insinuating that it was so strong that even the blind and the lame could hold it against any force David could send against it.

Then David turned a stratagem on them, offering the chief captaincy of his host to the man first to "get up to the gutter." Joab, the son of Zeruiah, along with his brothers, Abishai and Asahel, was the first one to accept David's offer. Throwing a rope over his shoulders to help others, he climbed up the wall like a squirrel, fastened it, and by its help others followed, entered the citadel and took it. David added it to Jerusalem, but it was ever afterwards called the "city of David."

Then David, true to his contract, gave Joab the chief captaincy of the host. Though not such a man as Napoleon Bonaparte, yet his inordinate ambition led him to shed innocent blood. He slew Abner, the captain of the host of Israel, and Amasa, the captain of the host of Judah, in cold blood. For this double murder David condemned him to die, yet he never executed him; not only did he let him live, but he let him command the army all his life. Yet when he anointed Solomon in his succession, he charged him to execute Joab, because he had, in two different instances, shed the blood of war in time of peace. David knew that God would send awful judgments on Israel in case he did not avenge that innocent blood. Therefore, when David died, Joab ran to the temple and laid hold of the horns of the altar, the last resort of a Hebrew in peril of his life. They told Solomon. He said he understood it, but could not do anything; therefore he had them bring him away and execute him.

If you would go to Jerusalem, they would tell you it stood on four mountains: Zion, the highest of all, in the southwest; Moriah, in the southeast, separated from Zion by the Tyrophœan valley; Bezetha, in the northeast, and Akra, in the northwest. Mt. Calvary is entirely without the city.

The Holy Land.

Fifty years ago there was not a single house outside the walls of the city, now the city without is much the larger. It is very beautiful, and nearly all built by Jews returning to their native land. The city is entered by eight gates, the Joppa Gate leading through the west wall near the northwest corner. The New Gate is the first one leading through the north wall as you go east, so called because it has recently been built by the Latin Christians, who erected a great convent there and needed it for their own convenience. Now we proceed eastwardly, a little beyond the middle of the north wall, and reach the Damascus Gate, through which the road to Damascus goes out. Soon we pass Solomon's quarries, which we enter through a gate under the wall from the north, finding ourselves in a great room under the mountain whence Solomon took the great and valuable stones to build the temple and the royal palaces, as under the ground they are soft and easily cut, but soon get very hard after they are exposed to the atmosphere. Passing on, we come to Herod's Gate, leading through the north wall. Going on, passing the corner and turning your face towards the south, you come to the Lion Gate, which you will recognize by the engraving of a large lion on either side of it. In the apostolic age it was called the Sheep Gate, because the great sheep market was near it; and since Stephen was stoned to death near that gate, through which they led him out, it is also called Stephen's Gate. Another gate also leads through the east wall, called the Beautiful Gate (Acts, 4th chap.), where Peter and John healed the cripple.

When the Mohammedans took the city, A. D. 634, some of their prophets predicted that the Moslem power would fall the moment that gate is opened, consequently it has never been opened since then.

The Mohammedans bury their dead on Mt. Zion and Mt. Calvary; the Jews, on Mt. Olivet; the Christians, on Mt. Zion. I saw very venerable tombs close up to this gate on the outside, that has not been opened during these long ages.

Following the east wall to the corner on Mt. Moriah, we turn our faces to the west and pursue the south wall of the city till we come to the Excrement Gate, called by this name as through it they carry out the offal of the city and cast it into the valley of Jehoshaphat. It is also called the Water Gate, because Jerusalem is above the water line, too high to dig wells —if you dig you will not get water—and so, during the summer (March 15 to November 15), when little or no rain falls and water gets very scarce, they go down through this gate into the valley of Jehoshaphat and get water from St. Mary's well and John's well, which never go dry.

Continuing our journey westward along the south wall, we come to David's Gate, on the summit of Mt. Zion, on the line between Jerusalem and the city of David.

When I first visited that country, sixteen years ago, there were no carriage roads except from Jerusalem to Bethlehem and Hebron. I went horseback. Five years afterward, in my tour I did the same thing, with the exception of the route from Jerusalem to

Jericho, the Jordan and the Dead Sea; thither we had a carriage road. Since that they have built them extensively over the country, and a new railroad from Haiffa on the Mediterranean to Damascus, so this time we did all our traveling by carriages and train.

(y) In our run across the wilderness of Judæa eastward to the Jordan, we were on the track of David when he fled from his son Absalom, who had so manipulated as to steal the hearts of the people, meeting them at the gates, kissing them and flattering them. The Bible pronounces him the most handsome man in the nation, but he had the misfortune to find it out. It made him proud as a coxcomb and vain as a coquette, he even wearing his hair long like a woman because it was jet black and exceedingly copious. It finally proved his ruin, actually hanging him fast in those oak limbs which caught it when his hard-mouthed mule, terrified amid the battle, stampeded under that densely tangled and limby oak.

David loved Absalom so that he was blind to his vanities and follies, which should have been his deep distress. He actually had fifty men run before him when he rode out in his carriage, and still it never aroused the apprehension of his father to recognize his Napoleonic ambition. Having laid all the plot to usurp the kingdom, and sent men into all parts of the country with trumpets to blow on a certain day, and to shout, "Absalom reigns in Hebron!" he simply went to his father and asked permission, on the appointed day, to go to Hebron to offer sacrifice, observing that it was a fulfilment of his vow to God. Therefore it worked like a charm. Before David had the slightest suspicion, he heard the trumpets blowing in Jerusalem and the people shouting, "Absalom reigns in Hebron!" Thus the insurrection broke out the same hour in all parts of the kingdom. David could only run for his life, so he took his flight eastward to the wilderness, having left the palace in the hands of the servant women. In his flight Hushai met him, anxious to help him any way he could; opportunely, because his grand old counsellor, Ahithophel, had gone with Absalom. David says to Hushai, "You go on, meet Absalom, and defeat the counsel of Ahithophel."

Sure enough, Absalom came from Hebron accompanied by a great host. Jerusalem was full of people shouting, "Long live King Absalom!" On arrival he took possession of the royal palace in a very pompous, demonstrative and carnal way, especially in his deportment toward the women whom David had left in charge of the palace. Then he and his followers held their council as to the tactics they should pursue. Ahithophel, to whom all were looking, as he was a father among them, delivered his counsel, urging them to hasten at once, before David had a chance to form an army, and bring all matters to an issue, settling affairs in the hands of Absalom. Taking his seat, he left the door open for others to give counsel. Hushai was clamored for. He rose, and begged leave to differ from the senior brother, Ahithophel. He observed that the men with David were all valiant and would fight like a bear robbed of her whelps, saying to Absalom, "Your father also is a valiant man," which

Absalom very well knew. "Besides," he said, "if you go now you will not get David at all, for he is off in a cave. You will meet a few men that will fight so valiantly that they will whip these raw recruits, produce a panic, and bring about a reaction utterly detrimental to the cause of Absalom." Says he, "I am for waiting till we rendezvous a great army and settle the matter at once, so that if any man deserts we will tie ropes around his house and drag it into the sea. And I suggest that Absalom in person shall lead this army."

They all said the counsel of Hushai was better than that of Ahithophel. Then the old man, brokenhearted, saddled his donkey, went home, and hung himself.

This delay gave David and his people time to cross the Jordan and fortify themselves, so they were in good shape when Absalom came around with his great host of undisciplined men. The result was their signal defeat and universal confusion among the dense oak trees. These trees had limbs thick and tough down to the ground, eminently fitted to tangle them up and produce incorrigible confusion and consternation.

In the heterogeneous bewilderment, Absalom's mule becomes unmanageable, stampedes under the entangled limbs, catches his head with its great mass of hair, and runs away leaving him hanging. Then men tell Joab about him, and he says, "Why did not you shoot him?" "Oh," says one, "I heard his father, when we started out, say to spare his son Absalom." But Joab rushed at once and dispatches him, then blows a trumpet telling all the people the war is over. And so Absalom's kingdom evanesced in its birth. But David almost died of grief, weeping and wailing, "Would to God I had died for thee, O Absalom, my son!"

When you visit Jerusalem you will see Absalom's pillar standing in the king's dale on the eastern slope of Mt. Olivet, in the valley of Jehoshaphat. They cast his body into a sink hole and threw a great heap of stones on it, this being his improvised sepulchre. Oh, what a warning to all young people! Who ever had such an opportunity as Absalom? Native beauty in the superlative degree, royal blood flowing in his veins; aye, everything heart could wish appertaining to this world. Yet dying such an untimely death in the bloom of his youth, with his soul crimsoned with the blood of his brother Ammon, and going into eternity a guilty patricide, as his own coronation meant the death of his father.

From Jerusalem to Jericho is down the great mountains all the way, as the former is 2,700 feet above the Mediterranean and the Dead Sea 1,300 feet below. The Dead Sea is the lowest spot on the globe, and 4,000 feet below Jerusalem. It is 47 miles long, 10 miles wide, and 1,000 feet deep. In the palmy days of Sodom and Gomorrah, Admah, Zeboim and Zoar, in the days of Lot, all that region in the fertile vale of Siddim was well watered. But the destruction of those wicked cities wrought a radical revolution in the physical condition of that whole country, turning it into a desert from which God has withheld the rains, and it has been without inhabitants, except as the wandering Bedouin pitches his tent for a day or two, and then goes on.

Ezekiel 42:12 gives a great light and hope on the forlorn condition of the desert region of the Dead Sea. That holy river flowing out on the right-hand side of the altar in the temple, and proceeding eastward, transforms the desert into fruitful fields and smiling gardens, till it reaches the Dead Sea; then it redeems the waters till they become sweet and delicious and swarm with fishes of every kind, while populous cities and thriving towns and villages spring up on every shore, and the entire vale of Siddim is transformed into an earthly paradise, as in the days of yore. At present no fish nor any animal can live in the Dead Sea; multitudes of fishes float down the Jordan into the sea, but they all die. Even birds flying in the air over the waters share the same fate. It is the awful curse sent on Sodom and Gomorrah still lingering till the arrest of Satan and the ushering in of the Millennium.

On the east coast, in full view of the shore, where visitors always dismount in order to look at the sea, you will find the ruined Macherus, King Herod's palace, where John the Baptist was imprisoned through the sympathy of the king, who "heard him gladly" and "did many things" responsively to John's faithful preaching, reforming his life so that many said he had turned a holiness man. When John boldly denounced the unlawful wedlock of the king and queen, Herod got convicted, but the queen got awfully mad, so the king had to shut up John in the prison to keep her from killing him through a hired assassin. Then when the daughter of Herodias captured him and all his magnates by her pantomimic solos, during Herod's birthday festivals, he promised her with an oath that he would grant her request even unto the half of his kingdom, not dreaming that the little, flirtatious girl would want the head of God's prophet. But she, in her bewilderment, went away to her mother, who leaped on the opportunity to execute vengeance on the preacher who had murdered her pride. Herod could not go back on his word without losing his own head, as the officers of his kingdom would have deposed him and, in all probability, have decapitated, so he sent and had John slain.

In Samaria they show the tomb of John in his great memorial church built by the Crusaders nine hundred years ago. The prophets Elisha and Obadiah lie side by side with him.

Now his head was gone so his disciples could not bury it, but they buried the headless body with great mourning, after the Jewish manner.

If you ever visit Damascus, you will see the tomb containing the head of John the Baptist in Mosque Rimmon, the largest in the world. How do you know the head is there? I only have the Mohammedans' ipse dixit. Of course Queen Herodias had the head and what she did with it we know not. The people of Damascus claim to have received it and to have buried it there.

(z) We visited the Jordan ford ten miles above

his influx into the Dead Sea. We call it the "ford" because Israel forded it there when God divided the swelling flood, but without this miracle it was no ford, but very wide and deep. In our journeys to the Holy Land, we always go to this ford commemoratively of God's stupendous miracle of dividing it and letting the Israelites go through dry shod.

Six miles west of the ford we reach Gilgal, the Israelites' first encampment in the land of Canaan, so named because Joshua there circumcised them all, saying, "I have rolled away from you your reproach, giving you God's mark." Here Joshua met the Lord, while waiting in prayer and prolonging the camp-meeting till the convalescence of the circumcised. An inferior general, in this campaign, would have attacked the weaker points whereas the wise always take the strongest points first in all the enterprises of this world.

God had promised Joshua (Joshua, chapter 1) that if he would only be very courageous no man would be able to stand against him all the days of his life; and Joshua had promised God that he would never turn back from any man as long as he lived. So now as he is walking in the moonlight, contemplating the towering walls of Jericho and soliloquizing fervent prayers in the deep interior of his heart, he sees a man standing with uplifted sword. Supposing him to be one of the giants come out to engage with him in hand-to-hand combat, he salutes him, "Who art thou? give an account of thyself." He responds, "I am the captain of the hosts of Israel." Then Joshua knows He is the Lord. He says to Joshua, "Take off thy shoes, for thy feet are standing on holy ground," then proceeds to give him His orders for Jericho. He commands him to march his army around it, blowing the rams' horns, and then to go back in their tents, neither shooting an arrow nor striking the walls with a battering-ram. This they were to do six days, and on the seventh, going out early in the morning, they were to march around it seven times, blowing the rams' horns. Then all of Israel were to shout aloud and He, the Lord, would knock down the walls. History says they uttered with stentorian voice, "Our God is mighty in battle!" and that while they were thus shouting the walls fell down flat, and they **passed over and took** the spoils for the Lord alone.

Meanwhile they spared the family of Rahab, the tavern-keeper, not as the English version says, "harlot." The Hebrew word "zona," translated harlot, primarily means a female tavern-keeper. This is corroborated by the fact that those godly men Joshua sent over stopped at her house. Again, it is a historic fact that she entered into wedlock with an Israelitish man by the name of Salmon. God gave them a son Boaz, who became the husband of Ruth the Moabitess. Tamar, the daughter-in-law of Judah, a Gentile, was also one of the mothers of our Lord, as you will see in the genealogies. These three Gentile mothers of Jesus encourage us from the fact that He was not a full-blooded Jew, but was really akin to all the Gentiles.

At Gilgal Saul stopped when he returned from his campaign against the Amalekites. Amalek had fought Israel forty years in the wilderness to keep them out of the land of Canaan. As that was the symbolic dispensation, it was important that they should all be destroyed and everything they had, in order to perfect and verify the symbolism. If we do not destroy everything that ever did fight against our sanctification, we will lose our experiences and finally break down. Therefore, to verify the symbolism, it was pertinent that Saul, in his royal capacity, representing all Israel, should go and utterly exterminate the Amalekites and everything they had. But he yielded to temptation, sparing the best of the herds for sacrifices and old Agag, their king, who symbolizes old Adam. When Samuel came along to Gilgal and saw these things, Saul told him he had fulfilled the word of the Lord. Then he said, "What mean the lowing of these cattle and the bleating of the flocks?" Saul said, "Why, the people would save the best of the animals to offer sacrifices." Then Samuel responded, "Obedience is better than sacrifice and to hearken more acceptable in the sight of God than the fat of rams; for disobedience is as the sin of witchcraft and covetousness like idolatry." Then he lifted up his sword and hewed Agag to pieces before the Lord. Christ is our Samuel, who takes the sword of the Spirit, i. e., the precious Word, and hews old Adam into smithereens.

Then Samuel rends his robe and says, "Thus God hath rent the kingdom from thee and given it to th neighbor." This sealed the fate of Saul, as afterward God no longer answered him in dreams or visions, by Urim or Thummim. In his desperation, he finally turned Spiritualist and went off consulting the witch of Endor. When she called for enchantments, as Spiritualists do now, God took the opportunity to send up Samuel with a message which was sad indeed. Said he, "To-morrow you and your sons will be with me," i. e., in Hades—Samuel in Paradise and Saul and his sons in Tartarus.

The walls of Jericho in the days of Joshua were shouted down and never rebuilt. The Jericho in the days of Christ was three miles south of its predecessor. The Jericho of the present day is two miles east of the Jericho of the days of Christ; it was built by the Crusaders nine hundred years ago. At old Jericho we have that great and beautiful spring called "Elisha's fountain," because he healed the waters. He found them bitter and cast some salt into them and they were healed and have been all right ever since. This fountain pours out water enough for a city of 500,000, abundantly irrigating all that country.

The beautiful Jordan valley is very productive. It is so low down that it has no winter, but gardens flourish the encircling year, producing all the fruits peculiar to the torrid, semi-tropical and temperate zones. Bananas grow there all right, also oranges, lemons, figs, olives and an endless variety of delicious fruits.

Running to Hebron, Caleb's old city, which he inherited, we passed the "Well of the Star" by the road, so named from an incident in connection with the Wise Men. They saw the star in the East and followed it till they stopped at Jerusalem, somehow there losing sight of it. It was out of their way to go to Jerusalem, as there they had to make a right angle to go to Bethlehem. They showed infirmity in not simply following the star, which would have led them directly to Bethlehem. We are prone to run after big places and big things. They, by going to Jerusalem, narrowly escaped serious trouble with Herod who had ordered them to come back that way, but God delivered them. Herod had encumbered the throne of Judæa for nearly thirty-eight years, and was determined to leave it to his family forever. He had murdered all the Maccabees, and even his own sons, Hircanus and Antipater, by his first wife, Mariamne.

When the Wise Men said they had seen the star proclaiming that the King of the Jews was born, Herod called the theologians and doctors to tell him where Christ was to be born, and they said in Bethlehem of Judæa. Then he told the Wise Men to go and search diligently and find the Child, then bring him word, that he might go and worship Him also. He really intended to kill Him, lest He might compete with his family for the throne. So the Wise Men, while tinkering with Herod at Jerusalem having lost sight of the star, started off to Bethlehem crying to God to reveal the star. Stopping at a well to drink, behold! they saw the star reflected in the water, and looking up identified it in the firmament. Then, keeping their eye on it they followed it till it halted over the manger hallowed by the world's Redeemer.

See how wonderfully God beats the devil. Joseph and Mary were the poorest people in the world, providentially that Jesus might be born in the deepest depths of poverty, down below every one else, so that no one can say, "I am too low for Him to love and save me." They were actually too poor to have a garment for Him (no factories then), therefore they picked up every old rag, washed it diligently, carried them all with them and sewed them together to make Him a garment. They were too poor to have a lodging, so He had to be born in the stable among the herds and flocks. They were too utterly poor to take that long journey into Egypt, which was absolutely necessary to save the Child's life, therefore God sent the Wise Men all the way from the East to bring them their traveling expenses—gold and silver, frankincense and myrrh, the former produced in the Himalaya Mountains of India and the latter in Arabia Felix.

We also passed Elisha's convent, memorial of his sleeping on the spot the first night after he fled from Jezebel. Now we came to Rachel's tomb, where she died of parturition on her way to Ephrata, Benjamin being born alive and Benoni deceased. The tomb stands by the roadside within sight of Bethlehem. Hence the Hebrew prophet repeats her wailing over the slaughtered infants when Herod massacred all the boy babies of Bethlehem two years old and younger, trying to be sure to get Jesus. "In Ramah there was a voice heard, lamentation, weeping and great mourning, Rachel weeping for her children, and would not be comforted, because they are not." Oh, how pertinent this outburst of love from the affectionate heart of a mother in Israel!

There we had a splendid view of Zelzah, the nativity of King Saul. The men of Ramoth-gilead having traveled from there all night to Bethshan, where the Philistines had nailed up Saul and his sons to the wall after they had fallen in the battle of Gilboa, took them down, carried them to their family sepulchre, and gave them a royal interment.

We next reached Solomon's three pools, twelve miles from Jerusalem, 300 feet long, 100 feet wide and 60 feet deep. Oh, the wisdom and enterprise of Solomon, thus providing an abundant supply of water for Jerusalem, whither he carried it by a stone aqueduct. And there we have the citadel built by Abraham Pasha of Egypt.

Moving along, we ran round the head of the beautifull valley of Berachah, where King Jehoshaphat had the people come and rejoice before the Lord three days, over the spoils they had gathered when the Edomites, Moabites and Ammonites all united against the Jews (2 Chron., 20th chap.), and Jehoshaphat marched his people out to meet them, but had them stand and sing the beauty of holiness and offer no fight. While they were thus singing jubilantly and vociferously the beauty of holiness, God put "ambushments among them," so that the Moabites and Ammonites turned their arms against the Edomites till they utterly demolished them. Then the ambushments continued and they turned against one another and fought on, of course thinking they were fighting the Jews, till they utterly smashed each the other. Then the surviving remnants took fright and ran for their lives, leaving the very earth groaning beneath the spoils, which it took the Israelites three days to gather. Then Jehoshaphat had them come to this valley of Berachah and rejoice three days before the Lord.

On our right we passed the ruins of a Christian city destroyed by the Mohammedans nearly two hundred years ago. On the left we passed Abraham's citadel. The magnitude of the stones in the ruin shows that it was no insignificant affair. You say, "I did not know Abraham was a warrior." Read Genesis 14 and you will see that when Chedorlaomer and the confederate kings came from Chaldea against the cities about the Salt Sea in the valley of Sodom—that is, Sodom, Gomorrah, Admah, Zeboim, and Zoar— and conquered and spoliated them, carrying away Lot and his family among the captives, Abraham took his own three hundred Bible students and one thousand men of Mamre, Aner and Eshcol, pursued them at double quick, overtook them away up near the head of the Jordan, a short distance this side of Cæsarea Philippi, assaulted and defeated them, and delivered all the captives and spoils. Bringing them back, Melchizedek, his pastor, met them and blessed them. To him Abraham gave one-tenth, as that was the law of the justified dispensation. If we do not turn over to God his tenth, we are robbers. (Malachi, 3rd. chap.) It is our glory not only to turn over to God His tenth, which belongs to Him, but to give Him our **nine-tenths** and throw ourselves in for good count.

We now found the carriage running rapidly down the valley of Eshcol where the grapes grew so exuberantly. That whole valley, running down to Hebron, is this day devoted to the production of grapes. A missionary living there told me that she makes five distinct eatables out of those grapes, **all exceedingly** delicious and nutritious.

Leaving our carriage in Hebron, we enjoyed a walk up the plain of Mamre, to the venerable oak so long honored to throw its shadow over Abraham's tent, where our Savior, nineteen hundred years before He was born in Bethlehem, accompanied by two angels, stopped and ate dinner with Abraham. This was the fourth time I have dined under that oak tree. You ask, "Can it live so long—3,800 years?" Oh, yes, the Palestinian oak, unlike the American, when it reaches maturity sends up sprouts which develop into trees, and so perpetuates itself indefinitely. When I saw it on this tour, one trunk was about dead, another about fully mature, another growing **vigorously,** and two more quite young and growthy.

We now went to the cave of Machpelah, **purchased** by Abraham for a sepulchre. In it sleep the holy family, Abraham and Sarah, Isaac and Rebekah, Jacob and Leah. It is overbuilt by a great Mohammedan mosque and guarded by Turkish soldiers. An attempt to go in would cost you your life. I have often looked on it from the outside, my prognostications contemplating the blowing of the trumpet, when these soldiers will fall like dead men, as on the third morn at our Savior's sepulchre, when the great archangel in flaming fire descended and rolled the stone away.

We stood at the pool of Hebron, where David hung up the amputated hands of Rechab and Baanah, who cut off the head of Ishbosheth, the king of Israel, and carried it to him expecting a great reward, but were sadly disappointed by the infliction of the retribution due the foul murder they had committed.

Hebron is a holy city, the inheritance of Caleb, who stood alone with Joshua in bringing the minority report when the spies returned from exploring the land for forty days. They made three reports to Moses and Aaron at Kadesh-barnea, where they all waited the forty days while the spies were gone. The unanimous report was: "It is truly a land flowing with milk and honey and abounding in corn and wine; verily all we ever heard of it is true." The majority report, brought in by ten of the spies, terrified all the people, certifying, "It is inhabited by formidable warrior giants, in whose presence we are but as grasshoppers, and it abounds in impregnably fortified cities, walled up to Heaven." Finally, Joshua and Caleb brought in a minority report: "We are fully able to go up and possess the land." The people believed the ten rather than the two and raised the howl, "Back into Egypt!" Meanwhile Moses and Aaron, Joshua and Caleb did their best to persuade them to enter the land at once; they had no river to cross—nothing to do but to go in and possess it. But they would not listen, and would have stoned them if God had not interposed in their rescue. Thus from the very border of Canaan they turned back toward Egypt, and wandered thirty-eight years, visited by fighting armies, destroying angels, fiery serpents and pestilence, and would have starved to death if God had not fed them with heavenly manna.

After this long wandering they got back to Kadesh-barnea, but the natives had then so fortified that it was impossible to enter there. Consequently, beset by formidable armies, they had to fight their way far up north, where they could only enter as God divided the swelling flood and let them in. God's time for us to enter Canaan is when a young convert, by way of Kadesh-barnea, where there is no Jordan to cross.

On our return from Hebron, we visited Bethlehem, and again looked on the manger in which Mary laid our Savior when He was born, and where the shepherds found Him, and whither the Wise Men came bringing traveling expenses for Him to escape the murderous doom quickly coming on all the boy babies.

We visited the room where St. Jerome translated the Bible, and went out to the shepherd's field, where the angels sweeping down from Heaven brought the glad news, "The Savior is born in Bethlehem."

Our guide pointed out the cave of Adullam, in which David hid from Saul. We looked over the beautiful hills, where David, when a little lad, was herding the sheep when the prophet Samuel, having sought the king among his elder brothers, sent for him and anointed him to lead God's people.

CHAPTER III.

Sacred Mountains.

The mountains, lifting their heights above the fogs to where the sun always shines, above the malaria, miasmata and mosquitoes, have in all ages inspired the people of this world as souvenirs of the Almighty. The mythologies of all pagan nations have invariably recognized the lofty mountains as the thrones on which their gods do sit, anon coming down and speaking to the people admonitions against their wickedness, exhortations to repentance, and benedictions on the true and faithful.

Our blessed Bible abounds in sacred mountains, the more prominent of which we briefly sketch by way of inspiration, edification and encouragement.

Pi-hahiroth and Baal-zephon chronologically head the catalogue of sacred mountains. I saw them as I sailed the whole length of the Red Sea in my journey around the world. We wonder why Pharaoh was so reluctant to give up his slaves. The explanation is simple. At that time there were so very few people in the world that men, women and children were valued above gold, silver, elephants, camels, horses, cal-tle, and everything else. Land was so plentiful that it had no value. The reason why there is no slavery on the earth to-day is not because the people are too good to buy and sell you, but because the world has an over-population of seventeen hundred millions of people. The result is that they are not worth anything and nobody will buy them.

After God had sent ten awful judgments on Egypt to break off the slavish chains that His people might go free, finally culminating in the alarming visitation of the destroying angels affrighting every home with the dead, so that the people forced Pharaoh to send Israel away, still reaction supervened and he pursued them hotly to bring them back. The sea rolls in front, these impassable mountains tower on either side, and the Egyptian army is pressing the rear to arrest them and take them back to their bondage. Oh! what a wail goes up from the host: "Why did you bring us out here to be killed by the Egyptians or taken back to bondage? Were there no graves in Egypt, that we might lie down and rest?" Then Moses responds with his stentorian voice, "Stand still and see the salvation of the Lord!" Oh, what a beautiful symbolism of conviction and conversion. In true conviction, the sinner is confronted by the impassable sea of his own sins, with mounts on either side higher than the skies, and the devil with his host and Hell with its fire and brimstone are at his back. Of course he can do nothing but stand still and see what God will do.

After that Moses walks out, lifts up that magic rod with which he wrought miracles, strikes the sea with all his might, and splits it from shore to shore, till it rolls away and the dry ground appears. Then he shouts uproariously, "Israel, go forward!" Leading the way, he runs and the hosts after him till they climb the bank on the other side. Pharaoh's army, following, are now nigh the middle of the sea, when, responsive to the wave of the magic rod and the mandate of Moses, it collapses and drowns them all. Meanwhile the hosts, led by Miriam the prophetess, shout uproariously, safe on the Asiatic shore.

Reader, will you not let God use you, His Moses, to lead penitents through the Red Sea with shouts of victory over sin and Satan?

Pisgah is a notable sacred mountain so conspicuous from Jerusalem that you see and recognize it every time you look toward the rising sun. I would certainly love to climb where Moses stood and view the landscape o'er, but it is a long journey, over Jordan and through the land of Moab, to that dizzy summit. A. J. Paine, my traveling companion in 1899, went to it. He saw the church which the Emperor Constantine built on the spot fifteen hundred years ago. No one lives there. He narrowly escaped the robbers.

Moses climbed the mountain alone, so no one would know his tomb, as they would have idolized him. God buried him, and he slept till Jesus needed him to stand by His side, along with Elijah, on the Mount of Transfiguration, there to represent all who will be transfigured through the resurrection, and Elijah, all who will be transfigured through the translation. Then He sent down Michael, the archangel (Jude 9), to resurrect him. Satan came roaring from Hell, determined to hold Moses in the dust. A terrible hand-to-hand combat ensued, in which the archangel was too much for the devil, who skedaddled back to Hell where he had more authority than he was about to get on Mt. Pisgah.

The Bible says that Moses could not enter the land of Canaan because he backslid at the waters of Meribah. The people murmured so because they had no water to drink, thus grieving the Holy Spirit and vexing Moses, that his patience there flickered. When he lifted up his rod to strike the rock, he said, "Oh, ye rebels!" He should have said, "Oh, my beloved brethren!" Though he backslid by imbibing impatience from the evil one, yet God sent the water all the same and satiated their thirst.

Take warning! God will honor His truth, dispensed through your ministry, using you to save and sanctify souls, and still you may backslide at the same time in your own experience.

Besides this backsliding, from which Moses soon recovered, there is a great, fundamental reason why he could not enter the land. He was God's lawgiver. His admission into Canaan would have symbolically involved the conclusion that we can be sanctified by keeping the law, which is utterly untrue and a dangerous heresy. It kept me out of Canaan nineteen years. Aaron had to die in the wilderness because he was the high priest and his admission would have involved the conclusion that we can be sanctified by ritual services and churchisms. Miriam could not reach it, because she was a flaming Holiness evangelist, and her admission involved the conclusion that the fire-baptized preachers can give us the experience, which is utterly untrue.

Sinai is a noted sacred mountain, symbolizing conviction, without which there can be no conversion, sanctification nor Heaven. The Gospel is the dynamite of God unto salvation to everyone that believeth. (Rom. 1: 16.) Take your stand on Mt. Sinai; ask God to give you thunderbolts, earthquakes, lightning shafts and cyclones, which you will heroically toss from the tips of your fingers till the wicked tremble and quake and believe the awful truth through their faith. The Holy Ghost, imparting a dynamite cartridge in the deep interior of the soul, and igniting it with a spark of heavenly fire, an awful explosion intervenes, actually blowing you up till you can neither eat nor sleep. Now conviction has settled down like a nightmare. If you want a revival, first preach the Sinai Gospel with all your might, till conviction lays its paralyzing grapple on all the wicked; then you will have workable material; otherwise all will be gum logs, neither splitable nor rivable.

(a) Then change mountains; run to Calvary, and standing on the bloody summit preach the dying love of Jesus to the broken-hearted penitents, till they all recognize and say:

> "I saw One hanging on a tree
>   In agonies and blood,
> Who fixed His eyes on me
>   As near the cross I stood.
> Sure, never to my latest breath
>   Can I forget that look;

> It seemed to charge me with His death
>   Though not a word He spoke.
> A second look He gave, which said,
>   'I freely all forgive;
> My Blood is for thy ransom paid,
>   I die that thou may'st live.'
> My conscience felt and owned my guilt
>   And plunged me in despair;
> I saw my sins His Blood had spilt
>   And helped to nail Him there.''

Thus confessing, praying and soliloquizing, the burden breaks loose, and goes rolling, leaping and bounding down Mt. Calvary till it rolls into a sepulchre at the base, and the pilgrim, light and elastic as the bird of paradise, goes leaping, bounding, singing, soaring, flying on his way.

Preach the Calvary Gospel to the truly penitent, till they actually believe the dying love of Jesus and see the problem of redeeming grace, luminous with heavenly light; then, through the faith the Holy Ghost imparts, a dynamite blast will ignite it with a spark of heavenly fire. The result will be a tremendous blowing up, blowing you all the way out of the brick-kilns and mortar-yards of Egyptian bondage, through the sea, and into the kingdom of God.

As the Calvary Gospel is fundamental in the plan of salvation, Satan, in all ages, has done his best to pervert, mystify and vitiate it. What a deplorable illustration of this fact we have at Jerusalem! The Bible says that Jesus was crucified on Calvary, outside of the city (so important, as He did not die simply for the Church, but for the whole world). Calvary means skull—it is one of the peaks of Zion having the shape of a human skull. I have just made my fourth tour to the Holy Land in the last sixteen years. This time we happened to strike the Eastern festivals; when forty thousand pilgrims from the ends of the earth were all thronging the Church of the Holy Sepulchre, which covers a whole square of the city. They crowded so that it was very difficult to get about, and our dragoman was all the time trying to keep us from getting run over, and also warning us against robbers. Some of our party got robbed. All this time they were packing and jamming the great Church of the Holy Sepulchre, believing it was Calvary, though there is no mountain there filling the description at all. None of them were going to the real Calvary except our party, whom I led thither, and perhaps a few others who found it out.

Sixteen years ago, when I first went to Jerusalem, Calvary was open and we could walk over it as much as we pleased, among the tombs, as it is a Mohammedan cemetery. (There were no Mohammedans in the world till the seventh century, therefore, when they buried their dead on it, they knew nothing about our Savior having been crucified there, and if they did, they do not believe in any Christ, but believe we are saved by the prophets, of whom they say Mohammed is the greatest.)

The Lord's tomb, as the Bible says, is in the garden at the base of the mountain. The whole world, in all ages, had been going to the great Calvary within the city, believing it to be the true one, till Doctor Gordon, twenty years ago, came to Jerusalem, and, with his open Bible saw their mistake and identified the true Calvary. As the people began to find it out and to go to it, the Mohammedans surrounded it by an impassable wall. Now the best we can do is to stand on an eminence and look at it. Fortunately the English have gotten control of the garden and the sepulchre; they have it all fenced by a stone wall, keep it in good order, and the whole garden filled with beautiful flowers and fruit trees. We held a meeting in the sepulchre, realizing the presence of our Savior though risen and pleading for us in glory.

You ask, "Brother Godbey, how did this awful mistake about Calvary ever supervene?" During the Jewish tribulation, A. D. 66-73, the Romans sold into slavery and carried into captivity every one that survived the sword, pestilence and famine. The Christians, who alone escaped, had to leave the country or they would have all been killed, because the Roman law made it a penalty of death for a Jew to be found in the Holy Land, or in any other country, traveling with his face toward Jerusalem. The city and the temple were utterly destroyed, and left without an inhabitant for fifty years, when the Emperor Hadrian, going thither, founded a Roman colony, Ælia Capitolina, so that the very name Jerusalem was dropped, and two hundred years rolled away during which there was no place on the earth called by that name.

When the Emperor Hadrian founded that Roman colony on the site where Jerusalem stood, and named it Ælia Capitolina, he bult a heathen temple on the site of Solomon's temple, and had his own statue set up in front of it. This temple stood there, and they worshipped idols in it, till the conversion of the Emperor Constantine, A. D. 321. Then he, accompanied by his royal mother, Queen Helena, went to Jerusalem and proceeded to hunt up the sacred places and mark them with suitable memorial edifices.

N. B. The Emperor had been a heathen all his life, utterly ignorant of the Bible and sacred history. He was converted suddenly and unexpectedly. While marching his army under the ensigns of the pagan gods, he saw a luminous cross in the air, superscribed "En touto nikia" ("In hoc signo vinces"—Latin; "Conquer by this sign"—English). Pursuant to this miracle, he at once halts his army, takes down the paganistic banners, and unfurls that of the cross, being thus suddenly converted to Christianity.

When Constantine and his mother came to Jerusalem, there was no one to give them information, because 250 years had rolled away since there had been a Jew in all of that country.

N. B. The primitive Christians were all Jews. Within a century the Church passed through a sommersault, eliminating the Jewish element and becoming all Gentile. Even the Jewish Christians, after the destruction of Jerusalem, all had to utterly escape out of the country or they would have been killed. Hence you see several generations had passed away since there had been any person in Jerusalem who knew the historic places. If Constantine had been familiar with the Bible, he could have corrected himself, but he had been born a pagan, and only so recently suddenly and unexpectedly converted to Christianity that he had had no time to familiarize himself with the Bible. When he and his royal mother proceeded to hunt up the sacred places, they had men digging up the debris, as the whole city had been desolate, i. e., transformed into a heap of ruins. On the spot where the great Church of the Holy Sepulchre now stands (where Constantine built it), the men were digging and excavating a diversity of things, when it is said they dug up three crosses. Then (it is said) they brought a sick woman to the spot, laid a cross on her, and it had no effect. Then they placed another on her, and she felt no change. Finally they placed on her the third cross and she was suddenly healed. From that miracle they concluded it was the cross on which Christ had been crucified, the other two being the crosses on which the two thieves were crucified. So in this way they identified Calvary and proceeded to build the great Church of the Holy Sepulchre. You see what an amount of fable and superstition there is about it.

The Emperor was so influential, in view of his office as ruler of the whole world, that the Church actually came to the conclusion that he was the re-incarnation of Christ come back to the world. In this way originated the post-millenial view of Christ's coming.

When we contemplate the world of idolatry which now floods the great Oriental churches, and is fast inundating the young Occidental churches, we are not surprised that God, in His providence, just permitted them to acquiesce in their own delusion, in order to keep that Pacific Ocean of idolatry and superstition away from the holy sepulchre, which is permitted to rest in peace in the garden at the base of Calvary, only being visited by a few Anglo-Saxon pilgrims.

Satan knows the Calvary experience bankrupts him forever, consequently he has laid under contribution all the myrmidons of the pandemonium to sweep it away in a flood of superstition and idolatry, so magnitudinous that no one can apprehend it without going and seeing it.

We now leave Calvary, the mount of conversion, and go to Zion, the mount of sanctification. Taking our stand on the summit, we preach inbred sin surviving in the heart of the regenerate, till they believe the truth enunciated and enforced by floods of indisputable Scriptures. Through their faith, the Holy Spirit imparts another dynamite cartridge, ignites it with a spark of heavenly fire, and there follows a grand explosion. It blows the believers in this Holy Ghost baptism clear away out of the howling wilderness, over the flood of Jordan, and into the land flowing with milk and honey and abounding in corn and wine, where they shout down every Jericho, march under Joshua's banner into the interior, stand on the battlefield of Beth-horon, see the sun halt over Gibeon and the moon over the valley of Aijalon, till Joshua can end the battle. Then they march under Joshua's banner into the great north, and meet the combined armies under Jabin, king of Hazor, at the waters of Merom, where we see those armies go down in signal defeat and all the tribes gather at Shiloh to receive their inheritance.

Now we leave Mt. Zion, where we have received the baptism with the Holy Ghost and fire, entire sanctification by the cleansing Blood, and have the victory, Christ crowned within and reigning without a rival. Then we cross the valley of Jehoshaphat and climb Olivet, the highest mountain in all the land of Canaan, from whose summit our glorified Savior ascended up to Heaven, and to which He is coming back ("His feet shall again stand on Mt. Olivet"—Zechariah, 14th chapter) to reign forever on the earth. We now take our stand on Mt. Olivet, and preach the transfiguration Gospel with all our might, till the people believe the wonderful promises in reference to our Lord's return to the earth to reign in His glory forever. They actually believe it in the deep interior of their hearts, and stand on tip-toe, stretching their eyes to see King Jesus coming in a cloud with a rainbow around His shoulders. We are thus transported by the exercise of transfiguration faith, till we, responsively to the archangel's trumpet, actually leap into the transfiguration glory, and soar away to meet the Lord in the air.

"Some morning fair I'm going away,
And we'll not come back till millennial day."

"Christ went a building to prepare,
Not made with hands,
And 'twill be decked with jewels rare,
Not made with hands.

"Put on the armor of our God,
Not made with hands,

> And take the path our Captain trod,
> Not made with hands.

Chorus: "I know, I know, I have another building;
I know, I know, 'tis not made with hands."

(b) Moriah, on which Abraham offered up Isaac, is a sacred mountain exceedingly prominent in biblical history. It occupies the southeast division of Jerusalem, separated from Mt. Zion by the Tyrophœan valley.

When David had achieved his wonderful success, subduing the enemies of Israel, and God so exceedingly blessed His people, he inadvertently yielded to the temptation of pride and ordered Joab to go ahead and number Israel. The great warrior on that occasion had better light than his king, therefore he begged him not to do it. Why was it such a sin to number Israel? Because not more than one in ten was a true Israelite, which is one who prevails with God. It is like the churches boasting of their numbers—i. e., the Methodists with their seven million. If they could only see the illuminations of the Judgment Day, they would never count them any more. David was strong-headed, and forced Joab to proceed and number Israel. Scarcely was it done till God sent the prophet Gad to David to rebuke him and to give him his choice between three awful retributions—a seven years' famine, three months of retreat before his enemies, or a three days' pestilence. David knew seven years' famine would sweep them all from the face of the earth; three months' defeat by his enemies he knew would utterly spoliate and slay his people; so he chose the last, and said, "Let me fall into the hands of God!" He knew that in the pestilence he would be dealing with God alone, and he would rather risk Him to have mercy on him than man.

Therefore the pestilence set in and swept terrifically, people falling dead all the time. Already seventy thousand had died when David becomes alarmed; it seemed like they all would die. He fell on his knees before God and cried aloud, "Do spare these sheep and execute the penalty on me alone; let me die!" God is moved with compassion, hears his prayer, and as He sees the destroying angel standing with uplifted sword over the summit of Moriah, He calls Him away, and David sees him go back to Heaven and knows that the plague is stayed. Then he runs with all his might, climbs Moriah, and calls to Araunah, who owned the threshing-floor on the ground, to sell it to him that he might erect an altar and offer sacrifice to the Lord. Araunah generously responds, "With great pleasure I donate it to you for that noble purpose, giving you the oxen for sacrifices and the implements for fuel." David responds, "That is very noble in you, but I cannot afford to offer God a sacrifice that costs me nothing." Then Araunah says, "Set your price on it and take it."

David aimed to build the temple on Mt. Moriah, and God admired him for it, as though he had done it, but kept him at another work all his life so he never did build the temple. He left it to his son Solomon, who, assisted by Hiram, the king of Tyre, and others, built that wonderful superstructure. For its dedication Solomon slaughtered 22,000 oxen and 120,000 sheep. Oh, what rivers of blood, quantity for quality, symbolizing the bleeding Lamb of Calvary. Josephus says it was common to slaughter 250,000 lambs at a single Passover. The Passover ran fifteen hundred years. Make the calculation and you'll find 370,000,000 innocent lambs bleeding on Jewish altars in the Passover festivals alone, all symbolizing the Lamb of God that taketh away the sin of the world.

This temple was destroyed by Nebuchadnezzar, B. C. 587. The second temple was built on the same spot by Nehemiah, Ezra and Zerubbabel, B. C. 447, and destroyed by the Romans, A. D. 70. The spot remained vacant, except for a heap of ruins, for fifty years, when the Emperor Hadrian built on it the heathen temple to Jupiter. This was taken down by the Emperor Constantine, A. D. 324, and a Christian church erected on that hallowed spot. This stood till the Moslem conquest, A. D. 634, when Caliph Omar took the city. He removed the Christian church and erected the Mosque Omar. This stood till the capture of the city by the Christian Crusaders, A. D. 1099. They took down the mosque and erected another Christian church. This stood until A. D. 1187, when Saladin captured the city, took down the Christian church, and restored the Mosque Omar, which stands to this day. Oh, what a wonderful history has this sacred mountain!

Due north of Jerusalem rises great Mt. Scopus, on which the Roman armies camped during the siege of seven years, A. D. 66-73. This was the time of the awful Jewish tribulation, when the Romans denationalized and expatriated the Jews because they would crown those false Christs king of the Jews, and give them so much trouble. The Romans were very reluctant to destroy the Jews, as they were their best revenue payers, therefore they waited on them one-third of a century to become peaceable. Finally old Vespasian, sitting on a diamond throne in his golden house in Rome, looking out on five thousand senators living in silver houses, constituting his board of counsel in the government of the whole world, issued that famous edict of Hebrew denationalization and expatriation. He sent itinerant heralds to the ends of the earth, "viva voce" to proclaim this edict to all the people on the globe. Then the Romans proceeded at once to capture and sell all the Jews into slavery. As slaves have no nationality, but simply rank as property, of course that procedure blotted the Jews from the escutcheon of nations.

From that day they have had no nationality, and never will, till their own Brother, Jesus, shall come down on the throne of the Theocracy, which is the kingdom of the Jews, and will be the Millennium in the good time coming.

Thus notified by the imperial heralds, all nations went to Jerusalem to buy slaves. The Jews were always the most popular slaves in the world because they were the most industrious and ingenious.

The army soon cleaned up the whole country except Jerusalem, which is so impregnably fortified by nature; with the deep valley of Hinnom on the west, impassable to an invading army; Jehoshaphat on the east, crawling round Mt. Moriah and intersecting Hinnom with a smoothing-iron point, thus effectually fortifying the city on all sides but the north. Therefore the Roman army could only besiege it on the northern side. Gallus Celceus, with a great army came to Jerusalem in 66, camped on Mt. Scopus, and opened the siege.

Jerusalem has been besieged seventeen times and destroyed seven times. It has always been the speckled bird among the nations, feared and antagonized by all the kings of the earth. As the city of God and holiness, it has always been the rebuke of kings and nations for their wickedness, therefore they have always longed to get rid of it.

Gallus Celceus presses the siege two years, and finds he has made breaches in the wall with the battering-rams so that he can enter, but, to his dismay, he discovers that the Jews have taken the stone and built another wall in the rear, so, if the army should go in, they would be in a bag, and the Jews would close the breaches in the bag and shut them up and slaughter them like swine in a pen. Therefore he gets so discouraged that he writes to the Emperor that the city cannot be taken, and they will have to give it up. Vespasian responds, "Go home, you coward, and go to bed." Then, leaving his golden house, never to get back, he goes to Jerusalem, takes charge of the besieging army, greatly enlarged, and presses the war for two years more. When the grim monster takes him away, he is succeeded by his son Titus on the throne of the world and in the command of the Jerusalem army. Titus presses the siege three years longer, takes the city, and, as the temple was so beautiful, orders his soldiers to spare it, but he could not control them. They tore it all down, hunting hidden treasures, as the Jews were a famous moneyed people. Thus they verified the prophecy of Jesus in His valedictory sermon, preached on Mt. Olivet on the Wednesday afternoon before His crucifixion, certifying, "Stone shall not be left upon stone that shall not be thrown down." (See Matt. 24 and 25, Mark 13 and Luke 21.)

Pursuant to the words of Jesus in that same sermon, assuring them that not a hair of their heads should be hurt, the disciples all made their escape. Going out eastwardly through the wilderness of Judæa, crossing the Jordan, then turning north, they went up to Pella, a Gentile city belonging to Decapolis. It was thither that Jesus went when He preached in Gadara, cast the ten thousand demons out of the man, made that same man a glorious preacher, and sent him to preach to his own people. He would not do for an apostle as they were all Jews and the Gospel had not yet been given to the Gentiles. The Word says he preached throughout Decapolis, and history says he had great success, especially in Pella, where he had many noble Gentile Christians just ready to take their Jewish brothers into their arms.

This is our last historic view of the Jewish wing of the Gospel Church, then and there absorbed into the rapidly growing Gentile wing. Whereas the primitive Christians were all Jews and kept both Sabbaths, the last and the first days of the week, as long as they lived, the Gentile converts never did keep the Mosaic Sabbath and were not required so to do. (Acts 15.) The Jewish wing, there at Pella absorbed by the Gentile wing, with their departure out of the world constituted the evanescence of the Mosaic Sabbath out of the Gospel Church.

(c) Mt. Mizpeh, seven miles from Jerusalem toward the northwest, in conspicuous view from all the towers of the city, is celebrated as the place where Israel first set up the tabernacle in the land of Canaan, which was eventually moved to Shiloh (more central in the land), where it stood about five hundred years, till it actually went into dilapidation, and, doubtless, disintegration, being carried away as souvenirs.

The administration of the Jewish government became very corrupt in the days of Eli, the wickedness of whose sons brought on them swift destruction; and also brought to himself a broken heart and a broken neck, because he, knowing their wickedness, did not correct them. Consequently God permitted the Philistines, encamped at Shen, signally and repeatedly to defeat the armies of Israel, encamped at Mizpeh. The disaster become so fearful that the Israelites take the ark out of the tabernacle at Shiloh and carry it to the army to give it victory. On its arrival the men shout aloud till the mountains reverberate and re-echo their stentorian voices. Then the Philistines tremble and quake, and say, "What does this mean?" The answer comes, "Why, the God of Israel has come into their camp and they are shouting over Him."

Then they say, "Alas for us; we are ruined!" Then the five lords of Gath, Gaza, Ekron, Ashdod and Askelon go about among their people, exhorting them to go along, be men, to fear not and fight their best, assuring them that they will win the victory. Sure enough, they do decisively triumph over Israel. Eli, the high priest, is sitting in the gate at Shiloh and looking out toward Mizpeh for the courier to bring the news. There he comes. What is the news? Why, both of Eli's sons, Phineas and Hophni, have been slain in the battle. This was awful, but he stood it. But when the messenger proceeds to say that the ark of God is taken by the Philistines, the shock is too great, and, fainting, he falls back, breaks his neck and breathes his life away.

The Philistines are so strong and heroic that the Israelites then clamor for a king to lead them on the battlefield. The prophet Samuel, so true to God, does his best to dissaude them, but in vain. He tells them God is their king, but that does not satisfy; they want a visible man to go before them to fight their enemies. God acquiesces, not only granting them a king, but selecting him Himself.

In that country there is no rain in harvest. Consequently they never stack their grain, but carry it on a camel's back to the threshing-floor, and both the reaping and the threshing go on simultaneously. Samuel now tells them that God will send lightning and thunder as an evidence of His wrath, which would be a miracle in time of harvest, when normally rain never comes. So there at Mizpeh, during their camp-meeting in harvest time, the lightnings flash, thunders roar and the rains pour down. Meanwhile the people weep and wail, knowing that God is angry, and plead with Samuel to intercede for them.

Samuel anoints Saul, the son of Kish, king over Israel. Saul is a giant in stature, head and shoulders above all the men of Israel. This was a Divine mercy, as the Philistines whom they had to fight were a nation of giants. Saul fought them all the forty years of his reign, won many victories over them, and they never could have whipped him if he had been true to God. He was joyfully converted in his young manhood; "when Saul met the prophets, God gave him another heart." How clear and glorious his conversion! His great difficulty was that he could never sink his own interest into God's interest, so he spared Agag, i. e., old Adam, was forsaken of God, turned spiritualist, and finally committed suicide; thus eternally and irrefutably demonstrating the utter falsity of Satan's Hell-hatched doctrine, preached from so many pulpits: "Once in grace, always in grace."

Mizpeh was a celebrated camp-meeting ground. On one occasion the Philistines came to break it up, when, stampeding the host, except Samuel, who was sacrificing a sucking lamb (typical of the innocent Savior), they, coming with roaring trumpets and hideous battle-cries, only saw the fugitive army. Then God sends an awful hail-storm, dropping down the stones thick and fast, big as your fist, on the heads of the Philistines, utterly blockading their way with heaps of the slain before they reach Samuel. Panic strikes

Ashdod, Gath, Gaza, Askelon and Ekron, the five principalities constituting their commonwealth. Meanwhile the men of Israel are chasing them and cutting them down, with sword, spear and battle-ax, thus consummating a great and decisive victory.

(d) When David built his tabernacle on Mt. Zion, he went after the ark to put it there, appointing Uzzah and Ahio to take care of it while they carried it on a new cart. When the oxen stumbled, Uzzah laid hold of it and dropped dead, so alarming David that he stopped and put it in the house of Obed-edom. God wonderfully blessed this house during the three months of its abiding; then David, with his army in grand parade, came down and took it to Jerusalem, and put it in the tabernacle, where it stayed till Solomon built the temple. Then they carried it over and put it in the sanctum sanctorum (Holy of Holies). It remained in the temple till Nebuchadnezzar destroyed that building, B. C. 587. He then carried the ark, with all the valuable gold and silver temple furnishings, into Babylon, and put them in the temple of Aisroch, his god. There all these things remained until Cyrus, the Medo-Persian, emancipated the Jews, B. C. 457. Then Ezra carried all this valuable temple furniture back to Jerusalem. He had no army to protect him, and camped out every night on the journey, yet, though the gold and silver were worth millions of dollars, he was never molested by robbers. Thus the ark, with the other valuables, was deposited in the second temple, where it remained till the city was captured by the Romans, A. D. 73; then all of this valuable temple furniture was carried with the spoils to Rome.

In my recent tour I saw that triumphal procession sculptured on the Arch of Titus, showing how, after the seven years' war at Jerusalem, having achieved the complete victory, he entered Rome through that arch on a chariot drawn by four white horses, and followed by the triumphant army carrying the immense spoils of conquest, trophies of victory. These were followed by a long captive train, as the market at Jerusalem became so glutted with slaves that they could not sell them, thus leaving a vast number on their hands to be led captive to Rome and turned over as the crown slaves of the Emperor.

My eyes are no longer strong, and the sculpture is quite elevated on the arch, so, as I could not get very close to it, while the seven golden candlesticks, spreading out so widely, were very conspicuous, yet I could not, to my satisfaction, identify the ark of the covenant. However, there is no doubt but it was carried into Rome with the seven golden candlesticks and other temple valuables. As these symbolisms have all done their work, and we have reached the glorious types which they represent, and which constitute the victories and heavenly prelibations, the crowning glory of the Gospel dispensation, God has never, in His providence, as in by-gone ages, miraculously restored these symbols.

The Goths, Huns, Vandals and Heruli, wild, barbaric nations in the North, now great Russia, with her 325,000,000 Russianized subjects, fought three hundred years, and finally, A. D. 476, captured Rome. They spent a whole week gathering the gold and silver from the palaces, temples and shrines, and returned home common soldiers having become millionaires and using donkeys to carry their money. Thus you can see the final destination of the sacred and valuable temple furniture. It was carried away by these barbarians, and finally coined into money; just as when Oliver Cromwell was triumphant in England. He, going into a church, saw a number of silver statues and asked the sexton, "Who are these?" He responded, "Oh, they are the twelve Apostles." Then Cromwell said, "Take them down, coin them into money, and let them go around doing good, like their Master."

(e) Five miles due north of Jerusalem is the city of Nob, where the priests lived in the patriarchal dispensation. Three miles further north, you will see, on your right, Mt. Ramah, the home of Elkana and Hannah, the parents of the prophet Samuel.

Samuel was providentially given and supernaturally born, like Isaac. When a little lad, he stayed in the temple of Shiloh, his infantile conversion before the forfeiture of his justification having brought him so near to God that he heard His voice when the high priest could not hear it. Though only six years old, how meekly he responds, "Speak, Lord; Thy servant heareth." God help you and me to do likewise! If all would thus answer Him, the Millennium would come at race-horse speed.

Later Samuel had a celebrated Bible School at Naioth, in Ramah. It was really a brilliant prelude of the apostolic age.

When Saul became so jealous and suspicious of David that he wanted him killed, he said he would give him his daughter for thirty Philistine foreskins, he feeling sure David would lose his life before he could kill the thirty and get them. But David succeeded triumphantly and demanded his wife. However, Saul was the more determined to have him killed, therefore he sent men to David's home to bring him to him. But Saul's daughter (David's wife) had let him down through a back window, so he would make his escape. Then she dressed up a wooden effigy and put it in the bed. When her father sent for David, she reported him sick and said he could not go: Then Saul sent the men back to take him, sick or well, but, upon examination, they found he wasn't there; it was only that wooden effigy.

David had gone away to Nob, the home of the priests, where they had been living for ages immemorial, as they belonged to the patriarchal dispensation. There were eighty-two of them, under Ahimelech. David asked them if they had any arms. They said thed had none but the sword of Goliath, which he had taken in the battle of Elah. He said, "Give it to me," and took it. Meanwhile, his men ate the shewbread, which it was only lawful for the priests to eat.

While there David was recognized by the Edomite shepherd, Doeg, who went and told Saul how the priests of Nob had received David, fed him and his men, and furnished them arms so far as they could.

Therefore Saul sent and slew all the priests of Nob except Abiathar, the son of Ahimelech, who fled away, fell in with David, and remained with him to the end of his life.

From Nob David went to Ramah, only a few miles away, where Samuel's Bible School was in its glory, and its students wonderfully filled with the Spirit. When David arrived among them, the Holy Spirit fell on him and he at once began to prophesy, i. e., preach, with all his might. So Saul, having heard that he was there, sent soldiers to arrest him and bring him to him. On arrival, the Spirit fell on them and they broke out prophesying; they stayed preaching with all their might and forgot all about taking David. Then Saul sent another posse, but the Spirit also fell on them; they went to preaching with a boom and forgot all about taking David. Then Saul went himself, with a cohort to take David whether or no, but on arrival the Spirit fell on him and all his band and they, too, began to prophesy fluently, Saul himself being the biggest preacher of all and prophesying all night, so that he forgot all about taking David. Meanwhile David and his men made their escape out of the country, Saul later pursuing them.

Eventually David and the six hundred men who had by this time fled to him, and dedicated themselves to him, came to Keilah, and found it awfully infested by the Philistines, who were driving off their herds nd flocks, robbing their threshing-floors, and spoiliating their country generally. David, with his men, subdues the Philistines, drives them out of the country, and completely delivers the city and its environments from the nuisance, so that all the people were delighted to entertain him and his men, while their praise is on every lip, extolling them for bringing deliverance to the land.

When Abiathar fled from Nob and fell in with David, he took with him an ephod, in which were the jewels, Urim and Thummim, by which they could consult the Lord, who would answer them by changing the color of the light flashing out from those jewels.

David now knows Saul is hot on his track with three thousand men, so he takes that ephod and consults the Lord, asking Him, "Will Saul come down to Keilah? Will the men of Keilah deliver me up?" (1 Samuel 23.) The answer comes clearly; "He will come down, and the men of Keilah will deliver thee up."

Some people say that God's decrees are never changed. There you see them make a mistake. David immediately blew his bugle a double-quick skedaddle from the place. Saul heard that David had gone, and, as he was coming from the north and David fled away due east—and Saul, through his scouts, kept posted on David's movements—therefore, instead of going south to Keilah, he turned off in a southeasterly direction, on the hypotenuse of a right-angled triangle, taking the nearest route to head off David. So here you see these two decrees—that Saul would go down to Keilah and that the Keilahites would deliver David up—never did take place.

If David had been a predestinarian, he would have

given up in despair; but he was acquainted with God and knew that He meant, "Saul will come to Keilah if you stay; the Keilahites will deliver you to Saul if you stay." Hence you see that the moment he got the answer from God, he fled away; then, of course, the Keilahites could not deliver him up because he was not there to be delivered. The Bible is the most sensible book in all the world; it has no foolishness in it.

(f) The Mount of Temptation, lying west of old Jericho and exceedingly conspicuous from the place where John the Baptist held his great meeting, and baptized our Savior, deservedly ranks in the catalogue of holy mountains.

On the summit of this mountain the Greek Christians have a convent, with a name symbolizing "forty." It is the memorial of our Lord's forty days' temptation by the devil.

So soon as John, by baptism, had anointed Him for the high priesthood, thus inaugurating Him into His official Messiahship, so that He entered at once upon His ministry, the Holy Spirit led Jesus away into the wilderness to be tempted of the devil. Now that He is exposed because of His humanity, and becomes our substitute, He must fight our battle as it would have been encountered by us if He had never fought.

When Satan attacked Adam the first, he began with his physical being, by tempting him to satisfy his bodily appetite. He and mother Eve both went down into utter ruin, slain by Satan on his first round. If they had resisted the physical temptation, he would have proceeded to fire on their spiritual and intellectual being, but this was not necessary. It is only a fool who will shoot dead game. He had already slain them, and so saved two-thirds of his ammunition, and at the same time achieved the greatest victory in all the ages.

Adam the Second must pass through the same ordeals; therefore, preparatory to the temptation, that it may have its greatest possible efficiency, He fasts forty days, not suffering with hunger, because the angels were all around Him entertaining Him with their heavenly fellowship. At the close of the forty days, the angels retreated away and His soul rhapsody evanesced with His heavenly company; then His normal physical condition supervened with intense hunger, as He had perfect health. In this juncture of keenest and most craving appetite, Satan tempts Him to use His omnipotence to satisfy His intense physical craving by transforming a stone which abounds in that mountain, looking much like barley loaves, into bread. But you see He downs him with a single stroke of the spiritual sword, i. e., the Word of God (Heb. 4:12): "It is written, Man shall not live by bread alone, but by every word that proceedeth out of the mouth of God." You see Satan did not come back at Him, showing the omnipotence of God's Word.

People in this world live ignorant of their power. If you will only fight the devil with the sword of Christ, i. e., the Word of God, a single stroke will down him every time, and give you the victory.

Then he leads Him away to Jerusalem, forty miles, and puts Him on a pinnacle of the temple, and says,

"Cast thyself down; because it is written (Psalm 91), He will give His angels charge concerning thee, and in their hands shall they bear thee up, lest at any time thou shouldest dash thy foot against a stone." The devil adroitly left out, "Keep thee in all thy ways."

This was an assault on Jesus' faith, the basis of grace and of all spirituality; lose faith, and everything goes down. Satan there did his best to rob Jesus of His faith by fooling Him with presumption, his counterfeit for faith. Oh, the millions of people who have Satan's presumption instead of God's faith! Where they look for Heaven they will find Hell.

But you see Jesus again downs him with a single stroke of the sword: "Thou shalt not tempt the Lord thy God." So the devil is defeated on two battlefields and has but one more chance. So leading Jesus across the valley of Jehoshaphat and up Mt. Olivet, the highest in all the land of Canaan, he gives Him a panorama of all the time-honored kingdoms of the earth. As the world is round, we cannot see all places at the same time, hence the presumption.

When he gives Him this thrilling exhibition, I trow Satan alluded to their old comradeship, when he was a great archangel, so brilliant as to be cognomened "Lucifer," i. e., light-bearer. He likely observed: "As I have gotten into trouble and lost my place among the heavenly hierarchies, with hard toil I have endeavored to ameliorate my situation by the accession of this earth to my restricted dominions. But as you have come to antagonize me and to take it from me, I propose that we compromise the matter, renewing our friendship. To make the matter easy, I will just give this world up to you to reign over forever, and I will be content to reign in Hell, simply on the condition that you recognize my divinity" (i. e., fall down and worship him).

But here we see again how by a single stroke of the wonderful sword of the Holy Spirit, Jesus settles the devil again: "It is written, Thou shalt worship the Lord thy God, and Him only shalt thou serve." This consummated the victory and skedaddled the devil. He runs from the field like a sheep-killing dog that had been shot at. Why? Because he had exhausted all of his ammunition, and an empty gun is a useless burden. He could not and did not tempt our Lord's divinity, but only the humanity, which consists of spirit, soul and body. You see he tempted Him on all these lines, but Jesus routed him with a single quotation from God's Word. So can you, every time, therefore thank God and take courage. And go and tell everybody this news. It is awful to see the devil dragging millions into Hell as a sheer gratuity, for every one can conquer him on every assault —by a single stroke of this wonderful two-edged sword.

(g) The Mount of the Good Samaritan deserves our diagnosis and appreciation.

By the wonderful, redeeming grace of God in Christ, every human being is born a Christian, though having an evil nature, i. e., depravity. Psa. 51:5: "I was shapen in iniquity, and in sin did my mother conceive me," thus turning our faces away from God.

If not converted before we lose our infantile justification by personal transgression, pursuant to this hereditary depravity, we go right away into sin, like the Prodigal Son, and if not felicitously rescued from the hogpen, we will soon plunge into Hell. God's time for our conversion is while we are still in His kingdom, where we are all born by the normal grace of Christ, and before we ever sin out. Then, like the elder brother, we'll need nothing but sanctification to take all the fret and jealousy out of us.

Our Savior (Luke 10th chapter) tells about the traveller from Jerusalem to Jericho falling among thieves, who beat him almost to death. Eventually the priest comes along and does him no good; also the Levite proves another nuisance, but the good Samaritan pours in the oil to heal him, i. e., converts him, and the wine to sanctify him; puts him on his own beast and carries him to the tavern, i. e., the visible Church; pays the landlord, i. e., the pastor, an earnest of the bill, tells him to take good care of him and he will pay the balance when he comes again.

Jerusalem symbolizes the kingdom of God. By the glorious grace of God in Christ, everybody is born in Jerusalem, and has no reason why he should not stay there till the work is done and the glorious exchange for the New Jerusalem above the stars supervenes. But very few, like John the Baptist, the prophet Samuel, the apostle Timothy, the elder brother of the Prodigal, and your humble servant, have the good fortune to get intelligently converted before the age of responsibility.

When, pursuant to hereditary depravity, we commit known sin, we forfeit our infantile justification, thus leaving Jerusalem and going off down the great mountains to Jericho (which is down-hill all the way). We fall among thieves, i. e., evil habits, which rob us of our virtues, graces, intelligence, hope, and everything, thus beating us to death, i. e., exterminating our spiritual life and fitting us only for Hell.

As the priest here is the preacher, you see clearly that no preacher can do the sinner any good. He can only take him to Jesus, introduce him to Him, and leave him in His hands.

The Levite is the church officer. You see he does you no good.

The good Samaritan is Jesus Himself. The donkey on which the Samaritan mounted the man, low down, convenient, perfectly gentle and paradoxically stout, is the arm of Jesus coming right under the sinner, lifting him up and carrying him to the tavern, the visible Church, God's hospital, where the loving pastor receives him with delight and gets a great blessing for his soul, which Jesus always gives the faithful pastor when He commits to him a member. But He will give him a vastly greater blessing when He comes for that faithful parishioner. After the wise, prudent, patient, toiling pastor has finished his work, Jesus will come and take him to glory, and so flood the soul of the pastor that he will almost fly away to Heaven with Him.

Jericho is only about twenty miles from Sodom and Gomorrah, on the Jordan plain. It was built by the fugitives from those wicked cities when God rained down fire from Heaven and destroyed them. It was reprobated to the awful destruction which came upon it in the days of Joshua, as, far back in the days of Abraham, as you remember: "The iniquity of the Amorites was not yet filled." God waited on them four hundred years to repent, but they would not, and moved on to the evil destination of Sodom and Gomorrah.

As you travel along the carriage road from Jerusalem down to Jericho, you will pass by a capacious stone building for lodgers, and a kraal, surrounded by a substantial stone wall, for the protection of animals and vehicles. It is called the "Inn of the Good Samaritan," and is said to be on the spot where the robbers beat the traveler almost to death, and would have finished him but that the tread of people coming scared them away. It is on the mountain, and the presence of the Good Samaritan sanctifies everything where He goes.

(h) Mt. Bethel, fifteen miles north of Jerusalem, is luminous with inspired truth. There Jacob was converted. As "Beth" means home, or family, and "el," God, therefore it memorizes Jacob's happy conversion. His name means rascal, significant of the depravity in his heart, which began to crop out when he took advantage of his brother in his boyhood and cheated him out of his birthright, which entitled him to a double portion of his father's estate; and Isaac was a millionaire, as Abraham had transmitted to him his unbroken estate; thus temporal wealth symbolized spiritual riches.

God, for reasons not revealed to us, reversed the patriarchal law in their case, giving the birthright to Jacob instead of to Esau, even before they were born, (Rom. 9:11): "The children not having yet been born, neither having done anything good or evil, in order that the purpose of God might stand, according to election."

Hence you see Jacob was elected before he was born, and Esau reprobated; this not appertaining to Heaven or Hell, but to the progenitorship of Christ. Throughout the Bible there are two elections, i. e., that of grace, which means salvation or damnation; and that of the Divine progenitorship, which simply means the consanguinity of our Savior.

Some have misconstrued Hebrews 12, where "Esau found no repentance, though he earnestly sought it with tears;" leaping to the conclusion that his reprobation forever excluded him from the kingdom of grace and glory. It is a mistake. Esau was only reprobated from the progenitorship of Christ, i. e., the exalted honor of His personal consanguinity, yet Christ died for him as really as for Jacob. He died for every one, leaving not a solitary soul out of the Atonement. (Heb. 2:9.)

We have "huper pantos" defining the comprehensiveness of the Atonement. "Huper" means instead of, always signifying vicarious substitution. "Pantos" means every one. Therefore the argument for limited atonement is utterly untrue and falls to the ground.

The election of the progenitorship, running through both Testaments, is unconditional. Abraham was elected and his idolatrous relatives reprobated. Isaac was elected and Ishmael reprobated. Yet the Atonement was made for all, the non-elect as well as the elect. The election of grace is on the condition of receiving Christ, your vicarious, substitutionary Expiator and Mediator.

This faith you cannot exercise without radical repentance, involving utter and eternal abandonment to God, thus reaching believing ground, where the Holy Spirit will give you all-needed help to believe God's Word and, by simple faith, to take Jesus for everything. Then He saves you.

Elect is from "eklectos," from "lego," to choose, and "ek," out, hence it means to choose you out of a lost world that you may inherit His kingdom and glorify Him forever.

Jacob stayed at home, worked hard, cultivated the earth, made the living, waited on his mother, and was consequently her favorite. Knowing that Esau was the firstborn, and thus entitled to the birthright, a double portion in the estate, she was anxious for Jacob to get it, neither she nor Jacob knowing that it was already predestinated to him. Therefore they both did wrong by resorting to trickery in his behalf.

Jacob had already taken advantage of Esau, coming home from the chase faint with hunger, by buying his birthright with a good dinner. You have been astonished at Esau for selling it, but look around and you see Esaus on all sides, selling out their transcendent interest in the Kingdom to satisfy physical appetites.

Jacob having thus adroitly bought Esau's birthright, he ran on him a similar stratagem, cheating him out of his patriarchal blessing. Isaac was old and his vision dim. He leaned to Esau as his favorite, in contradiction to Rebekah, who leaned to Jacob. Then he said to Esau, "My son, go to the mountains and catch me some venison, and cook it tender and sweet so I can eat it, though my teeth are fallen out; then my spirit will revive and I will bless you."

While Esau is preparing the venison, Rebekah has Jacob prepare a kid, tender and good, which she diligently stews. Then she puts on him Esau's goat-skin gloves, as he was a hairy brunette and Jacob a smooth blonde. Night is fallen, then Jacob enters his father's room, and says, "Arise, father; eat your son's venison." Isaac responds, "Art thou truly my son Esau?" for Jacob was doing his best to imitate the voice of his brother. Then he, to his shame, answers his father in the affirmative. Then Isaac has him come nigh, that he may feel him. Putting his hands on the gloves, he says, "These are the hands of Esau, but it is the voice of Jacob." Despite his bewilderment, he concludes that Jacob is Esau, so eats the kid and confers on him his patriarchal blessing.

Scarcely has Jacob retreated from the room till Esau enters and presents his venison to Isaac. Then the father discovers that he has made a mistake. Esau lifts a loud and bitter wail, importuning his father to revoke the blessing from Jacob and confer it on him.

This Isaac could not do, because God had conferred it on Jacob before he was born, i. e., the blessing of the Messianic progenitorship. Then Esau, recognizing the strategy of his brother, says, "Surely he has the right name, Jacob (rascal), because he has already supplanted me twice; having cheated me out of my birthright, he has now stolen my blessing."

Rebekah and Jacob, knowing the awful temper of Esau, have already hurried him off in precipitate flight for his life, with no time to take anything for the journey but a staff with which to fight wild beasts and savages. Oh, how he runs all that long, dreary night! When tempted to slow down, imagination hears Esau on his track. He runs on the ensuing day like an antelope, and at nightfall, reaching a great spring rolling its limpid way from beneath the mountain, he drinks voraciously, then his human nature collapses. Despite the horrorism of roaring lions, screaming jackals, howling wolves, and his enraged brother, he is soon wrapped in ambrosial slumber. Dreams move in panorama before him. He sees a ladder resting on the earth and lodging among the stars. On it glorified angels descend and sanctified humanity climbs up to God. His heart is crushed with penitential grief for the sins which have bronght him this flood of trouble. Then the God of Abraham and Isaac hears his cry and floods his soul with heavenly illuminations. Waking, he says, "This is none other but the house of God and the gate of Heaven! Surely God is in this place." From that memorable hour the mountain has been called Bethel instead of Luz.

This was Jacob's regeneration, when he, by the supernatural birth, because a member of God's family. During our late tour in the Holy Land, we visited Mt. Bethel again, and united in prayer in Jacob's Church, built by the Christian Crusaders nine hundred years ago, on the spot where Jacob slept, dreamed and saw the ladder reaching up to Heaven, symbolizing Christ, who is our ladder up which we climb to God and Heaven.

Rising in the morning, Jacob prosecutes that long and wearisome journey to Mesopotamia, whence came his grandfather and mother. There he toils twenty years in the capacity of shepherd, the most lucrative business in the world at that time, as there were so few people, and the land superabounded so that it was not appropriated, and every man used all of it he would.

The Jews this day are the most industrious and enterprising people in the world, getting rich where others remain poor, and Jacob is their ancestor. Arriving in Mesopotamia with nothing but his staff, in the lapse of twenty years he became a millionaire. Then, when God called him back to his native land, it seemed like breaking up his father-in-law, his flocks and herds having so wonderfully multiplied.

He journed back to the valley of Succoth, between Mts. Gerizim and Ebal, where he pitched his tent and lived quite awhile. There Laban, his father-in-law, overtook him and called him to account for his stealthy departure. They came into a mutual reconciliation, entering into a peace covenant, confirmed by a heap of stones which they mutually gathered and piled up for a witness to their reconciliation.

On this journey, as Jacob approached the Jabbok, messengers meeting him certify that Esau is coming with an army of four hundred men. Jacob sends his herds and flocks, the servants in charge of them, his wives and children across the river, and he himself goes aside to pray God to protect him from his alienated and angry brother. When he gets to praying, God turns in the light, and he sees that Jacob is his greatest enemy, far more formidable than Esau. Oh! that memorable night of wrestling prayer, while his song goes up:

>"Come, O Thou Traveler unknown,
>　Whom still I hold but cannot see;
>My company before me is gone,
>　And I am left alone with Thee.
>With Thee all night I mean to stay
>And wrestle till the break of day.
>　In vain Thou strugglest to get free,
>I never will unloose my hold.
>　Art Thou the man that died for me?
>The secret of Thy love unfold."

So God wrestles with Jacob all night long, till He says, "Let me go, for the day is breaking." But Jacob says, "I will not let Thee go till Thou bless me."

During all the wrestling, the salient point God makes with him is for him to tell Him his name. Of course God knew his name, then why did he make him tell Him? Why, that he might confess, which God requires in every case. The reason Jacob was so reluctant to confess his name was because it is a Hebrew name that means "rascal," and it was an awful thing for him to confess to God that he was a rascal. Though he held on all night before he made confession, the very moment he made it God blessed him, knocking his thigh out of joint. As the thigh is the symbol of power, He thus manifested the crucifixion of old Adam, i. e., the death of Jacob the rascal. The moment "Jacob" died, "Israel" leaped into life, i. e., God changed his name from Jacob to Israel, which is a compound Hebrew word, and means a "prince of God," i. e., one that prevails with God. Therefore "Israelite" is God's name for His people in all the world, simply meaning one that prevails with God.

Whereas Jacob had named the place of his conversion "Bethel," which means "family of God," because there he was born from above and became a member of God's family, now he names that spot by the brook Jabbok "Peniel," from "peno," face, and "el," God, meaning the "face of God."

The Fergerson missionary work girdles the globe. I have preached in their missions in America, Asia, Africa and the islands of the sea. It is called "Peniel," because they profess and preach entire sanctification, which means that they are walking in the light of God's countenance.

When Jacob received his peniel experience his fear all evanesced away, so he went on his way to meet Esau. On meeting, instead of Esau killing him, he embraced and kissed him, showing that he, too, had spent the night with God, and that He had gloriously blessed him, flooding him with love for his dear and only brother. This was beautifully confirmatory of the fact that salvation was as free for Esau as for Jacob, his reprobation in the controversy with his brother only involving the Messianic progenitorship, which had nothing to do with salvation or damnation. It was a matter very dimly apprehended by those boys who fought over it so long.

"But," you say, "Jacob had won Esau by that ten-thousand-dollar present he had sent him." That conclusion is refuted by the fact that Esau modestly declined to take it, as he, too, had grown rich and become the leading man of all Eden, which God had given him. On his refusal to take it, he observed, "My dear brother, I have enough;" but Jacob insisted on his taking it as a souvenir of his love for him, so that he could no longer resist. Suffice it to say that the two brothers became firm friends, and so remained to the end of life, uniting in the interment of their father and mother in the family sepulchre, Machpelah, in Hebron.

As the Jews are pouring in from the ends of the earth and colonizing the Holy Land, by the erection of their beautiful new cities marking all the ancient historic places, they have come to the spot where the brothers met, and there built a beautiful city, Synadelphia (meeting of the brothers).

(i) In this expeditious survey of the sacred mountains, we cannot pass by Mount Juttah, the home of Zacharias and Elisabeth, and the birthplace of John the Baptist.

We pass in full view of this beautiful mountain, on our right, as we travel to Hebron, about twenty miles south of Jerusalem. During the ages of desolation which followed the awful Jewish trubulation, this place was lost sight of, and remained unknown till five years ago, when the Germans discovered it. They have built on it a magnificent convent, which shows very conspicuously from the carriage road.

The reason the place went into swift decay and oblivion was because, while Herod was murdering the boy babies in Bethlehem and suburbs, Zacharias and Elisabeth, fearing for the safety of their son, though no such an order had been made for Juttah, migrated away to the wilderness of Judæa and never came back, but brought up their son among those poor Holiness people, i. e., the Essenes.

There were three denominations in the Jewish Church—the Pharisees, orthodox; the Sadducces, heterodox, like the Campbellites and Seventh Day Adventists, repudiating spirituality; and the Essenes, poor Holiness people. As the last were poor, they lived in the deserts, where the land was so poor and unproductive for want of rain that they had all the room they wanted, and at the same time extraordinary religious liberties.

John the Baptist was the greatest of all the prophets, aye, more than a prophet, because he was the introducer of his Lord.

(j) As the Bible takes Mts. Gerizim and Ebal together, we do likewise.

Long before Israel ever reached the Promised Land, Moses told them, when they did, to go to these mountains and let six tribes stand on the one and six on the other; those on Gerizim speaking blessing with a loud voice, those on Ebal the curses, and all together responding in vociferous Amens.

As these mountains are so far apart, and separated by the beautiful, rich valley of Succoth, in which Jacob was living when he dug the well at that place which to-day bears his name, and from whence he sent Joseph on the errand to his brethren at Dothan, I used to wonder how the people could all hear. But when I visited those mountains and the intervening valley, I found them constituting a natural amphitheater, having the properties of a whispering gallery, so that the voice is distinctly heard throughout that vast space. The Mormon Tabernacle, in Salt Lake City, Utah, this day is constructed in a similar manner. Consequently the audience of eighteen thousand which it accommodates can distinctly hear throughout the building.

On Mt. Gerizim you will find the great Samaritan temple, a rival of that in Jerusalem. It was built by Sanballat and Tobiah, the governor of Samaria, when Nehemiah, Ezra and Zerubbabel built the second temple in Jerusalem after the return out of Babylonian captivity.

In Shechem, in the valley of Succoth, the old capital of the ten tribes under Jeroboam, I have often visited the Samaritan convent, and seen the oldest book in the world, i. e., the Pentateuch of Moses, which he wrote 3,578 years ago.

At the base of Mt. Gerizim you will find Jacob's well, where Jesus preached to the lone Samaritan woman who, though an abundant sinner, got gloriously converted, so that, forgetting her water pot, she ran away to the city, a mile distant, and stirred it all with her shouts, a great crowd then following her back to see the wonderful Prophet who had caused the paradoxical change. Then He stayed two days preaching, and many were converted.

The tomb of Joseph is in full view, at the foot of Mt. Ebal, where the children of Israel buried him after keeping his embalmed body 154 years in Egypt and then hauling the heavy stone coffin all the time they journed from Egypt to the land of Canaan, including the forty years in the wilderness. Then when Joshua, at Shiloh, divided out the land among them, giving each tribe its inheritance, they buried him in the portion of Manasseh, his eldest son.

The long forty years of the memorable march out of Egypt into Canaan, to the eyes of all nations exhibited the aspect of a great funeral procession, as Joseph's coffin, on a wagon drawn by twelve oxen (as those stone coffins are so heavy), headed all that long procession of three million, out of Egypt through the sea, peregrinating in the wilderness and finally through the Jordan into the land of Canaan, and away to Joseph's inheritance at the bass of Mt. Ebal, where you now find his tomb kept in nice order and visited by thousands of pilgrims from all parts of the world.

(k) Mt. Ephraim, which is exceedingly large, containing several hundred thousand acres of exceedingly rich land, belonged to the tribe of Ephraim (from which it is named). It deserves recognition in the catalogue of sacred mountains.

Ephraim was by far the largest tribe in Israel, so the name is frequently used representatively of all Israel. Joshua, the greatest military chieftain in the annals of history, having enjoyed forty years of constant practice, fighting the Amalekites and other barbaric nations in the wilderness, was an Ephraimite. You will find his grave in this mountain, in front of the hill Gaash, as described in the last chapter of his book.

Off to the east from Mt. Gerizim, beyond Mt. Succoth, you will find the tomb of Eleazar and Ithamar, the sons of Aaron the high priest, who in their time succeeded their father in the high priesthood, their elder brothers, Nadab and Abihu, having lost their lives in the wilderness offering strange fire to the Lord.

The original says "other fire." When the high priest offered the sacrifice, God sent down the fire from Heaven and consumed it. Nadab and Abihu thought they could do what their father did, and in his absence started to offer incense to the Lord. When the fire failed to fall from Heaven and consume the incense, as they expected, they had the audacity to put some material fire on it. The result was that it not only consumed the incense, but burned and killed them, teaching us the awful and most important lesson that, if we tinker with any fire except that of the Holy Ghost sent down from Heaven, we are in imminent danger of losing spiritual life.

We live in the midst of multitudinous sad and

mournful illustrations of this grand truth, people making spurious professions and dealing with strange fire on all sides.

Mt. Ephraim is covered all over with great olive-trees, as well as an infinite diversity of delicious fruit-trees.

Mt. Samaria was bought by King Omri from the man by the name of Shemer, and amid all the revolutions and mutations of the ten tribes, changing their capital three times during their short career (first Shechem, then Tirzah, and finally Samaria), the city on it by that name became the capital, and so remained till they were carried into captivity by the Babylonians.

Samaria is a very beautiful table mountain, and a lovely site for a city. The city is now a heap of ruins, occupied by a few paupers, with troops of roaring dogs (peculiar to the Mohammedans, in whose religion the dog is sacred) roaring everywhere.

The largest and most important building in the city is the Church of John the Baptist, built by the Crusaders in the eleventh century. It contains the tombs of John the Baptist, the prophet Elisha and the chamberlain Obadiah. The head of John the Baptist is said to be buried in the Mosque Rimmon in Damascus.

During God's awful judgments against Samaria on account of her idolatry, at one time the Syrians besieged Samaria two solid years, when famine so prevailed that women ate their own children. King Jehu was walking on the wall when a woman cried out to him, "O King, please make my neighbor bring out her son, that we may eat him. She and I entered into a contract to eat our sons, as we were both starving to death. We cast lots and it fell upon mine. We have already eaten him and are starving again, but she has hidden her son and will not bring him out."

Then the king rent his robe and put ashes on his body, thus demonstrating the greatest distress and calamity, and attracting the attention of all the people, who cried out, "What aileth thee, O King?" He responds, "I am going to kill the prophet Elisha to-day and then surrender the city to the Syrians." "Why, O King?" Then he responds, "Our people are starving to death and eating their own children."

Then, accompanied by some of his lords, he goes to the cottage of Elisha and tells him what he is going to do. The prophet says, "Can't you wait one day?" The king says, "Oh, yes, we have been waiting two years, and you have been telling us to hold on, that the Syrians will never be able to take the city. You have prophesied lies, for the people are eating their own children, and we have to surrender or all starve to death."

Then Elisha says, "To-morrow a measure of wheat and two measures of barley will be sold for a shilling in the gates of Samaria." A lord on whose arm the king was leaning contradicted the prophet, saying it could not be so cheap even if the Lord should open windows in Heaven and pour it down. To this Elisha responds, "You shall see it, but not eat of it."

That evening at nightfall four lepers came to Samaria to the leper gate, where alone they are permitted to enter, and considered among themselves how the famine was raging in the city and they even were starving on the outside. Deliberating on the propriety of going in where they would starve to death, or of staying out where they were already starving, it was suggested that they surrender to the Syrians, observing that they could but kill them, and they had better be killed than starve to death. Therefore they determined to surrender to the Syrians.

Entering the Syrian camp, they find no human being, but plenty of food, and as they were so hungry, they proceeded at once to eat. Then they entered another tent, and found not only plenty of food but valuables, even silver and gold. As they continued to explore the camp, they found it entirely deserted, and food, money, and all sorts of valuables there. So they concluded to go and tell the king.

He responds, "I know these Syrians. They want to call us out to enter the camp, then they'll rush on us and kill us." A man says, "There are yet four horses in the city that are not starved to death. Let us take them and find what has become of the Syrians." So they do, and they find the Syrians have utterly fled away out of the country across the Jordan and gone home. They also find the way strewn with garments and valuables of every kind, which the Syrians had started to carry, but in their pressure had to throw away in order to expedite their flight.

The solution of the problem was that God caused the Syrians to hear a noise of many chariots and horses, rushing to battle with tremendous roar. So they all said, "The king of Israel has hired the kings of Egypt and of the Hittites to come against us, and our escape is only in flight." Consequently they started off in a precipitate stampede, leaving their stuff all on the ground, except the most necessary and valuable, and as the noise increased and seemed to get nearer all the time as they ran, their alarm was so intensified that they threw away everything that would encumber their flight, and ran for dear life.

As the Syrian army was thus utterly scared away, so that they gave up the siege, leaving an abundance of food and vast spoils on the ground, the king of Israel had the food brought to the gates of the city to be sold. He appointed over the work that lord on whose arm he had leaned when the prophet told him there would be plenty of food in Samaria the next day; that wheat would sell a measure for a shekel and barley two measures for a shekel, and the lord had contradicted the prophet, saying it could not be so even if God would make windows in Heaven and pour it down. When they brought out the food and this lord proceeded to conduct the sale, the people were so hungry that they ran over him and killed him, thus verifying the words of the prophet, "You shall see it, but shall not eat of it."

(1) Mount Dothan belongs to the sacred catalogue. It is twenty miles from Samaria.

On one occasion, Ben-hadad, king of Syria, concluded that there were spies in his camp. Consequently he convened his senate to hunt them, giving as the reason why he knew their counsels must be infested by spies, that the king of Israel knew everything they plotted in the dead hours of the night, and intercepted all their plans so that they were unable to make any headway.

A man, rising, observes, "O King, you are mistaken. We are all true men, ready to die in the cause of our country. I can explain the trouble you mention. There is a prophet in Israel who tells the king everything you devise at midnight, so that all of your plans are intercepted and contravened." "Now," says Ben-hadad, "that is light on the matter, and I know just what to do. We will ascertain that prophet's whereabouts, and go at once and kill him." Then a man says, "If that is all you want, I can serve you now with all needed information. He is holding a protracted meeting at Dothan."

Consequently Ben-hadad dispatches an army with all expedition to Dothan, with orders to surround it in the night, to find the prophet the ensuing morning and cut his head off. It works to a charm. They surround Dothan by night, till there is no possible chance for any one to escape.

Then Gehazi, Elisha's boy preacher, rises early in the morning, goes out, and runs back affrighted, with tremendous voice ejaculating, "Father, we die to-day!" "Why, my son?" "Oh, because we are surrounded by the Syrians on all sides, so there is no chance for any one to escape." Then Elisha goes out, looks around, and come back, observing, "My son, that is so; the Syrians are all around us, but there is another army around us too, much greater than they." The boy says, "Father, there is nobody here but the Syrians." Then Elisha asked the Lord to open his eyes.

Immediately Gehazi looks again, and he sees great Mt. Dothan literally covered with chariots, filled with angels lifting up glittering swords, flashing the sunbeams and eradiating the mountain till it looks like a celestial flame. Then, the Word says, "He (the Lord) smote the Syrians with blindness." Not a good translation, as they all had their sight all right, but He dropped on them an optical illusion so that they misapprehended Elisha for their own commander, and forfeited their recognition of Dothan altogether, concluding that the guides in the night had made a mistake, led them to the wrong place, and that they still had to travel to reach Dothan. Therefore when Elisha walked out and issued marching orders, they all cheerfully obeyed, thinking they were still going to Dothan.

Elisha leads them directly to Samaria, the capital of Israel, and turns them over to King Jehu, who thinks of nothing but to execute them, asking the prophet, "What shall we do with them; shall we smite them?" But Elisha responds, "Oh, no, do not hurt one of them, but put all your cooks to work to get their dinners, for they are very hungry." Then oh, what a clattering of pots and what a rally of the cooks!

So they give the men a good dinner, and they all eat a Benjamin's mess. Then the king says, "What shall we do now?" "Oh," says the prophet, "hold on till I pray for them." After that the king says, "What shall we do with them now?" Elisha says, "Hold on till I bless them all." Then the king says, "What shall we do now?" and the prophet responds, "Send them home," so it is done.

When they arrive in their own camp and tell Benhadad their wonderful story—about their kind and cordial reception, their good dinner, the fervent prayers of the prophet and his copious blessings—Benhadad says, "The war is over; we do not fight a people that will treat us this way." And so the long and bloody conflict is quickly brought to an end by Elisha's signal acts of Christian philanthropy.

(m) Mount Gilead, one of the Gilboa range, and not the Gilead range (which is east of the Jordan where Elijah was born), deserves a prominent place in the sacred catalogue.

It so happened one time that all the tribes of Arabia, under the common cognomen "Midianites," had united against Israel and enslaved them, putting on their necks the heavy, galling yoke of bondage, and using their fertile lands to graze their war horses. They let them sow their wheat and barley for bread, and their millet, sesame and panic for their animals, but they would come in and reap the harvest and take it all, so in the land of plenty famine was looking them in the face on all sides. The hope of the nation had sunk into the gloom of an eternal night, since seven years of hard bondage had rolled away and the chains were tightening all the time.

But behold! an angel in human form salutes Gideon, a young, unaspiring, uninfluential man walking in the fear of God and rendering himself useful as a class-leader. When the angel notifies Gideon that God has put His hands upon him to deliver Israel, his faith staggers, till he verifies the call by the practical test of the fleece and the dew, abundantly illustrating and confirming the Divine intervention. Then he sends his ten boy preachers to traverse all the land and blow the war bugles, calling them to assemble in Mt. Gilead. Of course in that time of universal despondency, only the few who would rather die on the battlefield than bear the galling yoke of bondage respond to the bugle calls. Pursuant to the law of Moses forbidding them to take faint-hearted people to the battlefield, Gideon brings the matter before his thirty-two thousand volunteers, when twenty-two thousand confess faint-heartedness, cutting down his army to ten thousand. God then commands him to proceed with his elimination by taking the ten thousand down to the water to drink, and calling out all who take up the water in their hands and drink with great expedition, like the dog laps up water with his tongue; and to let all who drop down and deliberately drink by putting their mouths to the water, go away with the twenty-two thousand who had already confessed their faint-heartedness. There are left but three hundred, as ninety-seven hundred were removed by the second elimination, pursuant to the test at the water. The twenty-two thousand were not idolators, but orthodox Israelites; the ninety-seven hundred were converted, but not sanctified; but the three hundred truly enjoyed the perfect love which casteth out fear, i. e., they had passed the "scarey" line and gotten out into an experience where they could not be scared; they saw God in everything, and their faith wavered at nothing.

By this time the alarm was terrible, because the orient was luminous with the splendor radiant from the glittering panoplies of the Midianites, three hundred thousand of whom were coming to nip the insurgency in the bud, and settle the matter forever. They arrived too late in the day for decisive execution, but received ample information in reference to Gideon and his men. The 31,700 had retired beyond the mountain brow into a place of security, but within the sound of the battle, because Gideon knew the three hundred were going to stampede that tremendous host, and also that when the enemy is on the trot cowards are just as good soldiers as you can want. It takes flint and steel to stampede the devil, but when he gets into a precipitate skedaddle, cowards will rally, chase the fugitive foe, and do great execution.

While the Midianites all spread their tents and lie down to sleep, no slumber comes to the eyelids of Gideon's three hundred braves. As the midnight approaches, and they are all on their knees praying for the God of Israel to come down and deliver His people, Gideon says to Phurah, his boy preacher, "Let us go down to the host," then they stealthily walk down. They hear the deep breathing and the snoring of the enemy, when a soldier, suddenly awakening, says to his comrade by his side, "Did you see that?" "See what?" "Oh, I saw a barley cake come rolling down Mt. Gilead and strike a tent, and down it came; another, and it fell, and still another and another until the encampment went into ruin." His waking comrade responds with broken utterance: "Oh, I know what that barley cake is—it is none other than Gideon, the son of Joash, a mighty man of war, who is going to light on us to-night from the summit of Mt. Gilead, and we are all dead men."

Then Gideon and Phurah rise and go back to the three hundred braves still on their knees praying through to God for the intervention of His omnipotent arm, in verification of His covenant with Abraham, Isaac and Jacob. Then Gideon divides them into three bands, one hundred each, and gives his order for each to take with him a pitcher (i. e., a large earthen vessel in which they carried water from the fountain), a torch and a trumpet—the pitcher to hide the torch till the signal of battle, and the trumpet to blow; and at the signal they were to shout: "The sword of the Lord and of Gideon!" (Judges 7:18.)

He then sends them to the three points of an isosceles triangle, encompassing the vast host of Midianites. At a given signal, they were all to break their pitchers, dashing them down on the rocks with the utmost violence, thus producing an uproarious and prolonged clatter, and awakening all the soldiers in that region, who would be seized with the impression that they were assaulted by an overwhelming force of cavalry and war-chariots, and that this noise is the clangor of their steel-shod hoofs against the rocks. Then, lifting high their torches, a round hundred in each band—enough to light a mighty host to the scene of conflict—they were all to shout: "The sword of the Lord and of Gideon (their vociferous battle-cry)!"

The assault was too sudden for the Midianites to raise any lights in the army, and as the assault was made on three sides, encompassing the host, the awful alarm given superinduced a stampede. Consequently they all rushed together in the interior of that great plain Esdrælon, on which so many great battles have been fought, and, in the darkness of the night, colliding, each, thinking he has met the enemy, draws his sword and bathes it in the blood of his fellow, thus killing one another in piles and heaping the battle-field with mountains of the dead.

Meanwhile the 31,700 who had taken the cowardly side of the question, have heard the shout of victory and come to the fight with all their might; now that the enemy was put to flight, they were no longer cowardly, but brave.

The stampede is universal, the vast host making for the fords of the Jordan. Meanwhile Gideon, anticipating this victory, had not sent recruiting officers into the great tribe of Ephraim, through which the fugitives had to make their escape out of the country, but he sent out trumpeters to rendezvous them to intercept the flight of the panic-striken host, and to slay them as they attempted to get away.

The result of all this was the signal and overwhelming defeat of the Midianites, and the emancipation of Israel, so that they had peace and prosperity so long as that generation lived who had seen the great deliverance and known God's mighty works.

From Mt. Gilead we cross the plain of Esdrælon to Mount Little Hermon, immortalized by two resurrections.

On the southeastern slope of this sacred mountain, we have the city Shunem, through which the prophet Elisha passed in his evangelistic tours, and where he stopped ever and anon, till the good woman suggested to her husband to build a chamber on the wall for the lodging of the prophet, supplying it with a table and a candlestick, as well as a bed on which to rest.

This couple was unfortunate enough to be without an heir, a serious affliction in Israel, as they could not hold their inheritance in the Holy Land. But, responsive to the prayer of the prophet, God gives them a bright son. He grows up, and, while laboring in the harvest, receives a sunstroke and dies. The prophet then lived at Mt. Carmel, fifteen miles away from Shunem, the boy's home. Then the mother went after him with all her might, having laid her son on his bed in his chamber, and having faith in God to raise him from the dead through the instrumentality of the prophet, responsive to whose prayers he had been given.

On her arrival, as soon as the prophet hears her message, he gives Gehazi, the fleet young man, his staff to carry at once and lay on the child. But that did not satisfy the mother, who falls and lays hold of his feet in entreaty, so of course he goes with her. On arrival, going up into his chamber he prostrates himself on the boy's dead body, placing eyes, nose and mouth on those of the lad, and hands and feet on his. While lying there praying, the stripling sneezes seven times and rises into life.

On the northwestern slope of this same sacred mountain stands the city of Nain, where lived the widow with the son, who sickened and died, leaving her entirely alone in this cold, friendless world. Jesus, forty miles away at Capernaum (His adopted home after His expulsion from His native city, Nazareth), beholding the scene, walks away accompanied by His disciples. The great procession is following the bier to the sepulchre. Coming up from a ravine, He steps in front of the bier, and beckons to the pall-bearers to set it down, to the unutterable astonishment of all, as it was a thing unheard of for anyone to interrupt a corpse on its way to the grave. Turning round, He lifts the pall from the face of the dead, exposing the countenance, black with that terrible Syrian fever which had cut short the young man's life; then He speaks with a voice so loud that all the multitude hear Him distinctly: "Young man, I say unto thee, Arise!" Those eyes open, the mist evanesces, they begin to sparkle, color comes into his face, and the ghastly pallor retreats away. He sees his mother, reaches out his arms, and she falls into his embrace.

By this time the funeral procession is all broken up, and they are running precipitately, like they were wild, and oh, how they shout! startling the people in the city who had never heard a shout at a funeral, but always weeping and mourning. They run up on the flat roofs of the houses, and stretch over to see what in all the world is the matter. Soon they recognize the whole crowd, right-about faced and moving back toward the city, shouting till the mountains reverberate the tremendous roar, "Glory to God in the highest for raising up a Prophet in Israel who has the power to speak the dead to life!" As the procession draws nigh, the people recognize the poor widow and Samuel, her noble son, arm in arm, leading the procession back to the city.

The Franciscan monks have built a beautiful church edifice on the spot where Jesus raised the young man from the dead. I have frequently been in it.

(n) Mt. Tabor, so celebrated in the sacred catalogue, is so conspicuous that he is in full view from many other mountains, and from the carriage roads crossing the plains you will always recognize him, because he is round as a potato hill. His history is simply wonderful.

As you will read in the Book of Judges, at one time the king of Hazor ruled over Israel for twenty years, with vigor and galling oppression, especially because he had nine hundred iron chariots armed with scythes, so that he could rush through an army and cut it to pieces on all sides. Israel had no such facilities, consequently she groaned in hard bondage. So many efforts to regain their liberties had been made, and proved abortive, that nobody had any faith. But now God laid His hand on Deborah, a mother in Israel, and raised her up to deliver the nation. She began her administration sitting under a palm-tree judging Israel, i. e., exercising the office of the people's ruler, which of course meant rebellion against the king of Hazor.

She sent recruiting officers about over the country to blow the trumpet to beat for volunteers, and to throw open the door for all who had the courage, to join the insurgency and to trust God to dethrone the usurpers and give Israel their freedom. The hope was so forlorn that only one here and there, who would rather die than bear the yoke of bondage, was venturesome enough to join the revolt.

Eventually ten thousand had rallied around this mother in Israel, then she sends away off to the land of Naphtali for Barak to come. He was considered the bravest man in the world, and hence his name, which means thunderbolt. When he came and she told him she wanted him to lead those ten thousand against the commander-in-chief of Jabin's army, his courage failed and he asked to be excused, observing, "To be sure my name is thunderbolt, but there is no hope for us. It would simply mean to die for nothing, because our enemies are too strong for us to do anything." Then Deborah says, "If I will lead the army, will you be my second?" and he responds, "Yes, till I die." Then she says, "We will go ahead with the war against Sisera."

So now she astonishes everybody by leaving Mt. Carmel, fortified by a great wall, where we would naturally conclude they would abide and operate on the defensive, and giving the order to descend the mountain and meet Sisera with his formidable host and nine hundred scythe-armed iron chariots on the open plain. It looked like the Israelites would stand no chance at all, but all be cut to pieces by those scythe-armed chariots. But they deliberately marched down the mountain, entered the plain of Megiddo, and marched against the hosts of Sisera.

Behold! God sends an awful hailstorm, dropping down stones big as your fist on Sisera's army, killing the men in piles and so affrighting the horses drawing those scythe-armed chariots that they become utterly unmanageable, dashing everywhere. The hail so blinded the people that order was utterly impossible, and the confusion became incorrigible. Meanwhile the rain fell in torrents, flooding the plain with waterspouts, and so overflowing the river Kishon that it spread out like a sea, flowing with blood, and nobody thought of anything but to escape for life.

N. B. The hail did not fall in the army of Israel.

In the terrible bloody flood and awful disaster of the hailstorm, knocking the people dead on all sides, Sisera runs for his life, with Barak on his track. He enters a Kenite village. (These people were descendants of Hobab, the brother-in-law of Moses, who visited him in the wilderness, and who declined Moses' earnest invitation to go with the Israelites to the Promised Land. Moses said, "Come thou with us, and we will do thee good: for God hath spoken good concerning Israel," but Hobab answered in the negative. However, he afterwards changed his mind and went, and these Kenites were his descendants.)

When Sisera was running through the Kenite village, faint with fatigue, Jael, a young woman, invited him into her house and gave him a bowl of rich, cold milk to drink. His physical exhaustion and the soporific potion soon lulled him to sleep. Falling down on the dirt floor, his deep breathing soon convinces Jael that he is fast asleep. Then, taking a large iron spike used to fasten the door, and a wooden mallet, she puts the point upon Sisera's temple and strikes so forcefully that she dashes it through his skull and brain and down into the ground, thus nailing him fast, and he breathes his life away. Then she goes to the door and sees Barak running with all his might, and shouting, "Have you seen Sisera?" She says, "Come in, and I will show you the one you want." She leads him into a back room and there he sees the greatest military man in the world, who had held Israel in bondage for years, lying dead.

This of course consummated the victory and set Israel free; then they had rest forty years. Thus you see how this great victory was achieved by a mother in Israel and a daughter of Zion; the former leading the embattled host, and the latter, with her own hands, slaying the champion of their enemies. I have often seen Harosheth of the Gentiles (Judges, 4th chapter), where Sisera lived and kept his army.

(o) Carmel is a celebrated sacred mountain, wonderfully identified with Hebrew history. It is ten miles long, cylindrical in shape, and very conspicuous from land and sea.

This mountain has wonderful celebrity in the biographies of Elijah and Elisha, the great prophets of Israel who filled the land with their miracles. If you ever travel in the Holy Land, you will certainly visit this mountain and enter the great Convent of Elijah on the west end, overlooking the sea. You will also, for hours and days, enjoy a conspicuous view of the convent on the east end, where the notable debate (1 Kings, 18th chapter) took place between Elijah and the false prophets, and in which he so decisively triumphed over them that the vast multitude of people saw that he was right and they were wrong. This was because God so decisively answered him by fire, which consumed the sacrifice, the wood, and even the rocks, as well as the twelve barrels of water which were poured on to convince the people that there was no concealed fire to ignite the sacrifice. Consequently a wonderful revolution transpired among them, so that, in obedience to the mandate of Elijah, they arrested the false prophets and slew them, thus revolutionizing the government and turning it over to God, who alone has a right to rule.

God sent Elijah to restore the law, which Israel had long violated, and sinned against so grossly and egregiously that He finally let the Babylonians carry them into captivity. He sent Elijah and succeeded him by Elisha, and if Israel had repented under their preaching, they never would have been carried into captivity.

Elijah wrought seven great miracles, and as Elisha, his successor, received a double portion of his spirit, he wrought fourteen. But the people were so blinded by the false prophets that they survived all the mighty works of God's prophets, and so persisted in idolatry that God permitted Shalmanezer to carry off Israel, B. C. 720, and Sennacherib, at a later date, to finish them.

It would seem that the awful fate of Israel would have saved Judah from a similar doom, but it did not. Consequently, despite the wonderful prophecies of Isaiah, Jeremiah and Ezekiel, they persistently ever and anon collapsed into idolatry. Though Hezekiah traveled all over the country destroying idols, and Josiah did the same, yet they would hold on to them in spite of God's prophets, until at last they were made captives.

(p) Mt. Nazareth lifts its lofty summit high up into the blue sky, and from it pilgrims enjoy a splendid view of Carmel, Tabor, Little Hermon, Gilboa—where Saul and his sons fell on the battlefield—Giliad, and Great Hermon, far away in Syria and covered with snows.

When our Savior returned to His home in Nazareth from John's great revival at the Jordan, where John baptized Him, and went into that old synagogue where He had worshipped for thirty years, He began to preach with the Holy Ghost sent down from Heaven, as He had received Him in the symbol of the innocent dove flying down from Heaven and lighting on Him. His humanity in the preacher needed the enduement of the Holy Ghost, which is the sine qua non of Gospel preaching. Therefore when He proceeded to preach, the truth and fire so electrified Him and burned them that they rebelled against Him, rose up, and were going to cast Him down from a precipice and kill Him. But His divinity came to the help of His humanity, rendering Him invisible, so that He passed away to Capernaum, there making His home (doubtless in the house of Peter, who lived there), while He preached in Galilee those two and a half years of His ministry.

We went into Joseph's carpenter-shop, and saw in statuary Joseph and Jesus wielding their tools and executing their mechanical work, while Mary sat by and looked on them. The Holy Spirit certainly wonderfully helped the artist in his manufacture of the statue of Jesus. It represents Him as about fifteen years of age, and invested with a simplicity, beauty, clemency and loveliness absolutely unutterable.

Nazareth was so insignificant as not to receive a single mention in the Old Testament. It was really the butt of ridicule and reproach. All of that was providential, in order that our glorious Christ might come from the bottom of society, so that no one could say, "He belongs to the nobility, and will not descend to notice me."

The place has been wonderfully improved and built up during the present generation. Since I first saw it, sixteen years ago, the Germans have built a great convent and Bible School there, high up on the mountain, and the Latin Christians have recently built a great edifice nearer the summit.

(q) Mt. Capernaum, hanging over that city on the north bank of the Galilean sea, is notable for our Savior's wonderful "Sermon on the Mount," and especially the Beatitudes He enumerated. (Matthew, 5th, 6th and 7th chapters.)

There is a great misunderstanding relating to the Mt. of Beatitudes. As a rule pilgrims visiting the Holy Land have accepted the testimony of their guides, who have generally told them that Hatton, on the west bank of the Sea of Galilee, is the Mt. of Beatitudes where our Lord preached His wonderful sermon and selected His apostles. You have only to read carefully Matthew, Mark and Luke (who give you the inspired history) to see that it cannot be Mt. Hatton. Jesus was in Capernaum when He ascended the mountain, accompanied by His disciples, whereas Hatton is ten miles distant across the sea. If He had gone thither, we would surely have the record. Those three inspired historians, without a dissenting voice, settled the matter that it was Mt. Capernaum, which hangs over the city and requires no sea voyage to be reached.

The reason why this mistake has been indulged in is because Capernaum, during the ages of desolation, utterly perished, and centuries rolled away when they could not know where it had been. Sixteen years ago they were just beginning to discover it by excavation. They have been at it ever since and have extensively uncovered it. As it was down by the sea, surrounded by mountains, and that sea is seven hundred feet below the Mediterranean, it was covered up with debris accumulated on it from the surrounding highlands. They will still go ahead with their excavations, and at the same time be rebuilding it.

A great synagogue, doubtless the one built by the

centurion (Luke, 7th chapter) has been uncovered. In Matthew, 11th chapter, you read: "Woe unto thee, Chorazin! woe unto thee, Bethsaida! for if the mighty works, wrought in thee, had been done in Tyre and Sidon, they would have repented in sackcloth and ashes long ago. It will be more tolerable for Sodom and Gomorrah in the day of judgment than for you. And thou, Capernaum, art exalted up to Heaven, but thou shalt be cast down to Hell."

He Himself lived in Capernaum; His presence is Heaven, hence Capernaum had Heaven, but did not repent.

The reason why these cities went into desolation was the visitation of these awful woes. They are now reviving, ominous of His near coming. While Capernaum, responsive to these woes, along with Bethsaida and Chorazin, went into utter desolation, Tiberias, on the west bank of the sea, survived in a depreciated condition.

A. D. 1187, a great battle was fought on Mt. Hatton between the Crusaders and Saracens. The former were signally defeated and driven out of Palestine, and the latter achieved a great and decisive victory, under the leadership of the great Saladin. This battle, with its decisive victory, gave such notoriety to Mt. Hatton that it was pronounced the Mt. of Beatitudes, and this statement has been transmitted, people traveling in that country accepting the testimony of their guides. Meanwhile Capernaum went down unnamed, desolate, covered with debris, and unknown, till very recently. But the Bible settles all controversies; you have nothing to do but to read and follow it, and you will see that the mountain rising up and towering over the city of Capernaum is the Mt. of Beatitudes.

(r) The Mt. of Transfiguration has been more involved in bewilderment than any other in the sacred catalogue. For long ages it was believed to be Tabor. If you travel thither, you will actually find the three tabernacles which Peter suggested to build—one for Jesus, one for Moses, and one for Elijah—built there. But these tabernacles were built by the Crusaders in the eleventh century, too late for them to know anything about it.

They, with all the Christians of the early centuries, followed Origen, the greatest scholar and writer of the apostolic age. His father and grandfather were both preachers, and both suffered martyrdom. As he lived in the third century, his grandfather must have been converted by the apostles. Origen was the author of about sixty books explaining the Bible. He says Tabor was the Mt. of Transfiguration. This conclusion is confuted by the fact that there was a town on the summit of Tabor at that time, while they "went apart," i. e., Jesus took Peter, James and John and went up into a lonely mountain apart, having left the nine others down at the base. Hence it could not have been Tabor, because its summit was occupied and they could not have been alone there through the night, as the Word says. Besides, Mark 9:30 says that when they came down from the mountain they traveled through Galilee to Capernaum.

Our Savior had taken His apostles away to Caesarea Philippi, in southern Syria, to reveal to them His Christhood. If He had done it among the Jews, they would have crowned Him king and the Romans would have killed Him, whereas He still had six months of His ministry, and it was high time that His apostles should have positive information from His own lips, assuring them of His Christhood. When He made this revelation to them, it filled them with bewilderment, inquiry and trouble. He then and there certified to them His tragical death to be at Jerusalem, and His glorious resurrection and ascension, so blighting their sanguine hopes of His coronation as "king of the Jews." Three times He positively certified these facts, in order that the prophetical curriculum might be perfect, as it is the basis of universal faith. Yet, if He had then let them believe Him, they would have rushed into a bloody war to protect Him, every apostle a recruiting officer and Peter commander-in-chief, whereas He wanted nothing of that kind. Therefore the Holy Ghost kept the truth of His statements hidden from them, so that they never understood them until after He had risen from the dead.

Our American Sunday-school lessons pronounce Great Hermon the Mt. of Transfiguration, but that is a mistake. Hermon is forty miles north of Cæsarea Philippi, which city was the northernmost terminus of our Savior's evangelistic peregrinations. Besides, Hermon is too cold to spend the night on his summit, as they did on the Mt. of Transfiguration.

Then, where is that mountain? The name is not given in the Bible. Our Lord knew that it would be filled with idolatry, as they have done with the Church of the Holy Sepulchre in Jerusalem, therefore He just left this mountain unnamed. He was on the border of Cæsarea when He delivered His last message to His apostles, and after six days ascended the Mt. of Transfiguration and then, descending, travelled through Galilee to Capernaum.

I have traveled that whole route, down the Jordan valley all the way to Capernaum, on the shore of the Sea of Galilee. Mountains tower on either side of the Jordan valley; on the left, the foothills of Great Hermon, and on the right the great Anti-Lebanon range all the way.

As Jesus and the Twelve were walking along leisurely and He was teaching them, pursuant to His custom, there were mountains at all times for them to ascend and pass through the wonderful scenes of the Transfiguration, Jesus Himself putting on the effulgent glory which now radiates from His person in Heaven. That wonderful scene lasted all night, and at daydawn they came down to the nine others awaiting them at the base of the mountain.

Such is the wonderful interest in and glory thrown around the Mt. of Transfiguration that the fallen Church would have flooded it with idolatry if the chance had been given.

Moses and Elijah retreated away before the scene was over, thus manifesting the resignation of their delegated and departing power and authority, and leaving Jesus alone; everything turned over to Him for time and eternity.

In regeneration we receive a new heart and get rid of our sins; in sanctification we receive a clean heart and get rid of inbred sin; in glorification, which is the third work of the Holy Ghost, we survive sins of ignorance, i. e., get rid of all infirmities, and this mortal puts on immortality. Sanctification gives us Christian perfection and qualifies us to live in this world without sin; while glorification, which we cannot receive till we evacuate these bodies, confers on us angelic perfection and prepares us to live in Heaven.

(s) Mt. Lebanon in Syria was included in God's land-grant to Israel (Joshua, 1st chapter), and is transcendently eulogized by the prophets: ''The righteous shall grow like the palm-tree and flourish like Lebanon.''

It is generally thought that the dates transported to this country are sweetened with sugar, but that is a mistake. The mysterious power of the tropical sun imparts all of that sweetness. The palm-tree grows up one hundred feet high without a single limb and there produces his copious crop of delicious fruit.

Before I was in Egypt (the palmery of the world in the date harvest), I was in a puzzle to understand how they gathered the fruit. In 1905, I was in the midst of the date harvest, and I was surprised to see them, with their bare feet, walk right up those trees one hundred feet high, and, lifting up a great willow basket with a string, gather the fruit and let it down.

In the palmy days of Israel, Mt. Lebanon abounded in great cedar trees, much larger and the wood much more compact and clearer of limbs and knots than I ever saw in any other country. The soil is very fertile and productive of all the delicious fruits earth commands and heart can wish, but these cedar forests have long ago evanesced before the farmer's axe, so that you may pass over that mountain and look in vain for cedars, which are still there, but not in sight of the railroad.

In your travels in the Holy Land, when you reach Beirut, down by the sea (the juvenile successor of Tyre and Sidon of ancient fame), just go up to the Protestant College, where the American Christians will be glad to see you; enter the museum, and you'll see beautiflu specimens of the Lebanon cedar. Externally it does not resemble the American.

In A. D. 1860, an awful massacre was perpetrated in Damascus and the surrounding country, the Turks murdering fourteen thousand Christians in cold blood, most of them in their own houses, and heaping the Christian quarters with the dead. When it first broke out, the Christians fled for refuge and wanted to hide in the Mohammedan houses, but they would not take them; consequently they could do nothing but die for Jesus and receive a martyr's crown.

When the awful news reached Christendom, as France was nearest, she sent an army of ten thousand to Damascus at once. On arrival, they arrested the governor and all his officers, and demanded of them the murderers of the Christians. They, however, plead ignorance, saying the Druses did it, but they could not identify the guilty ones. Then they hung the governor and all his officers, not for doing it (because they did not believe he and his men had done it personally), but for letting others do it; thus holding them responsible for not protecting the Christians.

When the news of this action reached Constantinople, the Sultan appointed another governor and corps of officers, advising them all, on their arrival at Damascus, to join the Christian Church, believing that would be essential to their personal safety, and so they did. Then the Christian Powers forced the Sultan to give the Christians an asylum in his empire, whither they might escape in case of danger. Therefore he granted them a beautiful territory belting great Mt. Lebanon and including the railroad which, by the rack and pinion system, i. e., with cog-wheels, runs over that great mountain. This Christian asylum includes a territory of two or three thousand acres, and has at present a million of people, all Christians, and officered entirely by Christians. Its name is Zedleh, and that of its capital, Babda. It is a most lovely and delightful home for all persecuted Christians.

They have an army of eight hundred soldiers, well drilled and constantly ready to give the officers all-needed assistance in the protection of the people.

The Christian Powers—Britain, France, Germany and Russia—in this matter acted very wisely, as no Christian is safe in a Mohammedan country. Their Koran (Bible) teaches them that they are to swim to Heaven in the blood of their enemies, and they count all the people in the world their enemies who do not accept the Koran for their authority and Mohammed for their prophet. The Mohammedans are a very dangerous power in the earth, for, if they could, they would exterminate all others in blood. If any of their members get converted to Christianity, they will kill them if possible.

Sister Murray, our faithful missionary in Hebron, Palestine, told me that a bright young man in that city got converted in their mission. The Mohammedans paid no attention to it, so that he thought they were going to let him alone. They waited a whole year, till all suspicion of danger had evanesced, then a band of men decoyed him into a cave and cut him all to pieces.

She also told me the case of a Mohammedan woman who got converted to Christianity. Then her husband got some of his brethren to pay them a little visit, and they took her into her room and cut her all to pieces. When they arraigned her husband for the murder of his wife, the jury decided that she was his property and he had a right to do as he pleased with her!

Hence you see the great importance of this Christian commonwealth Zedleh on lovely Mt. Lebanon, an asylum to which all Turkey's persecuted Christians can escape and be safe.

That mountain has every variety of climate: down on the sea level, on the southern slopes, tropical fruits peculiar to the torrid zone, grow. Then, ascending, we reach the semi-tropical, where the olive, fig, May-apple, pomegranate, etc., abound. Then we reach the vine, flourishing everywhere and burdened with the most delicious grapes I ever ate, literally piling the earth with the delicious fruit. Farther up, wheat, barley and all the cereals flourish. Meanwhile, we everywhere see the mulberry waving its beautiful leaves, which leaves feed the countless millions of toiling worms as they spin their beautiful sik threads of diversified colors. These supply the great factories which there abound, manufacturing the beautiful silk goods in which the people clothe themselves like queens and kings, and shipping their goods to all nations, thus supplying the ends of the earth with the most beautiful, comfortable and durable apparel.

CHAPTER IV.

LAND OF UZ, AND SYRIA.

Sixteen years ago, when I first traveled in the Orient, I either rode a horse or a donkey or traveled on foot everywhere I went, as there was but one carriage road, and that was from Jerusalem to Hebron, and a solitary railroad from Joppa to Jerusalem. This time (1911) I only rode the donkey amid the ruins of old Memphis and the tombs of Sakara, in Egypt, and nowhere mounted a horse, as I found the Holy Land, Syria and the Land of Uz well supplied with carriage roads and railroads.

It was estimated that forty thousand Christian pilgrims were in Jerusalem when we were there. Oh, what an inestimable blessing these rapid improvements in the roads of these countries!

When I made the journey in 1905-6, we not only visited the Bible lands, but traveled around the world. They were building a railroad from Haiffa, a Mediterranean port, to Mecca, Arabia, the Moslem holy city, whither the Koran requires every pilgrim to make at least one visit in life. The Sultan had this road built for the especial convenience of Moslem pilgrims.

If the Lord lets you visit the Holy Land, do not stint your time at the Sea of Galilee, so celebrated in the biography of our Savior. On its northern bank, in Capernaum, He made His home in the home of Peter for two and a half out of the three years of His wonderful ministry. You see in the Gospels how He sailed over that sea very often, and how Satan sent so many storms to retard Him, thus inadvertently opening wide the door for Him to magnify His divinity by commanding the wind and the waves.

I always carry with me my Greek Scriptures, and in my visits to this sea I have diligently followed our Lord in all His voyages, seeing where He crossed it at almost every angle of the compass, landed in different countries, and worked miracles. This time we spent four days sailing over and treading the banks of this beautiful and lovely crystal sea.

The reason why it is subject to storms is because it is seven hundred feet below the Mediterranean, i. e., the level of the watery world. This normally superinduces its environment to be by highlands on all sides, except a solitary break on the north to let in the Jordan and another to let him out from the south. After utterly losing his identity in the sea, he flows out at this point of egress with no perceptible increase in volume.

I felt it a great blessing to drink the holy waters of that sea, which are fresh, sweet, limpid, sparkling and delicious, and especially do I delight to bathe in the same.

As the western winds sweep over the Atlantic

Ocean for thirty-five hundred miles, and through the Mediterranean for two thousand more, impinging against the Palestinian coast after an unbroken flight of fifty-five hundred miles, and largely retaining their force for the twenty-five miles to the Sea of Galilee, there they encounter the vacuum, in view of its depression those seven hundred feet below the Mediterranean. This superinduces a dip in the aerial currents, so that when they impinge against the mountains on the other side, the normal trend is to move laterally around the sea in a circle, thus developing an aerial cyclone.

Though I have sailed much on that sea and we have had some strong winds, as a rule its surface is smooth as glass and without a solitary ripple. Hence the conclusion that Satan busied himself in the days of Christ, sending those storms (as he is the prince of the power of the air—Eph. 2:1).

I was delighted when I reached the sea this last time to learn that the new railroad from Haiffa to Mecca has tapped it, and consequently I was relieved of that long and laborious horseback ride to Damascus, which I took in 1899, narrowly escaping from serious peril by robbers.

When we stopped to lodge at Cæsarea Philippi, a Christian city, our dragoman complaining of headache, we employed a substitute to take us on some important explorations on one of the peaks of Hermon, hanging over the city. While this man knew how to escort us, he could not understand a word of English and we could not understand his language; therefore he could only obey the dragoman and serve us as guide like a deaf mute.

We had passed through the city of the Druses (those wild Mohammedans who murdered the fourteen thousand Christians in and about Damascus, A. D. 1860). We had heard that they had been in a war with the Christians of Cæsarea Philippi two or three years. (In the Turkish Empire the Government is so corrupt and weak that her subjects can wage war with one another with a degree of impunity.)

On that mountain Herod the Great built a large temple, in the exploration of which we were much interested. Napoleon Bonaparte also built a great citadel on the same mountain. In the midst of the explorations our mute guide got wonderfully excited, and began to pull us and motion to us to get away from there. We thought he was just lazy and wanted to wind up his job, so we paid no attention to him. Eventually we saw armed men on horseback galloping round, so, knowing that there was something wrong, we went back with our guide. Our dragoman was delighted to find us alive, because he had been awfully affrighted over the alarm in the city that the Druses had come and that they were going out to fight them.

The fact was, the Druses had not come, but the people saw us strangers at a distance and thought we were Druses, and so reported. So you see we were in imminent peril, and likely to be fired on for Druses.

Having again enjoyed a delightful visit to the

beautiful Sea of Galilee (sixteen and a half miles long, eight and a half miles wide, three hundred feet deep, and abounding in fishes, on which we lived fat), we now left our German hotel in Tiberias and made our last embarkation, to sail south and take the train at the station for Damascus. The country is so rough and so infested with robbers that we all hailed the iron horse as a glorious Godsend, and a felicitous relief from the laborious equestrian tour.

We ran up the beautiful river Yamonk, along which Abraham, Isaac and Jacob often traveled on their camels; 'tis said that when Abraham came out of Chaleda into Canaan he traveled along this river from head to mouth. It was May the first when we were there, so that the barley harvest was spreading its golden waves on either side, beautifully interspersed with the green wheatfields, which are harvested in June. And all along the track and round about we saw the roses of Sharon blooming in their beauty, felicitously variegated by the magnolias in gorgeous bloom.

As the Sea of Galilee is seven hundred feet below the watery world, and the river Yamonk has a great deal of fall, our run was a constant climbing, the iron horse manifesting his toils by his incessant puffing. The majestic crags reached their arms above our heads and kissed the azure skies. Eventually our dragoman called our attention to a beautiful waterfall far away in the distance, and said it was a part of the same Yamonk River which we were ascending. I knew then that tunnels abound or we could never reach the altitude of that cataract. Soon our train was running from side to side, crossing the river and dashing through tunnels, but incessantly making decided headway in the achievement of altitude. We actually ran under that very waterfall, and saw it leaping in sparkling beauty and reflecting the rainbow around our heads. In the prosecution of this climbing tour, we formed a complete loop, circling round and crossing our track, but meanwhile achieving a decisive victory in the way of altitude. No tongue can tell the beauty, grandeur and sublimity of scenery enjoyed by the traveler over this route.

On looking around I see the mountains beneath our feet, for we have transcended them all and reached a lofty plain of lovely highlands. The train stops at a station and takes a little rest. Then our dragoman, with stentorian voice, roars in our ears: "You are now in the Land of Uz, Job's country." During my former horseback tours, my dragoman had pointed it out to me in the distance, and oh, how glad I am to get there!

(t) My soul leaps for joy upon receiving the information that I am in the Land of Uz. Now a wonderful panorama moves in stupendous reality and absorbing erudition before my contemplative eyes. Sunday rolls around and we all go to meeting. Amid the sons of God Satan takes his seat, elegantly dressed and looking very harmless. God says, "Satan, hast thou considered My servant Job, that there is none like him in all the earth; a perfect and upright man who feareth God and escheweth evil?" Satan modestly responds, "I am just walking about over the earth, up and down, and going to and fro. As to Job, of course he is good to you, since you have paid him so well to be good."

N. B. The devil has no confidence in your religion or mine. When he severed his connection with God, the last scintilla of spiritual life evanesced away and left him enveloped in the midnight of Hell, full of carnality and nothing else. He believes you and I serve God through carnal motives, and he believed that Job was actuated through carnality alone. So he says, "You have set a hedge about him and made him a millionaire; therefore he can certainly afford to be good to you." Then God responds, "He is in thy hands; do what thou wilt, but touch not his person."

Now Satan puts all his wits to work and lays all the machinery of the bottomless pit under contribution. He stirs up the Sabeans, i. e., Sebeians, i. e., Shebeans, far away in that rich country bordering on the Red Sea and Persian Gulf, the most distant terminus of Arabia. It was their beautiful and intelligent queen who came all the way to visit King Solomon, to satisfy herself in reference to those paradoxical reports appertaining to his wisdom and glory which had reached her in her far-off-land. She could not believe them, but they so electrified and thrilled her with solicitude and curiosity that she rode on a camel's back five thousand miles (round trip), that she might see and hear for herself. When she came and saw the glory of the temple, the splendors of the royal palace, and, sitting at Solomon's feet, heard the wonderful wisdom flowing from his lips, her heart melted, and she said that everything she had heard was true, and that the half had not been told her. So, making him a contribution of one million dollars, she returned to her own land.

It was these Shebeans whom Satan stirred up to make a raid into the Land of Uz, to assault Job's ploughmen preparing his rich lands for the ensuing crops, to capture the five hundred yoke of oxen and five hundred donkeys grazing hard by and drive them away, and to slay the servants with the edge of the sword.

At the same time, utilizing his co-operative myrmidons, he stirs the Chaldeans to make a raid into the Land of Uz and capture Job's three thousand camels, then grazing and recuperating for caravan service. As this country was so very productive, the commercial interests were really magnitudinous and manipulated entirely by those caravans in which Job utilized the three thousand camels. The Chaldeans captured them all, slaying the herdsmen with the edge of the sword.

At the same time Satan had sent out another cohort of myrmidons, to raise an awful sandstorm in the great desert of Arabia, and suffocate Job's seven thousand sheep as well as the shepherds in charge of them. The same cyclone swept on and caught the house of his eldest son, in which his seven sons and three daughters were celebrating a birthday anniversary, in its precipitate whorls, lifting it high in air, whirling it round and round like a pair of winding blades, and letting it fall on the earth with an awful crash, slaying them all. Meanwhile Satan runs such an awful bluff on Job's good wife as to completely capsize her faith so that she could not live, but had to evanesce away.

The couriers run from their respective scenes of fell disaster, and tell Job all about it in unbroken succession, dove-tailing on one another. Job hears them all through, then demonstrates his great grief by the Oriental method of rendering his lamentation. Shaving his head, and falling on the ground, he says, "Naked am I now, and naked came I out of the womb of my mother. The Lord gave and the Lord hath taken away; blessed be the name of the Lord." "In all this Job sinned not, neither did he charge God foolishly."

The meeting day has rolled around again, when behold! Satan comes and sits down among the sons of God. The second time God interviews him: "Satan, what do you think of my servant Job? He is without an equal in all the earth; a perfect and upright man, who feareth God and escheweth evil." Satan responds, "Skin for skin; everything will a man give for his life. You touch his body and he will curse you to your face." God says, "Satan, he is in thy hands; do anything you please to Job but take his life; you cannot do that."

Then Satan proceeds at once to cover Job with devouring ulcers, that awful black leprosy, the terror of the Orient. Even a rumor that it was in Egypt in 1899 caused the Turks to arrest me when I sailed thence to Beirut, Syria, and to hold me in a quarantine prison for ten days, medicating me and disinfecting me at my own cost, because the whole Turkish Empire was quarantined against Egypt. All this just on account of the rumor that the Black Death was there, whereas I never could hear of an authentic case.

Though Satan wrapped Job in these devouring ulcers from top to toe, will you hear him testify and praise the Lord? He says: "I know that my Redeemer liveth, and that He shall stand at the latter day upon the earth: and though after my skin (his skin was already eaten up by vermin, even as in the case of King Agrippa at Cæsarea—Acts, 12th chapter) worms destroy this body, yet in my flesh shall I see God: whom I shall see for myself, and mine eyes shall behold, and not a stranger (E. V., 'not another')."

The meaning is that when the Lord appears He would not be a stranger to Him, as he always knew Him. Here Job preached the resurrection of the body and the second coming of Christ far back in that early day.

During Job's deep affliction, three great presiding elders of the Arabic country—Eliphaz, Bildad and Zophar—come to see him, confessedly to sympathize with and comfort him in his deep affliction, but really proving his tormentors. They stoutly and heroically proclaim and maintain that these terrible afflictions were righteous judgments sent upon Job to castigate him for his wicked presumption in claiming perfection, which, said they, is not within reach of mortals, but for God alone. Their speeches were very elaborate and learned, and certain preachers have been using their arguments against the Holiness people in all ages. Strange that the people do not know that their arguments are all false, for, as sanctified people are always ready to appeal from man to God, so Job appealed and God came at once in a whirlwind.

He turned that debate into a Holiness meeting. Looking Eliphaz, Bildad and Zophar in the face, He says to them: "You have not spoken that which is right concerning Me, as my servant Job has," thus condemning them and vindicating Job. Then He called those three presiding elders to the altar to seek sanctification, saying, "Now offer a sacrifice of seven rams and seven bullocks, and my servant Job shall pray for you." (Seven, in the Bible, means perfection, because Christ is the incarnation of all perfection; He is perfect man and perfect God. Three stands for God—Father, Son and Holy Ghost; while four stands for man— north, south, east and west, the cardinal points.) Consequently this was a perfect consecration and Job proceeded to pray for them.

Meanwhile Elihu, a young Holiness evangelist in perfect sympathy with Job, but who had been utterly crowded out so that he could not get in a word till God came in a whirlwind and turned the debate into a revival, exhorted and shouted over them. As he had been running over so long, but not allowed to speak, when the revival came he just said there was no use trying it, he would burst wide open if he did not speak:

therefore he set in shouting with all his might, patting them on the back and saying, "Go ahead; you will get it, for I got it just that way."

(u) The Lord gave me sanctification fifteen years before the Holiness Movement met dear old Dixieland, in which I was born and reared; consequently God used me to pioneer the Holiness Gospel from the Atlantic to Mexico, while there was only a solitary light here and there in many localities in the great North. It was my glorious privilege to serve as John the Baptist throughout the sunny South.

God used me in the different states to pioneer the Holiness Movement. In the great empire state of the Southwest (Texas), I preached holiness from Louisiana and Arkansas to the Rio Grande, and from the Gulf to the Panhandle. It is the greatest prairie on the earth, five hundred miles long and two hundred wide, with soil a dozen feet deep and as black as a crow. At a railroad crossing in Hill County, Hillsboro, the county-seat, sprang up like a mushroom in the night.

They called the Holiness Gospel a "Northern phantasm." Therefore while the panic was sweeping the country, lest this "Northern phantasm" break up the churches, all the Protestant churches of Hillsboro held a convention and united for mutual security against the common enemy, the Methodist Church being in the lead numerically, financially and influentially. (That name—"Northern phantasm"—was quite a misnomer, as I am not a Northern man.)

Despite the confederacy against the "Northern phantasm," curiosity so electrified the Methodist pastor that, sub rosa, he boarded the train and traveled forty miles to my meeting to spy out the thing. God's lightning was in the air; people were falling on all sides, praying through and shouting the victory uproariously. Then sure enough, the lightning struck him; down he came and prayed through. He shouted around a few days and then said to me, "Brother Godbey, I can never go back to Hillsboro alone; you must go with me." Says I, "I cannot; I am too crowded." "But," he says, "you are going, for I have prayed through and heard from Heaven, and God tells me you are going." "Of course I am," was my answer, as I knew that he had heard from God and the thing was settled. Therefore I wrote postponing my appointments, and giving a date for the meeting to begin.

On arrival in Hillsboro, I met the first box of my "Christian Perfection," a book which the Lord has wonderfully used. I opened it and sent by mail quite a number of copies as presents to my ministerial brethren and especial friends. Among others, I sent one to the presiding elder of the district in which I was laboring.

We began the meeting in Hillsboro at night. The ensuing day the pastor came to me at the dinner-table, weeping, and said, "Brother Godbey, I have bad news. My Board have notified me to meet them this afternoon because they are going to shut you out of the church." I was then an old presiding elder, and so posted in the laws of the church, which give the pastor complete control of the edifice until the Conference takes him away. I told him: "Go meet your Board. Open the 'Discipline' and read to them the law of the church, giving the pastor complete control of the house, and say to them, 'Brother Godbey has no meeting in our house. The meeting is mine and he is one of my humble helpers. If you close that house, you'll lock out your pastor, in open violation of the law, and I will prosecute every one of you in the next Conference for maladministration.'" They saw that he had the deadwood on them, therefore they telegraphed at once to the notoriously anti-Holiness presiding elder.

Meanwhile he had received my book and read it till conviction struck him. Then he had called in his wife and they had been reading and praying alternately for God to sanctify them, and they were both on their knees when the telegram reached them. He boarded the early morning train for Hillsboro.

Beginning the meeting early, we had opened the altar at eleven, and nearly every one in the house except a few who had the experience had poured up to it. Just as we went to prayer, I saw that presiding elder enter the door, and saw in his face like in a mirror the Holy Ghost working mightily. He marched down the aisle, fell at the altar, and oh, such praying I have seldom heard! A half an hour of fire-baptized prayers pulled Heaven down. A wave rolled over the altar, bearing a dozen to fifteen sweeping over Jordan into Beulah Land with tremendous shouts of victory; among them, the presiding elder.

That afternoon it would have done you good to see the sanctified pastor and elder, arm in arm, pass the plaza to the Board meeting. Characteristic of Northern style, shouting uproariously, they walked into the meeting, and the presiding elder said, "Brethren, I must notify you that you sent for the wrong man if you want that Holiness meeting closed, for I am for running it without a break till Gabriel blows his trumpet."

That threw all the fat in the fire, so they opened an anti-Holiness meeting in another church, the carnal Methodists and all other anti-Holiness people attending it.

Two daily papers in the city took opposite sides. The result was that the meetings monopolized everything, all the people dividing out on one side or the other. One of the city pastors, a college graduate and standing at the front of his denomination, was preaching to the anti-Holiness crowd. It so happened that he preached a sermon on Job which captured everybody who heard it. They pronounced it an unanswerable argument. He took all his proof from Eliphaz, Bildad and Zophar, Job's false comforters, whom God condemned when He came in the whirlwind responsively to the appeal of Job and turned that debate into a Holiness revival.

It is a mistake to think that every word in the Bible was spoken by God Himself; some of it is the words of the devil, and a considerable quantity is the words of bad people. The Bible is God's signboard pointing the way to Heaven, so that we may all travel it; and the way to Hell, so that we may all shun it.

When the sermon on Job raised so much town talk,

the anti-Holiness people clamoring that it was actually unanswerable, many said they "would like to hear Godbey answer it," and asked me if I would. I responded, "With great pleasure." Therefore the time was appointed for me to answer it and the anti-Holiness preacher adjourned his meeting and came. The audience was immense. I had in my hand the paper which had published the sermon in full, and held it up before them so that I would be certain not to misrepresent him. Meanwhile I gave him a convenient chair so that he could hear every word without an effort, and told him he was welcome to as much time as I used, if he was disposed to reply to me, as I wanted him to have perfect freedom to fortify himself against all possible misunderstanding.

Then I held up the paper with the sermon and said to the people, "In the providence of God, history repeats itself. A long time ago God and the devil had a debate. Job was their subject, God certifying to the devil that he was a perfect man, and the devil not only saying but assiduously laboring to show that he was not a perfect man. I never saw Job; I know nothing about him except what God tells me in the Bible. I say to you people that Job was a perfect man, just because God says it. Brother Jacobs says he was not a perfect man, as I suppose, because the devil says it. So you see we have the same debate now, and I am glad to be on God's side of it, and sorry that Brother Jacobs is on the devil's side."

As I thus showed up the debate, and the people all saw that I was on God's side and Brother Jacobs on the devil's side, instead of answering me, he took his hat and left the house, and I have never seen him since.

The revival swept on and God wrought mighty works, and out of it developed the largest camp-meeting in the world—Waco, Texas. In its palmy days, before 150 camps were organized in that great state, it had four thousand tenters and twenty thousand auditors.

The leading man in the Board of that Methodist church never did come to meeting, but so much lightning was left in the air that it struck him after we closed at Hillsboro, and in the ensuing camp-meeting in August he was the Ajax of the battlefield, running around the camp-ground with his mouth open like an alligator and roaring like a lion; thus vociferously witnessing to the wonders of full salvation.

I was giving a Bible reading to a large audience in the early morning, when some one shouted from the crowd: "Why do you not write those 'Commentaries'? We are afraid you will die and we will never get them." I responded, "I must go to the Holy Land first, because the land and the Book are so identified that no one is competent to write up the one without a knowledge of the other." He responded, "Why do you not go?" I answered, "I have not the money," and went on and finished the lesson. Then this man came forward and said, "Brother Godbey, I have $1500 in the bank and no especial use for it. The Lord tells me to give it to you to go to the Holy Land, so you may have a check for it." Thus God used that noble saint to augment my circuit by the addition of the Old

World to the New, enabling me truly to say, like Wesley, "The world is my parish."

(v) The Bible says that after Job convalesced out of all his sickness, God gave him back double all he had before, i. e., 1,000 yoke of oxen, 1,000 donkeys, 6,000 camels, and 14,000 sheep. You wonder why He didn't give him fourteen sons and six daughters, thus doubling his family. That puzzle is settled in the fact that his children were godly, and when Satan's cyclone killed them all, they still lived on in a better country than the Land of Uz, though I admit that even now that land is really charming. Therefore when the cyclone slew them and they all lived on in Heaven, and God gave him seven more sons and three daughters (doubtless by his second wife after the first passed away, her faith collapsing but, as we hope, being squeezed into Heaven by the fiery baptism in the dying hour—1 Cor. 3:11), you see plus his first set of children he had fourteen sons and six daughters.

If there were any books before the flood, they all perished in the deluge. Moses, as a rule, is recognized as the oldest author in the post-millennial world. I have repeatedly seen and handled his Pentateuch, still preserved in the Samaritan convent in Shechem, Palestine. Moses wrote it 3,578 years ago. It is admitted that the Book of Job is nine years older than the Pentateuch, which was written about the time Israel left Egypt for the Land of Canaan.

There is a query appertaining to the Book of Job. Some say Job wrote it himself, and others that Moses, while a shepherd in the service of his father-in-law

Jethro, visited the Land of Uz, and wrote the Book of Job as dictated to him. This is the more plausible theory, as there was so little learning in the world at that time; but Moses was reared up at the court of Egypt, and the Bible says was educated in all the wisdom of the Egyptians and was mighty in word and deed. To be mighty in word is to be a great scholar; to be mighty in deed, a great warrior. The case is very clear that Pharaoh's daughter adopted Moses for her son, and gave him the very best education within the competency of the magicians, then the most learned people on the globe. They educated Moses for ruler of the kingdom, believing him to be the veritable son of Pharaoh's daughter. Therefore the argument in favor of the Mosaic authorship of the Book of Job has the preponderance of weight.

History says that Job lived 140 years before his awful afflictions, and after his convalescence out of them 140 more, equal in all to 280 years.

As we ran along through the beautiful and charming Land of Uz, so level and nice and the soil rich as the Garden of Eden, eventually the train halted for dinner at Mecca Junction, a beautiful new village built of nicely hewn stone since the railroad came thither, and certified to be on the spot where Joshua fought the battle of Edrei and defeated Og, the king of Bashan. (Num. 21: 33.) It is now Mecca Junction. There we changed our course from the northeast to the northwest, and ran on to Damascus.

(w) We ran in sight of the spot where Jesus met Saul of Tarsus, with his soldiers on his way to Damascus to arrest and punish all the disciples there found. It was off to the left quite a distance. In 1899, when accompanied by Rev. F. M. Hill, my son-in-law, Rev. J. A. Paine, of Meridian, Cal., and three Christian Arabs—our dragoman, muleteer, and the owner of the horses we had hired in Damascus—suddenly our dragoman called us to halt, and notified us that we were on the spot where Jesus appeared to the persecutor, and where he fell and cried out and the Lord said, "Why persecutest thou Me?" Brother Paine constantly carried his Bible swung around his neck, shot-pouch fashion, so he could open it ad libitum, as we were constantly reaching hallowed places and wanted to read for our edification. Now I told him to turn to Acts, 9th chapter, and read the inspired history of Saul's conversion. Then we lifted up our hearts in prayer, testified for the Lord, shouted His praises, thanked God, took courage, and went on our way rejoicing.

We arrived in Damascus with nightfall and hastened away to our lodging.

Damascus is the oldest city in the world, having been founded by Shem, the eldest son of Noah, soon atfer the flood. Many cities subsequently founded have reached great notoriety and actually led the world in their day, and are now a heap of ruins, but here is Damascus, the oldest of all, still standing, the capital of Syria, with a population of 300,000, and pronounced one of the most beautiful cities in all the world.

The greatest false prophet the world ever knew (Mohammed), who this day has 175,000,000 followers, on arriving in Damascus, climbed a lofty mountain overshadowing the city, surveyed it with enraptured wonder and appreciation and said, "This is the paradise of the earth!" Perhaps it is the best-watered city in the world, as the beautiful, limpid rivers, Abana and Pharpar, both flow through it, clear, cold and delicious, as they descend from the snow-capped summits of the Anti-Lebanon range.

While sojourning in the city, drinking those beautiful, crystal waters, and seeing them flowing everywhere, irrigating the beautiful gardens of the city, I was no longer astonished over the deportment of Naaman the leper, the George Washington of his nation who had delivered them from all their enemies. When the little Hebrew damsel serving in Naaman's house frequently said, "Would to God that my master were in Samaria, that the prophet Elisha might recover him of his leprosy!" (it was only appearing in one place and he had not yet been consigned to the asylum for lepers, but was administering the government), eventually Ben-hadad the king hears about the talk of the little damsel, and it makes such an impression that he concludes to try it, as Naaman was the most valuable man in the nation and, if not healed, he would be exiled for life. Therefore the king outfits Naaman with a twenty-thousand-dollar present—gold, silver, and ten changes of raiment (very valuable, as they had no factories at that time), and he and his servants, mounting a retinue of camels, went away to the land of Israel. There Naaman hunted up the prophet's cottage, called him out, told him his business, and offered him the money and the ten changes of raiment. The prophet, however, courteously declines them all, and saying, "Go dip seven times in the Jordan," turning around, he walks into his cottage. Naaman receives this message as an insult, gets very angry, turns his camels' heads toward home and starts away in a rage of wrath, feeling that, after he had come so far and brought such a valuable present, the prophet had treated his royal majesty with contempt. So he goes on, vociferating, "Are not the waters of Abana and Pharpar better than all the waters of the Jordan?" Then his servants gather around him and reason with him: "Master, if the prophet had told you to go and do some great thing, you would have done it, but now you are mad and raging because he only told you to go and wash in the Jordan, a little thing that anybody can do. You know that God alone can cure the leprosy, which is sure to kill you soon or late if it is not cured by Divine intervention. In obeying the prophet, you have nothing to lose and everything to gain."

Then Naaman's anger abates and his reason returns. At once he turns his camel's head toward the Jordan, and the whole cavalcade move straight to it, dismount, and prepare for the dipping. While Abana and Pharpar are clear as crystal, the Jordan is always muddy, because he flows so rapidly as to keep the black mud constantly stirred up. Hence Naaman took gross offense at the prophet for telling him to wash in the muddy Jordan instead of the beautiful, limpid rivers of his beloved city, the idol of his patriotism.

Now all is ready, and as the Jordan is so swift and deep it is a very dangerous stream, but his servants give him all needed attention and help. So, accompanied and assisted by them, he wades in and plunges under the water. Coming out, they all look for the leprosy and find no change whatever. Then he repeats the very same modus operandi, comes out, looks and finds the leprosy unchanged. So he goes ahead till he has plunged under the water six times, and coming out finds no change whatever—the stubborn leprosy has not budged a solitary iota. Now the case is very simple, only one more chance; so, plunging in, he comes out, looks for the leprosy, and, to his unutterable astonishment and delight, it is absolutely gone, not a vestige of it left. Whereas the leprosy rots your body as it proceeds, thus working out a loathsome living death in which you rot by inches, not only is the leprosy itself gone from Naaman, but not an atom of rotten flesh is left. On the contrary, the vacuum formed by the removal of the rotten flesh is filled up by new, bright, perfectly healthy flesh and there is not a trace of leprosy left in his entire organism.

The solution of this wonderful problem is easy. Seven represents Christ throughout the Bible. The first six dips Naaman just had the water and that was all, and you see he got nothing, showing that water has nothing to do with salvation and never did have. Millions hug the delusion of water regeneration, and lose their souls. Naaman tried it six times and got nothing; he tried Christ once and got everything.

Peter walked on the sea, began to sink the moment

he got his eye on the water, and would have sunk to the bottom if Jesus had not caught him. So look out, all you hydrolators, i. e., water worshipers, as you are in great danger of losing your souls. Beware of trying to get anything to help Jesus save you, because He needs no help and the offer is an insult to His omnipotent majesty. Take Jesus for everything in the plan of salvation, and you get everything, leaving you but one job, and that will last forever; it is on the shouting line.

This time I was accompanied to Damascus by five noble Holiness preachers, who had never before made this tour and seen the sights, though it was my fourth trip. I was delighted going with them to see everything.

We went to the house of Ananias, whom the angel called to the house of Judas to pray for Saul's penitent soul. The room is used for a Christian church by the Greeks. There you see a large and beautiful picture of Ananias baptizing Saul. It is in harmony with all of the paintings, sculpture and statuary in the Bible lands, and represents Ananias as pouring the water on Saul's head.

On Sunday morning we went to the service in the Greek church on the spot where the house of Judas stood. We much enjoyed visiting those hallowed places. We went into the Mosque Rimmon, said to be the largest in the world, and saw the tomb which is said to contain the head of John the Baptist, as you know Herodias received it when it was cut off and the disciples did not get to bury it with his body in the great church which bears his name in Samaria, where now they show his tomb along with those of Elisha the prophet and Obadiah, Ahab's chamberlain. We visited the tomb of Saladin, the greatest military chieftain on the globe in his day, nine hundred years ago. Though he was a Mohammedan, and drove the Christian Crusaders out of Asia, he was distinguished for wonderful magnanimity and generosity. When, in a certain raging battle, his horse was shot from beneath the commander of the enemy, Saladin sent him another. When he conquered the Crusders and drove them out of Asia, he astonished them by letting them keep all of their church property.

When General Lee surrendered to Grant, the latter refused to take his sword, but sent it back to him, observing that General Lee was too brave a man for him to take his sword. When the Southern soldiers all surrendered, of course their horses were confiscated to the Government, by the law of all nations, but Grant kindly donated them to the men, observing, "You men will need your horses to make a crop." When he was approaching the end of his life, he had them telegraph to two Confederate generals to come and serve as his pall-bearers. Therefore the scene was very beautiful, the Blue and the Grey mixed together carrying the great Union General's remains to the grave, showing that the war was over and that all was at peace.

When Saladin the Great saw the end of his life coming, he told them to make his shroud and have some one carry it on a flag-pole through every street of the beautiful city of Bagdad (his captital), waving it over the heads of the people and shouting aloud, "Look here, all ye people, this is all that is left of Saladin! He stood at the front of the world, its master spirit in his day, but he can take nothing with him but a shroud!"

The mechanical arts in Damascus are really wonderful. When you visit the Orient, do not fail to go through the bazaars and look at their merchandise. But enter their factories and you'll see wonders indescribable.

(x) Leaving Damascus, our train ran up the beautiful river Pharpar all the way to its limpid source amid the snowy summits of the great Anti-Lebanon range.

The gardens of Damascus are wonderfully productive of all the vegetables and fruits peculiar to the semi-tropical and temperate zones, as they are so thoroughly irrigated by both the Pharpar and the Abana rivers, therefore Damascus is well supplied with a great variety of delicious fruits, among the latter being olives, figs, dates, oranges, lemons, and a vast variety of delicious and nutritious nuts.

The building timber of that country is the poplar, which grows up very quickly in such rich, well irrigated soil. They use it all the time for the frames and roofs of houses. It grows very dense and needs but little room, as it runs up so very tall and slender. They are all the time cutting them out and using them, thus making room for others to grow. It reminds me of the bamboo in India, which grows tall so quickly and is so stout for building purposes. The vine also flourishes and abounds in that country.

As we ran along, we saw Zenobia's temples and her aqueduct, which she built to carry the water from the Abana and Pharpar rivers away to Palmyra in the desert, her beautiful capital. At the death of her royal husband Odenathus, she not only took his place on the throne and administered the government with success and efficiency, but she mounted her war horse and went away prosecuting conquests in Egypt and other countries, till the Roman Emperor, Aurelian, with great reluctance, marched his army against her. He confessed his deep regret when he felt forced to march his army against that beautiful and noble woman, but his duty as executive of the Roman Empire constrained him to do so.

We also again passed Abel's tomb, which had repeatedly hitherto been pointed out to me.

We see from the rivers of Eden—Pison, Gihon, Hiddekel, and Euphrates—that the Garden of Eden included Egypt, Palestine, Syria and Mesopotamia. The Oriental meaning of "garden" is not a cultivated piece of ground, but what we in this country call a park, abounding in primeval growth, fruits and flowers.

The Pison is the Jordan, as it means "overflowing," which is peculiar to that stream. The Gihon, which means "rushing," is the Nile of Egypt, rushing out and flooding the whole country. The Hiddekel means "rest," and is symbolical of the placid and gentle Tigris, flowing between Syria and Mesopotamia, whereas the Euphrates, the northern border of the land-grant which God made to Abraham and Israel, still retains its Bible name.

LAND OF UZ, AND SYRIA.

After the subsidence of the flood, it seems that Noah and his family went to Syria, as Shem, his eldest son, founded Damascus soon after the flood, and they show us the tomb of Noah on the plain of Bekah, about ten miles south of Baalbec. As Baalbec plainly shows its ante-diluvian origin, its identity with the city which Cain founded in the land of Nod is very obvious. This co-operates with the identity of Abel's tomb in that country, as the Bible says that God expelled Cain from the human home because he killed his brother, and he went into the land of Nod and there built a city. Nod is a Hebrew word, which means "wandering," therefore Cain simply wandered away and built that city and found his wife (his sister). As he lived nearly a thousand years, she had plenty of time to grow and become his wife.

When we passed over the summit of the Anti-Lebanon range, our train ran down on the west side very rapidly till we reached the plain of Bekah, which begins a short distance northeast of the ancient cities of Tyre and Sidon, and runs north all the way to Bagdad and on to Babylon, having an area of a hundred million acres of very beautiful, rich land. Through this runs the ancient caravan road from Egypt to Babylon, the first great thoroughfare in the world, along which not only the camel caravans did convey the commerce of the greatest nations on the globe, but the armies marched through the ages. The reason why Egypt had so much war was because they were right on that route.

(y) Baalbec was the city Cain founded when he went to the land of Nod. It stands on the plain of

Bekah, twenty-eight hundred feet above the sea level, and is defended on the west from the pirates coming out from the sea by the great Lebanon range, and on the east from the armies of the continent by the great Anti-Lebanon range.

The citadel is surrounded by a gigantic wall 14 feet wide at the base, 8 at the top, 100 feet high, and 1000 yards (i. e., more than half a mile) in length, counting all sides of it, with no windows nor doors and only entered by a subterranean passage through the foundation, 100 yards long, so that a few people could protect it against a large army, as they could get in only by the subterranean passage which was so long that the defenders could kill them all before they got through. It was built of great stones, some of them weighing one million pounds and being placed away up high, thirty or forty feet above the ground.

The whole superstructure confirms the conclusion of its ante-diluvian origin, as there is no power on the earth to-day that could build it. The ante-diluvians lived a thousand years and were several times stronger than people in our day. Besides they had an animal, the mastodon, much larger and stronger than the elephant, which weighs ten thousand pounds. This animal was doubtless used in moving those exceedingly heavy stones. He has never lived on the earth since the flood.

Within the citadel they had the Pantheon, a vast temple containing 250 shrines of different gods, where everybody in the world had a right to come in and worship any god he preferred. In the citadel they also had the temple of Baal, the sun-god. It was wonderfully large and supported by many cylindrical columns, which, elevated far up on great pedestals, make the magnitude of the temple, especially in altitude, very wonderful.

Within the citadel the Roman emperor built the temple of Bacchus, the wine-god, which is a wonderful superstructure, showing the finest architecture you ever saw.

This city of Baalbec was erected in honor of the sun-god, the most popular divinity ever worshiped on the earth. Cain was his worshiper and to him he made his splendid offering, which God rejected. Whereas Cain worshiped the god of nature, and made his offering to him, Abel worshiped the God of grace and offered to Him not a vast array of fruits and flowers like Cain, but simply the bleeding lamb, symbolic of the innocent Savior.

The world went off after the sun-god and moon-goddess and worshiped all the stars, none of which has any power to save them from their sins, consequently the pagans of all nations have actually worshiped and poured out their sacrifices to gods which are utterly impotent to save them.

In the beginning of the world, the gold and silver mines (which have never been exhausted) were so productive that they not only piled up money, but made great life-sized images of their gods. The first banks in the world were the temples of their gods, and that is the reason why they built this citadel at Baalbec so strong, to make it robber-proof even against invading armies. The nations of the earth could take their money there and it would be perfectly safe. Baalbec was not only the greatest temple in the world, but the safest bank in all the earth. I doubt not but it was founded by Cain and used in the ante-diluvian times. Then after the flood they rallied to it again, improved the buildings, and kept on through the ages.

As Egypt is the oldest nation in the world, she took an interest in Baalbec, and we see some architecture there now which is actually Egyptian.

The Phœnicians, whose great and beautiful cities, Tyre and Sidon, are close by, came to the front of the world. Then they led the way, and pushed forward the work at Baalbec during their pre-eminence among the nations.

After Alexander the great conquered the world, Baalbec fell into the hands of the Greeks, who changed the name to Heliopolis, which it retained through the Grecian age and also through the Roman age, which followed. When the Arabs got it in the seventh century, they changed the name back to Baalbec.

When the Emperor Constantine was converted to Christianity, A. D. 321, he took special interest in Baalbec, doing his utmost to discontinue all the idol worship in that place which had been its metropolis in all ages from the days of Cain.

Under his influence Christianity, which had been introduced by the apostles, was revived. Philip had received Baalbec as his field of labor and, going thither, preached heroically till bloody martyrdom set him free. Not only the apostle suffered martyrdom there, but quite a number of others. St. Eudoxia, who was a native of the place, born of pagan parents, and who became an exceedingly bright Christian, suffered martyrdom at Baalbec, as did also St. Barbara, also a native and born of pagan parents.

After the Emperor Constantine, who gave a great impetus to Christianity, came Julian the Apostate, so called because he went back to the old pagan religion and did his best to exterminate Christianity out of the world. During his reign blood flowed in different parts of the world, and especially there at Baalbec.

St. Cyril nobly sealed his faith with his blood at Baalbec. The persecutors actually took the Christian virgins, brutalized them and then killed them. Cutting them to pieces, they fed their flesh to swine and because the swine would not eat it, they mixed barley with it until they did eat it.

Baalbec is wonderfully blessed with a great spring flowing out from the snowfields of Mt. Lebanon, clear, bright, limpid, beautiful, and copious enough to supply a city of a million inhabitants.

They carried this water in an aqueduct to the great cities Tyre and Sidon, which in their palmy days stood at the front of the world.

At different times Baalbec has suffered terribly from earthquakes, which shook down the temples and damaged the great and substantial walls of the citadel.

In 1759 a great earthquake shook down the magnificent Temple of the Sun, and many others, damaging them exceedingly. This has been the capital and metropolis of idolatry since the days of Cain, thus leading off idol worship among all the nations of the earth.

We do not wonder that God was opposed, and shook it down, thus letting the whole world know that the whole thing was Satan's delusion and fortification.

Baalbec at one time had about seventy rural towns associated with it, and under its government, which never was civil, but always sacerdotal, i. e., simply a government by the priest, the high priest of Baal being the chief executive.

The reason why the kingdom of Israel went so fast into idolatry was because she was so near Baalbec, the greatest citadel of pagan worship in all the world. For that reason she was carried into Babylonian captivity 120 years before Judah, which should have taken the alarm from the fate of her sister kingdom, and avoided the same by her loyalty to God. How strange that she did not, but persisted in her idolatry until she plunged into the same awful doom, her chief city (Jerusalem) and its temple being destroyed, and the people carried into Babylonian captivity.

(z) We now ran over great, beautiful and fertile Mt. Lebanon, wrapped in vineyards and olive orchards. The railroad runs all the way through the Christian province Zedleh and through its capital Babda. The Christian Powers forced the Turkish Government to turn over this lovely mountain asylum to the persecuted Christians, whither all can fly in time of danger, and receive all needed protection, as they have a standing army of eight hundred always ready for action, and all Christendom is in constant readiness to fly to their relief at a moment's notification.

Beirut, on the seacoast, is a new city, the daughter

of modern civilization, the commercial successor of Tyre and Sidon, in their palmy days mistresses of the world.

As Beirut is a modern city, you need not look for ancient curiosities. Be sure you visit the Protestant College, founded and conducted by Americans. When I was there, its venerable president, Dr. Bliss, eighty-eight years old (ten years my senior), had just returned from America.

You would also do well to visit the tomb of Bishop Kingsley, of the M. E. Church, who, while on duty in the city, was called from labor to rest.

You would also do well to visit the pottery. I sat and looked on about a solid hour, and saw them making the earthen vessels of different kinds and a diversity of sizes. My attention was especially directed to the water-pots which the women carry on their heads with great ease and adroitness, as they do not have to hold them. It was always a wonder to me why they did not fall and break to pieces. With these they carry the water from the fountain, frequently a great distance.

As I sat and saw the potter making them so rapidly, I thought of Romans 9: 34, which is simply the Pauline commentary of Jeremiah, "Hath not the potter power over the clay of the same lump to make one vessel unto honor and another unto dishonor?" This is the Calvinistic battering-ram, but misapplied all the way through, as there is not a vestige of absolute predestination about it. As I looked at the potter I saw plainly he had but one goal in contemplation, and that was financial security. The Greek word "timee" in this passage has no meaning but financial remuneration. The potter does not discriminate the character, size or use of the vessel he makes. He asks but one question in his own mind, "Will it pay?" An affirmative answer is all the encouragement he wants to go ahead and make the vessel. A dishonorable vessel is one that gets spoiled in the making so that the potter loses his time and labor, as he cannot sell it for anything. I saw a great lot of these vessels on the ship which carried us, going to market. Some of them were broken and could not be sold. Some of them had been left in the pile of rubbish at the pottery utterly worthless, and could not be sold, because the clay marred in the potter's hands, hopelessly spoiling the vessel.

I saw great quantities of the clay spread out and drying in the bright sunbeams of that semi-tropical clime. The removal of the clay out of the bank to the pottery symbolizes the conversion of the sinner, in which he is taken out of Satan's clay-bank into God's pottery. There the clay is comminuted, dried and sifted. This is sanctification, eliminating out of the soul everything that will not do for Heaven.

After the vessel is made they put a beautiful gloss on it, not only to protect it from abrasions but to magnetize the eye. This is the third work of the Holy Ghost, glorification, which we will all receive when this mortal shall put on immortality. How can there be any defalcation in case of the omnipotent Potter? Because God has left the will perfectly free, He lets you go down to Hell before He will save you without the reciprocation and co-operation of your own will. The reason why He ever makes a failure in the salvation of a soul is because such an one, by his free will, contravenes God's work, which is absolutely necessary to his salvation. The potter sets out to make an honorable vessel, i. e., a sound one, that will command the money every time. The only reason why he ever fails is because the human will contravenes the Divine manipulations, thus defeating God's work. God never set out to make a bad man or an unholy woman, but every time it is His purpose to make an upright man, a godly woman, who will do His will on earth as the angels do it in Heaven.

In regeneration the Holy Ghost gives us a new heart, thus making us a vessel unto honor; in sanctification, He gives us a clean heart, thus perfecting the vessel unto honor. Subsequent life is the period of character-building in which the hand of the omnipotent Potter is still on us, fortifying us against Satan's assaults and getting us ready for the glorious climax when this mortal shall put on immortality. Then He will put on us the heavenly lustre, so we will outshine the sun in the bright upper world and accumulate more gorgeous splendor, through the flight of eternal ages.

CHAPTER V.

Heavenly Ages.

"In the beginning God created the heavens and the earth." (Gen. 1:1.) The word for God here is "Elohim," from "Eloah," god. Thus you see the first verse in the Bible recognizes the Trinity: Father, Son and Holy Ghost. The Bible is clear, revealing the unity of the Divinity and at the same time the trinity in unity. The Trinity is accommodatory to our finite conceptions. We cannot comprehend trinity and unity, though we may approximate it.

I have been preaching fifty-eight years in my humble way, and at it all the time. In the providence of God, this is my seventy-second book. My life has been crowded with incessant labor. "How did you ever get time to write so many books?" you ask. I have not written them, but dictated them. I am book editor in the morning by dictation, Bible teacher in the afternoon, and preacher at night. Here you see three personalities, yet I am only one little man.

We have water flowing in the river, we have it solid in the ice factory, and we have it vaporous in the air; yet it is all the same compound of oxygen and hydrogen, but existing in three distinct forms.

The Holy Ghost is the Spirit of the Father (Acts 5:4-9), and He is also the Spirit of the Son (Acts 16:6, 7), for Jesus repeatedly affirms the identity of the Father and the Son, Isaiah actually pronouncing Him "the everlasting Father."

(a) There is a period after Genesis 1:1. When God created the heavens and the earth is not revealed. It simply says "in the beginning," hence you see, for a vehicle of time on the track of eternity, with His omnipic fiat, He created a vast mass of amorphous matter, about seven thousand millions of miles in diameter, with His own hands giving it a rotary motion, having conferred on it the centripetal and centrifugal forces, the latter predominating over the former.

Meanwhile, pursuant to the force of gravitation, contraction was incessantly progressing, eventually bringing it down to the orbit of Neptune, three thousand millions of miles from the sun. There, responsively to the centrifugal force, a great amorphous mass rolled off and, responsively to the centripetal and centrifugal forces, assuming a spherical shape, formed the planet Neptune, sixty times as large as this earth, with its four beautiful satellites; and it has been revolving there ever since.

The condensation still continues, responsive to universal gravitation inherent in all ponderous matter, till it got down to the orbit of Uranus, eighteen hundred millions of miles from the sun. There another great mass rolled of, forming the planet Uranus, eighty times as large as this earth.

Then the condensation continues till we reach the

orbit of Saturn, nine hundred and nine millions of miles from the sun, when a very large mass was disengaged, forming the planet Saturn, eleven times as large as this earth, attended by eight beautiful moons and three great, brilliant, luminous rings.

The condensation continues, responsively to universal gravitation, till we reach the orbit of Jupiter, four hundred and ninety-five millions of miles from the sun, when an immense mass is disengaged from the primitive integer, which formed the planet Jupiter, —four times as large as this earth, with his majestic belts and beautiful moons.

Then the condensation continues till it reaches the orbit of the Asteroids, when another large mass rolls off and forms another large planet, two hundred and fifty million miles from the sun. This planet underwent an explosion, disintegrating into an indefinite diversity of fragments, of which the fifty-two largest, pursuant to the inalienable laws of gravitation, formed planets known as the Asteroids; while the small fragments, in view of their lightness, were thrown so far away as to forfeit their elipticity, so that their orbits became parabolic, never returning into themselves, but wandering farther and farther, till, captured by the gravitation of some planet, they fall on it, many of them having fallen on this earth. I have often seen them, because they become luminous when they strike the atmosphere, and we call them "shooting stars." They consist of meteoric iron, some of them found in South America weighing nine hundred tons. Of course, more have fallen on Jupiter and Mars than on any other planet, as they are contiguous to the Asteroids on either side.

The condensation of the primitive integer still continues till we reach the orbit of Mars, one hundred and forty-five millions of miles from the sun, when there is another disengagement, forming that planet, whose magnitude forms one-sixth of the earth.

Now the condensation goes on till it reaches the orbit of Earth, ninety-five million miles from the sun, when a mass rolls off which, pursuant to universal gravitation, assumes a spherical shape and forms this Earth.

The condensation continues till it reaches Venus, sixty-nine million miles from the sun, when another mass rolls off forming that planet at which we often look, calling it the "evening star."

The condensation continues till we reach the orbit of Mercury, thirty-nine million miles from the sun; when another mass rolls off, forming that planet.

Now the elimination having continued till the centrifugal and centripetal forces have reached their equilibrium, there is no more elimination, but the primitive integer, constituting the sun, having so condensed as to become luminous, shines on in its gorgeous glory and transcendent magnitude, as he is a million times as large as this earth.

(b) You see the statement at the opening of the Bible, "God said let there be light, and there was light." The smaller a planet, the sooner it will become luminous by contraction, resultant from the force of gravitation. The fact that the sun is not mentioned till the fourth day, quite awhile after this light comes, precludes the conclusion that it was solar light, and involves the hypothesis that it was transmitted from the superior planets, Neptune, Uranus, Jupiter and Saturn. The sun is so large that it took him a long time to become luminous.

The conclusion that the days of creation were twenty-four hours is utterly untenable, because there was no sun to measure them by his rising and setting, as he never appeared till the fourth day.

The Hebrew word "yom," translated "day," simply means a period of time. 2 Peter 3:8 tells us that God's day is a thousand years. These creative days were all God's as man had not yet been created. The thousand years are not definite, but simply mean a long period of time.

Much trouble in biblical study simply arises from ignorance and foolishness. The idea prevails that disbelief in the twenty-four-hours days for creation is infidelity. The infidelity is on the other side. The Bible is its own dictionary. As these are God's days, and it says that God's days are a thousand years, the question is forever settled that these were demiurgic days, i e., long, indefinite periods.

(c) We are especially interested in this earth, which is our world. God created it for us and gave it to us, but Satan captured it, taking it out of our hands. Christ came to our relief and is certain to secure it to us forever. The fiery baptism at the end of the millennial age (which follows the present) will sanctify it wholly. (2 Pet. 3rd chapter.) Then God will recreate it, investing it with heavenly similitude (Rev. 21st and 22nd chapters), restore it back to Heaven, where Satan found it, and broke it loose in view of adding it to Hell, to add it to his restricted dominions.

After its sanctification and renovation, God will restore it to His saints (Matt. 5:5), who will possess it forever, shining and shouting through the flight of eternal ages. Our wonderful Savior is not going to leave Satan a solitary vestige over which to boast. He is going fully to restore humanity, spirit, soul and body, all who will let Him, and gloriously sanctify and glorify this earth. It will become a favorite in all celestial worlds, as it is the battlefield of God's empire, where His Son met the hosts of sin and Hell, heroically fought and gloriously conquered. Consequently the immortal intelligences from millions of unfallen worlds, through the flight of eternal ages, will, with infinite delight, come hither to see the old battleground, while we will verify that beautiful Beatitude, "The meek shall inherit the earth." Do not think it will be a prison, as we will all have our transfigured bodies and move with angelic velocity. Thus we will wing our flight from world to world, with adoring wonder eternally contemplating the beauty, grandeur and sublimity of God's stupendous work.

Oh, how unutterably glorious to be a participant in this wonderful redemption reaching spirit, soul and body, and the very earth which God created for our home in the celestial universe. We are now living in Satan's age of the world, in which we have very little of it, and the most of us none at all, but we can sing our triumphant anthem,

> "No foot of land do I possess,
> Nor cottage in the wilderness,
> A poor wayfaring man
> I wander to and fro,
> Camp awhile, content below,
> Till I my Heaven gain."

Even here, while Satan still reigns over the earth, our omnipotent Christ so redeems and gives us the victory that we sing jubilantly,

> "I've reached the land of corn and wine
> And all its riches freely mine;
> Here shines undimmed one blissful day,
> For all my night has passed away.
>
> "My Savior comes and walks with me
> And sweet communion here have we,
> He gently leads me by His hand,
> For this is Heaven's border land.
>
> "A sweet perfume upon the breeze,
> Is born from ever-vernal trees,
> And flowers, that never-fading grow
> Where streams of life forever flow.
>
> "The zephyr seems to float to me
> Sweet sounds of Heaven's melody,
> While angels in their white-robed throng
> Join in the sweet redemption song.
>
> Chorus:
>
> "O Beulah Land, sweet Beulah Land,
> As on thy highest mount I stand,
> I look away beyond the sea,
> Where mansions are prepared for me,
> And view the shining glory shore,—
> My Heaven, my home forever more."

(d) Now this earth, having first undergone disengagement and evolution out of the primitive integer, pursuant to the laws of gravitation, assuming a spherical shape, revolves around the integer (which becomes the sun) ninety-five millions of miles distant, performing a revolution in 365 1-4 days; as the normal result of condensation eventually becoming luminous by the development of heat. Before the invention of Lucifer matches, the blacksmith lit his fire in the forge by suddenly striking a piece of iron a violent blow, by which it became luminous. Therefore every planet, as the ultimatum of condensation, becomes luminous. Hence there was a time when this earth actually shone like the sun. After cooling off by the radiation of heat into space, eventually the circumambient vapor so condensed as to precipitate into water on the surface. Consequently the time came when the whole earth was covered with water. "The Spirit of the Lord moved on the face of the water."

The earth is this day a ball of fire with a thin crust on the exterior not so thick in proportion to its size as the shell of an egg, and perforated by four hundred volcanoes, sending up smoke and flame, and ever and anon superinducing earthquakes and pouring out rivers of lava.

As we sailed along over the Mediterranean Sea last month, we passed by Strombroli, which has been constantly afire for 150 years. These volcanoes are safety-valves, permitting the pent-up steam to escape and thus preventing an explosion. If they were all closed, soon the earth would explode and be transformed into a volcano enveloping the entire surface.

When the volcanic ages supervened, the earth lifted up vast mountain ranges and sunk down into intervening valleys. When you draw a band around a hat too tightly, it will produce ridges in one place and depressions in another. So when the crust of the earth first consolidated, the contraction of the volume was not complete. Consequently the surface became too large for the sphere and depressions and upheavals superinduced great irregularities in the surface, causing the lofty mountain ranges and the great intervening valleys into which the waters gathered, causing oceans and seas.

(e) The earth reached a degree of perfection in which she could produce vegetables, marine and terrestrial, before it was possible for air-breathing animals to live, as her luminosity had developed so much carbonic acid as to render it impossible for an air-breathing animal to live. As the vegetable kingdom is composed of carbon, oxygen and hydrogen, the latter two constituting water, therefore the great bulk of the vegetable world is carbon. The long ages when the earth shone like the sun had so highly charged the atmosphere with carbon that, when those volcanic upheavals elevated portions of the surface above the water, the vast forests sprang up, deciduous annual productions growing in a single season fifty or sixty feet high with trunks one foot in diameter, dying with the oncoming winter, and falling down in great piles, as they had grown so copiously.

After a series of years of producing these exhuberant crops of vegetable matter, physical revolutions in the world's surface, producing upheavals here and depressions there, would sink those regions thus piled with fallen vegetable growth so that the oceanic waters would overflow them and carry them in vast heaps into the subsidences. Then the sea would remain a long period of time and great strata would be formed on them, pressing them hard, and thus developing vast quantities of stone coal in the earth, so valuable in the oncoming ages of human habitation on the earth.

Long ages before man was created innumerable animals, especially aquatic, lived on the earth. I have climbed the great mountain ranges in the different grand divisions of the globe, and have seen the highest mountains in the world, Everest, 29, 002 feet high, also Chunchenginga, 28,046 feet high. In all my peregrinations on the earth, I have found sea-shells on the highest mountains, showing plainly that the ocean had been there long ages and that these marine animals have lived and died and undergone petrifaction, and afterward great volcanic upheavals lifted the surface above the clouds. In this way we see that the whole earth has at some time been the oceanic bed. Three quarters of the earth's surface are now the oceanic bottom receiving the debris of thousands of rivers, pouring down their fertility, thus making it all rich as the garden of the Lord. The Bible says, in reference to the on-coming celestial ages of the earth, that there will be no more sea (Rev. 22nd chapter), the sanctifying cremation of the earth having utterly removed it.

(f) The great Japanese Empire, with 50,000,000 of people and a marvelous record for heroism on the battlefield, having in the present generation conquered two of the greatest empires of the globe, i. e., China and Russia, has been largely created through the instrumentality of coral insects.

The lowest order of animals are radiates, having the form of a star. These abound in the ocean, which in the great home of the animal world. I have seen whales one hundred feet long and twelve feet through the body.

The first five days of creation passed away before a human being was brought into existence. In those early ages man could not live on the earth if he had been here. The carbonic acid would have killed him instantly, meanwhile the ocean abounded in animals, when no air-breathing animal could breathe on the earth. As man is the highest order of creation, his organism is the most complicated. Truly he has been pronounced "a harp of one thousand strings," and the puzzle of the ages confronts philosophers and sages to solve the problem of his keeping in tune so long.

The great coal-fields had to be produced and deposited in the earth to run the machinery of the human ages, the grand culmination of all, to which all preceding ages were subordinated, and this wonderful and speedy growth of the trees that formed the coal mines took carbon out of the air and deposited it for fuel in the crust of the earth long ages before God ever said, "Let us make man."

(g) The Bible tells us that God created all things on land and sea in the six days, climaxing His stupendous work with man. Then He rested on the seventh day from all His work. Now the question arises, What was the duration of the seventh day? Theologians and pilgrims have, through all the human age, been wondering how long Adam and Eve lived on the earth before they fell. N. B. They just lived through God's Sabbath. 2 Peter 3: 8: "One day with God is a thousand years." The days of creation were all His days, therefore we may conclude that His Sabbath was one thousand years. Indefinite as to all these days being creative periods.

"Oh," you say, "is it possible that Adam and Eve lived on earth one thousand years, living with God and knowing no sin?" You see the normal conclusion is a thousand years. "But," you say, "they would have gotten old in that time." N. B. If they never had sinned, they never would have gotten old, but would have bloomed in immortal youth forever. The infirmities of age are the soul progeny of sin. When they had been duly tested and tried, and their probation expired, guided by instinct, they would have had access to the tree of life, the normal effect of whose fruit would have been the elimination of mortality out of them, as they had been created mortal but designed for immortality, which would be the enduement of the fruit growing on the tree of life.

In case they had kept their first state, in due time

having access to the tree of life, whose fruit would have eliminated all mortality out of them, then translation would have, in the finale, forever emancipated them from probation. When we get to Heaven, I trow it will be our privilege to hear father and mother Adam and Eve, to our infinite edification, tell much of their downfall and life in Eden.

(h) The reason why we cognomen this chapter "heavenly ages" is because God was alone on the earth. His presence is Heaven. When I say He was alone, I simply mean that there was no disharmony whatever and His sweet will, which makes our paradise, filled the created universe. Of course the angels were here because they shouted uproariously when worlds rolled out from shapeless chaos, as above described.

Satan was then unknown in the universe, as God never created him; but He did create the archangel Lucifer, so named because of his brilliancy and glory, as Lucifer means light-bearer of Heaven. He was on probation, like all created intelligences. Unfortunately, he kept not his first estate, but dared to set up independently of God. That moment the Divine life evanesced from his spirit and left him enveloped in hellish midnight. Having once lost his hold on God, it was impossible for him ever to regain it. From that day to this, he has been doing his best to get the greatest possible following. Before he ever came into Paradise, God perfectly had His way. He created Adam and Eve because He wanted company and came daily and walked with them amid fadeless flowers and never-fading fruits of unfallen Eden. Therefore we pronounce all the ages "heavenly" which preceded the fall. God was present and managed everything in perfect harmony with His sweet will.

> "To Thee and Thee alone
>   The angels owe their bliss;
> They circle round the blazing Throne,
>   And dwell where Jesus is.

> "Not all the harps above
>   Can make a heavenly place,
> If God His residence remove,
>   Or but conceal His face.

> "To Thee my spirits fly.
>   With infinite desire, and yet
> How far from Thee I lie!
>   O Jesus, raise me higher."

(i) During the heavenly ages there were no deflections whatever from the Divine will. The seventh day was God's Sabbath, because He rested from all His work, and it still would have been running if Satan had not broken it. "Sabbath" is a Hebrew word and means rest. Applied to man, it means the perfect rest of the soul in Jesus, which we never can have till saved from all sin.

CHAPTER VI.

Satanic Ages.

The invasion of Eden by Satan broke up the heavenly ages, which had been moving along without the slightest friction since creation's dawn. In 2 Corinthians 4, where the English version calls Satan the "god of this world," it should read the "god of this age." We are all living in the satanic ages, which began with the fall and will run till he is arrested by the apocalyptic angel. (Rev. 20:1-4.)

Satan immediately adopted war for his religion. God's religion does its best to fill Heaven with people. Satan's religion does its best to fill Hell with people. It has been estimated that people enough have been killed in wars to populate the world fourteen times. We now have 1,700,000,000 of people on the earth. The above estimate gives you one thousand millions killed in wars. Truly the earth is rapidly becoming a graveyard from the rising of the sun to the going down of the same. Only a few days ago I saw them digging a grave and taking out the bones of a body that had been buried there in the long ago, in order to make room for the one they were preparing to bury.

When the battle is raging, they have no time to prepare for eternity. The moral effect is to stir up their evil tempers and make them fight like dogs, bears, and lions, horrifically ripening them for an awful Hell.

I was gratified when recently traveling in the Old World to hear of the Peace Conference held by all nations in Italy, in order to do away with war throughout the whole earth, and that our President Taft was the leader. It is certainly ominous of better days.

(j) The arrest of Satan by the apocalyptic angel (Rev. 20:1-4) will wind up his age upon the earth: "I saw an angel come down from Heaven, having the key of the bottomless pit and a great chain in his hand. He laid hold on the dragon, that old serpent, who is the devil and Satan, and bound him one thousand years and locked him up, that he should deceive the nations of the earth no longer till the one thousand years be fulfilled."

The reason why the world is so wicked now is because Satan is going forth in a great rage, knowing that his time is short. The flood was a wonderful harvest for Hell; the Jewish tribulation (A. D. 66-73) was another; but the great tribulation will be by far the most copious harvest that Hell has ever reached or ever will reach because there will be so many more people in the world.

The post-millennial invasion of the earth by Satan will not re-establish his reign on the earth, as you see he makes a failure and it ultimates in the glory of Christ.

The afflictions of Job were exceedingly conducive to the glory of God. Job was not afflicted for his own sake, but for yours and mine, that we may have an example of perfect patience. Satan certified in God's presence that Job was serving Him through carnal motives. When He turned him over into his hands, the falsity of his attitude was abundantly revealed and reacted as a sunburst on the world in all ages.

The millennial centuries have been sweeping along one thousand years, the glory of the Lord covering the earth as the waters the seas. Meanwhile Satan is muttering in Hell: "Oh, yes, you Son of God, you have things your own way because I am a poor prisoner and have no chance. You know I beat you in the fight for six thousand years, having the long end of the rope and the broad side of the battlefield; but now you are giving me no chance. I know the people of that world; they have no bottom. Give me a chance, and I can upset them so quickly as to make your head swim."

So you see it was for the glory of Christ to give him a chance. Therefore he lets him out and he proceeds with the utmost audacity and the most sanguine anticipations of sweeping success.

In his powerful oratorical appeals, he gets Gog and Magog to follow him. Gog means the kings and Magog the royal families. (Ezek. 38th chapter.) They are the Japhethites, i. e., the descendants of Noah's youngest son. (Gen. 10th chapter.) They had submitted quietly during the millennial reign, as they could not help themselves. Now Satan lays under contribution his powerful oratory to disaffect them against the millennial administration, telling them that they had been cheated out of their kingdoms and crowns the thousand years; he brilliantly descants on the pre-millennial ages, when they sat upon thrones and ruled the nations, and assures them that he had thus enthroned, crowned and sceptred them, at the same time assuring them that he can do it again, restoring to them all their kingdoms and crowns. Thus he imparts carnality back into their hearts and they rally round him a great host like the sands of the sea for a multitude.

(k) N. B. During the millennial ages, our Savior will be here, the Healer of disease, and no one will say, "I am sick." Consequently the world will rapidly increase in population. As the curse of sin will have been removed in the expulsion of Satan and all his myrmidons out of the earth, no longer will millions of money be wasted for strong drink, tobacco, gambling, and debaucheries, and the earth will be so much more productive than during the ages blighted by sin, that she will be competent to support the teeming millions and even billions. Consequently the royal families will constitute a mighty host.

At present the rulers of the earth are nearly all white people, i. e., Japhethites. Satan will make an awful raid on Africa. She has two hundred millions now. I trow by that time she will have two thousand millions; but Satan will get no followers in the Dark Continent. When those old Ethiopians shall have leaped up on the burning sands and shouted full salvation a thousand years, they will throw their mouths open like alligators and roar like lions till they stampede him from the Dark Continent.

Asia has eight hundred millions; at that time I trow it will have eight thousand millions. They have always been distinguished for their immobility. Satan will there make a complete failure; for those old almond-eyed Chinamen, fire-baptized Indians, and heroic Japs, having shouted full salvation and flashed the pentecostal fire a thousand years, will skedaddle old Diabolus from the Orient.

The truth of it is, when the angel arrests the devil and locks him up in Hell, his armies will all be driven from the earth and not permitted to tempt the people during the millennial reign, therefore Satan will come along as he entered Eden.

You see in the finale that Satan coils his royal army around Jerusalem, like a huge boa-constrictor, confident of victory, when God turns fire on them from Heaven and utterly discomfits them all, precipitating Satan into the lake of fire where the Pope and Mohammed had anticipated him one thousand years.

An exegesis of his signal failure is found in his utter divestiture of religious influence, as his counterfeit religions had all been swept away about the close of the Armageddon wars, evanescing from the earth with the fall of Babylon.

Therefore Satan's post-millennial invasion of the world really ultimated in the glorification of the Christ, confirmatory of the conclusion that his kingdom fell when he was arrested at the beginning of the Millennium.

Everything God permits to take place is ultimately a blessing to His true people. Romans 8:28: "All things work together for good to them that love God." You could not have "all things" and leave the devil out, as he is not only a "thing," but a big one. Hence you see God even makes the devil a blessing to His true people, who are environed by His providence, till neither men nor devils can reach them. Satan and his host, excarnate and incarnate, may do what they will to God's elect, and by the time it reaches them it will be God's blessing instead of Satan's curse.

CHAPTER VII.

MEDIATORIAL KINGDOM.

God, from all eternity, saw the revolt of Lucifer, the fall of man and the illimitable woes following down the ages, and provided the remedy. When the news reached Heaven, "All ruined in Paradise below," the angels hung their golden harps on weeping willows and sat down to bewail the appalling doom of a lost world. Fain would they all embark in the rescue, but hopeless despair stalks like an avenging spectre and the mournful wail rings out, "No hope!" Meanwhile the Son of God walks out on celestial plains and proclaims His espousal of the lost cause. Never before was Heaven so astonished. When the news reached Hell, certifying the espousal of the lost cause by the Son of God, the exultant jubilee roaring in full blast, sky rockets flaming, and all the myrmidons shouting, "Oh, the victory!" panic sweeps the pandemonium like lightning shafts and cyclones. Never was Hell so astonished before.

(1) When Satan fought the battle in Eden, he achieved the greatest victory known in the ages, because the countless millions of unborn were all in Adam.

Therefore in him he slew the whole race. Eve was no exception to the unity of humanity in Adam, because she was but a transformation of Adam's rib. First Corinthians 15:22: "In Adam all die, but in Christ shall all be made alive." Here you see that every human being died in Adam, temporally, spiritually and eternally, so it seemed that the last hope had gone down in the gloom of an eternal night. See how wonderfully our glorious Christ got the run on the devil! Hebrews 2:9: "By the grace of God Christ tasted death for every man" (English version); true reading, "every one." "Huper pantos." "Huper" means instead of, the very word used throughout the Bible for the vicarious, substitutionary Atonement. "Pantos" means every one, therefore "man" is not correct.

"When do we become one human being?" you ask. The moment soul and body united constitute personality. Therefore you see clearly that the mediatorial work of God in Christ normally reaches every soul the monent vitality supervenes, which is far back in the prenatal state, five or six months before the physical birth.

Therefore you see how wonderfully our Savior got the run on the devil. While all died in Adam seminally, every one is raised from the dead by the omnipotent Christ the moment he becomes a human soul. Thus, God, from all eternity, provided the remedy. (Rev. 13:8; 17:8.) Here we have two unequivocal Scriptures showing up the consolatory fact that God foresaw the awful ruin and provided the remedy from the foundation of the world.

Oh, the unspeakable wisdom, goodness, mercy and lovingkindness of our unspeakably gracious and glorious Heavenly Father!

You saw clearly from the above Scriptures that, by the superabounding grace of God in Christ, every human being is born a citizen of the Kingdom and only gets out by sinning out. The prodigal son and his brother were born in their father's house, i. e., the kingdom of grace. The elder brother never did get out, but was there safe and all right when the prodigal got back.

To be sure, he badly needed sanctification, to take the fret and jealousy out of him, but not to convert him, for this had been done in his infancy before he lost his infantile justification. Otherwise he would have gone away into sin and landed in the hogpen along with his younger brother. You see plainly by the record that he had never backslidden out of his infantile justification like his younger brother. He said to his father, "I have never at any time transgressed thy commandment." The very fact that the father accepted his testimony is demonstrative truth that he was correct. The verb is in the imperfect tense, showing that the father still continued to entreat him to come into the meeting. There the curtain falls over the scene. I believe he did come in before it was over, got sanctified in that glorious holiness meeting, and before the final benediction, immortalized himself as the highest jumper and loudest shouter.

When the father met the prodigal and kissed him that kiss was his justification. He immediately called for them to bring the best robe and put it on him; that was none other than the robe of entire sanctification, washed and made white in the blood of Calvary's Lamb.

(m) There is universal need of light on the relation of all the infants to the Kingdom. They are not born sinners, but Christians, with an evil nature in them, turning their faces away from God, so, if not converted, i. e., turned round and introduced to God before they reach responsibility, they will go headlong into sin like the prodigal son on to the hogpen, and plunge into Hell.

"If we walk in the light as He is in the light, we have fellowship one with the other, and the blood of Jesus Christ His Son cleanseth us from all sin." (John 1:7.)

This applies to every person in all the ages and nations. God does not require us to walk in light which He does not give us. Souls are only lost for rejected light. Heathens, Mohammedans, Catholics (Greek and Roman), Jews, and all other people who walk in all the light they have, and seek all they can get, and do the best they know, will receive the efficacy of the cleansing Blood mentioned in the Scriptures and make their way to Heaven. Mark it down, there is a great possibility for every human being in all the world to be saved.

The great argument for evangelizing the whole heathen world (nine hundred millions of pagans, four hundred millions of Catholics, and three hundred millions of Mohammedans and Jews) as quickly as possible is because the great commandment of our Lord dispatches us at once into this magnitudinous work. We must not only talk salvation everywhere we go, and do our best, but either go into the regions beyond or send, because otherwise we cannot be justified. The "sine qua non" is not on their side, but on ours. If we do not obey, we forfeit our justification and become backsliders. If they walk in all the light they have, and do their best to get more, they will be saved; not without Christ, because the Holy Spirit is in all the earth and He is the Spirit of Christ (Acts 16: 6, 7), and "Christ is the true light which lighteth every man that cometh into the world." (John 1: 9.)

(n) How does the light of Christ shine on people who have never heard of Him? N. B. The Holy Spirit is the excarnate Christ and He is everywhere verifying the word of John the Baptist that Christ, the true light, shines on every person that cometh into the world, so that none have an excuse for their damnation, as all could be saved if they would. Yet we dare not be delinquent in our efforts to carry the Gospel to every human being.

You will find in First Corinthians 15: 23-25, that the mediatorial kingdom runs on without a break until the end of time, when Christ shall vacate the intercessory throne for the judgment seat. The conclusion will be His adjudication of the whole world, for as

He has redeemed all by His blood, He will finally judge all in the great day. It is very consolatory to us to know that we will be judged by our own dear brother Jesus, who loved us and gave Himself for us, and is doing everything possible to save us.

During the long, rolling centuries while the Roman Empire ruled the whole world, when a province revolted, the Emperor would send out a proconsul to suppress the rebellion and bring the province into loyalty. Then they built a triumphal arch for the conqueror's reception, exhibiting his mighty achievements chiseled on it by the skilful sculptor. In the great and notable day of his triumphal ingress into Rome he would enter on a chariot drawn by four white horses, under the triumphal arch emblazoned with the splendid artistic manifestations of his glorious achievements. The subjugated armies, with their kings and queens, were led along to adorn the triumph, and the rich spoils of conquest were displayed on all sides.

(o) This is the only revolted world in the celestial universe. God's own Son volunteered to imperil His life and redeem it by His own blood. Therefore when the war against sin and carnality shall have been consummated so as to eliminate all disloyalty and antagonism out of the celestial empire world without end, Satan and his incorrigible followers, demoniacal and human, having been banished into the lake of fire in utter darkness far beyond the circle of the illuminated universe, so that the combined illumination of seventeen hundred millions of glowing suns will never reach them with a solitary ray, and they never can get back to trouble the peace and mar the glorious and perfect harmony of the celestial universe; the Son of God, having completed His mediatorial work and restored this revolted world back to her place as a true and loyal member of the heavenly empire, as the world will never again be inhabited by mortal people on probation, and the mediatorial work being now gloriously and forever consummated, will surrender up His commission to God the Father, who will be all in all forever. This is not incompatible with the eternal Sonship, as you read in Isaiah that, even in that capacity, He is the everlasting Father, and the government shall be on His shoulders.

When the Roman Empire ruled the whole world, people would come from the ends of the world to attend the triumphal ingress of a conqueror who had toiled and fought many years, in constant peril, for the restoration of a revolted province. This is but a faint illustration of the grandest ovation to be in the celestial universe; when the last battle shall have been fought, and victory perch eternally on Emmanuel's banner. Reader, be sure you are there and ring out your jubilant voice in the song:

> "All hail the power of Jesus' name,
>   Let angels prostrate fall,
> Bring forth the royal diadem
>   And crown Him Lord of all.
>
> "Ye chosen seed of Israel's race,
>   A remnant weak and small,
> Hail Him who saves you by His grace,
>   And crown Him Lord of all.

> "Ye Gentile sinners, ne'er forget
> The wormwood and the gall;
> Go spread your trophies at His feet,
> And crown Him Lord of all.
>
> "Oh, that with yonder sacred throng
> We at His feet may fall;
> We'll join the everlasting song
> And crown Him Lord of all."

(p) When I was preaching in Boston, dear Holiness people asked me if the pre-millennial coming of the Lord was harmonizable with His perpetual intercession till the final Judgment. I answered in the affirmative. If we don't take the word of the Lord and walk in the light appertaining to every truth, we will suffer spiritual detriment. N. B. The mediatorial work of Christ was efficacious from the foundation of the world. (Rev. 13:8 and 17:8.) It was just as efficacious in case of Abel as in case of the martyrs of the apostolic age.

When they asked John the Baptist if he was the Christ, he answered, "No, I am the voice of one roaring in the wilderness, Prepare ye the way of the Lord and make His paths straight." Go back to Isaiah 53rd chapter, and you find it says, "Prepare ye the way of Jehovah." Hence you see the Jehovah of Isaiah is the Christ of John the Baptist. Hear Paul's testimony (1 Cor. 10:11): "They tempted Christ and were destroyed by serpents." Go to the Pentateuch and you read that they tempted Jehovah and were destroyed by serpents. Therefore you see the Jehovah of Moses was the Christ of Paul.

These two brightest witnesses in all the world ringing out their testimony at the front of both dispensations settle the matter beyond all controversy that the Jehovah of the Old Testament is the Christ of the New; excarnate in the former and incarnate in the latter.

In the last month I again ate my dinner under the memorable old tree on the plains of Mamre where our blessed Christ and two angels, in the form of men, ate with Abraham nineteen hundred years before He was born in Bethlehem. He also appeared to Nebuchadnezzar in the fiery furnace in Babylon eight hundred years before His advent in Bethlehem.

It was necessary that His incarnation be postponed till learning had spread over the world and it would be faithfully chronicled in history so they would hold it with a giant's grip. If it had taken place in the early ages, it would have been lost in the fog and mists of superstition and mythology. While He was in this world, whether an infant in the arms of His mother or working miracles in Galilee, He was none the less our Mediator and Expiator.

His coming on the throne of His millennial glory will be no more incompatible with His mediatorship than His riding the donkey into Jerusalem. From Abel to the last human being ever born into the world, His mediatorial office is perfectly efficacious.

CHAPTER VIII.

Post-Edenic, Ante-diluvian Dispensation.

The ante-diluvian dispensation was evidently 2,656 years instead of 1,656 years, as the English version has it. This is the Septuagint record, made by seventy learned Jews, called together by Ptolemy Philadelphus, king of Egypt in Alexandria 288 B. C., and quoted by our Savior. It is also confirmed by the Egyptian pyramids built by the ante-diluvians.

I have climbed Cheops to the apex, said to be 550 feet high and covering thirteen acres of ground. Coins have been found in it giving its date as 3,700 years B. C. According to the English version chronology, putting the Christian era A. M. 4004, it would make the erection of this pyramid in the year of the world 304. You see that would not do as at that time there were very few people in the world, whereas calculations have been made reaching the conclusion that erection of this pyramid would require the work of one hundred thousand men twenty years or twenty thousand men one hundred years.

The Septuagint chronology would put the work one thousand years after Adam was created, when it would be feasible, because they lived one thousand years and were all giants and much stouter than the present generation; besides they had an animal, the mastodon, several times larger than the elephant (which weighs ten thousand pounds), and they doubtless used him in moving great stones. He has never lived on the earth since the flood, therefore one may rest assured that the ante-diluvian world was 2,200 years long.

If they had any books they all perished in the flood.

Moses, who wrote the Pentateuch 3,578 years ago, is the oldest writer known.

The Book of Job is certified to have been written nine years before the Pentateuch, but the facts favor the conclusion that Moses wrote it as dictated by Job, when he visited him while serving his father-in-law as shepherd, when, it is said, he went to the Land of Uz and saw Job, after he had convalesced from his great afflictions and God had so wonderfully restored him personally and doubled everything Satan had taken from him.

The ante-diluvians had starlight, continuing down to the Mosaic dispensation, when the moon rose, adding her beautiful, silvery effulgence to the glory of the glittering constellations. Day dawned with John the Baptist; the sun rose when Christ was born in Bethlehem; the noonday culminated at Pentecost, the glorious Sun of Righteousness with healing in His wings reaching the celestial zenith and going not down, but abiding and transmitting His noonday effulgence to the ends of the earth.

Post-Edenic, Ante-diluvian Dispensation. 265

So long as the Sethites, i. e., the holiness people, kept separate from the Cainites, the worldly idolators, things moved on gloriously and they were blessed by such preachers as Enoch, who was gloriously sanctified at the age of sixty-five, walked with God three hundred years without a break, and received the honor of a chariot ride to Glory without seeing death. The Jewish Talmuds, i. e., written histories, tell us that he was king, and so enraptured with the divine fellowship that he habitually went away alone and would remain days together in communion with God, and eventually he absented himself for his retirement and periodical talks with the Lord and stayed so long that they went to hunt him, but never could find him. The precious Word gives us the solution, that God took him. He was the seventh from Adam, but the Talmuds say that Adam lived till the time of Enoch and then died, and that Enoch, Seth and Methuselah served as his pall-bearers, and all the people in the world at that time attended the funeral and manifested their filial love by great mourning.

The record is clear appertaining to the cause of the awful and fatal ante-diluvian apostasy. You remember down about the sixth chapter is the statement that when the sons of God saw the daughters of men, that they were fair, they took to themselves wives. Then the statement very soon follows that the world was filled with violence, i. e., wickedness, and soon the statement comes that their days on the earth should be only 120 years, when the flood would come and destroy them all.

"Sons of God" means the holiness people, descendants of Seth; "daughters of men," the children of Cain, who worshiped Baal, i. e., the sun god. The city he founded, Baalbec, became the capital and metropolis of the paganistic world, as the sun god was the most popular divinity on the earth the first four thousand years of the world. The majority, with their riches, went to Baalbec and worshiped the gods of nature instead of the God of grace, whose followers in all ages have been a small minority.

The ante-diluvian dispensation would have done well had they only kept separate from the world. Even this day we have the same trouble everywhere.

When the godly people intermarry with the ungodly, it, as a rule, proves their ruin. The woman says, "Oh, I will marry him to save his soul." Be sure you get him saved before you marry him. If you can not then, you are sure not to succeed afterward. Our common hereditary depravity puts us all on an inclined plane. The wicked have the down-hill pull and in nine cases out of ten will beat the righteous, whose only chance is the up-hill pull.

The Lord never let me raise but one daughter. She was happily converted at twelve, gloriously sanctified at sixteen, and went out with me, helping me with the meetings. When I found those Blue Grass dudes waiting on her, I said, "Effie, I am not willing for you to keep the company of those ungodly young men." She responded, "Father, I do not want their company, but what shall I do? They are our neighbors and I must treat them politely." I responded,

"Now do what I tell you. When your beau comes, meet him at the door, escort him into the parlor, give him a chair, go to your organ and sing a full-salvation song performing on the instrument. When you begin to sing and play, that will be the signal for your mother and her company, if she has any, to come in. When you have sung a few songs, call all to prayer, make your beau a special subject, and thank the Lord for giving you a chance to pray for him." She responded," ",All right, father, I will do so with pleasure." Reader, how many visits do you suppose each dude made? Methinks you respond, "Just one." You are correct.

The years go by and I am home again, and my dear wife says, "Mr. Godbey, do you know that Effie has never had a beau since we prayed them all off four years ago, and it suits me well, for she is our only daughter and I do not see how we could do without her. I hope to see her remain single as long as I live." Two years roll away and I am at home again, and daughter this time brings up the subject, and informs me that four sanctified preachers are waiting on her and she will be obliged to me if I will take my choice, giving me their names. I respond, "Effie, they are all good enough for us; I have no objection to any of them; but Brother Hill was happily converted in my service when a boy and I have never heard anything wrong about him, and as I am better acquainted with him than the others, he is my choice." She leaps, and claps her hands, and praises the Lord, and says, "He is mine too." So very soon we all went into the

Methodist Church and witnessed the solemnization of their matrimony.

The destruction of the ante-diluvians by the flood was a signal act of mercy, as it was impossible for them ever to be saved. They had lost their hold on God and the tide was so strong that they were like a great drove of stampeded Texas cattle running away and sweeping over every obstruction.

(q) Noah preached to them 120 years with all his might and had no converts outside his own family. He certainly deserves great credit for standing so long alone, for that he was alone is settled in Genesis 7:1, where God says, "Come thou and all thy house into the ark, for thee alone have I found righteous in this generation."

Long life is a wonderful blessing when we are saved all right. Good old sanctified Bishop McTiere, presiding over my Conference twenty-seven years ago, when we had no evangelists by Conference appointment, told me that he believed in evangelists, and that I was the man for the work, and, with my consent, he would put me in it, but not without, for he had no way to give me any financial support from the Church. I said to him, "Bishop, your will is my pleasure. As to support, I am more than willing to trust God alone, who promises to feed me like the birds and clothe me like the lilies."

Then he took me out of the Conference, put me in the evangelistic work, and gave me the whole connection (which means the whole world) for life. I have been in it ever since; crossed the continent times immemorial, preaching from ocean to ocean, from the Gulf to British America and four times have travelled in Europe, Asia and Africa, helping the missionaries, and preached my way round the world.

I have been preaching fifty-eight years and am seventy-eight years old. It seems but a few days. If I only had some of that wonderful ante-diluvian longevity, as I feel that the Holy Ghost through that bishop actually gave me the world for my field of labor. Oh! how I regret to leave it! I have wide-open doors enough for one thousand men.

I think about coming eternity, which is so very nigh, when we can embark on enterprises requiring thousands of years with perfect safety, and push them through for the glory of God, our merciful Heavenly Father who is willing that we should live a thousand years in this world, and so permitted the ante-diluvians to do, but Satan took advantage of it and made it the greased plank to precipitate them into Hell by the wholesale. Oh, how he preached to them, "You need not get religion now; one hundred years from now, just before you die, will be plenty of time to get ready to die and go up to Heaven with a shout, and meet father and mother Adam and Eve, Abel and Seth, Enoch and others gone on before." The consequence was they postponed until their hearts got so hard and their lives so wicked that they utterly grieved away the Holy Spirit and could not be saved. Genesis 6:3: "My Spirit shall not always strive with man."

You see they crossed the dead line, sealing their doom so they could not be saved. If God had not interposed at the time He did, the last hope would have been forever gone, because while showing so great patience and perseverance, preaching to the people 120 years without a flicker, you see that Noah displayed great weakness even after the subsidence of the flood. We know he was saved all right, because his name appears in the faith roll. (Heb. 11th chap.) If he had gone down, the hope of the world would have sunk into the gloom of eternal night and this world would have been simply a hogpen in which to fatten souls for Hell. Thus Noah was rescued and honored to become the second father of mankind. We all know we are the children of Adam and we are equally the children of Noah, for God used his three sons Shem, Ham, and Japheth, to repopulate the world.

CHAPTER IX.

Post-diluvian Patriarchy.

Philosophers have denominated man the "religious animal." This is corroborated by the fact that no nation has ever been found without a consciousness of the supernatural and recognition of the Divinity. Satan very adroitly takes advantage of this innate principle in humanity, so manipulating as to get them to worship him. He even had the audacity to tempt our Savior to worship him when he led Him up to the summit of the highest mountain and gave Him a panorama of all the kingdoms of the whole world and proposed to give them all to Him if He would only fall down and worship him. Jesus signally repelled and skedaddled him from His presence by a single stroke of the spiritual sword, i. e., the precious Word of the Lord: "Thou shalt worship the Lord thy God, and Him only shalt thou serve."

(r) The primary organization of the Church is the family. God recognizes the Church in all ages. Antecedently to Moses, it was simply in the family; the father, the prophet, priest and king; and the mother, the guardian angel; sons, daughters, servants and sojourners, the members. Abraham, Isaac, Jacob, Joseph and his brothers, as well as Job, Melchizedek, Zerubbabel and others were preachers of the Gospel in the patriarchal dispensation.

Balaam, when first we hear of him in the Bible, was an intensely conscientious prophet of the Lord, most solemnly ascervating his determination to speak nothing but what God gave him. Unfortunately he yielded to the temptation of Balak's gold, so that God conferred on the donkey he rode the gift of tongues, so that he actually spoke to him in a human language, rebuking his wrath kindled against him, when, to avoid running against the angel that stood before him to prevent his going to the palace of the Moabitish king, where he would suffer that awful temptation, he wheeled away and struck his foot against a stone wall.

You find no more brilliant, beautiful, rich and sweet eloquence enunciated by inspiration than the prophecies with which God used Balaam to augment the precious volume of Holy Writ. Yet, yielding to the temptation of Balak's gold, he became apostate, and receives a mournful mention in the catalogue of the slain in the Moabitish war, fighting against Israel.

Melchizedek was a brilliant example of an inspired prophet as well as an officiating priest identified with the patriarchal dispensation.

Bible readers have been much bewildered over the adjective applied to Melchizedek by Apollos in the Hebrew Epistle. You say, "Brother Godbey, I thought Paul wrote Hebrews." Read the last chapter of Second Thessalonians and you see Paul certified that his name is in all his Epistles. You do not find his autograph in Hebrews, hence you cannot believe that Paul wrote it; as it has no signature, we do not positively know its authorship; however, I believe, with Dean Alford and the abler critics, that Apollos wrote it. Paul's word settles the controversy against his authorship beyond all defalcation. Besides, Paul wrote in a very plain way, lest the people might confide in the wisdom of man rather than in the power of God. Paul was the most learned man in the world, but declined to use excellency of speech and human wisdom, lest the faith of the people stand in the wisdom of man rather than in the dynamite of God. Apollos was not only a man of great learning, but Paul himself (Acts 18) pronounces him the most eloquent man in the world. The mere question of authorship has nothing to do with the value of that beautiful, eloquent Epistle, because, regardless of human authorship, it is the inspired Word of God. They never signed Paul's name to it until six hundred years ago, when the Pope ordered them to consign it to Paul. But he did not know, and gave the order as he does many things, entirely haphazardly and without any authority.

In that beautiful Scripture it says that Melchizedek "was without father, without mother, without beginning of days, or end of time." Under the patriarchal dispensation, God called the preacher, as in the Gospel age. Apollos takes up the ministry of Melchizedek, a celebrated prophet of the Lord and Abraham's pastor. (Gen. 14th chap.) He lived at Knob, the sacerdotal college, where the priests were educated. They continued till the reign of Saul, who had them all killed (eighty-one in all), Abiathar alone escaping, joining David, and remaining with him to the end of his life.

Those adjuncts, "without father, without mother, without beginning of days or end of time," simply appertained to Melchizedek's priestly character. Under the Mosaic dispensation no one could officiate as priest unless he belonged to the Aaronic family. In the Gospel, i. e., the priesthood of Christ, there is no restriction whatever. The father may be a drunkard and the mother a prostitute, but if God calls, the children have as much of a right to preach as if their parents had preached the Gospel before them.

George Whitefield was the greatest preacher in the world in his day. He crossed the Atlantic ocean seventeen times, finally finding a grave at the mouth of the beautiful Merrimac River in Yankee Land. He was born in a brothel, having no father to take care of him. After he reached the zenith of his wonderful power, they could find no house competent to receive his congregation, but built him a scaffold in an open field, where fifty thousand people would come to hear him preach and listen spellbound two solid hours, by his trumpet voice so transported that they scarcely knew whether they were in their mortal tenements.

There were so many Aaronic priests that Abiah divided the time among them, so as to give them all a chance.

As a man, Melchizedek had father and mother, like other people, lived his time on the earth, and passed away, as we are all so quickly hastening to the end.

> "Art is long and time is fleeting
>   And our hearts, though stout and brave,
> Still, like muffed drums, are beating
>   Funeral marches to the grave."

(s) Jethro was a prophet-priest, identified with the patriarchal dispensation. See how God honored him in the change of dispensations from the patriarchal to the Mosaic, even having Moses wed his daughter Zipporah and, in His providence, having Moses live in his family forty years, a faithful and appreciative student at his feet. Although he had been brought up at the court of Egypt, trained to govern the business, drilled in military tactics, and, as history (Ingraham) says, had become a great tactician and led the Egyptian armies, especially in the Ethiopian wars, yet Moses had much to learn as well as much to unlearn. Meanwhile God used Jethro to teach him primary truth, and to culture him in humility, meekness, faith and perseverance, as day after day he led his father-in-law's flocks over the rugged mountains, grazing them in the fertile valleys and protecting them from the wild beasts and savages.

God Himself was teaching him the great primal truths of righteousness and holiness, and especially perfect meekness; finally getting him ready for that wonderful epoch in his life (as in yours and mine), i. e., the baptism of the Holy Ghost and fire, which he received in glorious affusion at the burning bush, being astonished because, though wrapped in flames, it was not consumed. This wonderful fiery baptism does not consume our souls, but simply purifies them by consuming and destroying all depravity; yea, the very last vestige of Satan's cloven foot, giving us a clean heart and a right spirit, and filling us with the blessed Holy Spirit.

(t) When Moses was leading the great nation of Israel through the wilderness to the Promised Land, Jethro came to see him, bringing with him Zipporah his wife and his two sons. When he saw Moses so encumbered with labor, all the people coming to him to adjudicate their affairs, Jethro said, "My son, this will wear you out. You cannot bear it." Then he prayed God to relieve his son-in-law of his intolerable labor. He heard his prayer, and put the spirit of prophecy on seventy chosen men in Israel, who simultaneously began to prophesy, thus startling the people, who thought that was the office of Moses and they had no right to exercise it. Therefore they all ran to Moses, telling him the thrilling news, and thus giving him a chance to correct it.

As the Spirit fell on them all at once, the nearest couriers of course reached him first, and others arriving from all directions and overflowing with their messages of information at once began to tell their story, so in a few minutes the whole seventy are vociferating around him, producing babel confusion, so bewildering him that he leaps and shouts aloud, "Would to God that every man in Israel did prophesy!"

History repeats itself over and over. The world is full of that same superstition this day. I can truly say with Moses, "Would to God that every man in

Israel (and woman, too) did prophesy!" i. e., preach.

We see how the patriarchal dispensation developed into the Mosaic, the latter dove-tailing into the former. We see the matter beautifully developing in Jethro's family, when Hobab, the son of Jethro and brother-in-law of Moses, was visiting him in the wilderness. Moses said to him, "Brother, come go with us to the Promised Land, as we are now journeying thither, and we will do thee good, for God has spoken good concerning Israel." Though he answered in the negative, yet, reconsidering the matter, he changed his mind and went, became an Israelite and lived in the land of Canaan, his family receiving the cognomen Kenites.

The seventy elders whom God used Jethro to call through his prayer, Himself not only answering the prayer but selecting the subjects, afterward developed into the Sanhedrin, of which Nicodemus, Joseph of Arimathea and Saul of Tarsus were members.

So you see how, in the family of Jethro, Moses and Aaron, the patriarchal evanesced into the Mosaic dispensation. It was not done away with, but augmented and practically superseded. When the child has learned the alphabet, it moves on into reading science and literature, still using the alphabet more than ever; not as a study, but as the indispensable instrumentality in the prosecution of all the branches of the most thorough education; all the while the alphabet constituting the foundation. So the patriarchal dispensation is the foundation of all religion. When the foundation of a house decays, it falls down. In a similar manner, all religion goes into wreckage and ruin when the family altar is given up.

CHAPTER X.

Egyptian Dominion.

The Nile is the longest river in the world—forty-three hundred miles; rising far back beyond the equator in the Mountains of the Moon. The maxim "Caput Neilon reperire" (to find the head of the Nile) was synonymous with impossibility for six thousand years. Finally, in 1891, the head of the Nile was discovered. Another trite maxim prevailed through the ages: "Neilon doron Egyptos" (Egypt is the gift of the Nile), as that country is all desert except what the Nile has made flowing through the long ages antecedently to the creation of man.

The Garden of Eden, as you see, consisted of what is now Palestine, Egypt, Syria and Mesopotamia. The Pison River is the Jordan; the Gihon, the Nile; the Hiddekel, the Tigris, and the Euphrates still retains its name. As these rivers water the Garden of Eden, you see they take in the above-mentioned countries, which constitute the Eden park, as the Hebrew name does not mean a cultivated garden, but a native park.

This region is the center of the world, clustering

about the greatest sea on the globe. The Nile, by his semi-annual inundations, overflows the entire valley, depositing a stratum of fertility and thus developing a soil ten to forty feet deep, the richest in the world. Besides, the climate of Egypt is neither cold winter nor hot summer; but perennial springtime, and summer, with never-fading flowers and never-failing fruits; no rain falling, because the surrounding deserts absorb the clouds, giving perpetual sunshine; and as the whole country is down on the sea level, with no mountains to repel the sea breezes. it is forever refreshed with the hygienic zephyrs from ocean and sea.

These wonderful gifts of a beneficent Creator, so copiously lavished on this country, make it the garden of the globe and the granary of the world, i. e., producing four crops every year. From the beginning it magnetized the human race, concentrating them in Egypt, where they first developed nationality; building the pyramids before the flood, which stand to this day as monuments of ante-diluvian enterprise, and will stand to the end of time. For the same reason, immediately after the flood, they gathered in Egypt, first populating that country as they multiplied. Consequently it was the first to develop nationality and to organize civil government; antecedently, human administration having been restricted to the family, peculiar to the patriarchal ages.

As Egypt became the leader of the world in the development of nationality, fortified by the organized government, God selected her to protect the holy family of Abraham, Isaac and Jacob during the generations of minority, until Israel could develop into nationality and competency to protect herself.

As Satan had captured the world in the first battle fought in Eden, when the whole race was seminally in Adam, and he conquered and lassoed him, the lord of the earth, and in that way he spread the conquest of Hell over this entire planet, so appropriating it to himself as to make it a hell-feeder "ad infinitum," consequently war is the great and perpetual employment of humanity during Satan's reign, which will continue till his arrest by the apocalyptic angel (Rev. 20:1-4), when he will be taken out of the world, locked up in Hell, and the glorious millennial reign of Christ will cover the earth as the waters the sea.

(u) Thus God, in His condescending mercy, availed Himself of the first nationality that developed on the earth as a protector of His people. He used Egypt as an asylum of security till they could develop into competency to protect themselves. Slavery was, in His providence, signally utilized as an auxiliary to the efficiency of the asylum, as that relation kept them out of wars, so that they could all live and multiply.

The world has never known such prolificy as characterized Israel in Egypt. Going thither seventy-five souls, in 215 years they developed into a nation of three millions—a glorious miracle of the Lord, unparalleled in the history of the world.

Labor is hygienical, especially in that genial climate, where there is neither burning summer, chilling winter, nor falling rains. Really the bondage was exceedingly auxiliary to the paradoxical rapidity of their multiplication. God is the healer of the body. He gave them miraculous health, co-operated by physical labor, which kept them out of dissipations and irregularities, as well as the destructiveness of war, which, in all ages, has been constantly cutting down the nations.

Eventually Satan succeeded in superinducing the abuse of their power, especially when he manipulated the destruction of the male children by the midwives. When he made a total failure with them, he finally resorted to military power to impede their multiplication, which was so great that Pharaoh and his magnates became alarmed lest the Hebrews would become a greater people than themselves. Then God interposed in their behalf, leading them out of bondage, when they had developed into magnitude sufficient to protect themselves against the belligerency of surrounding nations. Hence the great utility of Egyptian dominion was the protection of the holy family till they could develop into nationality. Conducively to this, God permitted Jacob to have four wives, so all the twelve tribes of Israel could be launched in the same generation.

We are astonished at the pertinacity with which Pharaoh held his grip on the children of Israel. N. B. At the beginning of the world the great continents and beautiful islands were inhabited only by wild beasts; even in the days of Abraham and Job, land was not appropriated. It was so abundant that all the people could have all they wanted without appropriating it.

(v) Now, the poles of the financial battery having undergone a somersault, they are diametrically reversed, land having become the most valuable property in all the earth, and people, who, even down through the Roman ages were so exceedingly valuable that all nations owned slaves, having acually become worthless, so that slavery has gone out of the world— and the Christians are shouting over the glorious victory of God's kingdom on the earth. They are mistaken. If slavery paid financially, it would fill the world to-day as in the olden time. N. B. Seventeen hundred millions of people this day over-populate the earth, and that is the reason why men, women and children are not worth anything and never will be again. I am speaking simply from a financial standpoint. As to actual slavery, Satan is still running it in multitudinous and diversified ways in the interest of his kingdom, conducively to the rapid population of Hell with human souls.

CHAPTER XI.

Mosaic Mediatorship.

The Bible says there never was such a man as Moses, i. e., an equal to him; who spoke to God face to face, as for example, the forty days he spent on Mount Sinai when he received from Him the law.

Moses was the greatest prophet the world had seen, but more than a prophet, as he was a mediator between God and man. God calls him the "meekest man," i. e., the most humble and lowly the world had seen. This we have abundantly demonstrated when he asked God to excuse him from preaching to the proud and learned court of Pharaoh; apologizing for himself that he had a slow tongue. Nobody else in the world would have said his tongue was slow. It is an expression of his profound humility and meekness. We see the same in Paul, when he certified that he was the least of all saints, while he was really the greatest saint on the globe, with the most gifted intelligence and the finest learning. The same was true of Moses. He had been educated in all the wisdom of the Egyptians, standing at the front of the world, and there is no doubt but that his was the greatest intelligence and scholarship on the globe in his day.

(w) Soon after the autocratic decree for the ejectment of all the Hebrew male infants into the river had gone forth and was being enforced by the soldiers, Amram and Jochebed, Levites, were honored with a son. Knowing their environments and the eminent peril which hung over them, they hid him three months, when they see the utter impossibility of keeping him concealed any longer. Then they ostensibly obey the royal mandate to cast him into the river, i. e., they diligently manufacture a water-proof ark of rushes, lined with cement, and commit him to the great river in the dead hours of the night.

In the present tour, I again visited the place where tradition says Moses was born, and also the rock against which the ark was found resting when the king's daughter, accompanied by her two maid servents, went down to the river with the first gleam of Aurora to enjoy her morning bath. Seeing the ark, she commanded her maid servants to investigate it. They shout to her, "Oh, it is a Hebrew baby." She commands them to bring it to her. There is no doubt but he was the finest looking baby in the world, as the Greek says (Acts 7th chap.), "He was beautiful unto God," i. e., beautiful in the very highest sense, i. e., in the Divine estimation.

When she looks on his face she is charmed with his wonderful beauty and brilliancy. At the same time he breaks out crying and thus touches her heart with profound sympathy. History (Ingraham) says that her husband had recently fallen in the Ethiopian war, leaving her childless, and, as her father was quite old, without a son, and the crown would come to herself, she was anxious to have a son to whom she could transmit it. Therefore she feigned maternity, sending away those servant girls to regions unknown, as they alone knew the origin of the baby.

Moses' little sister Miriam, six years his senior, had kept her eye on her imperiled little brother from his commitment to the treacherous river. When they took him out, she drew nearer, looking with profoundest solicitude for the issue impending, asking the king's daughter if she wants a nurse. Then, responsive to her affirmative question, she runs back to her cottage and tells her mother and father, who come at once and take him into hand and nurse him for the queen.

Meanwhile Amram very soon has the good fortune to receive the superintendency of the royal garden, quite a lucrative appointment. Consequently Moses was nursed by his own mother in the royal mansion. History certifies that, as the king's daughter feigned maternity, publishing abroad that the Lord had given her a fine son, the whole matter received notoriety with the understanding that he was her own son. Of course his mother would keep the matter a profound secret. Thus you see how wonderfully God defeats the devil in all his devices.

As Pharaoh had become alarmed over the paradoxical multiplication of Israel, lest some powerful leader might arise among them, break the slavish chains and lead them out of bondage, now you see he has the very one who is going to do all this, in his own house, and with his own money is richly remunerating his own mother and father to nurse and take care of him. The consequence is, Moses was brought up in the royal court and educated in all the learning of the Egyptians, taught by the magicians, the most learned men in the world in that day, and we read in Hebrews that he became mighty in word and deed. To be mighty in word is to be a great scholar, while to be mighty in deed is to be a great warrior. Moses was educated for the kingdom, consequently they gave him the most culture not only in science and literature, but in military tactics.

(x) During his leadership in Israel, on one occasion when Aaron and Miriam thought he was rather usurping authority, as they did not understand his mediatorship, by way of castigation, they tantilized him with marrying the Ethiopian woman.

This statement stands isolated, without a word of explanation. History comes to our relief, certifying that, while Moses was commanding the Egyptian army, in the long siege of Thebes, the king's daughter, from the palace tower overlooking the Egyptian camp, saw Moses drilling his soldiers and culturing them into military tactics, and even at that distance fell in love with him as he was so fine looking. Thereupon, sending a message to him, she proposed to open the gates to his army on condition that she receive his hand in wedlock. In that way he took Thebes, the capital of the Ethiopians, and the last rival of the Egyptians, thus winding up that long war with the victory for the latter. As we never hear from her any more, the mind naturally conjectures that when the war was over and the Egyptian army returned, perhaps she preferred to remain in her own country, or she might have died; as the case is very clear that Moses was unwedded when he left Egypt and travelled away into Midian, when he became the shepherd of Jethro, wedded his daughter, and lived with him forty years.

As we see in Hebrews 11th chapter, there developed a crisis in Moses' life when he refused to be called "a son of Pharaoh's daughter." History says that his royal mother was so fearful that he would never receive the throne of Egypt, for which she had reared him in her succession, that, when he was thirty-five years old, she did her utmost to prevail on him to receive the crown. He begged her to excuse him, and, as he had already been serving as royal regent to relieve her, assured her that with great pleasure he would continue to do so; thus bearing all the burdens of government as if he had already been crowned and sceptered. Finally she is so importunate that he yields, and they are preparing for his inauguration and coronation, when God revealed to him a wonderful vision. In it he saw a midnight scene in which were soldiers out ransacking the Hebrew dwellings, finding the boy babies and casting them into the Nile. Then he sees a man and woman make a water-proof ark, put a baby in it and commit it to the river, and it floats down till, reaching an eddy, and resting against a great rock at the bank, the king's daughter and the maid-servants, coming for an early bath, discover the baby, take him out, and she feigns maternity and adopts him as her own son.

Thus God revealed to Moses the scene and finally communicated to him the fact that he is that baby, born of Hebrew parents, but reared up by the queen in the royal court, and taught to believe that he was her own son. Thus, his Hebrew origin having been revealed to him, he comes into the presence of his royal mother and tells her all about it. When she finds that he actually knows that he is a Hebrew and not her son, she begs him hard to keep the matter secret, and as they already thought he was her son, to let them still call him her son and crown him king to reign over the land, as she knew they would not let him reign unless they thought he was her son, as they had always understood.

Here comes up a thrilling ordeal. If Moses will receive the crown as the son of Pharaoh's daughter, he will reign over all the land of Egypt. If he divulges his Hebrew origin, of course the Egyptians will never let him reign. He deliberately settles the matter. Leaving the royal palace, he goes away to the land of Goshen, determined to undertake the deliverance of his enslaved and down-trodden brethren. Seeing an Egyptian abusing a Hebrew, he interposes in behalf of the latter, thus actually entering upon the office of civil magistrate and undertaking to protect his people. But accidentally he kills the Egyptian; then, looking all around and seeing no one in sight, he buries him in the sand. Going out the next day, he sees two Hebrews in a quarrel and interposes as a peacemaker, when the one abusing his fellow thrusts him away, saying, "What do you mean? Are you going to kill me like you did the Egyptian yesterday?" Then Moses knows that the matter is found out, and as his own people do not recognize him as their deliverer at all, and will not rally to him and appreciate his services and their own emancipation out of bondage, of course the authorities will get after him and kill him. So he flees away from the country for his life.

Moses was not saved then, but had actually been brought up in Egyptian idolatry. He was a great military man, and when he found out his Hebrew origin and his identity with that enslaved people, as he was naturally very brave and a stranger to fear, he volunteered to go among them in the capacity of a deliverer, aiming to lead them out of bondage by physical force. All of which was utterly contrary to God's plan, to deliver them by His own omnipotent arm.

(y) Then he fled out of the country to save his life, far away into Asia, where he had never been; God's providence leading him to the house of Jethro, the preacher of the Gospel in the patriarchal dispensation then in force. God, in His great mercy, used Jethro not only in giving him a home and a wife, but to acquaint him with the God of Abraham, Isaac and Jacob, and to get him intelligently converted. Then, after seeking sanctification forty years in the solitudes of great Mt. Horeb, thus having reached perfect submission and abandonment to God (which is believing ground for entire sanctification), finally, at the burning bush, he received the baptism of the Holy Ghost and fire. This was preparatory for his great and wonderful labor and responsibility in the emancipation of Israel out of Egyptian bondage, for their leadership the forty years in the wilderness, and the stupendous miracles which God wrought through his instrumentality.

When God sanctified him, baptising him with the Holy Ghost and fire at the bush, He immediately commands him to go back into Egypt and preach to Pharaoh and his court. God had also already put His hand on Aaron, and he had travelled all the way from Egypt and come to the spot where He baptized Moses with the Holy Ghost and fire. When Moses tells God that his tongue is slow, He tells him to go and meet Aaron, his brother, who had just come hunting him, and that he should be his mouthpiece. Therefore they both go at once back into Egypt.

Forty years make great changes, consequently Moses finds none of the people who had been living there when he got into trouble and had to run away for his life because he had killed the Egyptian. Let any of us take a period of forty years in our own lives—it will put us in our graves or work out great changes, revolutionizing our environments.

Now Moses and Aaron go before Pharaoh and his proud court and preach the everlasting Gospel; at the same time demanding the emancipation of Israel.

What say the Scriptures of Pharaoh? Romans, 9th chapter: "For this cause have I raised thee up, that I might show forth My power in thee, that My name might be proclaimed in all the earth." There is a great misunderstanding in reference to Pharaoh. The Calvinists take him to prove their doctrine of absolute predestination, concluding that God had raised up Pharaoh that He might make him the subject of those awful judgments, desolating his country, destroying his people, and finally drowning him in the Red Sea and sending him to Hell to show forth His power. That is all a great mistake. "Oh," they say, "the reason why he would not let Israel go was because God hardened his heart." The same sun that softens the wax hardens the clay by its side. "God is not mocked," neither does He mock any one. The Gospel received, softens the heart and saves the soul. The same Gospel rejected, hardens the heart and expedites the damnation.

God had given Pharaoh the world. He stood at the front; he had the men and the money to send the Gospel to every home beneath the skies. God's purpose in reference to him was that he should receive the Gospel and be saved, but Pharaoh, like millions of others, rejected the Gospel at the hands of Moses and Aaron, God's best preachers, and lost his soul. "That My name may be proclaimed in all the earth." If Pharaoh had been converted to the God of the Hebrews, he was the very man to send the good news of the true God and salvation to all the people in the world at that time, as there were so few of them. Oh! what a sunburst on the whole world would have radiated out from the conversion of the man whose word was law, at the mention of whose name the people trembled.

When Pharaoh rejected the Gospel, God proceeded to confirm His truth, as preached by Moses and Aaron, by a diversity of miracles, and to punish the wicked rebellion of Pharaoh and the idolatry of his people by ten awful plagues, sent on the land as castigatory judgments, not only to bring them to repentance, but to stand before the whole world and all future generations as righteous judgments revealing the indignation of God against idolatry and every species of indignity and abomination; standing out before the people as a solemn warning to repent of their sins and prepare to meet the righteous Judge of quick and dead.

God said to Moses, "Stretch out thy rod over the river and it shall turn to blood," and so it did, and the people were everywhere digging for water because in the rivers and fountains it had all turned to blood. Then Pharaoh would profess repentance under the castigatory judgments and again harden his heart, and God would send other judgments. He filled all the land with frogs; they were everywhere; even in breadtrays and kneading-troughs, and in all the rooms of their houses. When Pharaoh professed repentance and asked Moses to take away the frogs, they died, and they heaped them up in piles, so they stank and brought pestilence into the country. Pharaoh hardened his heart again, and God turned the dust into lice. After another reaction, He filled the whole atmosphere with flies, to the awful annoyance of every living thing, and after another reaction of Pharaoh He sent the plague of the murrain on the cattle, so that all the cattle of the Egyptians died. Then, as Pharaoh again hardened his heart, Moses was told to toss dust into the air and it became boils on both man and beast. After this, God sent the hail, which destroyed the crops and killed the animals and people. Another reaction supervened and He sent the locusts to devour every green herb and utterly desolate the land. After Pharaoh had again consented to let them go, he undergoes another reaction, and God sent darkness to fill all the land, a sooty blackness in the air that could be felt. Finally He sends the destroying angel to cut down the firstborn throughout all the land, making every house a Bochim of weeping and the air to rend with mournful wails over the dead which abounded indiscriminately. Only in the land of Goshen, where Israel dwelt, came none of these plagues.

These ten awful castigatory judgments withered, blighted and desolated the land everywhere; especially the awful havoc of the destroying angel so alarmed the people that they everywhere ran to Pharaoh importuning him to let Israel go ere their God destroyed them all. Finally he gives his consent and orders them to get away as quickly as possible. Then the Hebrews all gather from all parts of the country and march out under the leadership of the cloud by day and the fiery pillar by night.

They travel three days and come to the sea confronting their onward progress; while mountains impassable on either side and Pharaoh with his army in the rear combine to precipitate them into utter desperation. They cry out to Moses, "Were there no graves in Egypt that we could be buried there instead of bringing us out here to be destroyed by our enemies?" Then Moses shouts aloud, "Stand still and see the salvation of the Lord." Lifting high that magic rod, his old shepherd staff, he strikes the sea a violent blow, splitting it from shore to shore. Then leaping into the breach he shouts uproariously, "Israel, go forward!" Pharaoh and his army pursuing them, responsively to the outstretching of Moses' rod, the divided sea again collapses, drowning them all, meanwhile the hosts of Israel shout the victory on the shore.

The wonderful life of Moses is divided into three sections of forty years each. The first forty were at the court of Egypt, preparing to rule the world pursuant to the life-long aspirations of his foster mother but which he declined when he ascertained that he was a member of that race of toiling slaves, despite all the pleadings of his foster-mother, reminding him that Prince Joseph, a Hebrew, reigned over Egypt sixty-one years. To this he responded, "Joseph reigned as a Hebrew, but I will have to reign as an Egyptian, claiming to be your son when I am not; from the ostensible fact that the Egyptians will never again suffer a Hebrew to reign over them, as they have been humiliated, degraded and disgraced by slavery."

The forty years of Moses leading Israel were wonderfully memorialized by incessant miracles wrought through his instrumentality. The rod and staff which he had carried while a shepherd God wonderfully magnified when he threw it down on the ground and turned it into a serpent so that he fled from it with affright. Then when God told him to take it by the tail, despite his alarm, he took it, thus daring, regardless of his fear, to obey God. Behold! it turned to a rod in his hands.

It was really necessary that Moses should die in the wilderness, because he was the giver of the law. If he had entered the Promised Land, it would have signified the possibility of sanctification by legal obedience, which is untrue. In a similar manner, it was impossible for Aaron to enter the land, because he was the high priest, and it would have signified the possibility of sanctification through the ritual and churchisms. For a similar reason, Miriam could not enter the land, because, as she was a flaming holiness evangelist, it would have signified the possibility of getting sanctified through the baptized evangelist. "Joshua" is a Hebrew word which means Jesus. He alone could lead them into the land; thus symbolically signifying the great cardinal truth that Jesus alone can sanctify us.

We last hear of Moses on the Mount of Transfiguration, whither he had been brought by Michael the archangel to represent all who will be transfigured through the resurrection; whereas Elijah by his side represented all who will be transfigured through the translation.

Jude tells us about the great hand-to-hand combat which the devil had with Michael over the body of Moses on Mt. Pisgah when he raised him from the dead; but, suffering signal defeat, he was glad of a chance to retreat back to Hell where he had more authority than he was about to get on Mt. Pisgah.

The reason why the people in all ages have gone headlong into idolatry, worshiping the sun, moon and stars, is because they find it so difficult to walk alone with an unseen God; only one here and there has grace to do it. Idolatry is worshiping the creature instead of the Creator. This native incapacity to satisfactorily apprehend and appropriate God superinduces the necessity of a visible mediator, especially during the pre-Messianic ages.

(z) The Book of Hebrews was never written by Paul, as he certifies in Second Thessalonians that his autograph is in all his Epistles, which settles the question forever against the Pauline authorship of Hebrews. It remained without a name till six hundred years ago, when the Pope ordered Paul's name to be assigned to it. Though nameless, Dean Alford, with the abler critics, gives it to Apollos. I believe that is correct, because it is written in the eloquent Apollonian style. Regardless of its human authorship, it is true because God inspired the writer, as it is flooded with internal evidence of its inspiration.

This wonderful Epistle lays great force on the perfect expiation of Christ and the imperfect expiation of Moses. Josephus says that it was a common thing to sacrifice 250,000 lambs during a single Passover, thus quantity symbolizing quality, and all typifying the bleeding Lamb of God on Calvary. Solomon slaughtered 22,000 oxen and 120,000 sheep when he dedicated the temple; thus you see rivers of blood flowing, all symbolizing the precious blood of Calvary's Lamb that taketh away the sin of the world.

I have been reading my New Testament constantly in the inspired Greek more than forty years. The Latin captions of several chapters in Hebrews specify the perfect expiation of Christ and the imperfect expiation of Moses. Again, the precious Word tells us Moses was our schoolmaster to bring us to Christ, that we might be saved by faith. The Mosaic expiation was simply typical, symbolical and adumbratory of the great and perfect expiation which Christ alone can give. The great trouble with the Church to-day is the fact that they are groping amidst types and shadows, instead of rejoicing in the grand victories achieved by the glorious Antitype. The Mosaic institutions were only established to lead us to Christ. Now that He has come, the types and shadows all fly away. Paul, in Colossians, beautifully shows up the fact that all the Mosaic ordinances were nailed to the cross with the body of Christ.

It is a melancholy sight to see the rank and file of our contemporary preachers plodding along in the dispensation of Moses, three thousand years behind the age. That is the reason why we make so lamentably slow progress in the world's evangelization.

CHAPTER XII.

Phoenician Dominion.

Phœnicia always had a small territory, like England, a little bit of a country, but she ruled the whole world. Egypt was the first nation to stand at the front of the world, during the reign of the Pharaohs. Phœnicia was the second at the front of the world, during the palmy days of Tyre and Sidon, great cities on the east coast of the Mediterranean, the greatest sea in the world.

Egypt had invented a system of writing by hieroglyphics, which abounds in her catacombs and on her monuments everywhere. It was really writing by object lessons, i. e., pictures instead of letters. The Phœnicians heroically took hold of the Egyptian hieroglyphics and succeeded in the invention of letters; thus laying the foundation of the literature that fills and floods the world to-day.

(a) Those ten terrible castigatory judgments which God sent on the Egyptians, to humble their proud hearts and to break the slavish chains that His people might go free, caused Egypt to suffer awful financial detriment, as you see how the growing crops were destroyed by the hail and the locusts, the people by the pestilence, boils and blains and destroying angel, and the animals by the murrain. These awful castigatory judgments depreciated Egypt financially and numerically, meanwhile Phœnicia was booming ahead constantly on the upward trend. Therefore she eclipsed Egypt and came to the front of the world where she remained during the palmy days of Tyre and Sidon.

While Jesus was preaching (Matt. 11th chap.), sailing on a ship over the sea of Galile, He cries out, "Woe unto thee, Bethsaida! Woe unto thee, Chorazin! for if the mighty works which have been wrought in thee had been done in Tyre and Sidon, they would have repented in sackcloth and ashes long ago. And I say unto thee, it will be more tolerable for Tyre and Sidon in the Day of Judgment than for thee. And thou, Capernaum, art exalted up to Heaven, but thou shalt be cast down to Hell, because if the mighty works wrought in thee had been wrought in Sodom and Gomorrah, they would have repented long ago in sackcloth and ashes."

The reason why Jesus says to Capernaum, "Thou art exalted up to Heaven," was because He lived there and He is God and His presence makes our paradise. Therefore while He lived there they had heaven. The reason why it will be more tolerable for Tyre and Sidon and Sodom and Gomorrah in the Day of Judgment than for those Palestinian cities where Jesus preached is because they were heathen cities and never had the Gospel, hence you see that in the Judgment Day people will all be judged according to their opportunities; as God only requires us to walk in the light we have, and the light He gives us will be the measure of our responsibility.

Far back in the primitive ages of the world, when there were no factories, and the most of people clothed themselves in the skins of animals, as clothing could only be made by hand and required so much labor, those wonderfully ingenious Phœnicians got the run on the whole world in the manufacture of clothing, so that the kings of the earth went to them for their apparel. They found a fish in the sea containing a coloring principle, which would impart the beautiful deep red like the rose of Sharon—the scarlet red— and they used it to color the clothing which they made. Consequently it became the current fashion throughout the whole world for the kings and queens to dress in the Phœnician red.

As the gold and silver mines at that time were fresh, and so productive, and so few people in the world, they only cultivated the very best of the land which was very rich and productive, and the kings and people who were financially able to live like kings would pay paradoxical prices for those beautiful red garments, which all their subjects reverenced in adoring wonder as they saw them sitting on their thrones. Consequently the kings, princes and potentates of all nations sent to Tyre and Sidon for their clothing. It was carried by caravans on the backs of camels to the ends of the earth. Therefore these cities became wonderfully rich.

(b) And the Phœnicians were the greatest navigators in the world, leading the way in ship-building, so they scoured the Mediterranean, exploring it round about. As it has ten thousand miles of sea-coast, and they established colonies in all of the countries washed by this great sea, the result was that, in wealth, commerce and learning, they came to the front of the world and remained there through the on-coming centuries.

Isaiah and Ezekiel in their prophecies terribly expose and denounce the pride, vanity and vice of Tyre and Sidon. Oh, how they scathe, peel, and anathematize them! Sure enough, the awful woes denunciated against them have long ago transpired and their glory has evanesced away, till there is no such a people on the earth at this present day. They exist only in the chronicles of by-gone centuries. Tyre, the leading city of the world, and Sidon, her sister close by, are in those prophecies terrifically denounced and the appalling judgments of the Almighty very brilliantly described; even certifying that Tyre shall become a rock on which the fishermen shall dry their nets. That has been and is now signally fulfilled.

Alexander the Great besieged Tyre fourteen months, till she actually moved the city out on an island in the sea, meanwhile building a mole on which to travel to it. Different peoples—Persians, Arabians, Saracens, Tartars, and Moslems—all in their turn desolated and subjugated Tyre and Sidon, till those withering and blighting prophecies were literally fulfilled. This great nation, Phœnicia, for centuries at the front of the world, eclipsing everything in power and glory, came down low in the dust and has actually evanesced away until there is no such a people now in the whole world.

Phoenician Dominion.

After they had signally verified the awful predictions of the Hebrew prophets, Sidon began to improve; she began to revive about twenty years ago and has been slowly rising ever since, and to-day has about 15,000 inhabitants. Tyre, the mother of Sidon and the nation, and against which those horrific prophetic thunderbolts were hurled, actually verified them all, drinking the cup to its bitter dreg and becoming a naked rock on which the fishermen dried their nets and do to this day. All her wonderful shipping having evanesced away, she came down to a population of only 150, but five years ago she began to revive, and has been slowly rising ever since, till to-day she has a population of about 500.

Among the colonies which were sent by the Phœnicians, the Cathagenians were exceedingly prominent in history, on the northern coast of Africa. Carthage became so great that for centuries she even rivaled Rome. Hannibal, the great Carthagenian, crossed the Alps in the rigor of winter; lighting down on Rome as unexpectedly as if he had risen from the earth. He fought the battle of Cannæ, in which eighty senators of the blood royal were found among the slain, and the mistress of the world trembled for her doom. Cato, the great Roman statesman, made it a rule to wind up every speech in the Senate with the words, "Carthago delinda est" ("Carthage must be destroyed"). The Romans fought her constantly for 143 years, finally succeeding in her destruction.

CHAPTER XIII.

HEBREW DOMINION.

Phœnicia was included in the land grant God gave to Israel. (Josh. 1st chap.) It so happened that she never, never fought Israel and in the conquest of the country they never fought her. We see how (Acts 12th chap.) King Agrippa was exceedingly angry with the Tyrians and Sidonians, but when he went down to Cæsarea on the seacoast, the seat of the Roman government, they prevailed on Blastus his chamberlain to intercede for them, because their country was supported by his, and he delivered a powerful oration and the people, carried away with it, shouted aloud, "It is the voice of God and not of man!" God was so grieved because Herod took the glory to himself that He smote him with that black leprosy in which vermin eat up the body; so that he died.

We find Hiram, the king of Tyre, helping King Solomon to build the temple, hence you see Egypt was the first at the front of the world, Phœnicia next, and the Hebrews the third; the Phœnicians, their immediate predecessors, having co-operated with them, and so practically turning over the supremacy of the nations to them.

(c) David, the greatest military chieftain in the world in his day, brought Israel to the front by his military power and prowess, and held her there by the sword till succeeded by his son Solomon, who perpetuated the Hebrew dominion by his wisdom. Go to Jerusalem now and travel in the Holy Land and you still see monuments proclaiming the glory of King Solomon.

Go into Solomon's quarries and see where he had the valuable stone sawed and taken out for the temple and the royal palace, away down under the city; immense quantities having been removed, so that we find there a great vacuum 600 yards long, 50 feet wide, and 20 feet high. The stone beneath the earth, where the sun never struck it and the air has not struck it much, is soft and easily sawed up in the desired dimensions. When taken out it becomes very hard and lasts forever. Down under Mount Moriah, on whose summit the temple stands, in a similar manner Solomon had the stone cut out, forming a great area for a carriage depository and stables for his horses. A dozen miles south of Jerusalem we reach Solomon's Pools, three in number, 300 feet long, 100 wide and 60 deep, containing an abundant supply of water for Jerusalem, whither he carried it by stone aqueducts.

Solomon had no wars to amount to anything, as he ruled by the power of his wisdom instead of the sword.

(d) In symbolism, David symbolizes the uncrucified Christ, all his life hounded and beleaguered by his enemies, while Solomon symbolizes the risen and glorified Christ reigning forever.

What about Solomon's many wives? That is misunderstood. Nowadays it is the custom to send a man to every foreign capital to represent our government and her interests. When I am at Jerusalem I always visit the American consul. If I needed anything, he would take care of me as an American citizen, and, if necessary, send me back to America. In the Solomonic age, instead of sending a man to a foreign court, they would send a woman, the sister or daughter of the king or some member of the royal family. As Solomon, by his wisdom, stood at the front of the world, they sent to him their consuls from the ends of the earth, and in that way he had so many wives. It was state policy, rather than carnal propensity which superinduced the vast multiplicity of wives. His wonderful influence over the nations is manifested in the case of the Queen of Sheba, who came from the uttermost parts of the earth to behold his wisdom and contemplate his glory. When she had seen and heard, her heart melted within her, and she said, "When I heard the report in my own land, I did not believe it; yet I was so filled with curiosity that I came to see and hear for myself. I am constrained to say all that I heard in my own land is true, and the half has not been told." So she donated him $1,000,000 and returned to her own country, having ridden a camel five thousand miles to satisfy the longing of her heart to hear the wisdom and behold the glory of King Solomon.

If you are sanctified, the people will come from afar to hear your wisdom and behold your glory. Since Solomon symbolizes the sanctified experience, why did he lose it? The Bible says he was led astray by his strange wives, i. e., they were heathen, and he built temples at Jerusalem for their gods and went with them to meeting and was thus led astray. Do you believe he was ever reclaimed? I do. I believe he wrote Ecclesiastes while under deep conviction for reclamation, and the Songs of Solomon after he was restored.

His name does not appear in the faith roll (Heb. 11th chap.) for good reasons; as his life was so bad in his backsliding after God had actually appeared to him twice and spoken to him as he did to Moses on Sinai, it would have been unsafe to put his name in the faith roll.

1 Kings 10: 18, 19: "Morever the king made a great throne of ivory and overlaid it with the best gold; the throne was round behind, it had six steps and two lions on either side and on either side of the throne are staves and a great lion on either side." David never had a throne; his throne was simply his right to rule in the theocracy, but Solomon made this wonderful throne after David had gone to Heaven. Ivory is white and symbolizes the negative side of the sanctified experience, which is a clean heart. It was overlaid with the best gold. Gold throughout the Bible symbolizes the Holy Ghost, who always fills a clean heart. It had six steps. The first step into the sanctified experience is solid, intellectual faith in God's Word, certifying the reality of the experience. If you do not believe in it, you never can seek it. The second step is a spiritual conviction for it, so deep and real that it will not flicker. The third step is resolution—"I will have

it or die." The fourth step is the radical consecration which abandons all to God for time and eternity—"Casting all your care on Him." The fifth step is the faith by which you receive it and dare, without feeling, on the simple Word of God, to believe for it. The sixth step is the baptism of the Holy Ghost and fire which Jesus gives you, when you utterly and eternally abandon to God and believe on Jesus according to His Word.

As you are climbing the ladder to reach this golden throne, two lions are standing on either side to help you, these are the twelve tribes of Israel and the twelve apostles, representing both dispensations. They are your helpers while climbing up the stairway to your seat on the golden throne of the sanctified experience. When you sit down on the throne, two great lions, i. e., Jesus and the Holy Ghost, stand on either side of you, fight your battles, defeat all your enemies, and give you the victory perpetually.

The throne is round in the rear; i. e., you have a beautiful, well-rounded experience of entire sanctification. You are free from fanaticism in all its forms and phases. Reader, if you are not now seated on the throne of King Solomon, and reigning along with Christ, you see in the above in beautiful simplicity the way to get there.

CHAPTER XIV.

CHALDEAN DOMINION.

While Israel always boldly professed to worship Jehovah, yet they would worship other gods too. Therefore God found it necessary to let the Babylonians carry them into captivity, in order to cure them of their incorrigible predilection to worship the materialistic divinities of polytheistical idolatry. Therefore God found it necessary to let the Babylonians take them and keep them seventy years. Truly it had the desired effect, because they never afterward went into the polytheistical idolatry, i. e., worshiping the sun, moon, stars and mythological characters. It is a demonstrated fact that the Babylonian captivity did cure them of paganism, so they never did go into it afterward.

The pagan religions had no cross in them to crucify the Adamic nature and really, instead of fighting carnality, they actually deified the unhallowed lusts and vile predilections of the unregenerate heart.

(e) Nebuchadnezzar carried them into captivity B. C. 587. Shalmanezer had carried many out of Israel into Babylon 120 years antecedently to the deporation of the Jews, Sennacherib having carried the remainder away during the interim between the above deportations.

When Cyrus the Medo-Persian issued his proclamation at the end of the seventy years' captivity, in fulfillment of Jeremiah's prophecies that the Chaldeans would carry them away and after seventy years send them back, only 50,000 out of five or six millions returned. This supervened from the fact that they had scattered about through the world-wide Chaldean empire, gone into business, and were not ready to leave their diversified local interests.

The idea that the ten tribes were lost is a mistake. They had lost their tribehood, because many of them had been in captivity two hundred years when the emancipation proclamation was issued, and they had scattered abroad and so mixed up that they did not know their tribehood. I often meet Jews now who know not to which tribe they belong. On the day of Pentecost, we see "devout men" were at Jerusalem from every nation under Heaven. (Acts 2nd chap.) They still retained their membership in the Jewish Church and had come to enjoy that great holiness camp-meeting.

When I traveled around the world I found the Afghans in Central Asia, claiming to be the lost tribes of Israel. I also found the Japanese in Eastern Asia, making the same claim. When I was in Jerusalem, April and May of the present year (1911), I found a great colony in the suburbs of the city claiming to be the Gadites. They are rapidly gathering from the ends of the earth into the Holy Land. Ezekiel, in his last eight chapters, prophesies the gathering of all the tribes into the land of Canaan in the latter days. He actually locates them all, giving them their inheritances.

(f) The hand of God is on all nations and always has been, causing them to fulfill His promises. Five hundred years B. C. there lived in Persia a great and good man, Zoroaster, doubtless walking in all the light he had in that land darkened by ignorance, idolatry and superstition. This man taught some beautiful truths and was a great reformer in his day, really a bright and shining light in that dark heathen land. He taught the worship of fire. In Bombay, India, there are this day 500,000 Parsees, followers of Zoroaoter. They keep literal fire and never let it go out; thus symoblizing a beautiful and glorious truth, that we should never let the fires of the Holy Ghost go out.

In India at the same time, 500 B. C., there lived a great and good man, a brilliant teacher of some beautiful truths; his name was Buddah. Though he opposed idolatry and spent his life teaching sublime truths, they deified him after he had passed away, and this day 400,000,000 of people (the Buddhists) are his followers. There is even a sprinkle of them in America; they actually have a church in Cincinnati, Ohio, called the "New Thought Temple."

Buddah was a great and good man in his day and opposed idolatry, but they deified him after his death. If he were living now, he would be an enthusiastic disciple of our Christ, as he would have then if he had heard of Him.

At the same time, 500 B. C., there lived in China a

great and brilliant teacher of beautiful and sublime truths. Confucius was his name. He had extraordinary light, opposed idolatry and proved a great and profitable teacher in his day. But the people have idolized him since his death.

There is no doubt but the dispersion of the Jews throughout the Chaldean empire really scattered the light which flashed out to these great, prominent and influential leaders of the people in the three most prominent countries of the Orient of that time—Persia, India and China. Thus we see the wonderful hand of God in all ages and nations, fulfilling the prophecies and pushing on the interests of His kingdom. The Jews have always been the most migratory and enterprising people in the world. They are this day dispersed in every nation under heaven and everywhere are teaching about the God of Abraham, Isaac and Jacob. So the Chaldean dominion not only delivered the Jews from paganistic idolatry, for which they had such an awful predilection, but dispersed them throughout the whole world, they going to the ends of the earth and witnessing to the one great Jehovah God of Abraham, Isaac and Jacob.

CHAPTER XV.

MEDO-PERSIAN DOMINION.

When Nebuchadnezzar conquered the world so swiftly that Daniel describes him as moving on eagles' wings to the ends of the earth, having conquered all, he concluded that it would be for the good of the world to have their religions all unified. We have the same thing to-day. The Christians of all nations desire union, but know not how to get at it. The truth of it is, there is no available union, except that of the Holy Ghost in Jesus.

> "Brethren all ,who disagree
> That would have charity to ylease us;
> Union there can never be,
> Unless that we b eone in Jesus;
> One as He is one in God,
> In spirit and in disposition;
> This the Holy Scriptures tach,
> 'Tis plain without an exposition."

Pursuant to his grand enterprise of religious unification, Nebuchadnezzar had a golden image ninety feet high (worth millions of dollars—if he had not owned the world, he could not have commanded so much gold), set up on the plains of Dura and all nations called together. Then his commandment was proclaimed by hundreds of heralds: "When you hear the sound of the flute, harp, dulcimer, sackbut, etc., all fall down and worship the golden image." In that way he was going to unify the religions of the world. He had good motives, but did not know God.

When they informed him that Shadrach, Meshach and Abed-nego did not fall down, he got awfully mad, and proclaimed that they would give him another chance, and if any of them then refused, they should be cast into the fiery furnace, heated seven times above the ordinary. So they try it again and these Hebrew boys refuse to worship his golden image. Then he had them cast into the furnace which was so hot it slew their executioners who had to carry them near enough to tumble them in, as they could not walk because they were bound all over with iron chains. When Nebuchadnezzar looked in and saw them leaping around unhurt by the fire and shouting like angels, and a Fourth One with them, looking like the Son of God, he calls them all out, makes his confession, and becomes a convert to the God of Israel.

As Daniel was prime minister, he was absent on government business; otherwise he would have been cast with these youths into the fiery furnace.

The wonderful experience of Nebuchadnezzar when he became insane and wandered among the beasts those seven years, and God miraculously restored his mind and re-enthroned him, corroborated by the example of the Hebrews and the preaching of Daniel, all conspired in the conversion of Nebuchadnezzar to the God of the Hebrews. Therefore we have an inspiring hope that this great man, in the good providence of God, was actually admitted into the Kingdom.

(g) It seems that he left no son and was consequently succeeded by his grandson Belshazzar, in whose reign Cyrus, the Medo-Persian, sweeping along with his conquests over the world, eventually laid siege to Babylon. Belshazzar was not enterprising like his grandfather, who had conquered the world, but he was voluptuous, seeking only the pleasures of the world.

During the great annual festival in honor of their gods, Cyrus having besieged the city and, in company with his officers, ridden around it sixty miles examining the wall, 350 feet high and 87 feet broad, and having found no weak place anywhere in it, and having labored in vain to scaffold over it with those tall palm-trees abounding in that country, had given up in utter despair.

But having learned of the day on which the Babylonians were all accustomed to give way to drunken revelries and bacchanalian debaucheries, he had his soldiers dig an abyss to receive the river Euphrates, which flowed through the center of the city under the wall supported by great arches. Thus he diverted the Euphrates from its channel into that abyss, and meanwhile with his army passed under the wall into the city, as in their revelries the Babylonians had forgotten to close the great iron gates leading from the river bed up into the city; otherwise they could not have entered.

It was the night of doom for Belshazzar, he and

his thousand lords having no idea that Cyrus could enter the city. It was surrounded by that impregnable wall, with all the necessaries of life inside, enough to endure a siege of twenty years, and a million acres of rich garden lands replenishing the supply; so he entirely ignored Cyrus, feeling sanguine that he would soon give up in despair and go on his way. Then he sees an armless hand writing strange letters on the wall; is seized with panic, his teeth chatter, his knees knock together, and he calls for the wise men of Babylon to explain the writing. They all signally fail. Finally the grandmother tells him that in the days of his grandfather there was a man in the captivity of Judah who had wonderful wisdom in solving dark sentences and unraveling enigmas. He has him called in, and Daniel reads the writing: "Thou art weighed in balances and found wanting; thy kingdom is numbered and finished; God has given it to the Medes and Persians."

In their revelries the Babylonians brought in the sacred vessels spoliated from Solomon's temple in Jerusalem, and were drinking out of them the ruby wine in honor of the gods of Babylon. While the scene is moving before their eyes, a crash is heard at the door. Cyrus and his army march in. That very hour Belshazzar is slain and the kingdom turned over to the Medes and Persians, while seventy thousand men swelter in their own blood in the streets of the city.

(h) God's great utility through the Medo-Persian dominion was the restoration of the Jews back to

Jerusalem. Cyrus took the money out of the royal treasury to rebuild the temple and restore the walls, in fulfillment of Jeremiah's prophecy that after seventy years' captivity, they would all be brought back.

Jeremiah wrote his prophecies and his lamentations in the grotto that bears his name in Mt. Calvary. I have often been in it. It has room enough for several families. We read in his prophecy how the princes interceded with the king Jehoiakim to kill Jeremiah because they said his prophecy was weakening the hands of the fighting men. So he had him arrested, put in prison, and dropped down into a deep well without water but with mud in the bottom, into which he sank down to his waist, and would soon have perished but that a colored man managed to get permission of the king to lift him out and save his life.

Hananiah was boldly contradicting him, prophesying that they would conquer the Chaldeans. Jeremiah looking him in the face, said, "This year thou shalt die." So he did die in the seventh month of that year.

Though Ezra carried back to Jerusalem all the sacred vessels of the temple which Nebuchadnezzar had taken away, worth millions of dollars, yet he had no armed force to protect him, camping out every night with those immense treasures, yet they were never molested.

You see how wonderfully God has been in the revolutions of the world in all ages, using the Chaldeans to cure the Jews of paganistic idolatry, and the Medo-Persians to restore them back to their own country and rebuild the temple and the walls of the city. They founded the second temple 490 years before Christ was nailed to the cross, as Daniel had predicted in his ninth chapter: "Seventy weeks till Messiah shall be cut off."

CHAPTER XVI.

Grecian Dominion.

While all the world was in heathen darkness except the little Jewish nation, to the astonishment of the ages the Greeks moved away from them and went to the very top of creation; in poetry, oratory, philosophy and the fine arts transcending all nations, so that the kings of the whole world sent their sons to them to prosecute their education at the feet of their philosophers.

God's hand was in it all. While the Persians had every other nation in their iron grip, the Greeks were actually so brave that they could not be conquered. Xerxes came against them with two million five hundred thousand men, the largest army ever mustered on the earth, and the greatest fleet in the world. Feeling perfectly sure of victory on land and sea, he had his throne erected on a lofty mountain overlooking the Bay of Salamis, where the naval battle would take place, and in full view of the plains of Marathon, where the land forces would meet.

In the first place, Leonidas with three hundred Spartan braves held the straits of Thermopylæ against the whole army three days, and they never could have entered if they hadn't discovered a mountain pass. Then the three hundred braves fought on till they were all dead, as Spartan law made it a penalty of death to retreat.

When Xerxes on his throne saw the Greeks on their few little ships boarding his magnificent vessels, firing and sinking them, and news came from Marathon, "All routed in utter confusion and precipitate skedaddle," leaving his throne, he joined his fugitive hosts, all running for their lives.

The temple of Nikee, which the Greeks built to the goddess of victory in commemoration of that wonderful achievement, stands to this day in a perfect state of preservation. I saw it again on this tour.

(i) Soon after this wonderful victory, when Philip, the king of Macedonia, died, leaving an army of thirty-five thousand men, and thirty-five thousand dollars in the treasury, Alexander assembled his army, ordered the money box capsized, and divided equally among his men, giving each one a dollar. They said, "King, what have you left for yourself?" He responded, "My hopes." They say, "What are your hopes?" He responds, "To conquer all the world," and he inspires his little army with the same enthusiasm.

Then they start out and everything goes down before them, magnetizing all that hear the thrilling news. The king of Persia, two thousand miles distant in his palace, soliloquizes, "If I let him alone, someone will soon kill him." But Alexander moves on, everything going down before him. After while Darius, the world's monarch, says, "I will send a great army and surround those Greeks, bag them, cut their heads off, and scatter their bones." So they surrounded Alexander on the fields of Granicus with an innumerable host, a hundred file deep, assured that it would be impossible for a man to escape. No firearms then; they fought with swords, spears, battle-axes, bows and arrows. The Persians close in on them and make the assault; a whole day passes by in flowing blood, and the battle winds up leaving forty thousand Persian soldiers dead on the field and Alexander had not lost a man. The miracles are not all recorded in the Bible. You see clearly a miracle here on the plains of Granicus.

This shocks the Persians so that they almost believe the Greeks are immortals come down from Heaven, and so they wait a long time before they try Alexander again. Meanwhile everything is going down before him. Then the king, with the princes of all nations, gathers an army innumerable as the sands of the sea, and surrounds him on the plains of Issus. A battle ensues in which a hundred thousand Persians are left dead on the field while Alexander's loss is simply nothing. His men are much scarred up and bloody as butchers in the pen, because they had killed so many, but perfectly victorious on all sides, whereas the grand army of the world was utterly confused, and all who were alive stampeded in all directions.

The battle of Issus shook the whole world from center to circumference; revolutionizing all countries as by the shock of an earthquake; so years roll away before they attack Alexander. Meanwhile he is pushing his conquests everywhere.

(j) Finally they determine to make one more desperate effort. This time all the nobility of the different nations turn out, as 'tis normally presumed that the rulers are the best fighters. This time they surround him on the plains of Arbela, with an innumerable host, like the sand of the sea for multitude, and the stars innumerable. A battle of a whole week ensues, winding up with three hundred thousand Persians dead on the field and the Greeks perfectly victorious on all sides. Among the slain were all the nobility, so there was not a man left influential enough to head another campaign, and this innumerable army was flying in utter confusion in every direction, thinking only to escape with their lives.

Darius, the world's monarch, took fright early in the engagement and fled to the most distant country in the world, India, with Alexander on his track, running with all his might. He overtakes him in south India, where I preached when I was there. I was four times in Hydroabad, which Alexander founded and which, with its province, now contains eleven millions of people. When Alexander overtook Darius, the latter turned and proposed peace, saying to him, "Grecian, I will do you right. I'll split the world in two, giving you half and I will keep the other." People who have not been in India have no conception of the solar power and glory; the sun was then in the zenith. Alexander pointed to him and said, "Could this world have two suns?" He himself answered in the negative,

"They would burn it into a desert," and then observed, "Neither can it have two kings, so I take it all. You are welcome to eat at my table as long as you behave yourself. If you do not, you will wish you had."

I preached in India three months, running everywhere without guide or interpreter. How was that? Because England has ruled that country 150 years; consequently the English language is known everywhere.

When Alexander conquered the world he put the Greeks in every country under heaven. Three hundred years rolled away and God sent His Son into the world, and He sent His apostles into all nations to preach the Gospel. The normal effect of government is for the rulers to transmit their language to their subjects, so it was in case of the Greeks. They transmitted their language to every nation under heaven. When Jesus came into the world, He preached in Greek and so did all His apostles.

(k) You see plainly that the glorious utility of Grecian dominion was the transmission of a "pure speech," in fulfillment of the prophecies, to all the nations of the earth. Why did the Greeks come to the top of the world in learning and actually become the teachers of all nations? It was to qualify them to formulate that wonderful language which is itself a miracle, mechanical as a timepiece or a musical instrument; so you can only put it together as God has ordered and consequently no danger of misunderstanding it if you will be honest and walk in the light.

The English language would not do for a revelation,

because it is a mongrel from all languages, indiscriminately thrown together in a heterogeneous mass and may be turned and twisted according to the caprices of sophists and false prophets. It is a great language for common use, having already grown from twenty-three thousand to two hundred thousand words, and the Lord is now miraculously preparing it for the pure speech of the nations during His glorious reign on the earth.

You have nothing to do but read the history of bygone ages in the light of prophecy, providence and the Holy Spirit, to see the hand of God on every nation, turning them as He turneth the river of water.

CHAPTER XVII.

Roman Dominion.

The king of Alba, jealous of two twin boys, Romulus and Remus, because they had a little royal blood in their veins, had them exposed in their infancy to be devoured by wild beasts, which abounded in the primeval forests on the banks of the Tiber, near a cave in which there was a wolf den. The mother wolf, instead of eating them, fell in love with them. (Go to the Capitol in Rome and you will see the memorial wolves.) She carried them in her strong mouth to her cave, put them in her warm bed, wrapping her long shaggy hair about them to repel the chill of the night already received, and fed them on her nutritious milk. They grow rapidly, become shepherds, and constitute the nucleus of a band, which soon swells into a tribe, as every homeless tramp falls in with them.

Then a serious trouble confronts the band—they have no women. They then manipulate a pantomimic rural exhibition, and invite the Sabines, the nearest colony. They turn out liberally with their women and children. In the midst of the entertainment, which captivated all and proved thrillingly interesting, pursuant to preconcerted plans, every fellow having spied out his wife, at a given signal, he jumps, seizes her and holds her tight. This breaks up the exhibition with a row, a fight and a stampede, as the Romans prove too much for them. The Sabines, in raging animosity over the rape of their women, rush home and prepare for war with all possible expedition. Meanwhile every Roman makes good use of his time, courting his captured wife and getting her reconciled to live with him. Soon the Sabines come with an army to fight and rescue their women. The battle is in array, the fight is on, and the blood is flowing. Then the women rush into the midst of the conflict between their new husbands on the one hand and their fathers and brothers on the other, hugging and kissing them simultaneously, and begging them to give up the fight, be at peace and let them alone, as they want to stay and live with the men who had captured them. The women win the day, perfectly reconcile the angry competitors, who not only consent to the matrimonial alliances of their daughters and sisters with the Romans, but unite with them, thus trebling their number.

With this providential and insignificant beginning, they launch out for the conquest of the world, adopting war for their religion. They open the doors of Janus temple to signify war, and close them to serve as the index of peace with all the world.

(1) Then 753 years roll away, during which the temple of Janus was never closed but twice; first during

the reign of Numa Pompilius; and secondly, immediately after the first Punic War. The third time was at the close of this period, after the terrible battle of Pharsalia between Cæsar and Pompey, the great rivals of the Roman world, when the latter went down, leaving the former, on a diamond throne in a golden house, his crown radiant with rays of an unsetting sun and his sceptre sweeping the circumference of the globe; five thousand senators in silver houses dwelling on those triumphant mountains, constituting his council chamber in the administration of his universal empire.

The pacification of all the world was a necessary prophetic fulfillment to corroborate our Lord's advent into the world, as He was the King of peace. That is the reason why He entered Jerusalem riding the donkey, which is the symbol of peace, as it is too slow for war and never so used. For that reason it would not do for Jesus in his triumphant entry into Jerusalem to come on a fine horse. Thus the Romans, in that long bloody series of wars in which the sword was never sheathed but twice in the 753 years, wound up with the glorious blessing of peace resting on every nation under heaven—the conquered peace which comes to stay.

(m) We see how God so miraculously used Alexander the Great with his little Greek army to conquer the world and give them that wonderful language which he had miraculously made through the instrumentality of the heathen Greeks, who labored on it heroically a thousand years; thus giving the world the most significant, comprehensive, vivacious, melodious, euphonic, inflexible, incorruptible and mechanical language ever spoken beneath the skies; His own vehicle in the transmission of His own blessed, wonderful, infallible, heavenly truth to all nations, for time and eternity. They ruled the world long enough to give them their language, as Alexander, when he conquered the world, put his own people in every government under heaven.

When God wants a school He astonishes all with the magnitude of His methods. The normal effect of government is the transmission of the language to their subjects. The Greeks never thought of such a thing. God first used them through rolling centuries, subsidizing philosophy, poetry, and the finest oratory in the world, science and literature in the patient and indefatigably laborious work, culminating in this miraculous language, destined to become the depository of the transcendent eternal truth, revelatory of the wonderful and paradoxical redemptive scheme to all the world.

When Alexander was moving along, carrying his conquests to the ends of the earth, in due time he came to Jerusalem. Instead of coming out with swords, spears and battle-axes, they came in a solemn religious procession, headed by the high priest, carrying the Scriptures, and the long phalanx of clergymen in sacerdotal robes. When they met him, the high priest opened his Bible and read from Daniel that wonderful prophecy in which God actually gave Alexander's name "Grecian"—certifying that he would bear rule over the whole earth. Of course Alexander rejoiced in the prophecy, received their prayers and blessings, and left them in the enjoyment of the liberties God gave them in the theocracy.

When Alexander was scattering the Greeks all over the world, investing them with the official administration of every nation under heaven, they never dreamed that they were really doing the work of teachers, teaching their subjects their own language that they might receive the truth of God and be saved, and yet that was verily true. Thus every Greek officer in all the earth was God's teacher of his own language, that he might get his subjects ready to receive God's wonderful salvation, receive the glorious supernatural birth, enter the kingdom of Heaven and live forever with God, glorified angels and redeemed spirits.

Alexander lived but a little while after he had finished his work and made the Greeks the rulers of the whole world; thus actually making them the gratuitous teachers of the Greek language to all the people they ruled.

The result of this wonderful world-wide revolution and the appointment of the Greeks in the efficient administration of every nation, i. e., using them as teachers of their language to all the people throughout the world, was that, in the lapse of three hundred years, the Greek language was known throughout the whole earth, and it was really the learned language of all nations.

(n) Now the great work which God, in His providence, miraculously wrought through Roman dominion was the consolidation of all nationalities into one universal empire, with the strongest government ever known to mortal man, i. e., a military despotism.

Sixteen years ago when I began to travel through Europe, Asia and Africa, I had to carry a passport from the United States Government, to give me liberty to travel and fortify me against arrest and imprisonment. I was happy in this my fourth and last tour to find no use for my passport; cheeringly ominous of the Lord's near coming to reign over the whole earth, when there will be no obstruction by national boundaries. Thus my heart leaps with joy to see the glorious dawn of the long-prayed-for millennial day, in which,

> "He shall have dominion,
> O'er river sea and shore,
> Far as the eagle's pinion,
> Or dove's light wing can soar."

In by-gone ages the normal state of things has been universal belligerency, so that a person could hardly travel beyond the sight of his own capital without liability of arrest as a spy, because all nations were fearful of strangers. Now I travel all over the world alone, amid the thronging millions. Though a stranger, I am free and at home and in no danger of arrest or imprisonment.

While the Greek language, which God used Alexander the Great and his Greek officers to transmit, became the learned language of every nation under heaven, yet the apostles, when they divided out the whole world among themselves and each one went to his field of labor, pursuant to our Lord's commission (Matt. 28: 19), would have been arrested, imprisoned and probably held in a loathsome jail the fleeting remnant of their lives, had not God, in His merciful providence, provided that great Iron Kingdom, so brilliantly prophesied by Daniel, in the clear illuminations of the Holy Spirit, revealing the Roman power, with great iron legs walking through every land, and as the centuries rolled on, subduing every nation under heaven, and so felicitously consolidating all into one vast military despotism, the strongest grip ever put on the nations of the earth. This universal despotism concentrated at Rome, whence great roads were built, cutting down mountains and bridging rivers; thus facilitating the travel of all nations to Rome. This we recognize in the inspired history of the Pauline peregrinations into all nations. You observe how Paul could go anywhere and everywhere, simply by claiming his Roman citizenship. When under arrest in Jerusalem, he forced Festus, then Roman governor, to take him out of prison in Cæsarea and send him to Rome, even at his own expenses.

The apostles divided out all the world among themselves, each one going to his field of labor; Paul and Peter preaching at Rome till bloody martyrdom set them free. (Paul, however, in the capacity of general superintendent, traveling into all nations.) The two Jameses both suffered martyrdom in Jerusalem; Mark went to Egypt; Matthew, to Ethiopia; Matthias, to Abyssinia; Thomas, to India; Andrew, to Armenia; Jude, to Tartary; Philip, to Syria; Bartholomew, to Phrygia; Simon Zelotes, to Britain; all preaching heroically till bloody martyrdom liberated them for the Glory Land.

If the Romans had not conquered all the world, the apostles, and the hundreds and thousands of evangelists who in the apostolic age arose up and went everywhere preaching the Word (Acts 1:8), would have been arrested and imprisoned when they attempted to cross any of those old national lines, which had divided the whole world into principalities, satrapies, tetrarchies and dukedoms, even to the uttermost parts of the earth.

(o) While the Romans were fighting those 753 years, they had not the faintest conception of the great providential work God was doing through their instrumentality. They were simply actuated by ambition, avarice and the spirit of conquest. Some great things you see God can do through the instrumentality of unsaved people. Other things He can do through His own servants on the justification plan, whereas He can do just anything He pleases through wholly sanctified people. They have utterly and forever given up their own will, sinking it so deep into the Divine as to utterly lose sight of it. Consequently they are resting sweetly in Jesus, ringing out the delectably obsequious acclaim, "Speak, Lord, thy servant heareth."

God is so anxious to bless everybody and to do all possible good that He never misses an opportunity, but even uses the wicked, who will not let Him save them (as He cannot save against the will, as in so doing He would; "ex necessitate," dehumanize one), to do mighty works, such as you see in all the chapters in this book captioned "Dominion." As you read them over, you are electrified and edified in contemplation of His wonderful mercies and benefactions; through the instrumentality of the heathen nations and unsaved people nominally bearing the cognomens peculiar to His kingdom in the different ages and nations.

CHAPTER XVIII.

Johannic Precursorship.

When the prophet Malachi went to Heaven, God, for reasons to us unrevealed, became reticent, permitting the long period of four hundred years to roll away without speaking to His people through human voice. It was an awful test of their faith; meanwhile the great rank and file, from the high priest down to the synagogue sexton, degenerated into dead formality and hollow hypocrisy. But a few faithful spirits did walk with the Lord. Luke 1:5, 6: "Zacharias and Elisabeth were both righteous before God, walking in all the commandments and ordinances of the Lord blameless."

Good old Simeon had walked in the light of His countenance about a hundred years, till the infant Christ was brought into the temple for dedication; the Holy Spirit having revealed to him that his mortal eyes should behold the Lord's Messiah; so taking Him in his withered arms, he dies of joy. Good old Anna, serving as the guardian angel of the temple eighty-four years, is also blessed to behold the infant Redeemer and to heroically testify to all the people in the temple.

This long, dark period, with only a star gleam now and then and anon the brilliant flash of a meteor, evanesced away, and only left the darkness more appalling.

When Herod massacred the boy babies in Bethlehem, Zacharias and Elisabeth at Juttah, about a dozen miles distant, taking prudential warning, migrated away to the wilderness of Judæa and returned no more. Fortunately they brought up their son among those poor holiness people the Essenes, living there because there was plenty of room and the land so cheap that they could have their own cottage in the wilderness. As you travel through it now, you see the hermit houses hewn out in the precipitous cliffs and entered horizontally from the paths cut through the defiles and canyons.

Consequently John was happily converted through the instrumentality of his saintly father and mother before he forfeited his infantile justification, and gloriously sanctified and filled with the Spirit. Therefore we have in him a beautiful paragon Christian normal to God's order, which is a "bona fide" conversion antecedently to the age of responsibility, thus effectually fortifying against the temptations superinduced by hereditary depravity, which turns the face away from God, so that the moment accountability is reached the normal trend is to go away into sin, like the prodigal son, and recklessly from bad to worse, till you land in the hog-pen, the next station to Hell.

God's order is conserved in the elder brother, who, like John the Baptist, the prophet Samuel and hundreds of others, got converted antecedently to the forfeiture of his infantile justification. Consequently he stayed at home all his life, augmenting the rich patrimony (i. e., double portion) transmitted from his father by faithful toil, honest enterprise and good management, till he is now a millionaire; in ostensible contrast with his younger brother, who spent all in riotous living, and, though saved by the skin of his teeth and sanctified wholly when he received the bloodwashed robe, is still poor in spirit, having had no time to lay up treasures in Heaven.

(p) John was a hermit prophet, like all others in that barren desert, living in the cheapest and most simple way on the locusts and wild honey. It is vain to deny that John did eat the animal locust, as the Greek word "achris" has no other meaning. I have seen them so abounding that I could fill a bushel basket with them without moving three steps. They were big, fat, lazy, slow to get out of my way, and no trouble to catch. The Bedouin Arabs gather them by great camel loads, carry them away to their tent villages and eat them. If they have salt, they are living like kings; if they have none, they eat them all the same.

John's rearing out in the desert, hermitizing, gave him an iron constitution, lungs like a bellows, and a voice like a lion; enabling him to hold spellbound his wonderful audiences of ten thousand people. When he reached majority (thirty years under the Levitical law), and began to preach with the Holy Ghost sent down from Heaven, everybody who heard him was thunder-stricken and lightning-bolted, so they had to run and tell others. Fast as they heard him they ran to the ends of the earth telling the thrilling news, till the cities were emptied and the wilderness populated by the thronging multitudes, pouring out from dewy morn till dusky eve; the rich on their camels, the middle class on donkeys, and the poor crowding their way barefoot over the rocks, all pressing like a mighty wave of the sea into the desert to satisfy the curiosity that had raised the Hebrew world and many curious Gentiles on tiptoe, as they almost unanimously believed him to be the Christ of God anticipated for 4,500 years.

Turn your eyes and you see crowds of priests, with the long roll of the prophecies, holding them up before their eyes, day and night investigating to answer the question clamored from every lip, "Is not this the Christ?" Finally they appoint a delegation of priests and Levites to wait on John and ask him outright, "Art thou the Christ, or do we look for another?" He frankly responds, "I am not the Christ, but the voice of one roaring in the wilderness, Prepare ye the way of the Lord and make His paths straight."

The English version "crying" is not a correct translation of "booontos," which simply means to bellow like an ox when he throws his great mouth open and lowes out the continuous long sound of "o." You have all frequently heard the ox lowe. The Greek word here simply means the lowing of an ox, showing that John had a loud, heavy, strong voice like the roaring thunder; whereas "crying" would imply a feeble, shrill voice, like a woman or a child. John had the thunder's peal and the lion's roar. As neither that generation, nor their parents, nor their grandparents, nor their great-grandparents had ever heard an inspired prophet preach, but only the dead chanting of the clergy, the rise of John the Baptist was like a thousand thunder-bolts unsheathed from a cloudless sky, therefore the greatest revival the world had ever known broke out under his preaching.

(q) Though he answered the question, "Art thou Elijah?" in the negative, he simply meant that he was not the prophet Elijah raised from the dead. He did not mean that he was not the second Elijah of prophecy for whom the Jews were looking immediately before the coming of Christ. Jesus (Matt. 17th chap., Mark 9th chap., Luke 9th chap., and in other places) tells us outright that John the Baptist was the Elijah to come, therefore that matter is forever settled in the affirmative.

A few years ago the Holiness Movement was in a dilemma between Dowie and Sanford, each one claiming to be Elijah, and controverting each other like dogs fighting over a bone. Oh, what a spectacle for the myrmidons of the pit, when they saw these two great Holiness evangelists fighting over the crown of the second Elijahhood, which John the Baptist has been wearing among the angels 1879 years! Those men in their papers were constantly quoting Malachi 4th chapter, "Behold the day cometh, that shall burn as an oven; and all the gay, all the proud, and all the wicked, shall be stubble: and the day that cometh shall burn them up, saith the Lord of hosts, and shall leave neither root nor branch. But unto you that fear My name shall the Sun of Righteousness arise with healing in his wings; and ye shall go forth, and grow up as calves of the stall. Ye shall tread down the wicked; they shall be ashes under the soles of your feet in the day that I shall do this, saith the Lord of hosts. Remember ye the law of Moses My servant, which I commanded unto him in Horeb for all Israel, with the statutes and judgments. Behold, I send Elijah the prophet before the coming of the great and dreadful day of the Lord: and he shall turn the heart of the fathers to the children, and the heart of the children to the fathers, lest I come to smite the land (i. e., the land of Canaan) with a curse." ("Aerets" often means simply the land of Canaan.)

John's preaching shook the heathen nation from Dan to Beer-sheba and actually caused the thousands dispersed among the Gentiles to come and enjoy his meeting, i. e., Saul of Tarsus from Cilicia and Apollos from Africa.

His wonderful preaching with the Holy Ghost sent down from Heaven, revealed the awful wickedness of the nations and showed up the terrors of the law as Elijah had done seven hundred years antecedently, for they were on the same line, i. e., the restoration and enforcement of the law by the radical repentance of the people. His preaching shook everything to pieces, smashing their false hopes founded on ritualistic obedience in smithereens, uncapping Hell and shaking them over it, old and young, great and small; therefore he had a wonderful, shaking, up-rooting, overturning, cyclonic revival. The effect of it was for the fathers and mothers to repent before their children for neglect of duty and ask their pardon, and the children to plead with them to forgive them for their disobedience and wickedness which had broken their hearts with trouble and were bringing down their gray hair with sorrow to the grave. Such is the normal effect of a genuine Holy Ghost revival, such as God always sends responsively to the preaching of such men as Elijah and John the Baptist.

(r) The Seventh-day Adventists beat all the world at perverting, falsifying and misapplying God's Word. They are the people (as well as others of a similar character) described by Paul in 2 Timothy 3rd chapter: "Creeping into houses and leading captive silly women." The Greek means men as well as women, and, fully translated, it would read "silly men and goosey women," i. e., anybody who is stupid and blind enough to let them lead him. They creep into our Holiness Missions and scatter their Hell-hatched literature, teaching no-Hellism, no-soulism, and materialistic infidelity by the wholesale; but are careful to invest it, so far as possible, with the mantle of orthodoxy.

I picked up one of their books on the annihilation of the wicked, which they had left in one of Sister Fergerson's Peniel Missions for the people to read. I read it through. It was in proof that the wicked will all be annihilated and, like the animals, be no more forever. They did not write much, but crowded it with quotations from the Bible, so that unthinking people would swallow it all down and turn Seventh-day Adventists on the spot, whereas there was not a solitary word of truth in it. The whole book was falsification and perversions of God's Word; a horrifically wicked thing for a Judgment-bound soul to do.

The first Scripture in their catalogue is in the above quotation from Malachi: "Ye shall tread down the wicked, they shall be ashes under the soles of your feet in the day that I do this, saith the Lord of hosts." They headed the list with this, as it was their strongest. Annihilation is from "nihil," nothing, and simply means to make a thing nothing at all, which cannot be done, as both the philosophical and chemical worlds have demonstrated. You cannot turn something into nothing. You can change the form of it, but still it is there, as real and substantial as ever; as in this case the wicked are called stubble. They are burnt into ashes. Does that turn them into nothing? You know ashes are as real and substantial as stubble. So you see after the wicked are burned, they are not turned into nothing, but into ashes. Hence you see the utter falsity of the annihilation dogma. Not a single quotation had any reference to annihilation, but to destruction, which is a very different thing. A house is destroyed by fire. It is not annihilated. If you could weigh the ruin and the gases evolved, you would have precisely the number of pounds which the house weighed.

Satan is the father of lies and liars. He sends out his lying preachers to the ends of the earth; wolves in sheep's clothing, seeking whom they may devour. Beware of them if you would not make your bed in Hell. When you get there, you will be awfully sorry that you believed those lying preachers who led you to believe there is no Hell.

(s) John the Baptist was Heaven's sunburst on the fallen Jewish Church—Elijah the prophet sent back to warn them and restore the law which God gave to Moses in Horeb, and to bring the people back to it—those who repented under the preaching of John, radically, genuinely and substantially (multitudes repented superficially and it evanesced away). Jesus said John was a bright light and ye were willing to rejoice for an hour in that light. Here He speaks of the great stir under John's preaching, and with mournful wail deplores its evanescence in an hour.

The few who went to the bottom and struck the rock became the disciples of Jesus, and with Him passed through the awful Jewish tribulation; they alone escaping the unutterable horrors of perishing by the sword, pestilence or famine, or of being sold into slavery, or lead captive to Rome and turned over to the Emperor, the crown slaves of his majesty.

Matthew twenty-fourth and twenty-fifth chapters, Mark thirteenth chapter, and Luke twenty-first chapter, give you Jesus' valedictory sermon, which He preached on Mt. Olivet on Wednesday afternoon preceding His crucifixion, in which He predicts the awful impending doom of His nation, because they had rejected their Christ, and were consequently victims of the sword, pestilence or famine, or sold into slavery, or lead into captivity. Meanwhile the city and the temple were to be destroyed, not leaving stone upon stone that should not be thrown down. At the same time He tells His disciples (who were the few prophesied by Malachi that shall "grow up as calves of the stall, treading down the wicked as ashes under their feet") that not a hair of their heads should be hurt. Their hearts had been so richly blessed under the preaching of John that they were melted with redeeming grace and dying love; and their homes flooded with heavenly prelibations, so the "fathers were turned to the children, and the children to the fathers"—the normal effect of a glorious revival in all ages. Meanwhile the awful curse of death, desolation, slavery and captivity came on all the balance, during those terrible seven years of Jewish tribulation.

(t) The Romans waited long for the Jews to become peaceable and to cease to crown those false Christs rising among them, which was high treason against the Roman Empire. As they had conquered all the world and ruled the nations with a rod of iron, their maxim was rule or ruin. A nation they could not rule they destroyed, i. e., sold them into slavery, thus utterly taking their nationality away from them, as slaves are property like herds and flocks, having no nationality.

The Jews were always the most thrifty people in the world, getting rich while the Gentiles stayed poor. Therefore the Romans waited on them a third of a century to quit their insurgencies and become peaceable. Finally, A. D. 66, old Vespasian, on his diamond throne in his golden house in Rome, issued that famous autocratic edict of Hebrew denationalization and exportation, sending couriers out in every country under heaven to publish, "viva voce," the imperial edict. Then all nations prepared to go to Palestine and buy slaves for themselves, as the Jews were always the most intelligent and industrious people, and consequently the best slaves in all the world.

The Romans divided out the country into sections and sent armies into each to carry out the edict. They made expeditious work everywhere except at Jerusalem, which is very impregnably fortified by nature. The great mountain gorge Hinnom runs down on the west, impassable to an invading army; and Jehoshaphat on the east, which coils around Mt. Moriah, assuming a southwesterly trend till it intersects the valley of Hinnom, in a smoothing-iron point; thus fortifing the city on all sides except the north, consequently the Roman armies could only besiege it on the north. These great natural fortifications not only encompass it on three sides, but there are great walls built on top of these cliffs, thus rendering it doubly secure. On the north where there is no natural fortification, it was protected by a gigantic wall augmented by great towers, in communicating distance from each other; the whole length of the wall supplied with catapults and other munitions of war.

Jerusalem has passed through seventeen sieges and been destroyed seven times.

The Roman armies encamped on Mt. Scopus, north of the city. Gallus Celceus, with a great army, laid siege to the city and pressed it hard two years. With the battering-rams he had made such breaks in the wall that he was expecting to enter; but upon finding that the Jews had taken stone out of the mountain and built another wall in the rear, he, knowing that if they went in they couldn't reach the city on account of that other wall and that the Jews would fall in the rear, repair the other wall and then have them in a pen, where they would butcher them all like unrelenting sheep, consequently became so discouraged that he raised the siege and wrote to the Empror that the city could not be taken. Then the old emperor left his golden house in Rome, never to see it any more, went to Jerusalem, took charge of the besieging army, greatly re-enforced, pressed the siege two years longer and died at Jerusalem. He was succeeded on the throne of the world and in command of the Jerusalem army by his son Titus, who pressed the siege three years longer, took the city and the temple. Though he ordered the soldiers to spare the temple, they tore it down, in fulfillment of our Savior's prophecy, leaving not one stone upon another. The Jews were such a moneyed people the soldiers thought surely they would find in it hidden treasures.

During the siege, a million of people perished by the sword, pestilence and famine, and ninety thousand were sold into slavery; many having been left on hand whom they could not sell because the market was so glutted that they could not get a bid. These they led captive to Rome and turned them over as the crown slaves of the Emperor, who put them to building publis works, the first of which was the Coliseum—1,800 feet in circumference, 160 feet high, solid wall up to the eaves, and with seating capacity for 100,000 spectators; the largest theatre ever built on earth. It would cost this day $50,000,000; it cost the Romans nothing, because in that great captive team were found the most skilled mechanics and the greatest architects in the world, who received no pay. Here we see a fulfillment of the prophecies of Isaiah and Ezekiel: "They will sell you and no one will buy you."

(u) In our Savior's valedictory sermon on Mt. Olivet Wednesday before He was crucified, He not only prophesied the awful doom of His nation, and city, and temple, but He told His disciples that they would all escape and not a hair of their heads be hurt. It turned out verily so. He told them to follow the prophecy of Daniel, telling them, "When you see the abomination of the desolation (i. e., the Roman battle flag) set up in the Holy Place, fly to the mountains."

The temple is surrounded by thirty-five acres of holy ground, left bare for the occupancy of tents during their great annual festivals—Passover in the spring, Pentecost in the summer, and Tabernacles in the fall.

Now the question arises, How could they escape when the Romans had the city throughout, and it was a penalty of death to let a Jew escape? There was no chance but Divine intervention, which did take place. The manner is not revealed; God so hid them from the eyes of the soldiers that they all went away unseen.

They were obliged to go utterly out of the country, as the imperial edict made it a penalty of death for a Jew to be found anywhere in the Holy Land, or in any other country traveling with his face towards Jerusalem. He was to be taken up and killed. Therefore all the Christians, if they had stayed in that country; but they fled away eastwardly through the desert, across the Jordan, turned north and went out of Palestine into Decapolis, a Gentile country frequently mentioned in the Scriptures.

Our Savior once went into Gadara, which belongs to that country, where He met the legionaire, i. e., man with ten thousand demons, which He cast out, at the same time gloriously saving his soul and calling him to preach. Though he wanted to go with Jesus, as the Gospel had not yet been given to the Gentiles, He told him no, but sent him to his own people, and the Word says that he preached throughout Decapolis, which means ten cities constituting that commonwealth. History says he had glorious success in his field of labor and especially at Pella, whither the Christian fugitive Jews made their escape. Hence the Church, having begun all Jews, in less than a century underwent a radical revolution, becoming all Gentile. The fugitives from the destruction of Jerusalem met a glorious reception by the Gentile Christians in Pella with whom they united, thus surviving their Jewish peculiarities and becoming all Gentile.

In the beginning they kept both the first and the seventh days of the week holy to the Lord, denominating them "Sabbaths." The Gentile Christians kept only the first day of the week, never observing the Mosaic Sabbath, as they were not required so to do. (Acts 15th chap.) With the absorption of the Jewish wing by the Gentiles, the Mosaic Sabbath, with all other Old Testament institutions, evanesced, and was superseded by the new government and the Lord's Day.

(v) The crowning glory of John the Baptist was the introducing of the Savior to the people. He had already settled all their apprehension that he was the Christ, by positively telling them the contrary, and at the same time informing them that the Messiah was already on the earth and that he would introduce Him to them. This raised all on tiptoe, watching like hawks, so they would be sure to see Him if He came.

John's audiences had so grown that he had already moved to the Jordan, in full view of the wilderness, where he began to preach and baptize. There is no water in the wilderness but the brook Cherith, which never fails unless the drouth is extraordinarily severe, as in case of Elijah, when it held out three years and then failed. The great audience having so many camels, donkeys and horses and needing so much water for cullinary purposes, it became necessary to move to the Jordan, where they had plenty.

They did not go to the Jordan for baptism, for John did that in the wilderness, as Mark tells us, a proof that it was not immersion, for there is no immersion water in the wilderness. (I have traveled through it eight times.)

Now the meetings are at the Jordan fords, so called because Israel forded there when they entered Canaan, when God divided the flood and let them walk through dryshod. There is no ford except by the miraculous division of the river, which is fifteen feet deep at low water and much deeper during floods. Now John is preaching to an audience of about ten thousand, listening spellbound and all on the lookout for the Christ to put in His appearance, as John had told them He was all ready to do, and that he would introduce Him.

(w) Suddenly John lifts his stentorian voice like thunder; "Behold the Lamb of God that taketh away the sin of the world!" All eyes are turned and eagerly flashing to see the illustrious Personage. He and John were both born Jewish priests, who entered upon their office at age of thirty, which was majority. John, six months older, has already been preaching these six months. Jesus, reaching majority at his home in Nazareth, walks the ninety miles over the rough mountains to John's great evangelistic meeting at the celebrated ford of the Jordan, the brilliant souvenir in every Hebrew mind looking back to the wonderful days of old when God divided the swelling flood and led them through into the land flowing with milk and honey and abounding in corn and wine. John suddenly reaching out his hand, the entire multitude recognized the approaching Stranger, and the happy Baptist at the same time started to meet Him. The electrified multitude spontaneously gives way, thus forming an aisle through which they mutually tread, meeting each other. Oh, what a meeting! Never did men or angels before behold such a sight, the Son of God actually meeting the greatest prophet the world has seen in 4,500 years, since the bark of humanity was launched on the ocean of time. The meeting of Napoleon Bonaparte (at that time at the top of the world) and the Czar of Russia on a raft in the middle of the Tilsit River, amid the tremendous roar of artillery from either shore, was insignificant comparatively with the scene now contemplated by the enraptured multitude.

Jesus demands baptism at the hands of John, who modestly declines, observing, "I have need to be baptized of Thee, and comest Thou to me?" Baptism has no meaning but a purification. Jesus so defines it over and over and settles the matter forever. John was a fallen man, like every other son of Adam except Jesus, who took our nature, sin excepted. Heredity is paternal and not maternal, the mother only performing the office of gestation till the progeny is competent for the open air. Jesus had no earthly father, the Holy Ghost being His father (Luke 1:34), therefore John the Baptist needed a purification to eliminate the hereditary depravity out of him, as does every son and daughter of Adam's fallen race. This baptism Jesus alone could give. Jesus does not gainsay the testimony of John, certifying that he needs His baptism, but recognizes the fact. Meanwhile He observes, "Suffer it to be so now, as it becometh us to fulfill all righteousness."

The levitical law required the high priest to be anointed before he entered upon his office. Jesus was born Prophet, Priest and King, but John's baptism anointed Him for the high priesthood, so He could enter upon His office, as you see in Matthew, Mark and Luke. When on the arrival at Jerusalem He entered upon the office of high priest in the temple, driving out the buyers and sellers, and they demanded His authority, He referred them to John's baptism every time.

So, understanding that it was His anointing for the high priesthood, John said no more, but proceeded at once to pour the baptismal water on the head of his Lord. "Brother Godbey, I thought he immersed Him." Neither your thought nor mine is worth anything. God's Word settles everything for time and eternity. John says he handled the water and not the people. Mark 1:8, which includes the testimony of Peter the author and Mark the amanuensis; Luke 3:16, which includes the testimony of Paul the author and Luke the writer (Acts 1:5). This passage is the literal word of Jesus Himself, over which we would not dare to cavil. It involves also the testimony of Paul the author and Luke the amanuensis (Luke 11:16); also Hebrews 10:22 (as Apollos was the author of Hebrews, not Paul as you think. N. B. Paul says his autograph is attached to all of his Epistles, and it is not in Hebrews and never was until the Pope put it there six hundred years ago. So Paul did not write it. Dean Alford and the abler critics all give it to Apollos. but the book is all right in either case, as it is the inspired Word of God).

These five passages include the testimony of Jesus, John the Baptist, Peter, Paul, Apollos, Mark and Luke, and no one will dare to insinuate against the unimpeachable authenticity of them, which certify that John handled the water and not the people. How do we know that? Because "hudati," the word for water, is in the dative of instrumentality, positively certifying that John handled the water and not the people; thus settling all controversy forever. While fanaticism can certify anything, yet that does not make it true. There is not an insinuation in the Bible in favor of the conclusion that John immersed Jesus, or anybody else.

King James' translators did their work three hundred years ago, when the world was just emerging out of the Dark Ages, the thousand years during which not one man in a thousand nor one woman in twenty thousand could read or write. At that time they generally immersed them three times—first, right side down; then left side downward; and finally, face forward. The translators had all received the trine immersion and consequently had water on the brain, and there was so little learning in the world then, with them or anybody else, that they thought John immersed Jesus; and though they do not say He went down into the water, they do say, "He came up straightway out of the water." But it is a well-known fact that "apo" (the Greek word used) never does mean "out of," but "away from," simply certifying that after John baptized Him He went away from his meetings, lead by the Spirit into the wilderness to be tempted forty days. Besides, the old Jordan tells his own story; fifteen feet deep at low water, so muddy you cannot see an inch below the surface, and moving with the velocity of a mountain torrent so that a man cannot stand in it. He is in the rapids preceding his efflux into the Dead Sea.

John only preached about six months until Herod shut him in prison and never turned him loose but beheaded him. It says all Judæa, Jerusalem, and round about Jordan went out and were baptized by him at the Jordan. He could not have handled all those people (six millions) at that time. If he had been an iron man, it would have worn him out. He would have needed to be a hippopotamus to stand the cold river and it not kill him.

All the statuary and engravings represent Jesus standing and John pouring the water on His head. I saw them in the Catacombs of Rome, which were made A. D. 100-600. I have also seen them in St. John's Church in Rome. In the house of Judas in Damascus on the present tour I saw a picture of Ananias baptizing Paul by effusion. There is not a solitary voice in the Bible lands in favor of immersion. It is not in the English Bible. The only arguments they have are founded upon the prepositions "into," "out of," and "in," which are perfectly correctly translated "to," "from," and "on," i. e., at the Jordan; and in case of Philip and the eunuch, instead of saying "into" the water and "out of" it, a perfectly correct translation reads "to" the water and "from" it. I have been at the site of the eunuch's baptism eight times, there is nothing but a water-spout. They catch the water as it flows and use it, so that no stream runs away. There is no river nearer than the Jordan, sixty miles. The road run from Jerusalem south toward Gaza (Acts 8) back on the watershed; the Great Sea within thirty miles on the right, and the Salt Sea thirty on the left; the distance too short to accumulate water enough for a river.

There are two words in the New Testament which mean immerse—"catapontidzo" (Matt. 18: 6) and "buthidzo" (1 Tim. 5: 9), but neither of these words is ever used for baptism. The Bible was translated into Latin during the apostolic age. Immersion is a Latin word, while baptism is Greek. If immersion had been the practice, it would be in the Latin Bible. I am familiar with it and assure you it is not there, which is positive proof that it was not the apostolic practice.

(x) The people generally construe Romans 6: 6, "buried by baptism," to mean immersion, and also Colossians 2: 2-9. It it utterly untrue. The thing buried in these Scriptures is not the human body, but it says it is the "old man," i. e., depravity in the heart, which is first crucified, i. e., destroyed, then buried, not in water, but into the death of Christ, which is the atonement, the

> "Fountain filled with blood,
>   Drawn from Immanuel's veins,
> And sinners plunged beneath that flood,
>   Lose all their guilty stains.
>
> "The dying thief rejoiced to see
>   That fountain in his day,
> And there may , though vile as he,
>   Wash all my sins away."

This Scripture does not say that baptism is a burial, but the buryer, i. e., the baptism of the Holy Ghost, which Jesus gives, is God's sheriff, who ties the rope, hangs the criminal hereditary in every heart, and performs the office of undertaker, burying him into the atonement of Christ, into which all sin must be buried or the person having it enter Hell. In immersion we bury the body into water and raise it up. In Romans 6 and Colossians 2 it is the dead body of that old crucified man buried into the atonement and never resurrected. Raise him up and you are a poor backslider, "the last state worse than the first."

Whereas the Bible, corroborated by all history, settles the matter against immersion world without end, they often say we would better take it anyhow, so as to be satisfied. Satisfaction with anything but Jesus is idolatry and will prove Satan's greased plank on which to slide you into Hell. It is very dangerous to tinker with anything on which you may lean for security. The thing to do is to knock all the props away, leaving Jesus only, as He alone can save.

Having been happily converted in my mother's arms before she took off the baby clothes, neither she nor my preaching father understanding the relation of infants to the Kingdom, believed I was converted. Thus failing to apprehend my relation as a citizen of the Kingdom, they did not succeed in so teaching me to walk with the Lord as to enable me to keep my eye on Jesus and retain my citizenship in the Kingdom, consequently, though my outward life was irreproachable, I inwardly got away from the Lord, living an up-and-down life, sinning and repenting till the age of sixteen, when I was gloriously reclaimed in a Baptist revival. I immediately saw that I needed something more, i. e., sanctification, but nobody could tell me how to get it. Many said, "Get immersed and you will be satisfied;" consequently I forced a Methodist preacher, against his will, to immerse me with water, hoping to get the victory for which I sighed; but only finding a change from dry to wet sinner.

Soon I went to preaching, responsively to the call I received in that baby conversion, which never ceased to ring in my ears. In the providence of God, I was educated in a Baptist college, but I wandered in the wilderness nineteen years preaching fifteen of those years. Though I had no teacher, the Lord finally gave me the experience fifteen years later before the Movement reached Dixie Land, my field of labor. I verily believe if I had not tinkered with the big baptism, even in the absence of sanctified people to help me, I would have prayed through and struck fire in less than half of those nineteen years. No one gets the full victory till he loses sight of everything else and takes Jesus for everything he needs in time and eternity. He is omnipotent and needs no help. So long as we are looking to anything else and do not utterly abandon to God and take Jesus for everything, we do not get the victory. Finally, forty-three years ago (1868), in the midst of a glorious revival in which I was doing all the preaching and inwardly crying to God to sanctify me wholly, fill me with His Spirit, and give me the victory I so much needed, and for which my soul did sigh and my heart did cry, I received that blessing.

Having been born and reared a Methodist, I had little divinities with the Methodistic shibboleth. Having been reclaimed in a Baptist meeting and educated in a Baptist college, I had some Baptist gods, the greatest of all, the water god. By God's wonderful grace, eventually I found myself out in a large place, all of these gods having evanesced away, the big water god having passed into a fog bank, till I saw him no more. Then something wonderful happened; as I had never seen people sanctified, at first I did not know what it was, till I read Holiness books, and especially Wesley, Fletcher, Watson, Clarke, and the old Methodists. I reached the solution of the problem, and Jesus baptized me with the Holy Ghost and fire, burning up the freemason, the oddfellow, the college president and the Methodist preacher, leaving me no leader but Jesus, no guide but the Holy Ghost, and no authority but the precious Word. This baptism which Jesus gave me with the Holy Ghost and fire burned up carnality, politics and sectarianism, and gave me His omnipotent grace, by which I am utterly abandoned to God and sink away into His blessed divinity.

> "Oh, the blessing and the power
> That the Lord gave me then;
> I never shall forget
> I never can forget;
> Even now it is stealing over me again and again,
> It lingers with me yet."

(y) As Elijah had spent all his life praying and toiling to restore the law, John the Baptist was Elijah the Second, having in mercy been sent to the world to finish the work of his predecessor. He really, in his uncompromising enforcement of God's law, which He proclaimed on Mt. Horeb, lost his head. Herod and Herodias (his brother's wife) were living together in open violation of the law. John boldly and unequivocally condemned their illegitimate wedlock. Herod really got convicted under his preaching and the Scripture says that he heard him gladly. He so yielded to the light of conviction which shone into his heart under the preaching of John that he endorsed it and delighted to hear the unvarnished truth proclaimed. He admired the fearless, heroic spirit of John and it says, "He did many things," i. e., he reformed his life, righted it up in many respects, and turned a new leaf; so the people were clamorous over his reformation, reports going out that he was about to turn Holiness crank.

The case was quite different with the woman. She was so proud that John's awful exposure of her unlawful wedlock with the king made her exceedingly mad, so she would have hired an assassin to kill him if Herod had not had him shut up and in that way preserved his life. Therefore when her thoughtless, giddy little daughter, having by her pantomimic dance so pleased Herod and his magnates at his birthday feast as to provoke from him a reckless, enthusiastic promise to give her according to her asking, even unto the half of his kingdom, ran and told her mother, asking her advice, pursuant to the suggestion of Satan, she has her ask the head of John the Baptist. Though Herod saw his folly, it was too late, as the princes would not have permitted him to violate his oath; they would have taken off his political head and probably have actually decapitated him if he had gone back on his affidavit, which he had sworn in the presence of all his lords.

John the Baptist was like Elijah his predecessor,

who met all the prophets of Baal on Mt. Carmel, standing alone against the 450, so John lived a hero and died a martyr. His disciples came and took his body and buried it.

They show us his tomb with that of the prophet Elisha and chamberlain Obadiah in the great church of John the Baptist in Samaria. In Damascus they show us the tomb containing his head in the Mosque Rimmon, claiming that the head was procured from the queen who got it from her daughter and buried it there.

(z) The ministry of John the Baptist was Israel's glorious opportunity to repent, get back to God, and be ready to receive her Christ, introduced to the people by John. The first six months of his ministry, till Herod imprisoned him, were the most brilliant sweeping revival ever known on the earth; really a glorious souvenir of Elijah's victory over the false prophets, whom he met on Mt. Carmel, when he actually so triumphed over them all and aroused the vast multitude to repent and come back to God that they rose up, arrested and slew them all. After this wonderful victory, when Jezebel threatened him so violently, his heart failed him and he fled away. He has generally been censured for running from Jezebel, who said she was going to have his head taken off the next morning, but we do not know but it would have turned out even so if he had not fled for his life. Perhaps the people who had stood by him on Mt. Carmel would have reacted to some extent. We see the deplorable fickleness of Israel under the ministry of these two greatest prophets the world ever saw. Elijah had heroically labored all his life to restore the law in Israel, which had been ignored and trampled under foot. While we see the great victory on Mt. Carmel, as if they had given up their idolatry and unanimously turned back to Jehovah, yet we must remember that those people were soon afterward carried into Babylonian captivity, which never would have transpired if they had repented and reformed under the ministry of Elijah.

As John the Baptist was Elijah come back, not in person, but in spirit, power and work, they hailed him with enthusiasm, poured out by multitudes, hanging with breathless awe on his eloquent lips for days, weeks and months. As his wonderful protracted meeting continued six months, it actually seemed like they meant business and were going to be permanent, but Jesus said to them, "John was a bright and shining light and you wish to rejoice in that light for an hour;" thus reminding them of the transiency and instability of their professions, as out of that wonderful revival so few proved true, persevering on and identifying themselves with Christ the successor of John.

Those were days of unprecedented opportunity. If they had persevered in the repentance they manifested under John's preaching, they would have been ready for Christ, as it was really the mission of John to prepare a people made ready for the Lord. As the great Gentile world spread out before them, the whole nation would have been needed for its evangelization. God had sent Elijah, followed by Elisha, to preach repentance to them, restore the law and bring them back into loyalty in the succession of Abraham, Isaac and Jacob. Then He repeated the same great effort to reclaim them from their apostasy and bring them back to the law through the ministry of John the Baptist, that there might be a general repentance and reformation throughout Israel, thus bringing them to believing ground, where they could receive their own glorious Christ by faith and thus receive the immortal honors awaiting God's church-nation, i. e., the evangelization of the whole Gentile world.

CHAPTER XIX.

MESSIANIC DISPENSATION.

"He came to His own and His own received Him not; but to as many as received Him, gave He the privilege to become the children of God, even to those who believe on His name, who were born, not of bloods, nor of the will of the flesh, nor of the will of man, but of God."

When Jesus came to the Jews, His own people, the rank and file rejected Him; yet the faithful few received Him, i. e., the true disciples of John the Baptist, including the apostles, and a few besides, who gathered to the ministry of John the Baptist, and amid the great and alarming defection that so soon followed, when the revival tide subsided, thus by the ministry of John having been prepared for Christ, received Him joyfully. When John the Baptist pointed Him out, shouting uproariously, "Behold the Lamb of God, that taketh away the sin of the world!" they immediately pursued Him and became His disciples. As John said, "I must decrease, but He must increase."

(a) John had preached with all his might, "Repent, for the kingdom of Heaven is at hand." Jesus is the King of Heaven. His presence is the kingdom. John pointed Him out, so they could actually receive Him and enter His kingdom then and there and abide in it forever. Repentance was, in the days of John the Baptist and Jesus, this day and forever, the key to His kingdom. Hence it is very important to know what repentance is. It is a compound of two Greek words, "meta," change, and "noos," the mind. Therefore it simply means to have an exchange of minds; i. e., to get rid of the carnal mind and receive that of Christ. The Holy Ghost is the omnipotent Agent executive of this wonderful change.

The great demonstration made under the ministry of Elijah on Mt. Carmel and by the thronging multitudes during the six months' protracted meeting of John the Baptist in the wilderness and at the Jordan ford, expose their paradoxical superficiality by their lamentable transiency, leaving but a little band, honored of God to prove true, bear the banner, receive the crown and go to the ends of the earth proclaiming the wonderful news of salvation to the millions sitting in darkness and in the shadow of death.

Repentance is the only available precursor of the supernatural birth, which cannot be secured by bloods, i. e., animal sacrifices—Old Testament ritual—and this is equally true in reference to the New Testament ordinances, i. e., baptism and the eucharist. The rank and file of church-members in all ages have depended on these sacraments for regeneration; utterly in vain, like leaning on a broken stick. They will let you fall and the broken pieces pierce your hand.

While the ordinances are all right in their place, beautiful souvenirs of inward graces administered by the Holy Spirit, yet they are utterly destitute of spiritual, stability and availability. Neither can the supernatural birth be reached by the will of the flesh, i. e., your own carnal will, nor the will of man, i. e., the preacher or priest who administers the ordinances of the church. It never can be reached through any of these expedients, "but by the will of God," i. e., it is His work alone. When we meet the condition, i. e., radically repent of all our sins, leaving them forever, never to come back, and cast ourselves down at the mercy-seat, utterly and eternally abandoned to God, the Holy Spirit will witness to us that we are wholly given up to God, and we will know it better than anything else. This puts us on believing ground where, by the help of the Holy Spirit freely given, we are enabled to receive Christ by simple faith, our perfect and all-sufficient, atoning Savior.

In that case, God freely and fully cancels all our sins from Heaven's chancery, and the Holy Spirit, responsively to God's pardoning mercy, then creates within us a new heart and a right spirit, thus making us new creatures in Christ Jesus, and making all the world new to us; as there is a world without corresponding with the world within, the outward being the reflection of the inward. Consequently when God, by His blessed Holy Spirit, has wrought in us the new creation, everything without undergoes a revolution, putting on a new aspect homogeneous to the new world within.

(b) The world had waited 4,500 years for the coming of Christ. God had perpetuated the genealogy from Adam all the way down through the long run of the ages, so everybody could trace Him back to Adam and know that He was not an angel invested in a human body, and consequently incompetent to take our place under the law and redeem us.

The Greek and Roman poets had extensively written up their gods as taking the form of men and coming on the earth, going around among the people, mixing with them and preaching to them; but none of them could ever save any of us, because they could not become our vicarious substitute, taking our place under the law, paying the penalty and redeeming us from sin, death and Hell. Therefore the genealogy of Christ, running all the way back to Adam, was absolutely necessary. That is the grand utility of the Old Testament, which is the biography of Christ excarnate whereas the New Testament is the biography of Christ incarnate. The Jews were His own family, authenticated by history, from Adam down. Oh, what a glorious honor they enjoyed among all the nations of the earth; and what a wonderful opportunity lay before them!

God sent John the Baptist into the world to take up the great work of reviving and restoring the law in the succession of Elijah, in which case the people would all have repented, thus reaching believing ground for the reception of Christ by simple faith. Then He would have baptized them with the Holy Ghost and fire, as John had preached to them, and sent them into all the world to preach the glorious good news-that the Savior had already come and redeemed the whole human race and they had nothing to do but repent of their sins, give up their idols and receive Him, their glorious, all-sufficient, atoning Savior.

(c) Oh! how sad for the angels who had shouted at creation's birth, wept over the fall and swept down from Heaven when Christ was born in Bethlehem, told the shepherds the joyous news and looked forward with thrilling anticipation to the wonderful scene when all of the Lord's family would receive the pentecostal enduement of the Holy Ghost, go to the ends of the earth, and spread the good news of the world's redemption, till the nations sitting in darkness and the shadow of death will all hear, from the rising of the sun to the going down of the same; repent of their sins, renounce their dumb idols, which can neither see, hear nor feel; come by millions, enter the kingdom of God with shouts of victory, and flood the world with the glory of the Lord—how sad for them to see this work so long delayed! In that case the whole world would have been evangelized long ago and the glorified Savior have come back on the throne of His millennial glory, and established His kingdom in all the earth, actually bringing Heaven down. And, oh! how the angels who shouted at creation's birth, turned Heaven into a Bochim of weeping when the sad news of the fall reached them, as they have in all ages taken so much interest in humanity.

Oh, how appalling the scene, when Jesus, after all

these unutterable benefactions wrought by our loving Heavenly Father to make the plan of salvation a glorious success, "came to His own and His own received Him not." (1 John 1: 13.) But praise the Lord for the faithful few who had stood by Elijah in his faithful, life-long labor to restore the law, repented under the preaching of John the Baptist, and were ready to receive the glorious Messiah, "to whom gave all the prophets witness that through His name every one believing shall be saved."

(d) The whole world was wonderfully ripe for the Gospel when Jesus came. The polytheistic religions, with their multitudes of gods, had proved very unsatisfactory, and utterly incompetent to satisfy the longings of the immortal soul. Human philosophy had climbed the altitudes of Parnassus, drunk from the Pyerian fountain to its utmost capacity, and after all, proved incompetent to tell man either his orgin or his end. Consequently all heathen nations had conceived the lofty anticipation that the Creator of the world and all things in it would send from His effulgent throne a messenger to teach the people primary truth, in happy contradistinction to the mythical fables of their pagan divinities.

At Lystra (Acts 13th chap.) those heathens leaped to the conclusion that Barnabas was Jupiter, the chief Roman god, and Paul, Mercury, the god of eloquence, showing up the attitude of the heathens looking for God to send a messenger from Heaven. Never did a nation in all the ages enjoy so wide an open door and golden opportunity to actually capture the world, and win a crown of glory that would never fade away, but accumulate new lustre through the flight of eternal ages, as the Jews. But they sadly fulfilled the awful prophecy of Isaiah, "He hath hardened your hearts and blinded your eyes." God is here represented as doing it in divine retribution; when they had rejected His blessings, they became curses. The same sun that softens the wax hardens the clay. God's blessings which gloriously save the penitent believer harden the heart of the impenitent rejecter and expedite his damnation. Jesus wanted to save all the Jews, give them the baptism of the Holy Ghost and fire, and send them out to preach to all the Gentiles the glorious Gospel of life and salvation.

When a new President is elected, thronging multitudes are clamorous for official appointments and millions would be if they thought there was any chance to succeed. When Jesus came into the world, He came to His own people, not to mock, but to save them, and if they had received Him, as He had the whole Gentile world to evangelize, He would gladly have used them all in this world-wide evangelization. It would have suited the Jews precisely, as they are the most itinerant and aggressive people on the face of the earth. But their own persistent rejection of the light so blinded their eyes that they could not see.

(e) Human leadership has always been manipulated by Satan in the wholesale destruction of souls. The trouble with the Jews was that the high priest, the Sanhedrim and the influential officials rejected Him, and the multitude went with them in the fatal depreciation of their own golden opportunity, such as the world had never known. Oh, how the ages waited, groaned, sighed and cried 4,500 years 1or the coming of the Messiah to bring light, life, hope and victory to the suffering, Satan-deluded and Hellward-bound millions! But when He came, how unfortunately they followed their blind guides, the high clergy, and rejected Him, bringing on themselves ruin for time and eternity.

The awful tribulation (A. D. 66-73) desolated their land, slaughtered their people by sword, pestilence and famine, destroyed their cities, and spoliated their beautiful temple with its gold and silver and sacred vessels, which were carried away, never to get back. Then, worst of all, the people went plunging into eternity without hope and God; the surviving remnant all being sold into slavery and led into captivity among all nations, where they have toiled and groaned through the ages; scathed, peeled, persecuted and robbed by every nation under Heaven, responsively to their own awful imprecations when, standing before Pilate's bar. led by the high priests, they shouted aloud, "His blood be upon us and our children!"

No people on the earth have suffered like the Jews. They have been persecuted, enslaved and downtrodden by all nations as their own inspired prophets predicted: "You shall be the tail." God made them the leader of all the nations. When they rejected their Christ, they infelicitously vibrated to the opposite pole of the battery, becoming the "tail" of the world instead of the head.

(f) The vociferous acclaim of John, His forerunner and introducer, and Jesus Himself was, "Repent, for the kingdom of Heaven is at hand!" John preached no shoddy Gospel but bottom-rock repentance, i. e., the exchange of the carnal mind for that of Christ, which is consummated in the baptism of the Holy Ghost and fire, which crucifies the old man, destroys the body of sin and buries it into the "fountain filled with blood," so deep that Satan will never be able to resurrect it, making the last state worse than the first.

When the scribes and Pharisees, robed in their self-righteousness, claiming to be God's holy people when they were Satan's deluded counterfeits, came to John, demanding baptism at his hands, he positively refused, exhorting them, "Bring forth fruit meet for repentance, and say not within yourselves, We have Abraham to our father: for I say unto you that God is able of these stones to raise up children unto Abraham. The axe is laid at the root of the tree, and every tree that bringeth not forth good fruit, is hewn down and cast into the fire."

This plain preaching, instead of convicting and saving them, made them so mad that they did not receive his baptism. It was too hard for them in their beautiful robes to get down, wallow in the dust with the publicans and harlots, and weep and mourn, bathing their faces with scalding tears, then rise with shouts of victory and testify that they had prayed through to God, met Him in His condescending mercy, and been forgiven of all their sins. From this humiliating ordeal their proud hearts recoiled with indignation, consequently they perished miserably in the destruction of Jerusalem, going into eternity unprepared to meet the God whose Son they had rejected and crucified.

The Gospel is the same in all ages. The great delinquency to-day is at this point. Evangelical repentance, with a broken heart and a contrite spirit, accompanied by the utter abandonment of all sin, radical reformation from everything out of harmony with the kingdom of grace and glory, open confession of all sins and restitution of all ill-gotten gains, has lamentably gone out of the popular pulpits, till the pews are filled with proud, wicked, impenitent people who will not bear the plain, straight truth of repentance, regeneration, and the baptism of the Holy Ghost and fire which crucifies the "old man," buries him into death and raises up the "new man," created in the image and likeness of God (Eph. 5: 24) to walk in newness of life.

The awful apostasy of the churches has forced God, in the interest of His kingdom, to raise up the Holiness Movement, which this day girdles the globe, preaching the straight old Gospel preached by Elijah, John the Baptist, Jesus and His apostles; the Gospel of radical repentance, sky-blue regeneration, the baptism of the Holy Ghost and fire; crucifixion, destruction and interment of the carnal mind; investiture and infilling with the whole mind of Christ, all witnessed by the indwelling Holy Ghost.

The greatest danger of the Holiness Movement is in slowing down on fundamentals. The foundation is the most important part of a house; when it gives way, the house topples and falls. Therefore we must keep down on bottom-rock repentance, which was the battle-cry of Elijah, John the Baptist and Jesus, all vociferating it as the condition of entering the kingdom of Heaven.

(g) Jesus the King came to John's meeting before his imprisonment. John pointed Him out so that all could look on Him with their eyes. He inaugurated Him into His official Messiahship by baptism, thus clearing up the whole matter. The king takes his kingdom with him wherever he goes, represents it, opens the door, receives whom he will, and closes it against whom he will. You see in the preaching of John and Jesus, repentance was the only condition required, in order to enter the Kingdom. It is the same, yesterday, to-day and forever.

Genuine repentance is invariably accompanied by confession and restitution, as well as characterized by a broken heart and a contrite spirit. Its fruit is holiness (Rom. 6:22): "Being made free from sin, we have our fruit unto sanctification, and the end eternal life." That sanctification, as you see in this chapter (vs. 5, 6), is wrought by the baptism of the Holy Ghost and fire which Jesus gives, crucifying the "old man," destroying the body of sin, and burying it deep down in the Atonement, there to abide forever; buried into His death. This refers to Christ. Death is His atonement made for the sins of the whole world, and the normal receptacle of all sin. The sin that is not buried in that magnitudinous sepulchre of all sin must be buried into Hell, there to abide forever.

The kingdom of Heaven is the divine government, whose subjects not only obey the laws of the Lord but delight in them. (Psalm 1.) This kingdom fills Heaven and when Jesus the King came He brought it with Him, throwing the door open to every truly penitent, believing soul. As repentance breaks the yoke of Satan and rescues us out of his kingdom, faith receives the yoke of Christ and enters His kingdom, where the old man of sin, having been conquered in the battle of repentance and bound in regeneration, is crucified in sanctification, his body destroyed and buried deep into the fountain filled with blood, and all the debris accumulated in the spirit and mind by a life of sin and all the hereditary depravity are burnt up by the fires of the Holy Ghost, and the heart made clean and filled with the Spirit of God, so the life is a glorious victory over the world, the flesh and the devil, and a locomotive advertiser of the heavenly kingdom in all the earth and through the ages of eternity.

CHAPTER XX.

PENTECOSTAL DISPENSATION.

The Mosaic dispensation had three great campmeetings every year. The Passover, in April, commemorated the emancipation out of Egyptian slavery, when the destroying angel winged his flight throughout the land of Egypt, cutting down every soul on which he did not find the blood of the Passover lamb sprinkled; showing that God is no respecter of persons. Many of these where the angel saw the blood were the greatest sinners, and still he passed over them, and many where the blood was not sprinkled were clever, high-toned church-members, but he cut them down all the same because he did not see the blood. Hence this festival commemorating their deliverance from the yoke of Egypt applies to every soul in the world, in justification of those under the Blood, and condemnatory of all where He does not see the Blood.

Reader, be sure you keep under the Blood, as the destroying angel is constantly on the wing, the seventeen hundred millions of people now populating this world dying at the rate of one every second, sixty per minute, or about one hundred thousand per day. Therefore you cannot afford to abide even under the shadow of a doubt appertaining to the Blood question. If the angel comes to you and does not see the Blood, he cuts you down. He never stops to ascertain whether you are a church-member, genteel, ladylike, philanthropic, enterprising and clever; or a debauchee, down at the bottom of slumdom. In either case, it is all the same— if he sees the Blood, he passes you by; if he finds no Blood, he cuts you down, so keep this Blood problem constantly settled without possible defalcation, as your destiny hangs on it.

The Passover festival not only commemorated their emancipation and national birth (as slaves have no nationality, but are catalogued with herds and flocks), but it beautifully and brilliantly symbolizes our personal regeneration, the normal and inseparable concomitant of our justification from all unrighteousness.

(h) Fifty days after the emancipation out of Egyptain slavery and their national birth, God, amid thunder-bolts, lightning-shafts, earthquakes, and tornadoes, causing all the people to tremble and quake, gave them the law on Mount Sinai. The law says, "The soul that sinneth, it shall die." (Ezek. 18:4 and 20.) You see, in this one chapter, in order to write it inefaceably on all memories, the Holy Ghost puts it down twice; besides it runs through the Bible from alpha to omega, keeping all Bible readers constantly trembling before its infallible Author.

The law is irreversible. Jesus says in His Sermon on the Mount, "I came not to destroy the law and the prophets, but to fulfill." The people misapply and pervert the Scriptures to their own destruction. (2 Pet. 3rd chapter.) They say we are not under the law, but under grace. (Rom. 6:14.) N. B. Those two chapters in Romans (five and six) tell us how we get out from under the law; it is by having our "old man" crucified and the body of sin destroyed, so that we no longer serve sin. So long as the "old man" is on hand, you are under the law, and if you there abide, there is no place for you but Hell when you leave this world.

The Pentecostal festival is so named because Pentecost means fifty, and it was established just fifty days after Passover because that time elapsed in their journey out of bondage through the sea to Mount Sinai, where God gave them the law. Hence it commemorates the giving of the law and symbolizes their obedience to the law, which is the crucifixion of the sin-man hereditary in every heart. Hence their first great camp-meeting (Passover) commemorated their emancipation out of slavery and symbolizes our regeneration by the Holy Ghost; while Pentecost commemorates the giving of the law, and symbolizes our sanctification, the great second work of the Holy Ghost in the re-creation of wrecked humanity.

They also had the Feast of Tabernacles, in September, commemorating their journeyings in the wilderness through which they marched into the Canaan of rest, and this symbolized our glorification, which is the third and last great work of the Holy Ghost in the reconstruction of ruined humanity.

The first work of the Spirit is our conversion, saving us from personal transgression and giving us a new heart, competent to the new life God requires us to live. The second great work of the Spirit, entire sanctification, saves us from the Adamic sin and gives us a clean heart, thus qualifying us, by His abiding presence, to live a holy life. This third work of the Holy Spirit we cannot receive till this mortal puts on immortality in corporeal dissolution.

(i) The Pentecost fifty days after the Passover, which was April 14, came off early in June, and the Feast of Tabernacles in September, when the harvests were ripe and gathered into the graneries, matured so as to keep in any climate. In regeneration, the crop is pitched; in sanctification, it is matured; and in glorification, it is gathered into the heavenly storehouse.

This chapter is directly on the pentecostal experience. It is pertinent that we all know what it is since it is an indispensable "sine qua non," without which no soul would ever pass the pearly portals. Satan's plan is to flood you with foolishness, appertaining to all Christian experiences, as his only chance is to cheat, delude and fool you out of it; otherwise you pass out of his clutches forever. On regeneration, he has flooded the world with foolishness.

I was born and reared among Campbellites, who denied the personality of the Holy Ghost, making all manner of fun of Holy Ghost religion—not their people in common parlance, but their preachers in the pulpit. When they wanted a revival, they would start by preaching powerfully against the Holy Ghost and ridiculing all experimental religion, and so making fun of it that the people would be ashamed to come to a mourners'-bench. Then they would preach awful sermons on Hell, in order to get the Hell-scare on the people so they would act. Finally they would go to preaching what they would call the "Gospel," telling the people they had nothing to do but to reform their lives, come and join the church, confessing that Jesus Christ is the Son of God, get immersion in water for the remission of their sins, and that settled the matter, making them bona fide Christians—whereas there was not a word of truth in any of it.

Then the people, believing this the easy way to Heaven, whither all wanted to go, would come by dozens, scores, and hundreds, join the church, and get immersed, as Jesus says (Matt. 23rd chap.) making them twofold more the "child of Hell," because to the long, black catalogue of the deeds of their wicked lives, which still stuck to them, they added the abominable sin of hypocrisy by professing to be Christians.

When I was in Jerusalem a few days ago, during my fourth tour through the Bible lands and the historic countries of Europe, Asia and Africa, forty thousand pilgrims were there from the ends of the earth, giving the most incontestable manifestation of sincerity; whereas the great rank and file of them, along with their preachers, were utterly ignorant of personal salvation, following corrupt, lecherous priests, looking to them and diversified churchisms to save them, while they themselves were not saved. Thus Satan, the god of this age (2 Cor. 4:4—not as in the English version, "this world"), got them. He is not the god of this world because our wonderful Savior has included this world in His glorious redemption; to sanctify it by the fiery baptism (2 Pet, 3rd. chap.) and re-create it (Rev. 1st and 2nd chaps.), turning it into a heaven and restoring it back to its place on the plane of the ecliptic, Satan caught it in his fall, and has ever since been doing his best to add it to Hell. He is destined, however, to signal and ultimate defeat and ejectment into the lake of fire in "outer darkness," i. e., so distant that the combined illumination from seventeen millions of glowing suns will never reach it with a solitary cheering ray. This is the ultimate doom of Satan with all his followers, demoniacal and human. (Rev. 20:15.)

Regeneration and sanctification are the grand "sine qua nons" of Christian experience, without which there is no Heaven. Therefore the devil has laid all Hell and this wicked world under contribution to so pervert them as to cheat the people out of them, so he can slide them into Hell over the greased planks which fallen churches utilize in his interest, so efficiently in the population of the bottomless pit.

(j) In a similar manner, the devil is doing his best to counterfeit sanctification and cheat the people out of it. The greatest landslide from the infernal world he has been able to turn on the Holiness Movement is the counterfeit gift of tongues.

Twenty years ago the Lord gave me that book, "Spiritual Gifts and Graces," which He has so wonderfully honored; showing the nine graces by which we are saved, and the nine gifts by which we help to save others. Among the latter is the gift of tongues, i. e., languages, which the devil has so manipulated as to literally delude and cheat the people so as to get their eyes off of Jesus, and on to his jabber, and so give him a chance to actually rob them of their experience. Under this awful delusion, many good Holiness people, once, like John the Baptist, bright and shining lights, are now the victims of wild fanaticism; and the Holy Spirit, grieved away, evil spirits, having superseded Him, pass themselves off for Him.

This counterfeit Tongue Movement came to us from Spiritualism, which is devil worship. I preach throughout the world, not only the whole United States, but beyond the ocean, enjoying a vast field of observation. I know to my sorrow what I tell you. We have traced this so-called "Tongue Movement" into Spiritualism in numerous instances. In India, where the Lord has let me preach much, the devil worshipers have it. While God alone can give a language, Satan and his emissaries imitate God in everything. That is the reason why wizards, witches, necromancers, jugglers, wicked magicians, legerdemainers, spiritualists, sorcerers, and all sorts of diabolicisms do what they call "speaking with tongues," i. e., giving ejaculatory utterances, going into trances, and making all sorts of demonstrations.

The evil spirits which throng the air in vast armies Satan leading them (Eph. 2:1), can excite you, work on your emotions, stir up your sensibilities, so that you will leap, jump, shout, and give utterances which neither you nor anybody else knows, because they are no language; if they were, somebody would understand them. Here the finatical Tongue people depart from the Scriptures.

(k) They tell us it is an "unknown tongue," known and spoken by no one; consequently we need not expect anybody to understand them. N. B. There is no unknown tongue. Look in your Bible (1 Cor. 12th. and 14th chap..), where you find the unknown tongue. The word "unknown" is italicized, which is an honest confession on the part of the translators that it is not in the original, and they had no right to put it in the English translation. "Tongue" has no meaning in the Bible but language and the physical organ that articulates the language. There is no unknown tongue, from the fact that there is not an unknown language in all the world. There never was a language that some nation on the earth did not know and speak, and never will be. Therefore say no more about an "unknown tongue"—there is none, never was, and never will be. Of course there are many languages which you and I do not understand; but there are people who do, otherwise they could not speak them.

The "Tongue People" say that tongues are for a sign; the Bible does not say noises are for a sign. This meaningless jabber which they utter in their meetings is no tongue, but simply noises like birds, frogs, crickets, etc. It is simply the work of evil spirits counterfeiting the gift of tongues, as they do everything else that God does. That is Satan's business, as he is the great counterfeiter and the father of all other counterfeiters. He plays God and the Holy Ghost, deterfeiters. He plays God and the Holy Ghost, deceiving the millions who worship the devil, thinking it is God, i. e., the Spiritualists in this country, who claim to communicate with the dead, whereas the evil spirits who throng the air play their dead relatives and friends on them. Millions cognomened "Christians" worship the devil under delusion, thinking they are worshiping God. The heathens worship the devil understandingly, in order to appease his wrath, so he will not send calamities on them.

Among King Solomon's strange wives was an Ammonitess. As they worship Moloch, an evil deity, i. e., the devil, in order to appease his wrath, Solomon brought his image to Jerusalem and set it up in the valley of Hinnom and it remained there till the reign of Josiah, who took it away. It had the body of a man and the head of an ox. The image was hollow, and they built a fire in it like a stove, heated it hot, then sacrificed their children to Moloch by laying them in his arms and drowning their voices with music while they were burning up.

(1) The Tongue People confess judgment against themselves by grossly perverting God's Word, recklessly misconstruing and even flatly contradicting it. They say there was no sanctification on the Day of Pentecost, but only the baptism of the Holy Ghost. In this statement they flatly contradict Jesus, who defines "baptizo" (baptism) and "hagiadzo" (sanctify) by the very same word, "catharidzo," thus showing positively that they reveal the same blessed work of grace. (Luke 11: 39.)

When the Pharisee invited Jesus to dine with him. He proceeded to eat without washing His hands, to the astonishment of the Pharisees. Knowing the criticisms transpiring in their minds, He answered them orally, "You Pharisees make clean the outside of the cup and plate. while the inside is full of extortion, and covetousness, and impurity."

"Wash" in the Scriptures is "baptizo" (baptise); "make clean" is "catharidzo," so you see Jesus defines baptism as a purification. You find this definition in many Scriptures and really it is the only definition of baptism in the Bible.

Ephesians 5:25: "Husbands, love your wives with divine love, as Christ loved the Church and gave Himself for her, that He might sanctify her, purifying her by the washing of water through the Word, that He might present her to Himself a glorious Church, having neither spot nor wrinkle nor any such thing, but that she might be wholly unblameless."

In this beautiful Scripture "hagiadzo" (sanctify) is defined by "catharidzo" (purify). Take this passage in connection with Luke eleventh chapter and you find "baptizo" (baptize) and "hagiadzo" (sanctify) defined by the same word "catharidzo" (to pruify). Therefore they both simply mean to give you a clean heart, "without which no one shall see the Lord." (Matt. 5:8.) Therefore the baptism which Jesus gives with the Holy Ghost and without which no soul will pass the pearly portals, and sanctification, so prominent in the precious Word, both mean the same great work by which inbred sin is washed away, when the Holy Ghost, whom Jesus gives in the baptism, applies the cleansing Blood, and the refining fires, burn up worldliness in all its forms and phases, i. e., lodgery sectarianism, politics and all sorts of vanities, styles, habitudes and foolishness; enabling the soul to sink away into God so deep that, under faithful perseverance, Satan will never reach it with his black lasso; as he says in the above Scripture that he will present the Bride to Himself a "glorious Church, having neither spot nor wrinkle, nor any such thing." When Jesus gives you a pentecostal baptism with the Holy Ghost and fire, the blessed Spirit applies the Blood to the expurgation of all hereditary depravity out of the heart; meanwhile He uses the hot iron to remove all the wrinkles. When clothing is thoroughly washed, it would neither be comfortable nor sightly without the iron running over it, taking out kinks and wrinkles. When the Lord baptized me with the Holy Ghost and fire forty-three years ago, expurgating all sorts of hereditary depravity by the cleansing Blood, He wondefully used the hot iron eliminating the wrinkles. I had the Masonic wrinkle, Oddfellow wrinkle, Methodist wrinkles, Baptist wrinkles, ecclesiastical wrinkles (i. e., not free from churchisms), political wrinkles, etc. Oh, how they all evanesced and the Holy Ghost shoved the hot iron all over my soul.

It takes the Blood, the omnipotent elixer, to interpenetrate the fabric, as the powerful alkalis in the hands of the laundryman, ferreting out every atom of impurity and making the heart so clean that the omniscient eye of the Almighty fails to discover an atom of impurity. That purity is the condition of admission into Heaven (Matt. 5: 8), but if we are full of wrinkles, we would blush to meet the angels—not on account of sin, for that is gone, not a trace left; but on account of our ugliness, which is not sin, but the scars left by the heavy tread of sin. This is all swept away by the smoothing-iron of the Holy Ghost, eliminating all the wrinkles and irregularities.

(n) In the bold affirmations of the Tongue People, they certify that the apostles were all sanctified on the evening of our Lord's resurrection day, when He breathed on them saying, "Receive ye the Holy Ghost." In that way they get sanctification out of the pentecostal experience, making that experience simply the baptism of the Holy Ghost, manifested by speaking with tongues. They did speak with tongues sure enough, but our Tongue People do not speak with a tongue, because a tongue is a language and somebody could understand it. We have searched the world around to find people who can understand it. (myself having traveled around the world). We have sent my personal acquaintances across the oceans both ways and compassed the globe to find people who could understand them, but all signally failed.

Acts 15: 9: "The Lord hath granted unto the Gentiles the like gift as granted unto us, purifying their hearts by faith." Peter there uses the word "catharidzo" (purify) which Jesus defines with "baptizo" (baptism). Hence you see they received sanctification on that day because Jesus (Luke 11: 39) defines "baptizo" by "catharidzo," and in Ephesians 5: 25. He defines "hagiadzo" (sanctify) by "catharidzo" (purify). Therefore in these Scriptures, Peter,

Paul and Jesus all certify that the apostles were sanctified at Pentecost. The affirmation of the Tongue People that they were all sanctified when Jesus breathed on them the evening of His resurrection is simply a perversion, in order to get sanctification out of Pentecost and leave nothing but the baptism of the Holy Ghost, confirmed by the gift of tongues, which is their demoniacal jabber and no tongue at all.

They received real tongues at Pentecost, but none which somebody there on the ground could not understand, because "devout men from every nation under Heaven" were there. Consequently there were people on the ground who understood every language given on that occasion.

(o) The apostles were not sanctified when Jesus breathed on them, but reclaimed from a backslidden state. God's Word settles everything. Jesus said to them at the Last Supper (Matt. 26:30; Mark 14:29), "You shall all backslide in Me this night" (English version, "be offended"). The Greek "scandalidzo" used in all these passages has no meaning in the New Testament but to backslide. We know they did all backslide the night of His betrayal, because He says it, and that settles the matter forever. Their backsliding was not from God, but only from Him, giving up His Christhood.

Though He had three times positively predicted His tragical death in Jerusalem, in order that the prophetical curriculum might be perfect, as the faith of all ages must stand on it, the Holy Ghost so removed it out of their minds that they did not understand it, but believed, with all His disciples, that He would deliver them from the Roman yoke and reign over them in this world. When He rode the donkey into Jerusalem, and they all shouted so, they fully expected to crown Him king during the on-coming Passover. The Jews had borne the Roman yoke, so heavy and galling, a third of a century, and as Rome had her iron grip on the whole world, they had no hope of ever regaining their liberties but by the coming of Christ, who the prophecies said (Luke 1: 32) would sit down on the throne of David and rule over the house of Jacob forever.

The reason why the Holy Ghost took from them the understanding of our Lord's prophecies of His death and resurrection was to keep down an uprising which would have deluged the country with blood. Jesus had healed all who were brought to Him by their friends from the ends of the earth, so you could not find a blind, deaf, dumb or leprous person in all Palestine; besides they had brought the patients from foreign nations and He had healed them. With the rank and file of the people and the lower clergy He was exceedingly popular, so they would have fought, bled and died for Him. The officials, ecclesiastical and political, envied, feared and hated Him, believing that if He succeeded, He would dethrone them. If the apostles and His friends had known what they were going to do, they would have fought, bled and died for Him; every apostle would have turned recruiting officer, and Peter would have been commander-in-chief in the revolutionary army to protect Him against His enemies.

He did not want anything of that kind. He had come into the world to bleed and die for the people and save all from sin, death and Hell. When the apostles saw at midnight in Gethsemane His arrest by His enemies, they all took fright and fled away up Mt. Olivet, lest they might arrest them as His accomplices. It is generally thought that Peter alone backslid; this is a great mistake. He was the most commendable of all for staying with Him alone, when all the balance fled away.

John was the young man about whom we read as flying for his life with a linen cloth on his undressed body, i. e., in his night apparel, when the soldiers dashed after him, actually getting hold of his coat, but he was so active that he jumped out of his garment, leaving it in their hands and, running, made his escape. He must have been wonderfully fleet, to outrun all the Roman soldiers. Thus running away to the house of Rabbi Amos in the metropolis, he there procured a Jewish sacerdotal robe, invested in which, returning to the scene, he falls in with Jesus, walking by His side, the soldiers mistaking him for a Jewish priest and letting him alone; while Caiaphas, who knew him, declined to divulge his relative, as the word means he was akin to him.

Consequently John walked by Jesus' side that sorrowful night of His prosecution at the tribunal of Annas, the ex-high priest; of Caiaphas, the ruling high priest; beofre the Sanhedrim court, at Pilate's bar, in Herod's judgment hall, back again to Pilate, then up Calvary, while they were nailing Him to the cross, and on through those three awful hours of dying agonies; finally standing by Him till that Roman soldier, Philippus, comes with his spear, plunging it into His side, and tears His heart to pieces. Till John saw that His heart was ruined, he hoped that He would revive, come down from the cross, defeat all His enemies, receive the crown of David and Solomon and ascend the throne of Israel. History says that when John saw His heart torn to pieces by the cruel spear, his faith failed, hope fled and he fainted. There is no doubt but John was the last one to backslide, i. e., give up the Christhood of Jesus.

The other nine who fled in Gethsemane and came back no more, received an awful shock when they saw Jesus arrested and completely in the hands of His enemies, like any other man. They came no more to Him, but spent the night on Mount Olivet and the ensuing day viewed the crucifixion afar off. From His arrest, their faith in His Christhood was wavering all the time, and one by one they gave up, dropping Him down to the plane of the prophets, no longer believing Him to be the Christ.

Peter deserves great credit for staying with Him when they all fled. He was naturally one of the bravest men that ever walked the earth, actually brave enough, single-handed and alone, to have fought that whole army if Jesus had let him alone. When they assaulted Him in Gethsemane, drawing his sword Peter made at them, aiming to strike Malchus, their leader, a fatal blow, splitting his head open in the middle; but providentially the blow glanced him, cutting off his right ear. Jesus leaping to it healed it (His last beneficent miracle), then forced Peter to put up his sword, when he got awful scared and behaved badly, of course letting his faith evanesce.

Thus all the apostles fulfilled the Lord's prophecy at the Last Supper, "This night you shall all backslide in Me," i. e., give up His Christhood.

(p) When they all gave up His Christhood and dropped Him down to the plane of the prophets, in so doing they all backslid in Him, as He had prophesied they would, but still were holding to God and looking for Christ to come. As prophets cannot save anybody, themselves being but saved sinners, when they gave up the Christhood of Jesus and dropped Him down to the plane of the prophets, of course they had no salvation.

You see plainly their attitude in the conversation of Cleopas and his comrade that afternoon walking away to Emmaus, seven miles, when Jesus fell in with them, dropping an eclipse on their eyes so they did not recognize Him, and said, "What news have you?" They responded, "Are you but a stranger at Jerusalem that you do not know the news?" "What news?" ' About Jesus of Nazareth, a man, a prophet, mighty in word and deed, and we hoping that He was the one to redeem Israel; but we have given that all up, as our rulers have delivered Him up and they have crucified Him. Some of our women were this morning at the sepulchre and said they had seen a vision of angels who astonished them by saying He was alive." Then He began with Moses and swept through all the prophets and showed them how it behooved Christ to suffer and die by His vicarious expiation and enter into His glory.

By this time they had reached Emmaus and He walked on, testing their hospitality, but they constrained Him, stranger as He was, to stop and abide with them. At the supper table He reveals Himself to them when He breaks the bread and hands it around. Their eyes are opened and they recognize Him, when immediately He vanishes out of their sight. Their appetite leaves them, and they run back to Jerusalem, despite the darkness and the rough mountains, as the moon, full when He was crucified, had not yet risen.

They find the disciples all in a room barred up through fear of the Jews, but they gladly admit them. They were talking about His resurrection, as He had, in the early morning, appeared to the women and at a later hour to Peter. Then these two disciples tell their thrilling story, confirming the conclusion of His resurrection, when suddenly He stands in their midst with the words, "Peace be unto you," and going around breathes on them all, saying, "Receive ye the Holy Ghost." You have nothing to do but to believe the words of the Savior and the inspired writer, and you will know this was not their sanctification, as backsliders cannot be sanctified till they get reclaimed.

People foolishly say that nobody receives the Holy Ghost but Christians in sanctification. As the Holy

Ghost is the Executive of the Trinity, the Spirit of the Father and the Spirit of the Son, we receive everything from God through His omnipotent agency. If sinners do not receive the Holy Ghost as a Convictor, they will never be convicted, but drop into Hell. If penitents do not receive the Holy Ghost as a Regenerator, they will never be born from above nor enter the kingdom of God. If backsliders do not receive the Holy Ghost as a Restorer, they will make their bed in a backslider's Hell. If Christians do not receive the Holy Ghost as a Sanctifier, they will never be sanctified and never see the Lord (Heb. 12: 14), but backslide and find their doom, with all other backsliders, in the regions of woe. The trouble with the Tongue People is there minification of sanctification, whittling it down to a geometrical point, till there is not enough left to make soup for a sick grasshopper, much less to defeat the devil and bankrupt Hell, which is its glorious prerogative.

(q) When the Lord breathed on them that night and said, "Receive ye the Holy Ghost," He blessedly reclaimed them from their backslidden state in which they had remained all the time He lay in the sepulchre, having no idea that He was the Christ of God, the Redeemer of Israel, the Shiloh of prophecy and the Savior of the world. While, pursuant to their convictions, the Christ was immortal and could not be killed, but would sit down on the throne of David according to the prophecies and rule over the house of Jacob for ever, yet when they saw Him killed by His enemies, they utterly gave up His Christhood, dropping Him down to the plane of the prophets. This was perfectly harmoniacal with the persecutions He endured and the martyrdom which took Him out of the world, as the most of the prophets before Him had suffered martyrdom, and even recently John the Baptist, His forerunner.

While utterly giving up the Christhood of Jesus for the above reasons and relegating Him to the prophets, they unhesitatingly pronounced Him the greatest prophet that had ever been on the earth, because He wrought more mighty works than any of His predecessors. He did not publicly certify His Christhood among the Jews, because they would have crowned Him king on the spot, and the Romans would have killed Him. But it was absolutely important for Him to live those three years in order to launch the Gospel Church, by faithfully teaching His apostles the grand truths of His kingdom. Therefore they were much bewildered with reference to His Christhood, as He did not proclaim it, but left them to their own deductions from His works; whereas, in that very country, Elijah and Elisha had filled the land with all sorts of miracles, even raising the dead.

At 10 A. M., I stood in the city of Nain, where Jesus raised the widow's son from the dead, on the northwestern slope of Mt. Little Hermon. In the afternoon of the same day I stood in the city of Shunem, on the southeastern slope of that same mountain where Elisha raised the son of the Shunammitish woman from the dead.

(r) Reader, have you received your Pentecost? The Tongues People tell you if you do not have their gibberish, you have not been baptized with the Holy Ghost and fire. We find people who have that committing all sorts of sins—drunkenness, adultery, and even infidelity; showing that they are not saved, much less sanctified. It is but the strategy of Satan to cheat you out of your experience and your immortal soul. "Let him that thinketh he standeth take heed lest he fall." (1 Cor. 10:12.) Many of our dear Holiness people have gone after the gift of tongues and lost their sanctification, like the dog in Æsop's fable, which, carrying in his mouth a piece of meat while walking through the river, seeing his own shadow, which he thought was another dog with a piece of meat in his mouth, jumped at him to get his piece, thus letting go his own and finding himself with none at all. The one he jumped at was only a shadow; the one he had, he let go to get the other, and found himself hungry and with nothing to eat. This is the way Satan is fooling the people out of their experiences by all sorts of new-fangled hoaxes.

There is a third blessing we must all have to live in Heaven. It is glorification, which takes away mortality and infirmity and confers angelic perfection. We cannot get it while in these bodies. The Holy Ghost gives it to all sanctified people synonymously with the evacuation of these mortal tenements. So rest assured, sanctification, which saves you from original sin and fills you with the Holy Ghost, is the blessing you need to give you the victory, and enable you to stand in the hour of temptation and shout glory while the world is on fire. It is the high plane of perfect rest, above clouds, fogs, gnats, mosquitoes and malaria, where Jesus walks with you hand in hand, bearing all your burdens, fighting all your battles, winning all your victories, and giving you a heaven in which to go to Heaven.

"O Brother Godbey, I want more religion." The sanctified experience is the very place to get it; you are at your Heavenly Father's table groaning under all the good things of the Kingdom, with nothing to do but eat till you are satisfied; the angel waiters trooping round you giving you the most summary attention. You have a check on Heaven's bank for everything you need in time and eternity. You have nothing to do but check out all you want. God Almighty is President, Jesus the Cashier, and the Holy Ghost the Teller. Therefore do not be afraid you will break the bank; you cannot do it. The Bible is your check-book, full from lid to lid—33,000 promises. The more you draw, the brighter the smile on the face of the Cashier and the more alert and spry the Teller in pouring out every cent you call for, with a loving query, "Why did you not check for more?"

Sanctification is the biggest thing in all the world and gets bigger as days and years go by, and you grow in grace and the knowledge of the truth. Before you are aware, you find yourself electrified with your glorious balloon ride with Jesus. Some of these days, you will ride into glory before you know it and find yourself talking with the loved ones gone on before and now waiting you on the bright, shining side. Be sure you are ready. You must have the pentecostal baptism of the Holy Ghost and fire, to crucify old Adam, destroy the body of sin, bury him eternally into the death of Christ, fill you with the Holy Ghost, and give you the victory forever. If Satan fools you at this point, he'll defeat you in the arduous conflict and when you leave the world you will find yourself in Hell instead of Heaven.

"Brother Godbey, do tell me what my Pentecost is, so I can know when I get it, whether I had it and when I lose it." As Pentecost was instituted to commemorate the giving of the law, the meaning of Pentecost becomes very simple. It is the execution of the law. "What is that?" The law says, "The soul that sinneth it shall die." The law cannot be broken with impunity. If so, the government of Heaven would fall flat, and anarchy would fill the universe. Jesus, in His wonderful Sermon on the Mount, says, "Think not I have come to destroy the law and prophets, but to fulfill. Heaven and earth shall pass before one jot or tittle shall pass from the law till all be fulfilled."

Satan has filled the great churches of the world in all lands with the awful lying delusion that, because they are under the law and not grace, they can sin with permission. Christ came, bore all of our sins and made a perfect expiation for the whole world, not that the people can evade the law, but that the law may be fulfilled in every case; otherwise damnation is the doom of every soul. In the pentecostal experience the law is executed, and old Adam, the devil nature hereditary in every human being, is crucified and destroyed; thus fulfilling the penalty of the law. The reason why we read nothing about the "old woman" in the Bible is because Adam and not Eve is the representative of every human being. When Satan slew Adam, he slew the whole human race, as they are all unified in Adam; Eve being no exception, she being but a transformation of Adam's rib, therefore she sinned with him, as well as personally.

So your Pentecost is the execution of the law given at Sinai. When the sin personality in your heart is crucified, the law is executed.

Rome, the iron kingdom of Daniel's prophecies, the most prominent nation in all the ages, which ruled the world a thousand years, aye longer than any other nation, crucified her criminals in the most conspicuous places, in order to terrify others. Calvary is in the angle formed by the road running north to Damascus and the one running east to Jericho. So Mount Calvary is the most conspicuous place about Jerusalem. The multitudes have come from the ends of the earth to the great holiness camp-meeting at Pentecost. The accusation of the criminal was always superscribed on the cross above his head, so everyone could know the crime for which he died.

When the Jews condemned Jesus to die for blasphemy in saying He was the Son of God, they found themselves in a dilemma, because they had lost their government and did not have the power of capital punishment. Therefore they had to turn Him over to the Romans to execute Him. Then another dilemma stared them in the face, because blasphemy was not a penal offense in the Roman law, so they had an awful time to adapt the accusation to the Roman administration. This they did (He had often said He was King of the Jews) by charging Him with insurgency against the Roman Government, as no one could be king but Cæsar. When Pilate interviewed Him and asked Him if He was King of the Jews, He responded in the affirmative. Then he asked Him where His army was, as Rome was a great despotism and had no conception of authority without an army. When He responded to him, "My kingdom is not of this world, otherwise My servants would fight for Me," it terribly alarmed Pilate and confirmed the suspicion already on him that Jesus was one of the Roman gods in human form, as reports taught them that their gods often assumed human form and walked upon the earth. So while Jesus was hanging on the cross, His accusation above His head, written in Hebrew, Greek and Latin, was, "THIS IS THE KING OF THE JEWS."

(s) Crucifixion was a disgraceful punishment, and always inflicted for dark crimes, in order to intimidate evil-doers. As Paul was a Roman citizen, they could not crucify him, but decapitated him with the sword. In America hanging is the succession of crucifixion among the Romans. The United States Government never hangs a soldier, because he has enjoyed the honor of fighting for his country. If he is guilty of high treason or some other crime requiring execution, they shoot him.

Jesus became the substitute of every criminal in all the world, perfectly expiating all the sins of commission and omission; of ignorance and intention; whether original or personal, and all the multitudinous infirmities of all ages and nations; thus perfectly satisfying the violated law and so completely clearing up the condemnatory aspect of human iniquity as to preclude the apology of the damnation of a solitary soul.

While this grand truth looks the whole world in the face, let no one say that endless punishment is swept from the field and Universalism becomes orthodoxy. These conclusions do not follow as a legitimate logical sequence; from the simple fact that God saves no soul without the reciprocation and co-operation of the free will. This would dehumanize that soul and utterly defeat the great end for which our glorious Creator has brought into existence immortal intelligences, that He may have fellowship in the celestial universe. While the work of Christ perfectly satisfies the violated law, developing the possibility of universal salvation, it does not force it on any. When Satan fought the battle of Eden and slew our progenitors, he slew us all, because we were all in Adam (1 Cor. 15:22): "In Adam all die, but in Christ all shall be made alive." The death in Adam was a wholesale seminal mortification; whereas the redemption in Christ is purely personal, dealing with individuals.

However, Jesus leaves every one without excuse, by reaching every soul in all ages and nations, in the prenatal state, the very moment soul and body united constitute personality, which is five or six month before the physical birth. So we are all, as you see in the case of the prodigal son and the elder brother, born in our Heavenly Father's house, i. e., in the kingdom of God, and only get out by personal transgression. However, we are born with hereditary depravity in the heart (Ps. 51:5), turning the face away from God; Christians, but in a sinward attitude, so if not turned round and introduced to the Savior, the child goes spontaneously into sin, falling under condemnation and from bad to worse until it drops into Hell, if not reclaimed, from the hogpen or some other place on the road to the bottomless pit. By the wonderful grace of Christ, every human being is born a citizen of the Kingdom, and ought to be converted before the forfeiture of infantile justification, then sanctified to keep from backsliding.

Hence you see the wonderful victories of redeeming grace leave not the shadow of apology for the damnation of a solitary soul, yet salvation in not forced upon anyone. The free will must reciprocate and co-operate all the way through. The regeneration of the sinner, taking away his own sins and giving him a new heart; and the sanctification of the Christian, taking old Adam out of him and filling him with the Holy Spirit, are the great "sine qua nons" which all must have or everything will break down, prove a failure, and Hell will be the doom. Christ has made the perfect expiation and yet not taken away the law; He has only provided for its fulfillment.

There is no compromise with sin anywhere in all the Bible, and if you depend on it, you will lose your soul. God's method is destruction, "therefore we are buried with Him in baptism into death: that, as Christ was raised up by the glory of the Father, so we also shall walk in the newness of life. Knowing this, that our old man is crucified, that the body of sin might be destroyed, that we shall no longer serve sin." (Rom. 6:6.)

(t) This is your Pentecost, i. e., the crucifixion of the sin-man in your heart and that of every son and daughter of Adam's ruined race. Paul, in his bold imagery, calls it the "old man," because it is old as the devil, i. e., the fall of Lucifer. Isaiah 14:12: "How thou art fallen, O Lucifer, the morning star." His glory shone so brilliantly that he enjoyed the honorary cognomen "light-bearer." This evil nature, sin personality, in the heart must be crucified, which is the penalty for sin and corresponds with hanging the criminal in America. That crucifixion destroys the body of sin. They always let the body stay on the cross till it was dead, then they broke the limbs so there could be no artificial restoration of life. This dead body is buried not in water, as people vainly and foolishly think, but into the death of Christ, which is the atonement.

If the "old man" is dead, you will find it out, as he will not move any more. Satan will come to you as he did to Jesus, and find nothing in you belonging to him, then he will just go away. You will never get where Satan does not shoot at you, because that is his business; but you can get out of gunshot, so he will only waste his ammunition, as none of his cannon-balls will reach you. He fishes through my pond every day, but never gets a nibble by a minnow, as nothing in it wants his bait. Yesterday a banker counted twice over each time cheating himself out of twenty dollars despite my telling him meanwhile; yet I persisted in calling his attention until he saw it and thanked me. Satan said, "It is his own mistake; come away and let him alone, for you need the money," but nothing in me had the slightest leaning towards that filthy lucre.

John Wesley says, "A man insults me; instead of anger rising, I feel nothing but love for him. A woman solicits me; instead of feeling lust, I feel nothing but aversion. The people eulogize me; instead of feeling pride, I feel nothing but humility." These illustrations might be multiplied indefinitely, including every conceivable attitude in life.

You will never have perfect and abiding peace and rest while the sin personality abides in your heart. If God would let you enter Heaven with it, it would rise and trouble you there.

(u) This sin-man, old Adam, devil nature, must be crucified, utterly destroyed, and buried into the death of Christ, which is the great and glorious Atonement, so deep that Satan's resurrection trumpet will never reach it. As you see in Romans 6:6, and in many other Scriptures, the baptism of the Holy

Ghost and fire, which Jesus gives, executes this mighty work. That was the Pentecost in Jerusalem and it is yours when you get it. The Holy Spirit will witness to you when you have received your Pentecost, the sin personality being crucified, utterly destroyed, and buried away in the Atonement, the death of Christ, the blessed Holy Spirit, the omnipotent Agent, being the Executive of this stupendous work.

You cannot afford to rest in uncertainty at this point. The supernatural birth and entire sanctification, the baptism Jesus gives with the Holy Ghost and fire, must be certified by the Holy Spirit so indubitably that you know it better than you know you are alive. "Do tell me how to get it." Utterly and eternally abandon everything to God, your will and interest for time and eternity, abiding steadfastly in this complete and perfect submission, till the Holy Ghost witnesses to you that you are wholly given up to God, so clearly that you know it. In this attitude of perfect abandonment, the blessed Holy Spirit will give you all the help you need to believe on Jesus for entire sanctification under the precious cleansing Blood. He will baptize you with the Holy Ghost and fire, thus imparting to you the blessed Executive of the Trinity, whose office is the revelation of the glorified Savior to the soul, so that you keep your eye on Him your only Leader; the Holy Ghost being your only Guide, and the precious Word your only authority.

In this beautiful attitude of God's triple leadership, you can never get wrong; you are as sure of Heaven as if you are in it. If you have not the blessed witness of the Spirit to entire sanctification by the baptism which Jesus gives with the Holy Ghost and fire, the blessed Holy Spirit is on hand to give all needed help to make this utter abandonment in which you have nothing to do but receive your Pentecost by simple faith in Jesus to baptize you and give it to you. Then the Holy Spirit will witness to it and you will abide in perfect rest, a rest so sweet and deep that the troubles of life will never disturb it, as the inward disturbance all died with old Adam, and outward foes can never disturb you because the door is shut against them and you are not going to open it and let them in. Neither will the heavy tread of the grim monster disturb this perfect rest, nor the awful thunders of the Judgment Day, nor the terrible earthquakes of the resurrection morn, nor the mighty sweep of eternal ages.

Reader, have you this rest? Take it **now in Jesus.**

> "Long my yearning heart was trying
> To enjoy this perfect rest,
> But I gave all trying over;
> Simply trusting, I was blest."

CHAPTER XXI.

Moslem Dominion.

Mohammed began to preach in Arabia, A. D. 606. His preaching was rather condemnatory of the people, so they revolted and kicked at it and actually ran him away from Mecca, his native city. On his flight to Medina, chased by his enemies, he took refuge in a cave. They came to it and saw a spider's web built over its mouth and concluded that he was not in it, thinking the time too short for the spider to build the web after his entrance. Oh! what wonderful achievements and revolutions often hang on the smallest and most insignificant providences. That man launched an institution which swept over the Old World like an avalanche, burying everything before it; shaking the nations from center to circumference, deluging the world with blood, and sending millions into an untimely grave. If his enemies had only entered that cave and taken him, many battles would never have been fought and volumes of history never written. But seeing the spider's web they supposed he was not in it, and so went on their way.

Having reached Medina, he began that wonderful book, the Koran, i. e., the Mohammedan Bible, which a hundred and seventy-five millions of people read and believe now. While it endorses the Old Testament and adopts the patriarchs and prophets, it rejects the New; repudiating the Christhood of Jesus, but receiving Him and the apostles as prophets.

Mohammed claims that the archangel Gabriel was his patron, often meeting him and making revelations to him. Eventually, in the dead hours of the night, hearing a noise at his gate and going out, he finds the archangel Gabriel with the donkey which Jesus rode into Jerusalem. He stated to him that God had sent for him, that he might stand before Him and receive His message for the people in this world.

(v) Gabriel told him to mount that donkey and go with him. He found the donkey very skittish and difficult to manage, as he had never been ridden since the days of Christ, 550 years before, because there was nobody on the earth worthy to ride him.

They dashed through trackless ether with meteoric velocity, reaching the first heaven, where he found Adam and Eve, so crippled by the fall that they had gotten no farther. However, quite a host of people of a similar character were there with them, and groups of angels hovering round. Again, they mount and dart along quite a distance, and reach the second heaven, where they find more people and angels and some of the patriarchs and prophets. Then, moving on to the third heaven, they find a more worthy grade and angels of a higher order. Then they move on to the fourth heaven and find many patriarchs and prophets, saints and angels; and on to the fifth, where they find a great number; and finally to the sixth, where they meet a mighty host of patriarchs and prophets, angels, cherubim, seraphim, and heavenly hierarchies.

Then Gabriel looks Mohammed in the face and tells him he can go with him no farther, for he is not worthy, but he will have to go alone to the seventh heaven, to stand before the great God. So Mohammed darts away on Borac with meteoric velocity, dashing on and on, amid rolling worlds, blazing suns and glittering constellations, till a gorgeous splendor rolls its billows of light and glory all around him. It is the unspeakable effulgence flashing out from the majestic throne on which sits the Creator of the universe and the Judge of all worlds.

God proceeds to tell Mohammed that He has sent prophets and patriarchs into the world to persuade men to repent; but their work had been a failure, as all efforts to bring them to repentance by persuasion had proved abortive. Then He proceeds to tell him, "Now I send you, not to persuade them, but to compel them to repent, give up their idols, and worship the only true and living God in all the universe. Though I have sent many patriarchs, prophets, saints and wise men, and my Son Jesus Christ and His apostles to persuade them to repent, yet instead of repenting, they rejected their loving messages with contempt, stoned some of them, beat others, cast them out and slew them in many ways. Therefore I send thee, My last prophet, into the world, not to persuade them, but to compel them. So I put a sword in thy hand, with which to enforce repentance, truth and righteousness on the earth."

(w) This belligerent propagation of religion by sword, spear and battle-ax just suited the barbaric Arabs in the midnight of the Dark Ages. Mohammed's policy took those barbarians with glowing enthusiasm. They sweep over Arabia, enter Egypt, the great leading country of the world and the oldest nation, and it falls before them like the harvest before a multitude of reapers. The bloody wave rolls over the Holy Land, taking Jerusalem, A. D. 634. Then it sweeps over Syria and continues to roll its bloody wave over those countries of Asia and Africa where the apostles had established the Gospel. They sweep through northern Africa—Algeria, Tripoli, Tunis and Morocco—like a cyclone of fire, burning everything before them, and leaving but ruin and desolation in their wake. They cross the Strait of Gibraltar connecting the Mediterranean with the Atlantic ocean (only twelve miles wide), enter Spain and carry everything before them, ringing out the battle-cry, "The Koran and tribute, or death," and killing everybody who did not turn Mohammedan.

Like withering siroccoes they swept their pestilential gales, blighting everything they touched and leaving nought but ruin, death and desolation in their wake, till they overran all Spain, establishing **bloody Mohammedanism** everywhere.

Crossing the Pyrenees, they poured a deluge of blood and fire into France, with their mighty hosts of desperadoes—Arabs, Tartars, Turks, Syrians, Nubians, Copts, Ethiopians—one hundred thousand strong, carrying terror and dismay whithersoever they went. More than a hundred years of victory were perched upon their banners and they verily believed that it would continue till they conquered the world. They had really had no defeat of any consequence in the many countries they had overrun, and as Mohammed claimed that God had sent him to bring the world to repentance with the sword, he thus terrifically utilized the power of death to bring the world to God.

Of course such an enterprise would only be available under the black darkness which then surrounded the whole earth, as the nations of Europe, Asia and Africa (the whole known world at that time), had all gone into barbarism since the fall of Rome, A. D. 476, when the Goths, Huns, Vandals and Heruli, after three hundred years of war, had captured and spoliated the city. As Rome was the only upholder of ancient civilization, with her fall it passed away, schools everywhere going down and learning evanescing from the earth.

When this barbarical army, which had swept over the fairest portions of Asia and Africa, where the apostles had established Christianity, subjugated Spain and poured into France, sanguine of certain victory, Charles Martel, king of France, marshalled his hosts and gave them an awful fight, persistently keeping on and persevering with heroic indefatigability till he conquered them in the battle of Tours, France, A. D. 733. There he received the cognomen "Martel," which means hammer, because he hammered the Saracens till he broke them.

The victory of Tours marked a most notable epoch in the history not only of France, but of the world.

These awful Moslem wars were prophesied by John (Rev. 9th chapter) under the cognomen of the "first woe." There you see seven angels sounded their trumpets one after the other, till we come to the fifth period; the last three trumpets proclaimed calamities so terrific that they are denominated "woes."

(x) The chapter opens with the first woe: "I saw a star having fallen from Heaven who had the key of the bottomless pit." That star is fallen Lucifer (Isa. 14:12): How thou art fallen, O Lucifer, the son of the morning." When the archangel Lucifer, long before man was created, fell in Heaven, he became the devil and was cast out. Here we see that he had the key of Hell. When he set up for himself independently of God, He cast him out of Heaven and made him king of Hell, where he rules now and will forever.

Here we see him open the bottomless pit and locusts pour out, vividly described as having the heads of lions and the tails of great serpents, with scorpions all over them, going forth destroying the people. It says they will continue five months, i. e., 150 days, i. e., 150 years, as in these prophecies days stand for years.

MOSLEM DOMINION. 411

This measures the first great period of the Moslem wars, having for their object the extermination of all the people out of the earth who did not take their new religion—the Koran for their Bible and Mohammed for their prophet. It really looked like they would certainly take the whole world, as they swept on for 150 years an unbroken tide, overrunning everything, and killing everybody who did not take their religion. These great locusts, coming up out of the bottomless pit, with lion heads and mouths pouring out fire, and huge serpentine tails with scorpions all over them, were sent forth to destroy the people 150 years.

When Charles Martel made the long and persistent effort against them, rendezvoused all France and fought till he conquered them, he thus produced a reaction and rolled back the awful tide of death and destruction which had rolled over so many countries, bearing terror, dismay, and destruction in its wake. So finally, in the good providence of God, the Christians, under the leadership of King Charles of France, after long and desperate fighting, achieved the glorious victory of Tours, which revived the hopes of Christendom, which were then very small, as they had been driven out of Asia and Africa, where our Savior and His apostles preached and sealed their faith with their blood.

(y) These Mohammedans had captured Jerusalem and the Holy Land, taken down the Christian church that stood on the site of Solomon's temple, built the Mosque of Omar on that hallowed spot, and taken possession of all the sacred places. When the Christian pilgrims from Europe, going there to worship, saw everything in the hands of our Savior's enemies and how they themselves were often mistreated, the enterprise gradually took hold of them to go and rescue the Holy Sepulchre, the manger in which Jesus was born, and the other sacred places, out of the hands of the infidels, and so to deliver His patrimony from the False Prophet.

After the victory of Tours had turned the tide in favor of Christianity, the project of a Christian crusade, to recover the patrimony of our Savior out of the hands of the False Prophet, spread over Europe. The Pope approved the enterprise, and the saints everywhere seemed led in that direction. Consequently the Pope appointed Peter the Hermit, a flaming holiness evangelist, and Walter the Penniless, both fire-baptised monks, commanding great power and eloquence, to preach the Crusades through Europe. Oh! what a stir they everywhere produced, men, women and children enlisting to go to the Holy Land and fight for the recovery of our Savior's patrimony.

The Crusades lasted two hundred years, spread through Christendom, and finally, A. D. 1099, after two hundred years of fighting, they took Jerusalem, under the leadership of Godfrey of Bouillon. He was a brilliant Christian and a great warrior. I have often had his sword in my hand, which is still preserved in the Church of the Holy Sepulchre in Jerusalem. He must have been a giant, as his sword is so large and heavy. He called it the sword of Christ.

His tomb and that of Baldwin, the first king of Jerusalem, are in the Church of the Holy Sepulchre.

Though the Christian Crusaders fought two hundred years to conquer the Mohammedans and recover the Holy Land, and finally succeeded in capturing Jerusalem and taking possession of Palestine, they only held it eighty-eight years by constant fighting, as the Moslems never did cease from war against them, and finally, under the leadership of the great Saladin, they defeated them in the battle of Hattin, fought on that mountain on the west coast of the Galilean Sea, so that the Crusaders retreated out of Palestine and never got back.

Revelation, tenth chapter, gives this tragical history in brilliant prophecy. John, who represents the Church, sees an angel come down from Heaven and stand with one foot upon the sea and the other upon the land, and lift up his hand and swear by him forever and ever, that time should be no more; meanwhile holding in his hand a little open book. The prophet begs him to let him have the book. He first refuses it, but afterward consents to his importunity, telling him to come and get it, and it will be in his mouth sweet but in his stomach bitter. So he did take the book out of the angel's hand and ate it, and in his mouth it was sweet as honey, but after he had eaten it his stomach was bitter.

As the tenth century had been ushered in, the impression prevailed throughout Christendom that the world would wind up with that century, as it would complete a thousand years. A desire settled down on many Christians to be in the Holy Land when the Lord returned, hence that was a grand inspiration stirring up the Crusaders to go and drive the infidels out of our Savior's patrimony before He returned, and under the powerful preaching of those enthusiastic evangelists, Peter the Hermit and Walter the Penniless, who were sent out by the Pope to preach the Crusades throughout Christendom, and rendezvous the holy armies, to leave Europe, go to Asia, and drive the Mohammedans out of the Holy Land, thus rescuing the Lord's patrimony before His return.

So they fought on those two hundred years, finally taking the city, A. D. 1099, but though they were very enterprising, building churches in different parts of the country, especially on the historic sites, they were finally driven out, leaving a million of Christians bleaching their bones on Asiatic soil, and they have never gotten back, except simply going on pilgrimages, to tarry a short time and come away. Thus the great enterprise of the Holy Crusades, into which all Christendom embarked, and fought so long, finally proved a failure, as they were driven away and the False Prophet still treads that land. The Lord has led me to make four pilgrimages to it in the last sixteen years.

Hence you see how literally Revelation, tenth chapter, has been verified.

While they were rendezvousing the armies, under the powerful preaching of those eloquent, enthusiastic and influential monks, a wave of holy excitement seemed to roll over Christendom, amounting to ecstasy

Moslem Dominion. 415

and rhapsody, carrying everything before it, so men, women and children were leaving their homes and employments to volunteer in the Holy Crusades. Then the book of this prophecy, while they were reading it, was sweet in the mouth; but afterward, when they continued those pilgrimages amid toils, privations, untold sufferings and calamities two hundred years, and finally succeeded, apparently, got possession and established the Holy Roman Empire in Jerusalem and extended it throughout the Holy Land, determined to hold it till the coming of the Lord; yet their enemies never would let them alone to rest in peace, but fought on without a break and at the expiration of eighty-eight years so defeated them that they retreated out of Asia; then the book of prophecy which they had eaten was bitter in the stomach, nauseating them and giving them terrible suffering.

When the news of their signal defeat and the capture of Jerusalem by their enemies reached Rome, Pope Urban fell dead.

CHAPTER XXII.

MOGUL DOMINION.

Saladin was the greatest military chieftain on the globe in his day, the eleventh century, nine hundred years ago. As we travel in the East, we see many grand monuments of his enterprise. He built the mosque on the citadel at Cairo, said to be the finest in the world, 400 feet high, with magnitudinous dimensions, constructed of the finest marble, much of it alabaster. He also built Mosque Rimmon in Damascus, the largest in the world. He commanded the army that so signally defeated the Christian Crusaders on Mount Hattin, west of the Galilean Sea.

While he was the greatest man in the world, though a Mohammedan, he seemed exceedingly humble, generous and kind-hearted. He astonished all the Christians when he defeated them, driving their armies out of Asia, by his wonderful generosity, letting them keep all their church property, which they have to this day. I have repeatedly visited his tomb in Damascus.

Saladin's efficient personal leadership, having no equal on the earth, again gave the pre-eminence to the Moslems, after their signal defeat by Charles Martel in the battle of Tours, which was followed up and ultimately developed into the Holy Crusades, uniting all Christendom in that desperate effort to recover the Holy Land.

The upward trend imparted to the cause of Islam continued to move and spread over the earth till it culminated in the Mogul Empire, founded by Akbar the Great and Tamerlane the Tartar conqueror; the former the statesman, and the latter the warrior, the master spirits of the world, if they were barbarians.

This Mogul Empire brought India to the front of the world as the Moslem power had given Arabia the pre-eminence. Thus we see Egypt first of all in the pre-eminence; then Phœnicia; followed by the Hebrew dominion; then Chaldea, under Nebuchadnezzar, comes to the front of the world. He was soon superseded by the Medo-Persian under Cyrus the Great, which was followed by the Grecian, under Alexander the Great. Ere long this was superseded by Rome, the great iron empire of prophecy. After her fall, A. D. 476, the next country at the front was Arabia, under the leadership of Mohammed, the false prophet. The center of power ere long shifted to India, which reached the front of the world and the leadership of the nations under the mighty Moguls. Result from the great impetus imparted by Saladin and afterward perpetuated by Tamerlane, was that the Mohammedans revived and became stalwart in all the earth, and sanguine in their aspirations to verify the meaning of the banner under which all their armies were fighting, i. e., the Crescent. The growing moon, as you know, is first seen when new, a simple thread luminous from the sun, and gradually growing till she becomes a full orb. The Crescent is the Turkish flag to-day. In the beginning it signified that, starting out from nothing, their power would gradually increase until it took the whole world and would abide forever.

(a) The Mohammedan religion is very simple, in contra-distinction to the infinitesimal complications of paganism. The Brahman priests of India preach three hundred and thirty millions of gods. The empire has three hundred millions of people. So you see the Hindu religion has a god for every citizen and thirty millions besides for all foreigners that may sojourn in the land. The Moslem faith has but one great dogma, i. e., there is one God and Mohammed is His prophet. The minaret is built high over every mosque, so the priest can climb up and proclaim aloud the above creed five times a day, which is the signal for all the people to turn their faces toward Mecca, their holy city, and pray to God and Mohammed.

As they propagated their religion by the sword, they slew all heathens, Christians and everybody else who did not accept the Koran with the simple creed, one God and Mohammed His prophet.

Revelation 9:1-12 gives the first woe, which we have expounded in the preceding chapter on the Moslem dominion. This is the second woe (Rev. 9: 13-21), and you have it brilliantly and terrifically revealed. There is but one more woe, as there are only three and two of them are already passed. The third will soon be here, and it will prepare the way for the Millennium by eliminating out of the world all the unsavables and incorrigibles.

You see from Daniel and John that this momentous work will be wrought by the destroying angels (Dan. 7:9) and the Armageddon Wars (Rev. 19th chap.).

(b) This great second woe which came on the earth during the Mogul dominion, as you here read, followed the sounding of the sixth trumpet and the angel thus commands them to go and loose the four angels bound in the great River Euphrates. Those four angels are the four Turkish sultans bordering on that river, which are always stirred up for the great and universal conflict.

The time is here given as a year, a month, a day and an hour. That a prophetic day is a year, we find abundant proof. Daniel said (9th chap.), "There shall be seventy weeks after the founding of the second temple by Nehemiah, Ezra and Zerubbabel, till Messiah be cut off." History shows up the fact that it was just 490 years till Christ was nailed to the cross. You know seventy weeks are 490 days. Count up the year, month, day and hour and it just gives you about four hundred years.

Oh, how terribly Christianity has been tested and tried on the earth! The first woe runs 150 years, and the second 400 years, equaling together 550 years during which the False Prophet has fought Christianity with all his might, sanguine that they might succeed in its extermination from the earth. Here the warriors are enumerated to myriads and myriads i. e., two hundred millions, and it says, their power is in their mouths and in their tails. They are described as having tails like serpents, biting and destroying the people. The Scythian warriors were so skilled in the exercise of archery that, while riding at full speed, they would turn round on their horses and shoot with unerring precision, thus mowing down their pursuers, and making their defeat as fatal as their attack. Thus the four hundred years rolled away and they had spread their conquest over all the earth except northwestern Europe.

(c) Finally, A. D. 1683, they coiled their grand army of three hundred thousand veterans around Vienna, Austria, then the strongest city in Christendom, perfectly sanguine of success. They cut off all ingress and egress, but those imprisoned succeeded in getting word to Poland, at that time one of the great powers of Europe, and though she then relieved Austria, the latter afterward, to her shame, destroyed the Polish nationality, obliterating her from the escutcheon of nations.

At that time John Sobieski was at the head of Poland's affairs. Not only was he a great warrior, but a noble Christian, as the Poles were a very godly people. At once, responsively to the call of the Viennese, he proceeded to stir everything and to rally his warriors with the greatest possible expedition, therefore he succeeded in the rendezvous of seventy thousand Poles for the relief of Vienna. They hastened with all expedition, as the case was one of immergency. Arriving at Vienna on the Sabbath, at 4 P. M., Oct. 12, 1683, he delivered his army a powerful speech, in which he expressed a determination to relieve Vienna or leave his body on the field. He delivered them all the battle-cry which they were to shout while making the assault: "Not unto us, O Lord, but unto Thee be the glory!" Then he leads his host at sweeping gallop, shouting this battle-cry at the top of his voice. So they all dash violently against the Saracen phalanx with irresistible impetuosity, dashing through them with terrible havoc, blood and slaughter, and pouring into the city.

(d) It so happened in the providence of God that it was the time of full moon. She arose above the eastern horizon with her grand and beautiful full orb, inspiring all the Musselmen with vociferous shouts of victory because the growing moon is their banner, and as she gradually grew to fullness, so they believed that they would gradually prolong their conquest till they would take the whole world, all nations turning Mohammedans, giving up all their idols, worshipping the one God, and receiving unanimously His greatest, best and last prophet, Mohammed.

That vast army of three hundred thousand was utterly illiterate, knowing nothing about astronomy. Therefore when the earth came between the sun and the moon (as it was total eclipse and the earth so much bigger than the moon, she utterly hid her from view), when those ignorant, superstitious Musselmen saw the striking phenomenon, it scared them terribly, so that they screamed everywhere, "Do you not see?

God has forsaken us and our banner is fading from the sky!"

Thus panic seized them, their hearts melted within them, and they stampeded from the field, consternation prevailing more and more, and dismal affright settling down on them despite all the arduous efforts of their officers to rally them to the conflict and get them to stand the fire of the foe. The result was that the grand army of the Orient, flushed with a thousand victories and enriched with all the spoils of conquest, yielding to the panic, stampeded for their lives, leaving the very earth groaning beneath the burden of the spoils left on her bosom; not only herds and flocks superabounding, but silver and gold and all the spoils which they had gathered from a thousand conquered cities. Thus the Moslem tide that had been rolling on and on without a break four hundred years, and almost inundated the whole world, dashed against an impassable obstruction, rebounded, rolled back, and has been ebbing ever since.

(e) Daniel the eighth chapter is all on Mohammedanism, describing the False Prophet as a little horn, rising up and becoming great and towering and doing wonders, filling the world with wizards, witches, sorcerers and magicians. This day there are one hundred seventy-five millions of them in the world. I have been traveling among them the last sixteen years and I find them literally as Daniel prophesied.

The reason why Mohammed is described as a little horn is because his country, Arabia, though very large in area, is mostly sandy desert and has always been politically weak. While Daniel describes him as wonderfully magnifying, spreading out, towering, and subduing everything before him, so that nothing could stand against him (v. 25), yet he says, "He shall be broken without hand." How signally has this prophecy been verified and it is constantly receiving its fulfillment.

All Christendom united, fought two hundred years to break the grip of the False Prophet on the Holy Land, and, though with terrific loss of life and everything else involved in the perils of war, they took possession of Jerusalem and the Land A. D. 1099, yet the Moslems never ceased fighting, and at the end of eighty-eight years so signally defeated them in the battle of Hattin as to drive them not only out of the Holy Land, but out of Asia. Why was it? Daniel had prophesied that the False Prophet should not be conquered by human power, but by God's own hand. In this wonderful and notable battle, God actually, by His own providence in the total eclipse of the moon, came and affrighted them almost to death, until those three hundred thousand veterans, flushed with a thousand victories and with perfect confidence of success, having no idea that anything could stampede them, were so panic-stricken that they fled precipitately from the field, all dashing pell mell for dear life, and leaving the earth groaning beneath the spoils. Then and there God began to break the False Prophet, and He has been breaking him ever since.

(f) As they had been on the victory side four hundred years, carrying everything before them, and had really conquered the known world except the wilds of northwestern Europe, into which the few surviving Christians had fled for refuge, when they coiled around Vienna, the strongest citadel in Christendom, they felt perfectly confident of success and verily believed that, with her fall, all Christendom would surrender. But since that signal defeat, a whole dozen great empires and kingdoms have been wrested out of the hand of the False Prophet, Turkey alone surviving. She is the only upholder of the Moslem faith on the face of the earth, and she would not stand twenty-four hours were it not for the jealousy of her Christian neighbors, watching and rivaling each other, lest when the "turkey" is eaten up, they may not receive their share of the spoils, as each one wants the biggest piece.

This breaking of the False Prophet made a decisive advancement two years ago, when a revolution shook Turkey from center to circumference. The secret Committee of Union and Progress, cognomened "The Young Turks," revolutionized the government, imprisoning the old Sultan in his harem, taking the government into their own hands, forming a constitution and running it their own way, without the knowledge or co-operation of the Sultan. The truth of it is, the Sultan is dethroned, and this day a prisoner for life, the sceptre having departed, never to return. This is a grand epoch in the fulfillment of that notable prophecy (Dan. 8:25): "He shall be broken without hand."

(g) "God sits upon the circle of the heavens,

turns the seasons around, and keeps His hand upon everything, making the wrath of man to praise Him, and restraining the remainder of wrath." When He cannot make the wrath of man to fulfil the prophecies and praise Him, He just puts His foot on it and stops it.

"Brother Godbey, how can the awful falsehoods and cruelties of Mohammedanism glorify God?" By way of castigating corrupt Christianity. When Mohammed arose, A. D. 606, Christianity in the great East was awfully corrupt, not only having degenerated into dead formality and hollow hypurisy, but plunged deep into idolatry, having their images everywhere in their churches and bowing down before them, in positive violation of the second commandment of the Decalogue. Mohammed was the scourge of God, in His permissive providence, to chastise fallen Christianity in all the earth.

During the first three centuries of the Christian era, while they persecuted the Christians with all their might, doing their utmost to exterminate them from the earth—burning them at the stake and feeding them to the wild beasts in the Coliseum for the entertainment of the cruel multitudes thronging that largest theater ever built on the earth—Christianity remained pure, preaching sky-blue regeneration, entire sanctification, and the return of Jesus to the earth, with all her might. While they thought that they could certainly kill them all, that was the very thing to spread it over all the world, for the Christians went everywhere preaching the Word with all their might.

In A. D. 321, even the Emperor Constantine got

gloriously converted, to the unutterable astonishment of everybody. The persecutions had gone on by the authority of the Emperor, but while marching his army under the ensigns of the pagan gods, he sees before him, suspended in the blue sky, a golden cross radiating, the brilliant beams of an oriental sun, and superscribed "En tonto nika" (Conquer by this). He halts his army, takes down the pagan banners, and lifts up the cross to lead his army. His motives were perfectly pure, but Satan took advantage of them as the years rolled on, to fill religion with politics, which always ruins it.

God must have a true people on the earth at every cost. While Mohammedanism has deluged the world with blood, whitened it with bones and filled it with sin, yet it teaches a pure, hard monotheism, i. e., that there is but one God and He alone is to be worshiped. As Mohammed claimed that God had sent him commissioned from Heaven to propagate His religion by the sword, they killed everybody who would not give up their idols and content themselves to worship God alone.

(h) I am just now out of Jerusalem and the Bible lands, having returned from my fourth tour in the Orient in the last sixteen years. The Roman Catholics have 275,000,000 members; the Greek Catholics, 125,000,000. These four hundred millions of Catholics all have their churches supplied with graven images, and it was so before the rise of Mohammed, while there are nine hundred millions of heathens in the world bowing down before their idols. Mohammed couldn't see any difference between them, as they all had their images, and it appeared to him just like they were all worshiping idols. Therefore they treated them all alike, giving them their choice—to receive the Koran for their Bible, Mohammed for their prophet, and give up their idols, or perish.

While wicked people lose their souls on account of their sins, God makes them, and everything else, a blessing to His true people (Rom. 8:28): "All things work together for good to them that love God." You see how God actually used this awful, wicked, bloody Mohammedanism to destroy the idolatry which was about to capture His Church, as He must have a true people somewhere, to light the world.

CHAPTER XXIII.

German Dominion.

In 1640, as Prussia had run down in all respects, having long been on the decline, Austria, France and Russia entered into a syndicate, dividing out her territory, each furnishing a quota of soldiers to constitute the union army sufficiently forceful to successfully manipulate the projected dismemberment obliterating her from the escutcheon of nations. Frederick II., the incumbent of the throne of Prussia, a young, awkward, unassuming man, with no character as a military tactician, was looked upon as a mere official figurehead, having nothing in him. Therefore it was the opportune epoch for the long contemplated dismemberment of Prussia; as the Powers of the earth are this day diagnosing and contemplating the dismemberment of China.

Frederick the Great (as this is his cognomen in history, but it was not then, and nobody had a dream that he ever would receive the honorary shibboleth reached by so few), in a way known to none but himself, in the good province of God, succeeded in the invention of a new mode of warfare, paradoxical and unprecedented in the celerity of its movements; strikingly contrasted with the tread-mill "modus operandi" of the old German routine. You have heard the maxim, "Necessity is the mother of invention."

(i) The combination against Prussia was so formidable that his only hope was in his chances to disconcert and upset them by strategy, as an open field fight would settle his destiny at once, confirming the dismemberment of his government and partition of his territory.

Therefore when the grand army of those three great nations united invaded his territory, to make a finale of specifications entered upon in the syndicate, Frederick marched his army out to meet them just as if he had a hundred times as many soldiers, and made a feint at attack on the right wing of the mighty host. When the grand army proceeded to maneuver to meet the assault, and had gotten so far out in their routine plans as to be unable to change their policy, he suddenly changed his, and poured a literal avalanche on the left wing, now weakened by the concentration on the right; assaulting them so violently that, breaking the ranks and sweeping everything before him, he actually defeated them and put them on the stampede before their comrades could right about face and come to their relief. The result was confusion, so reckless and precipitate as soon to become hopelessly incorrigible, developing irremedial bewilderment and culminating in the capture of multitudes from each army, and the retreat of all who could get away.

The great generals they had on the field did hardly

believe the issue that supervened; they mutually counted and said it was a lapse on their part, and they would know how to watch in the future, and would certainly get the gentleman all right next time. So they took ample time to make deliberate preparations, greatly enlarging their armies in order to make sure and have enough to surround him with a thousand-file league, and so settle the matter in a short way. Eventually they came again. This time Frederick made his feint on the left, and they proceeded to move their forces, wisely and deliberately, putting the battle in array to make a sure thing of it. After they had gotten under march, orders had been given, and they were moving on heroically to meet him, they were so many and he had so few that they had to concentrate.

(j) Quick as the flight of an eagle, he changed his tactics, and poured all his forces on the right wing, now depleted for the concentration on the left, moving so precipitately as to utterly disconcert that old German routine; breaking the phalanx, capturing a big lot, and developing such an utter confusion as to beggar all efforts to hold them in check and to restore order. It got worse and worse till regularity was really out of all consideration; the mighty host being so confused that they could do nothing but try to take care of themselves. Frederick captured a great host of soldiers and officers and among them eleven generals, whom he received to his own headquarters, saluting them with the utmost kindness, ministering to them with his own hands like a **loving** brother and entertaining them like kings; meanwhile apologizing for not being prepared to render them more comfortable; observing, "Gentlemen, you must excuse me, as I did not expect you to come to see me so soon, nor in so large numbers."

The effect of this great battle at Leno was the knowledge of the fact that they had actually encountered the greatest military chieftain on the globe, to them an unutterable surprise, and a still greater surprise to Frederick himself; the events and environment and results showing up the fact that he was the greatest man in the world, though nobody knew it till those terrible ordeals supervened, developing the wonderful availability hitherto lying occult in the man. He was the Jehu of the political world, though he knew it not; neither did anybody else.

(k) When the prophet Elijah fled from Jezebel, because she so heroically threatened to have him killed, and he knew that she was the ruler of Israel in the name of her stupid husband, he ran far away into Arabia to Mt. Horeb, where God gave the law to Moses for all Israel, and which He had raised him up to restore. There while praying in the cave a tornado rushes by, tearing trees out by the roots and sweeping everything before it. Then an awful earthquake comes by, with heavy tread rending rocks, opening chasms and crashing the mountain. Then a hurricane of flaming fire moves by. God was not in the tornado, nor in the whirlwind, nor in the fire; i. e., the God of grace was not in it, though the God of nature was, in great power.

Then, covering his head with his mantle, Elijah stands in the mouth of the cave and hears a still small voice (in which he recognizes the God of grace), telling him to go to Israel and call Elisha, the Jordan farmer, to his own succession; to anoint Hazael to be king over Syria, and Jehu to be king over Israel. Therefore he walks all the way back (a journey of forty days), passes by Elisha plowing with twelve yoke of oxen (not to one plow, but to twelve plows running on his farm); and throwing his mantle on his shoulders, moves on.

Elisha understood it, and responds in the affirmative, "All right, I will leave my farm and go, but hold on till we offer sacrifice to the Lord;" then, turning back, he sacrifices a yoke of the oxen to the Lord. Then he leaves his farm forever, and goes with Elijah to preach the everlasting Gospel, to receive his mantle and perpetuate his work when the chariot lowers, and he, mounting, rides away to Heaven.

Meanwhile Jehu, with his staff officers, is in his room at Ramoth-Gilead, when a young prophet (sent by Elijah) walks in, taps him on the shoulder, and says to follow him into a back room. There, taking out a vial of oil, he pours it on Jehu's head with these words, "In the name of Elijah's God, I anoint thee king of Israel;" then leaping out at the back door, he runs with all his might (as he would have been killed if found out). Jehu walks back into the room where his officers are all waiting, who say to him,

What did that crazy fellow want?" (they still call the Lord's prophets crazy). He says, "He is not crazy, but is the Lord's prophet, and he anointed me to be king over Israel." Knowing that with him it was a word and a blow, every officer takes off his himation (outer garment), in contra-distinction to the tiphoon, which they wore next to the body, as they only had the two); for him to walk over (the most significant Oriental method of manifesting perfect submission).

Then Jehu shouts, "Every man to his chariot!" (giving no order to the infantry as they could not keep up). Quickly as the fire company, every man runs to his chariot and in a moment they're off, at sweeping gallop, Jehu in the lead.

Meanwhile Azariah, king of Jerusalem, is visiting Joram, king of Israel, in his palace at Jezreel; a sentinel standing on the watch-tower, looking in all directions to espy an approaching troop and to give notification. Jehu and his army are coming so rapidly that the dust rises in a cloud, which the sentinel recognizes far away, and so shouts, "A troop cometh!" Joram orders a courier to go at full speed and meet them. The sentinel now sees the troop and watches the courier till he meets him and sees him fall in with them. Then he shouts, "He meets them, but comes not again." (Jehu on his arrival roared at him, "Fall in line or you are a dead man in a minute," and so he did and came along with them.) Joram is alarmed and orders another courier to go with all speed. Now the troop is in plain review and the sentinel shouts, "The driving is like that of Jehu, he driveth furiously." The second courier meets him, and Jehu forces him into line. The sentinel shouts, "he meets the troop, but cometh not again."

They are getting so nigh that something must be done, so the two kings, with their bodyguards and commandable men, mount their chariots and start off to meet the troop drawing very nigh as they're driving so rapidly. Then Jehu, rising up in his chariot, shoots the king of Israel through his body with an arrow and he drops dead in his chariot. The king of Jerusalem, taking fright, wheels round and flies for his life, Jehu after him, and he kills him while running round the garden house. Then, looking up, Jehu sees Jezebel looking out from a third-story window, having painted her face and tired her head, hopeful to captivate Jehu. She shouts to him, "Had Zimri peace after he slew his master?" Jehu roars at the eunuchs by her side, "Throw her down!" They obey, precipitating her down on the stone pavement from the third-story window, so that she is dashed to pieces. Then they all enter the royal palace and eat their dinners.

When they get through, Jehu says, "We must go out and bury that woman, for she is the daughter of a king;" but when they go, they find nothing but her bones and jewelry, the dogs having eaten her flesh, in fulfillment of Elijah's prophecy to Ahab when he met him in Naboth's vineyard after he had been stoned to death by false accusation brought into the court by witnesses whom Jezebel had bribed to bear false witness against him, certifying that they had heard him blaspheme God and the king, the penalty for which was death by stoning according to the law of Moses. In that case the law turned over the property of the culprits to the government by confiscation, so Ahab, the head of the government, had nothing to do but go and take possession of it, as no process of law was necessary.

When the awful tragedy was transacted pursuant to the strategy of Jezebel to get Naboth's vineyard, for which her royal husband was crying like a little child after a toy, God spoke to Elijah and told him to go at once and meet Ahab in Naboth's vineyard. So he did, and looking Ahab in the face, roared like a lion, "The dogs that ate the flesh of Naboth shall drink the blood of Ahab and eat the flesh of Jezebel." Sure enough, when the Syrian soldier, at the battle of Ramoth-Gilead, drew his bow at a venture and God directed the arrow and it killed King Ahab, and they carried him home in his chariot, it was filled with his blood, which the dogs licked when they washed it at the pool. Now the same dogs have eaten the flesh of Jezebel in fulfillment of Elijah's awful prophecy.

The teachers in charge of Ahab's seventy sons in the royal college at Samaria, responsively to the letter received from Jehu, stating, "Your king is dead, select one of his sons, put him on the throne and fight for him;" terribly alarmed, after consulting among themselves and saying, "What can we do against a man before whom two kings have already fallen?" answer, "We will be your servants." Then he writes back to them, "If you mean what you say, send me the heads of all of Ahab's sons without delay." In due time a great camel arrives with a big sack on his back. They lift it off and find in it the heads of all of Ahab's sons, which Jehu piles up on either side of the royal threshold.

(1) Jehu has already written to the priests in charge of Baal's great temple in Samaria to assemble the people to witness his innaugural sacrifices on a certain day. Riding along in his chariot, he meets Jehonadab, the Bedouin chief, and shouts to him, "If thy heart is as my heart, give me thy hand." He reaches it out, Jehu grips it and pulls him up into his chariot, to ride by his side.

On arrival, they find the vast temple packed with the magnates and supporters of the idolatrous kingdom, who had come in to receive their new king, feeling sure that he would worship Baal, as his royal predecessors, from the days of Jeroboam, had done, because he had his innaugural sacrifice in his temple.

Jehu and Jehonadab enter the door, which soldiers, pursuant to orders, at once take into hand, permitting neither ingress nor egress; and walk down the aisle side by side. As all things are ready, they offer the sacrifice. As the smoke ascends in wreathing volumes and the rich perfume fills the temple, oh, what roaring shouts ascend and reverberate from the surrounding mountains, "Long live our good King Jehu!" Then the soldiers come in, close the doors after them, and keep them diligently, permitting no one to escape and begin the work of death, cutting them down on all sides till the temple flows with blood—with blood to swim in—and not one survives.

Thus Jehu cuts off opposition to his coronation, enthronement and administration, by having all the influential aristocracy, servitors of the idolatrous government, cut off. The result was he reigned over Israel twenty-eight years.

(m) Idolatry had proved the ruin of Israel; Jeroboam, who led off the revolt of the ten tribes, having set up two golden calves for the people to worship, one at Bethel, the other at Dan; i. e., at either terminus of his kingdom, so the people would not have to go to Jerusalem to offer sacrifice. His successors, Zimri, Omri, Ahab and Joram, and their confederates, all revelled in gross idolatry, so provoking the righteous judgment of God that the sword never departed from the royal family, and that awful prophecy of Elijah, which he spoke to Ahab when he met him in Naboth's vineyard, certifying that every male identified with his family should be cut off, was signally fulfilled in the decapitation of his seventy sons in the royal college pursuant to the order of Jehu.

They had no abiding peace, but constant perturbations, their capital changing three times from Shechem to Tirzah and thence to Samaria.

The solution of this incorrigible predilection for Baal-worship and other phases of gross idolatry was the near proximity of Baalbec, the capital and metropolis of Baal-worship in all the world. It is so near that the people of Israel could go and see the wonderful pomp and pageantry displayed, the grand processions and sumptuous festivals in which they were so delighted, and that popular religion had no cross, no yoke of Christ to keep them out of Bacchanalian revelries "ad libitum" and "ad infinitum" (freely and forever). Oh, how carnality loathed the law of the Lord, which made no compromise with sinful pleasures!

In that Oriental clime, the sky is so clear, and the sun shines with a brilliancy unknown in the Western world, therefore the sun god was the most popular divinity in all the world the first 4,500 years.

Cain was the great patriarch of natural religion, with no blood to redeem and no cross to bear, but a religion that interferred with none of the carnal pleasures.

God sent His wonderful prophets, Elijah and Elisha, to spend their lives in a heroic effort to restore the law and bring the people back to it, filling the whole world with stupendous miracles wrought through their instrumentality.

(n) Frederick the Great was the Jehu of the political world in his day. God would not let them blot out Germany, while the fervent, prevailing prayers of Luther, Melancthon, Zwingle and their conferees where still burning on the altar before Him. He has wonderfully used Germany to preach and expound His Word and to evangelize the world.

When I graduated in college fifty-two years ago, I proceeded to ransack the world for books and gather up a library from the ends of the earth at a cost of a thousand dollars. I sent to Germany for my whole Bible, in parallel columns, Hebrew, Greek, Latin and German, all before my eye at every opening. It has been my life study. King James' translation, though a great blessing in its day three hundred years ago, has, in the New Testament alone, two thousand errors. About all the heresies in doctrine now paralyzing the Church and sending millions to Hell originated from errors in translation, as there was so little learning in the world three hundred years ago, and during the long roll of a thousand years when not one man in a thousand nor one woman in twenty thousand could read or write, so, much error crept into the Scriptures.

The New Testament which King James' committee translated was written off by hand about the close of the fourteenth or beginning of the fifteenth century, and they had had all that time since the apostolic age to accumulate error. Meanwhile God had the pure, precious Word from the apostolic pen safe in the monastery of St. Catherine on Mount Sinai, built in the second century to commemorate the beginning of the law and discovered by Tischendorf, the faithful German saint, in 1859, the very year I graduated in college. This great scholar and noble pilgrim spent his life roaming over the Bible lands and hunting everything that could throw light on the Bible. King William of Germany, the most enterprising Christian sovereign in his day, furnished all the money to defray his traveling expenses and to pay the thousands of men whom he hired to dig in the ruins of cities, excavating to find everything that would throw light on the precious Word.

His attention had been arrested by the great parchment rolls in an old closet in the convent, so old that you could not see a letter on them to save your life, and so brittle that any effort to decipher them would have broken them into smithereens, and have ruined them forever. They had to lie there till the science of chemistry was discovered and the art of printing invented, as all the arts which now run the world by machinery came out of the sciences, in which Germany is in the lead.

While gazing on these venerable parchments in 1859, Tischendorf's attention was especially magnetized by one which bore all the testimonies of great antiquity. As no human eye could see a letter on them, they could have no idea what they were, as all books were written on parchment and rolled up. Just as God on that same mountain spoke to Moses, so He spoke to Tischendorf, while looking on that great old parchment, "This is Mine." Then he proceeded at once to buy it from the monks who kept the convent, who are always very jealous of relics. They positively refused to sell it, and it seemed that he was at the end of his rope. Pursuant to the maxim, "Every man has his price" (which is not true; I have none and cannot be bought; it is too late, Jesus has already bought me with His precious blood, so I am not for sale any more), Tischendorf bids higher and higher, till they can stand it no longer, but close in with him, receive his money and deliver him the parchment roll. It was the king's money which the man of God used constantly those forty years, amounting to a princely fortune. The Christian world never did know its indebtedness to King William and Tischendorf.

Now he throws his arms around it, returns to Germany after an absence of forty years, and commits it to those shrewd chemists who saturated it with their powerful alkalis, whose normal effect was to soften it up, nimble as a green hide. It was a great roll of sheepskins, having been nicely dressed, superscribed and rolled up. God in His wonderful providence, gave me a copy of the first book made from the parchment, and I have been using it all my life in the pure, original Greek, to the exclusion of all translations. A man who can drink at the spring would rather drink there than out of a bucket, even though he has carried the water himself. Responsively to the importunities of the Holiness people, I have translated for the benefit of the millions who cannot get to the spring, but I do all my drinking at the fountain.

CHAPTER XXIV.

SWEDISH DOMINION.

Four hundred years ago, Sweden controlled the Baltic Sea, as Britain now the Mediterranean. For that reason she is somewhat in the way, of other countries depending upon that beautiful little sea for their water outlet.

In 1687 it so happened that their king, Charles XII., was a minor, only eighteen years old, apparently a gawky stripling. Consequently the kingdom was in the hands of senators, serving as royal regents till the king reached his majority. Poland, Denmark and Russia all entered into a conspiracy to dismember the kingdom, partition the territory, and obliterate that venerable commonwealth from the escutcheon of nations. When the news reached the people, they received it as a death-knell, which it really was to their nationality. It seemed as if the angel of doom had come down from Heaven with his mighty trumpet, blowing it vociferously, and the dead were all rising and with the living, climbing the firmament to stand before the great white throne. Ominous gloom settles on every countenance. The merry laugh gives way to groans, sobs, and cries. They gather in the statehouse obviously for the last time till it shall be occupied by strangers. They are talking over their troubles, weeping, wailing, fasting, and praying, as they look into their national sepulchre and behold their winding-sheet.

(o) The boy king is with the crowd, but nobody expects anything from him. They weep over him as a child of sorrow and trouble, when he surprises all by rising and speaking, "Am I not king of Sweden?" "Oh, yes, my dear boy," is the response of many, "but what can you do?" "Give me the army and the navy and turn over the government into my hands, and I will show you what I will do."

It was death anyhow, and they had nothing to lose by giving the lad a chance, but everything to gain. Therefore they turned it all over to him and said, "Son, we pray for you night and day." Before those three great nations had time to rendezvous and organize the union army, to come take possession of the government and divide out the territory among the three, the boy dashed off with his army and conquered old Saxony, adjacent to Sweden. Then moving on before the others get ready to help, he pushes his conquest so expeditiously that he conquers all Denmark and adds it to his own country. Then he booms ahead, enters Poland with an army vastly enlarged under the encouragement of Saxony and Denmark added to Sweden, and he has an unbroken tide of victories until he overruns Poland and takes her in. Then he has nothing to do but to invade big Russia at his leisure.

With that the whole world wakes up to a thing of which they never dreamed, and opens their eyes to recognize the boy king as the greatest military chieftain on the globe. It was never so surprised as to find a beardless boy at the front of all nations, the master spirit of the globe, the greatest conqueror on the earth. And while it was the unutterable surprise of the nations, he himself was more surprised than anybody else; his greatness stole a march on him and captured him in his striplinghood, thus bringing Sweden and her boy king to the front of the world and making them the sensation of the nations.

(p) What is the solution? Why, those dear old Swedes prayed through to Heaven, and got hold of the omnipotent Arm, who can conquer through a child as easily as though a matured giant, as you see so wonderfully illustrated by David at the battle of Elah, when he slew the giant Goliath, and won the victory for all Israel.

Twenty-seven years ago, good old sanctified Bishop McTyere, of the M. E. Church South, presiding over my Conference, "per se" took me out of it, and put me in the evangelistic work, extra legally. As we had no evangelist and no such appointment, and consequently there was no way for him to give me any temporary support because I had no people, and simply could be a helper of the pastors, consequently he consulted me before he proceeded, telling me that he needed an evangelist, and felt impressed that I was the man, and with my consent, he would take me out of my Conference and give me the whole connection (which means the world) as my field of labor. I responded, "Bishop, I am here to take any appointment you give me; follow the Lord freely. As to support, I am more than satisfied with the Lord alone, since He has promised to feed me like the birds and clothe me like the lilies." So then and there he gave me the world for my circuit, and I have been traveling ever since; times immemorial preaching from the Atlantic to the Pacific, from the Gulf to British America, and four times having traveled and preached in Europe, Asia and Africa, circumnavigating the globe; preaching in both hemispheres and the islands of the sea, and never so much as insinuating any financial help. God has been everything to me; better than all the financial boards.

In my evangelistic peregrinations with all nations, I must turn over the banner of hospitality and benefaction to dear old Sweden. In all lands the Swedes have never been too poor to take me into their rented rooms, lodge, feed and help me press the battle and save souls. They have actually spoiled me, so I everywhere feel perfectly at home among the Swedes. They seem to me to stand on the top of hospitality, brotherly kindness, generosity, and superabounding beneficence. In the cities, where rent is so high and lodging so scarce, they come to me, give me the street and number, and tell me the cottage chamber is always ready.

Therefore I can explain the mystery of how the

stripling king tramped over the Triple Alliance of those three great nations, which had already agreed upon the division of their territory and were marshalling their armies to put all quibbles to everlasting quiescence, blotting out their nationality, though one of the oldest in the world, and relegating them with the nations of by-gone nations which you can no longer find on the face of the earth, as they have evanesced into nonentity.

CHAPTER XXV.

FRENCH DOMINION.

When a student in college, I read Cæsar's history of his own conquests in Gaul (now France), subjugating the great nations and organizing them into a Roman colony, two thousand years ago.

As the centuries rolled along and those barbaric nations were ousted from their moorings by the Roman armies, they became migratory, the aborigines (mostly Helvetians) migrated and the Francs (from the land of the Rohn) immigrated into the delightful and fertile Gallic plains, became the dominant people, and absorbing the surviving aborigines, developed into the great French nation.

Paris, their capital, has been pronounced the most beautiful city in the world. It is in the center of a great rich plain, on either side of the beautiful, limpid Seine, bearing on his swelling bosom the commerce of this mighty nation out into the great Atlantic ocean, over which it goes to the ends of the earth. They claim a population of three millions. It is built in the form of a star, radiating out from the center in all directions, thus giving indescribable beauty when you stand on a lofty tower in the center and look out to every point of the mariner's compass and contemplate the stellate symmetry, splendor and glory as it radiates far away till the eye is eclipsed in ether blue, the sky dropping down and resting on the fertile fields, smiling gardens and cozy mansions in all directions.

The French kings traced their genealogy far back into the mystic ages of remote antiquity, when they dwelt on either bank of the beautiful Rohn. From ages immemorial, they imbibed an awful heresy hatched in the bottomless pit and withering and blighting kings and subjects in all lands. That heresy is cognomened "The divine right of kings." The most eminent in the royal family was Louis XIV., who uttered these words, "If a man is born a subject, he has nothing to do with the kingdom; God will manage him." That is the very essence of Hell-hatched heresy.

Satan lost his spiritual life and glory, when a brilliant archangel, by setting up independently, thus becoming the rival of God. He is still in that attitude, doing his utmost to play God on the people; to pass himself for God. That is the reason why God calls him "the god of this age." (2 Cor. 5:17.) We are living now in Satan's age which will continue till the apocalyptic angel (Rev. 21:4) shall descend and arrest him, lead him out of the world, like a common criminal, and lock him up in Hell. Now take Louis XIV. assuming that a man is born a subject and has nothing to do, as God will manage him. "God is no respecter of persons."

All men are born free and equal. The very assumption that, if a man is born a subject, he has nothing to do with the king, turns over the government to Satan who is ready to pass himself for God, take you by the throat, and bind you in adamantine chains.

God wants to give us all His own freedom, which is the only real freedom in all the universe; everything else under that cognomen is Satan's counterfeit. God is free to do everything good and nothing bad, and He gives that very glorious freedom to every soul that will take it. He has to get out of the devil's slavery to take it; in this God is ready to give him all the help he needs, to break his slavish chains and set him free. Reader, are you free?

(q) As human government deteriorates with the run of the centuries down the stream of time, the French kingdom, founded on this political heresy, denominated "the divine right of kings," got worse and worse, till it ultimated in a political volcano bound to explode. It had drifted down to the deplorable attitude, when one-third of all the real estate belonged to the nobility and was free from taxation; another third belonged to the Roman Catholic Church, and was free from taxation; while the last third belonged to the laboring people and they had all the taxes to pay, burdens to bear and government to support. You see in that case a break was bound to come, no possible defalcation about it. It did come, A. D. 1789; when the political volcano actually exploded, tearing everything to pieces and rolling a bloody revolution over the land like a mighty sea.

The awful corruption of the Roman Catholic Church had driven many people into infidelity, led on by the master spirits of the nation—Tom Paine, Voltaire, and their disciples. They were great writers, through speech and pen doing their utmost to destroy Christian faith and take the Bible out of the world. Voltaire wrote his prophecy predicting that in a hundred years from that date there would not be a Bible in the world. When the hundred years rolled around, the very room in which he wrote that prophecy was a Bible depository. J. J. Rousseau was another brilliant infidel writer.

Consequently during the revolution they tore everything to pieces, the infidel philosophers got the government into their hands and managed things in their own way. They abolished the Sabbath, proclaiming every tenth day for recreation and rest. They closed the churches against all religious worship, using them as lecture rooms and playhouses. They sent men throughout the entire country, to superscribe on every graveyard, "Death is an eternal sleep." They had everything in their own hands three and one-half years, which time is known in history as the "Reign of Terror."

They were so suspicious toward the people lest they might be disloyal to them that they encouraged informers, and would take up people, report them as unfavorable to their government, imprison and kill them.

A man by the name of Guillotine invented a machine in the shape of an old style cutting-box, convenient for the decapitation of a person at a single stroke. During that awful Reign of Terror a million of people, men, women and children, lost their heads on the guillotine. It got worse and worse till the people became desperate and reckless, as they knew not what minute, pursuant to some evil report, they would be hurried away and have their heads cut off. They got so they did not care if they lived or died, so they rose up en masse and slew the terrorists—Danton, Murat, and Robespierre—the infidel triumvirate who ruled the nation.

(r) Here we see the fulfillment of Revelation 11th chapter, when the two witnesses were slain, lay dead three days and a half, then revived and flew up to Heaven. It says the two witnesses, the two olive trees; the tame olive tree (the Jewish Church), and the wild (the heathen world). Under the Gospel they get gloriously saved and united, thus they represent the two great works of the Holy Ghost in the heart, regeneration and sanctification. They are the two candlesticks in the two courts of the temple; the outer, the justified experience, and the inner, the holy of holies, the sanctified experience. The Word also says that, if you trouble them, fire will come out of the mouths and burn you up. That is true of the two great works of the Holy Ghost. When people get born from above and open their mouths in red-hot testimony, neither men nor devils can stand against them. When they get baptised with the Holy Ghost and fire, it is pre-eminently true that nothing can withstand the fiery testimony that goes out of their mouths.

In these prophecies, a day stands for a year, therefore the three and a half days precisely harmonize with the Reign of Terror in France, which represents the world, because Napoleon brought France to the front and held it there twenty-five years.

When, at the close of three and one-half years, the people rose up and killed the tyrants, then they returned to their government, re-opened the churches, restored the Bible, and took down the cemetery signboards, "Death is an eternal sleep"—hence we have the fulfillment of the two witnesses.

Brother Seiss of Philadelphia, whose writing was a great blessing to me in my boyhood, says in his books that these two witnesses were Enoch and Elijah, he predicting that they will come back to this world in their bodies, suffer martyrdom, and rise from the dead. The whole exegesis is entirely without proof, and assumed by that great and good man in order to sustain the hobby which he rode all the time, i. e., literalism. Great men are not free from mistakes; he gives this explanation because he has to literalize everything. Spiritualities cannot be literalized, neither can literalities be spiritualized. The Swedenborgians spiritualize everything. Brother Seiss literalizes everything. The truth is between the two. Let the spiritual soul remain, and the literal likewise, and you will have no trouble.

(s) The Goths, Huns and Vandals, wild, barbaric nations huddled around the North Pole, born amid the icebergs, were so inured to the cold that they were all right and comfortable amid winters which would freeze Italians to death. Consequently the utter incompetency of Roman soldiers to endure the winters of those high northern latitudes debilitated the force of the empire in those regions. As Rome had great macadamized roads built into every nation under heaven, these barbarians would journey to Rome, the world's metropolis, for curiosity. There they saw wonders which magnetized them. How the Emperor's golden house and the silver houses of his senators aroused their cupidity! Eventually, smelling the precious metals, they came in great armies, carrying with them terror and desolation. They actually fought three hundred years for the gold and silver they saw in Rome; finally taking the city in A. D. 476, and spending a whole week gathering the gold and silver from the palaces, temples and shrines. The common soldiers who, on entering Rome, were not able to buy their breakfast, returned home millionaires needing a donkey to carry their purse.

With the fall of Rome ancient civilization passed away, as she was the upholder of it. The barbarians, who could neither read nor write, conquered the world and took it into hand, so depreciating and discouraging learning that it evanesced from the earth. Civil governments declined and sunk into oblivion, the time coming on the earth when not a civil magistrate in the world could enforce his authority. Consequently marauding bands went everywhere robbing, and when necessary in order to the robbery, killing the people.

The people in every community would gather around the bravest, wisest, and most trustworthy man, who built his castle on the highest mountain, the people all building their tenements around it and uniting in the erection of a stone wall, robber proof, encompassing all. This popular leader being the business man among them, as so few of them had any learning, would have to attend to the legal phases of their interest and hold the titles for them. In process of time, generations coming and going, as a normal result the real estate would drift into the hands of their captain, while the rank and file would cultivate the lands and do the work generally. In this way all Europe drifted into the feudal system of lords and tenants, which developed into a kind of slavery, which many of the lords used to oppress the people.

During the stormy times of the French Revolution, in the latter part of the eighteenth century, Napoleon Bonaparte, a native of the island of Corsica, floated to the front, showing great ability as a brave soldier, an industrious, enterprising citizen, a wise officer and a valiant army leader. The dissolution of the government and the dilapidation of the social fabric opened the door for this brilliant young man to float into prominence. Finding the ship of state tossed by the revolutionary storm, compass and chart lost, the crew disorganized and inefficient, and the passengers all seasick, affrighted and discouraged, he comes to the helm, cheers up and organizes the crew, rights up the rigging, recuperates the machinery which had seriously gotten out of kilter, and steers the ship through the storm, effecting a safe disembarkation.

Thus the French Revolution ultimately brought

Napoleon to the front, making him first consul of France. Then he proclaimed himself the friend and protector of the poor, toiling people throughout all Europe, who had long been oppressed by those feudal lords. He did protect them during the quarter of a century while he was at the front not only of his own nation but of all Europe, and by his wonderful success on the battlefield he broke up feudalism in Europe. If he had been contented thus to emancipate the serfs and deliver the Cossacks from their yoke of oppression, he would have been eminently useful.

(t) When Napoleon had swept over Europe, Asia, and Africa in his brilliant military career, and actually been eminently useful in breaking up the feudalism which had oppressed the people a thousand years, and brought France to the front of the world (as she was more prosperous under his civil administration than ever before), as he evidently was one of the greatest intellectualities that ever lived in any age or country, if he had been contented to serve the world in a capacity of public benefactor, he had before him the widest open door of any man in the last thousand years. But he had been born plebian and he was ambitious to become identified with the patricians, i. e., the nobility. Therefore he divorced his noble wife Josephine and married Maria Louisa, the daughter of the king of Austria, thus adding to the splendors of his throne the lustre of descent.

Then he went off after big things. As everything on Continental Europe had submitted to him except Russia, he determined to conquer that great empire.

Knowing that French soldiers could not stand a Russian winter, he conceived the idea of using the great old Russian capital, Moscow, to protect them from the awful severities of the winter, which he knew his army could not stand.

But, although he made all possible preparations to get off in the spring, he did not get started till June, then spent the whole summer on his march, never reaching the Russian border until September, as the Cossacks met him and fired on him along the way, skirmishing and retreating simply to impede his march and to throw him into the winter, which they knew would be his defeat.

He meets the Czar on a raft in the middle of the Tilsit River, amid the tremendous roar of artillery on either side, the avowed end in view, to settle the affairs of the nations. Failing to make an adjustment, he marches on, directly toward Moscow, till the spires of the ancient capital glittered in full view. Then he runs into the grand imperial army, intrenched among the hills of Borodino, when suddenly an awful volley of heavy artillery is turned loose on him. The slain piled the hills and blood deluged the valleys through three days of terrible conflict. The Russian batteries are cleared of men three times over, and replenished, when an awful charge of cavalry, neighing of horses and clatter of the steel-shod hoofs against the rocks, is heard and the batteries are taken. Marshal Nay, the bravest of all, has dashed in with Napoleon's "Old Guard," which was his dependence in every awful emergency.

What is the result? The French have gained the day, as the imperial army has been defeated, and the last hope of defending the city has been given up. They make no more effort, and the French army comes into it and takes possession. They are having a jolly time, merry with dances and wine, when the alarm of "fire" is heard. They rally and extinguish it. It breaks out again and in many places in the city, so they find it impossible to keep it down; the Russians were burning their own city to keep the French army from entering it. Napoleon says it looked like an ocean of flame.

(u) The city has gone down in ashes. It is the first of November; winter comes in good earnest, and snow is falling a dozen feet deep. Napoleon mounts a sledge, and sets out for Paris, arriving thither the first of all, the mournful herald of his own defeat. The great French army is utterly broken up, caught by that terrible winter. They suffer, freeze, starve and die, receiving no interment but a snowbank by the roadside.

The effect on the political mind of Europe is most disastrous to Napoleon. They hold a convention and pronounce him the common enemy of Europe. Avowedly the friend of the poor, and seeking the emancipation of the downtrodden millions of the serfdom of the by-gone ages, yet they concluded that he is laboring to establish a universal empire to the downfall of all their governments; his great and brilliant dominion proving the end of all others. Therefore they all repudiate and drop him like a hot potato, the king of Austria forsaking the cause of his son-in-law. Then they exiled him to the Isle of Elba

(v) As the days speed their flight, reaction takes place in his behalf; he gets stronger and stronger, until the news comes that Napoleon has left Elba and is coming back to Paris. A grand army of his old friends goes down to meet him, greet him, and welcome him to his native land. His violation of the conventional decree consigning him to exilement on Elba raises all Europe on tiptoe. They at once prepare for war. The united army, under Arthur Wellesley, Duke of Wellington, meeting him at Waterloo, an awful battle is fought and Napoleon is signally defeated. The collapse on him is terrific and the reaction appalling. The combined Powers of Europe consign him to the barren rocks of St. Helena for life. He never gets away, but passes into eternity amid an awful storm raging at sea.

Meanwhile his gigantic mind topples and falls from its throne. In his delirium he wanders away to the battlefield, where he goes out of the world commanding the hosts amid the scenes of bloody conflict. On his dying bed he stated, "Alexander, Cæsar, Hannibal, Charlemagne and myself founded kingdoms with the sword; they have passed away not leaving a trace behind them. Jesus Christ founded a kingdom with love; it has stood through the ages and will stand forever."

(w) While people commit sin and lose their souls by multiplied millions, God brings good out of it all to His true people. He made Napoleon a great blessing to the world, using him to break up the feudalism in the Old World, which had been fastened on the people during the Dark Ages and had borne its sway a thousand years.

(x) Napoleon's great trouble was that of King Saul, who could not sink his own will fully into God's. After God had so wonderfully used him to emancipate the manacled millions, he could not stop there, but wanted the dominion of the world, like Alexander the Great two thousand years before him, who wept that there was not another to conquer.

CHAPTER XXVI.

ANGLO-SAXON DOMINION.

While Juluis Cæsar, the great Roman and a beautiful writer, his own autobiographer, was sweeping his conquests over Europe, at that time the wild west, two thousand years ago, having consummated the subjugation of Gaul (France), he came into Britain, subjugated the wild nations, and founded London (Londinium), which has been growing ever since. Though it now has seven and a half millions, it receives an annual addition of one hundred thousand—still the best-growing city on the globe. The mind grows dizzy contemplating its coming magnitude; destined in the near future to reach a billion of people, and it will doubtless retain the metropolitanship of the world indefinitely, unless eclipsed by Jerusalem during the millennial ages.

(y) The aborigines of Britain, i. e., the Angels (so cognomened because the word means angels, and explorers, seeing them at a distance, with their long, flowing auburn hair looking like angels, so denominated them), were Druidical in their religion, because they worshiped under the spreading oak, a convenient airy temple, and were called "Druids," from the name of the tree. Eventually they miscegenated with the Saxons on the Continent, consolidating the languages and forming the Anglo-Saxon, which originally had twenty-three thousand words, but now has two hundred thousand, having received accresions from multitudinous languages and especially the Latin and Greek.

(z) The great battle of Waterloo, fought by the English under Arthur Wellesley, Duke of Wellington, against Napoleon Bonaparte, ultimating in the signal defeat and final exilement of the latter, brought the Anglo-Saxons to the front of the world, where they have remained these ninety-six years and certainly bid fair to continue, as they are everywhere on the ascendant; in colonization, civilization, education, the arts and sciences, and evangelization leading all the world.

(a) God's wonderful providence in Anglo-Saxon dominion is the transmission of a pure speech to the whole earth, in contra-distinction to its six thousand languages now spoken by the different nations. This purity of speech is an indispensable auxiliary to the world's permanent and intelligent evangelization. God miraculously used the Greeks to make the language of revelation, in order to give the Gospel to all nations. He miraculously used Alexander the Great to impart this language to all the world, using the most feasible method, i. e., giving Alexander the dominion of the earth and through him putting the Greeks in every government under heaven, thus making them, though inadvertently and unconsciously, the constant, faithful and indefatigable teachers of their own beautiful language to all the people on the earth.

In a similar manner, He is now using the Anglo-Saxons to teach all nations their wonderful language; providentially, by His Spirit, moving the hearts of all nations to want their children to learn English. This is wonderfully illustrated in America, where we have a heterogeneous conglomeration of all the earth, responsively to Uncle Sam's cordial and unanimous invitation to come from the ends of the earth and enjoy the blessings of this great New World.

Responsively to this magnanimous invitation, we are a great and growing mongrel nation—English, Germans, French, Spanish, Portuguese, Italians, Greeks, Syrians, Egyptians, Danes, Poles, Swedes, Russians, Indians, Chinese, Japanese, etc. It is natural for all to love their vernacular tongue and with delight transmit it to their children. How can you account for the spontaneous contravention of this innate predilection of the human heart throughout this great nation?

(b) There is but one feasible conclusion; the hand of God is on all these diversified nationalities, leading them to prefer the Anglo-Saxon to their mother tongue. Consequently none of them want their children to study their own language, but they have them all learn English from the cradle. It is God's work, miraculously giving the English language to all these different nationalities so they will teach their people and, as we are rapidly becoming a missionary nation, actually go to the ends of the earth, carrying the pure Gospel of our wonderful Savior on the vehicle of the Anglo-Saxon language.

When I began my Oriental travels through the Bible lands, sixteen years ago, it was a common thing for me to ride on a ship where no one could understand my speech. I am actually incompetent to tell you the wonderful change which has transpired during this brief interval, only one-sixth of a century. I actually found the change really marvelous in the last five years. During my last tour (from which I have only been on this sacred mountain dictating these pages a fortnight), traveling on foreign ships, as I did not make a single run on the American line, I everywhere found them answering me in English.

As God miraculously used the Greeks to give the world a pure speech, preparatory for the first advent of His Son on the earth, so He is now miraculously using the Anglo-Saxons to disseminate the English language among all nations. While the Greek, so intensely mechanical and incorruptible that it cannot be misunderstood, is the very language for the safe and successful transmission of the precious Gospel treasure to all the world, the English, so loose, disconconnected and independent of all dialects, detachable and attachable "ad libitum," is the very thing to snatch up and preach the Gospel to all nations, as we find them everywhere scattered abroad.

(c) We all have great reason to lament the unfortunate separation of the U. S. from great Britain in the Revolutionary War of 1776. The intelligent

English people of all the earth join us in the lamentation over the separation, taking all the blame on themselves and imputing the sad mistake to the intellectual imbecility and periodic insanity of their king, George III., who exposed himself to the criticism of all nations by going to war with his own subjects, instead of settling all the difficulties (which were simply a family quarrel) in the family, by conventional arbitration, without firing a gun.

While there is no reason why we should not be united under one government, amid the present state of things, we should do our utmost, by prayer and good works, to practically effect a unification of all the Anglo-Saxons throughout the world, in order to bring into availability to the greatest possible efficiency the most perfect co-operation in the evangelization of all nations. The paradoxical spread of the English language throughout the whole world is a most prominent sign of the Lord's near coming.

(d) When I speak of the universal Anglicization, I do not mean that all nations will master the English language, which now has two hundred thousand words, but I simply mean that they will get some of it so they can answer you when you speak to them in Anglo-Saxon. N. B. The common people only use three or four hundred words, and great scholars only use eight or ten thousand. As this language is a mongrel, utterly unmechanical, you can use it any way you please. Therefore people understanding a few dozen words can communicate, and as preachers should be not only baptized with the Holy Ghost and fire, but with good solid common sense, they can actually preach the glorious essentials of Gospel truth in a few words.

This wonderful spread of the English language throughout the whole world I find exceedingly manifest in the books which the Lord has given to the world through my humble instrumentality, of which this "The Apocalyptic Angel," is the seventy-second. Fifteen years ago there was but little demand for them in foreign nations, because they could not get them translated into their own language so as to scatter them very extensively. Now they are circulating them in English in vast numbers in India, Africa, South America and the West Indies, because the people are so rapidly learning to read English. A missionary during this camp-meeting, told me he could use ten thousand of my books in his own field, which spreads extensively over South and Central America and the islands. We certainly have every reason to thank God and take courage when we see the wonderful utility with which He is honoring the Anglo-Saxons in all the earth.

CHAPTER XXVII.

MILLENNIAL KINGDOM.

Daniel 2: 45, 46: "I saw the stone which had been cut out of the mountain without hands strike the image on the feet and it became as the chaff of the summer threshing-floor, and the wind blew it away, and the stone filled the whole earth."

God, in the Old Testament, constantly calls Himself a rock, and in the New our Savior prominently alludes to Himself as a stone, on which those who build will stand forever, in contra-distinction to all others who unfortunately build on the sand, without a foundation, destined to hopeless wreckage in the oncoming floods, which are going to roll over this world, undermining, wrecking and engulfing every superstructure which is not built upon the everlasting Rock, our Lord and Savior Jesus Christ.

With the fall of Jerusalem, B. C. 587, the Theocracy went down to rise no more on the earth till brought back by our triumphant Christ, when He shall return on the throne of His millennial glory, and set up His kingdom, i. e., the Theocracy, in all the earth. The people got so wicked that they would not have God's government; despite the faithful and awful preaching of Elijah, Elisha, John the Baptist and all the Hebrew prophets, especially Isaiah, Jeremiah, Ezekiel and Daniel, they would not walk after the statutes and judgments which God gave to Moses on Mount Horeb, but would go off after the paganistic idolatries, which had swept down the ages from the days of Cain, the great patriarch of the sun god, Baal, and the moon goddess, Ashteroth, and the many divinities represented by all the stars, glittering in their beautiful constellations traversing the firmament night after night. The people just would worship gods whom they could see, while only one here and there was content to walk alone with an unseen God.

King Hezekiah was the great leader of the Holiness Movement in his day. He traveled all over Palestine destroying idolatry, thus heroically serving God not only in the capacity of a righteous ruler and heroic Gospel preacher, but as a bold iconoclast. He utterly destroyed the brazen serpent, grinding it into powder and throwing it into water so the people could not get at it. Of course he did it reluctantly, as it was a beautiful souvenir of a glorious deliverance, yet the people would burn incense to it. He traveled through all the tribes far and near, destroying idolatry.

(e) But Hezekiah's own son and successor, Manasseh, who reigned over Israel all told (including his absence when a suffering captive in Babylon) fifty-three years, went away into idolatry, and spent the most of that time worshipping the popular paganistic divinities and even persecuting unto death the worshippers of Jehovah, the God of his heroic father. When the Babylonians carried him into captivity and kept him there for an unknown length of time, they tortured him awfully. It brought him to repentance, so he actually went down to the bottom, sought and found his father's God amid his awful troubles, who not only gloriously saved him, but delivered him from his tormentors, restoring him to his kingdom in Jerusalem, after which he faithfully walked with the Lord to the end of his life. He did his best, but could not save his sons from idolatry, who followed the example of his own wicked life, instead of the good which he so much desired to bring into availability in their salvation.

Josiah was the last godly king of Judah's line, who traversed the country over and over serving God as an iconoclast, like Hezekiah, everywhere destroying the idols. He took away the image of Moloch out of the valley of Hinnom, which Solomon had put there to please the Ammonitish wife.

Despite all the heroic labors of sanctified prophets and kings, the people would not keep God's holy law, therefore God let the government of the world go into human hands. I trow Nebuchadnezzar was the greatest intellectualist in the world in his day, therefore God, in mercy, chose him to be the first human ruler after the fall of the Theocracy.

(f) Then he saw that gigantic image with golden head, breast and arms of silver, brazen abdomen and thighs, great iron legs and feet of iron and clay and the toes also iron and clay, and the stone which was cut out of the mountain without hands strike it on the feet and smash it into smithereens till the winds blew it away like the chaff of the summer threshing-floor. Then the storm spread abroad and filled the whole earth and will abide forever. The dream went from him and he could not recall it. So he sent for the wise men of Babylon, magicians, astrologers, Chaldeans, etc., asking them to expound the dream, at the same time being unable to tell them what it was. The result was that they altogether fell into the dilemma out of which they could not possibly extricate themselves. Meanwhile Nebuchadnezzar told them if they were true in their profession of receiving light and wisdom from the immortal gods, they would reproduce the dream and tell the interpretation.

While they all signally failed to reproduce the dream, they unanimously clamored, "O king, tell us the dream and we will tell you the interpretation." He certified to them that, if they were true, God would reveal them the dream, and the very fact that they could not tell it was the demonstrative truth that they were liars and counterfeits, so death for them and desolation of their homes would follow inevitably if they could not give the dream and the interpretation.

When Arioch, Nebuchadnezzar's minister, proceeds to the execution of the magicians on account of their failure, as Daniel, on account of his wisdom, ranked among them, therefore he takes him along with the magicians for the awful impending doom. But Daniel tells him he has had no chance, because he has not been before the king; he says to lead him in and perhaps he could satisfy the demands of the king and save the lives of all the magicians. Sure enough, when he stands before the king and the king tells him his great trouble because his dream has gone from him and he cannot strike a trace or track of it, Daniel tells him that his God has given him the dream and will restore it to him and give him the interpretation. Then he proceeds to tell him the dream, in which he saw that wonderful chronological image, adumbrating all the human kingdoms that would ever rise on the earth, assuring him that he himself (Nebuchadnezzar) is the golden head.

Here we see a great fact revealed in reference to human government, i. e., that it depreciates as the centuries come and go. We see it is gold at the beginning, which is the most valuable substance in the world; then, depreciating in value, it becomes silver. The deterioration goes on and it becomes brass; the same deterioration superinducing iron; afterwards the iron mixed with clay. Last of all, the stone kingdom, i. e., the Theocracy, returns to the earth and fills it all.

"Mountain" in the Bible means the Church. We have a long chapter in this book captioned "Sacred Mountains," in which we have written up about twenty-five of these holy mountains. God's kingdom is spreading over the whole earth and has felicitously reached this very spot which our glorified Brother Knapp cognomened "Mount of Blessings," where God has so wonderfully revealed His presence and doth, in signal, condescending mercy, abide night and day. In a similar manner, the kingdom of God is going to spread over the whole earth, till the Mount of Blessings will actually reach from pole to pole, from the rising of the sun to the going down of the same.

It says that the stone is cut out of the mountain without hands. That stone is Christ, who was born in Bethlehem, in the Church of the living God, which is none other than His holy mountain.

(g) As this gigantic image was seen in the northern hemisphere, where all the great kingdoms of the earth have risen, run their course and many of them, in fulfillment of this prophecy, have evanesced away, its back must have been toward the north pole and the face looking on the equator and the southern hemisphere. That attitude would put the right hand toward the west, and the left toward the east. The golden head of this image, as inspiration certifies, was the Chaldean Empire, which passed away with Nebuchadnezzar. It was superseded by the Medo-Persian, represented by the breast and arms of silver. This is followed by the abdomen and thighs of brass, which symbolize the world-wide kingdom of the Greeks under Alexander the Great, which has long ago passed away. Then we reach the great iron empire, symbolized by the legs, which traveled with the Roman armies into all the world, subduing everything before them and ruling the world longer than any other human power, a thousand years. The legs are followed by the feet, which represent Rome and Constantinople, and as they were iron and clay, it shows the progressive deterioration, just as clay represents the ecclesiastical element.

Constantine the Emperor, who was converted to Christianity, A. D. 321, founded Constantinople in order that he might be succeeded by two of his sons instead of one. As Constantine was the head of the political world and he proceeded to promote the Christians from the lions' mouth and burning stake to the royal palace, he thus inadvertently, without design or anticipation, mixed the clay, i. e., the ecclesiastical element, with the iron; thus continuing the deterioration in the direction of weakness and impending dissolution and evanescence. Now we come to the toes, as we are certainly living in the toe stage of the chronological image. Anglo-Saxony, i. e., Britain and America, constitute the great toe of the right foot, with their one hundred and fifty million of subjects standing at the front of the world this day; meanwhile the smaller toes represent the kingdoms of Europe and America. Asia means east, Africa means south, and Europe means west. The reason why America is not directly mentioned in the prophets is because she is included with Europe, being the western hemisphere. Therefore we recognize the right foot of the image as it faces the noonday sun, the great toe Anglo-Saxony, and the smaller representing all the kingdoms of Europe and America except Britain and Yankeedom.

(h) Now the great toe on the left foot symbolizes great Russia, with her three hundred twenty five millions of Russianized subjects, while the smaller toes typify all the kingdoms of Asia, Africa and Oceanica.

The greatest population of the earth occupies the oriental hemisphere, a half dozen times as great as populates the occidental. Yet, though America has only been known four hundred years, we have reached the time when she is exceedingly prominent in this chronological image, in which, along with Europe, she is represented by all the toes on the right foot. Some of the brightest and best Biblical exegetes have asked me, Why is not America included in the prophecies? If they would search more diligently, they would find she is fully and abundantly included. Read in Genesis, Noah's latter-day prophecies, "The Lord will enlarge Japheth and he shall dwell in the tents of Shem and Ham will be his servant." When Noah made his will after the subsidence of the flood, he gave Shem, Asia, the great continent, double the size of the others, pursuant to the patriarchal law giving to the firstborn a double portion of the estate. To Ham he gave Africa and to Japheth, Europe.

When Columbus discovered America in 1492, he found it sparsely populated, from pole to pole, containing twenty millions of Asiatics. They had migrated thither over Behring Strait, connecting the Atlantic and Arctic Oceans and separating Asia and America; evidently arriving hither long ago, as they had multiplied and were constitutionally a wandering, roving people, and actually peregrinated this vast continent from the arctic icebergs to Cape Horn. The Lord has let me travel much among the Asiatics as well as the Indians of this country. Even transient diagnosis leads the observer to identify their racehood and catalogue them in the great family of Shem, Noah's eldest son.

The children of Ham, four hundred years ago, were kidnapped by the Anglo-Saxons, brought to England and the other British Isles and to America, and held in bondage till the Civil War, when the United States President knocked off the shackles of bondage, but left them in their diversified locations to serve the old masters for hire. They gladly accepted the situation; their local attachments being very strong, they manifested no desire to seek a new home.

Therefore, here in America, we have the constant literal fulfillment of the Noachian prophecy. The Anglo-Saxons and other white races, Japhethites, are dwelling in the Indian wigwams, locally superseded by princely mansions; meanwhile the sable children of Ham still serve them. This is the literal fulfillment of the latter-day prophecies appertaining to America.

(i) Greece was the first country settled by white people in Europe, history certifying that Javan (which is the euphonic pronunciation of Japheth) was the pioneer of the land and the progenitor of their nation. Fable comes to the relief of history and expedites the population of the primeval wilds, which would have been so slow from the family of Javan alone, certifying that Cadmus was a pioneer of that country, who, when thirsty, wandering in the wild forests, found a great spring flowing out, beautiful, limpid waters; but behold! it was guarded by a sleepless dragon. The hero slew him and sowed his teeth; every one germinating, an armed man sprang up from the earth, and rallying around him, helped to subdue the wild beasts and settle the country.

The poet Ovid describes Ducalion and Pyrrah his wife (who were Noah and his wife) as surviving the flood, going out of the ark and feeling very lonesome, as all the people in the world were drowned and gone, and they were praying God to give them company. Then they proceeded to throw stones over their heads behind them as far as they could, and those thrown by Ducalion all turned to men and those by Pyrrah all turned to women. These were fabulous explanations of the wonderful rapidity with which the world became populated, after the flood destroyed them all.

(j) As "Adam" is a Hebrew word and means red, and "Shem" means brown, we recognize in Noah's family Shem as his real successor, as far as complexion and climatical adaptation were concerned, while Ham and Japheth, the one black and the other white, were providential adaptations to the other zones of the earth so that in the coming ages mankind could inhabit the entire globe. Black is an adaptation to the torrid zone (in which the most of the inhabitants of the earth live), about as large as the temperate and frigid zones combined.

When I was preaching in the torrid zone, where the sun had so much power that I had to wear a sun-proof topy on my head and carry an umbrella to keep the intense power of the sun from knocking me down and killing me, the natives, when they got ready to eat their noon lunch, would go out with no apparel on their body except the little about the loins required by the civil law, sit down under the burning sun, instead of in the equally convenient, cooling shade, eat and take their rest. This would kill white people, but it seemed hygienical to them and I am sure they enjoyed it exceedingly. If white men were to try it, if sun-stroke did not kill them instantaneously, its burning rays resting on the skin would blister it, and develop sores which if not protected from the sun, would never get well, but kill them.

The skin consists of the cuticle (the outside envelop) and the cutis vera (the true skin), which has nerves and intense sensation when punctured. Between them lies a net containing mucous. This mucous in the black man is black; in the red man, red; in the white man, white. Therefore there is no difference in the color of the human skin enveloping the different races; the cutis vera and cuticle both being colorless in all. But the paint in this ret mucosum between the cutis vera and cuticle, in the black man is "pigmentum nigrum" (black paint); in the brown man it is "pigmentum rubrum" (brown or red paint); while in the white man it is "pigmentum album" (white or colorless paint). Therefore the difference in the colors of people is not because one is a black skin, another red, another white, but owing to the color of this paint in that net lying between the cuticle and cutis vera, i. e., the outside envelop, which holds the blood, and the true skin, which is really a part of the bodily organism.

The reason why black is indispensable to people in the torrid zone where the millions live, is because it absorbs the solar heat, transmitting it into the body where it is hygienical; whereas, in case of the white man, it is reflected and instead of penetrating the body, its entire force rests on the skin and blisters it, developing sores all over the body, superinducing disease and death, as the skin is the great excretory which throws off the poisonous waste matter from the system, thus perpetuating health and life.

Before the flood, as all the people had to emanate from Adam and Eve, it seemed that they did not disperse throughout the whole earth. In the second launching of the human family, God trebled the progenitorship and, interposing His merciful providence, provided Ham for the hot regions of the torrid zone; leaving Shem in the old homestead with his genial semi-tropical climate, and adapting Japheth to the cold climates of the temperate zone.

(k) All people need the saving grace of God to eliminate out of them all race prejudices. Color in people signifies no more than in the animals, where it is not regarded. Therefore the kingdom of God, which is for all mankind, has no line appertaining to color, race, nationality nor even sexhood, as we read (Gal. 3:28): "In Him is neither male nor female." Therefore sexhood is unknown in the kingdom of grace and glory.

The Lord has wonderfully used my little book, "Woman Preacher" in repelling the fogs which had long wrapped the popular mind appertaining to the privileges of womanhood. I hope King James' translators repented radically before they went into eternity. I would have had my head cut off before I would have done what they did, when I was translating the Lord's Word (in His providence He has permitted me to translate the New Testament, which has a great circulation and has been wonderfully blessed, repelling the superstitions which gathered over the popular mind during the long roll of the Dark Ages).

Psalm 68:11 reads, "The Lord gave the word and the women who publish it are a great host." The translators three hundred years ago when there was so little light in the world, studying over that passage, concluded that a literal translation would not do; that it would ruin the women, who would leave their babies to squall and die, and their husbands to sweep and wash, nurse and cook, and they would go off preaching; thus breaking up the homes. Therefore they left the women out, an awful thing to do when God had put them in. That is a beautiful latter-day prophecy.

When I was traveling around the world and the missionaries were calling me everywhere to help them in their work, and I was running day and night (as my time was very precious and I was anxious to give them all the help I could), it was a common thing for me to come to a mission station and find a half dozen women doing the preaching and one man for the lackey jobs. When God created man He made him out of the earth; but He made woman out of man, therefore she is the second blessing in creation, having originated from the double refinement of the original material. She everywhere vindicates her moral and spiritual superiority. There are more women in Heaven than

Hell and there are more men in Hell than women: this follows as a logical sequence from the ostensible and indisputable fact that there are so many more godly women than men in this world, which is the index of the next.

My heart leaps for joy when I see this latter-day prophecy revelatory of the women going forth in great armies and preaching the unsearchable riches of Christ. They have more leisure than men and more grace, and this leads to the conclusion that we should encourage them to go forth preaching the Gospel in all the earth; as the Lord is nigh, it is very important to get all the people within our reach ready for His glorious appearing.

(1) In the fourth chapter of Daniel we read a wonderful episode in the biography of Nebuchadnezzar. His conquest of the world was so expeditious that Daniel describes him as going on eagle's wings. He conquered the world and, making Babylon his capital, fortified it impregnably, so he could rest in peace, fearless of all the world; having surrounded it by that stupendous wall 350 feet high and eighty-seven feet broad. The city was a beautiful square sixty miles in compass, surrounded by that impregnable wall fifteen miles long on the north, south, east and west. He had poured out the resources of the world to beautify his magnificent capital.

Then comes a day beautiful and bright, the sky clear and cloudless, and the sun looking down and, with his effulgent beams, reflecting the gorgeous glory, as if ten thousand suns had broken out from worlds of clouds to augment the unutterable spendor which flashed from the artistic beauty radiant from towering spires, Gothic domes and Corinthian columns. Everything about Nebuchadnezzar seemed to be magnifying glory. His heart is lifted up in pride as he soliloquizes, "Is not this great Babylon which I have built for the enhancement of my glory and the magnification of my power?"

God was grieved because of the pride and vanity which filled his heart, so, touching that gigantic intellect, it tottered and fell from its throne in his extraordinary mind, and blank lunacy settled down on his cranium. He leaves his beautiful palace, wanders away among the beasts, domestic and wild, roaming "ad libitum," with no reason nor intellect to elevate him above the herds and flocks in whose midst he stalked abroad, and laid down and slept when his body got weary. His person is neglected, his apparel soiled, his locks unclipped and his beard unshorn. People were watching him, as he was monarch of all the world, while they followed him with their love and hoped for his convalescence out of the fatal dementation which, for reasons to them utterly inexplainable, is now his melancholy fate. Seven years pass over his head, nightly bathing his unshorn and uncombed locks with the dews of heaven. In the deep soliloquies of his heart he talks to the great Builder of the universe, who had taken him from the dust and promoted him to the loftiest seat, the broadest privileges and the brightest honors within the realm of mortality. The eye of the Almighty had been on him. He is a problem of Providence and prophecy, mercy prevails, God reaches down His hand, and again lifts his gigantic mind back to its throne in his gigantic cranium, restores to him his reason, and pours on him the light. He sees the folly which he committed when he claimed the glory of his wonderful achievements for himself, which glory belonged to great God alone. He humbles himself before God, and repents in dust and ashes. The passers-by recognize the serenity of his face and the radiance of his contenance which in former years sent the lightning of conviction round the world, preparing the princes of the earth to quake before the majesty of his conquering tread.

The news reaches the royal palace, where his nobility had been administering the affairs of his world-wide kingdom in the capacity of royal regents, in hopeful anticipation of his convalescence from the mental trouble which had been his unhappy lot for so many days and years. This news of his convalescence sends a "gaudaumus" throughout the palace and the metropolis. They dispatch a delegation with barber and implements, laundry and royal investiture away to the ranch where he had peregrinated and whither he had roamed among the beasts of the earth these seven years; dreaming and believing to-day that he is a camel, and eating with them; again, that he is an ox, and eating with them; and so during the days and months of his unhappy dementation.

Meanwhile his hopeful and appreciative subjects, reverential of his royal majesty, have not the courage to interrupt the monarch of all the earth in his insane caprices, playing the ox, horse, dromedary and donkey. Now that his reason is returning and his gigantic intellect has again ascended the throne, and, to all appearances, he is normal and all right, and of course in his nudity and uncouth physique does not want to be seen by the magnates of his kingdom, therefore they send on the committee accompanying the barber in advance, to trim, wash and dress him and get him ready for the grand parade of statesmen, courtiers, magicians, poets, orators, and soldiers, official as well as rank and file.

They bring with them a royal litter. Now that he is trimmed, washed, dressed and invested with the regalia of his royal majesty, mounting him on the shoulders of his tallest men, elevated on the royal litter, high above the heads of the happy procession, with every musical instrument tuned and roaring, they return in pomp and pageantry to the royal palace, amid banners flying on all sides and every conceivable demonstration of public joy.

(m) Nebuchadnezzar has actually passed through that awful experience of insanity and come out, in the good providence of God, gloriously restored, his intellect, hitherto the transcendent one of the earth, recuperated by the long rest and brightened by the splendor of God's wonderful providence and the radiation of His blessed Spirit. Thus he has been enabled to see the vanity and folly of the pride and egotism which had deluded his mind and corrupted his heart. So he profits by the awful experience of these seven years spontaneously degraded with the beasts of the earth. He now has light and grace to drop the curtain over the past and make a new departure, henceforth to walk in the light.

In this wonderful providence appertaining to Nebuchadnezzar, we see worlds of truth and beauty, which we need to understand the mysterious problem of humanity. Well does Alexander Pope, in his "Essay on Man," say "the proper study of mankind is man."

Nebuchadnezzar, at the fall of the Theocracy, B. C. 587, succeeded God Almighty on the throne of the world. (I simply mean that God's government is the Theocracy which went down with the fall of Jerusalem, 587 B. C., and human government succeeded it.) This was symbolized by the chronological image which stood before Nebuchadnezzar, with golden head, silver breast, brazen loins, iron legs, and feet and toes of iron mixed with clay.

As Nebuchadnezzar was the golden head, he was the first ruler in man's government on the earth, during the Chaldean dominion; followed by the Medo-Persian, that by the Grecian, that by the Roman, and that by all the kingdoms into which the Roman Empire on its fall was disintegrated, and which stand to this day.

We are now in the toe stage of human government, the last of all, and are expecting that "stone," which is the millennial kingdom of our Savior, the identical Theocracy which went down B. C. 587, and was superseded by human government.

That stone (Dan. 2:45, 46) cut out of the mountain, i. e., Christ, was born in the Church, which is the mountain which is coming back to strike the image on the toes, which are the kingdoms of this world. The glorious millennial kingdom of our Lord will strike these toes and knock them into the chaff of the summer threshing-floor, i. e., utterly demolish them, till they will evanesce away never to return; meanwhile this stone fills the whole earth. It does not say it will roll on and on leaving a vacuum behind it, but it will spread out and fill the whole world, till the glory of the Lord shall cover the earth as the waters cover the sea.

(n) You see that the human government symbolized by the chronological image will constitute an interregnum in the Theocracy, which went down with the fall of Jerusalem, 587 B. C., and the Chaldean kingdom under Nebuchadnezzar, with a golden head, deteriorating to silver, brass, iron and finally iron mixed with clay, shows how human government is always best when it begins and gets more corrupt till it actually falls to pieces and breaks down. Read history and you will find that has been the case in all ages of the world. Man has always been a failure—he failed in Eden, and fell; he failed before the flood, and had to be destroyed for his wickedness; he failed after the flood, and soon landed in Egyptian slavery; he failed in the Mosaic dispensation, under the most favorable circumstances, and got so utterly blind that he did not know his own Christ when He came, though he had been watching and waiting for Him 4500 years. So blind and ignorant had Satan made him that he mistook his own Christ and killed Him.

It is the same thing over and over in every age

and he is now failing in the Gospel dispensation, getting worse in Church and State and more corrupt, and fast ripening for the great tribulation that will soon come in awful destruction on the earth, in order to eliminate out of the world all who will not do for the glorious millennial reign.

The truth of it is, God alone is competent to rule a nation or a church. Man's government is best at the start and gets worse all the time until it perishes of its own corruption.

"Brother Godbey, you discourage me." I am glad of it, that's what I want to do, so discourage you that you will give up human rule altogether, both political and ecclesiastical, and take God alone for your Ruler in State and Church. Till you do that, you will have nothing but failure, break-down and disappointment.

(o) How long will it be till the stone shall strike the image on the feet and knock it into the chaff of the summer threshing-floor, i. e., the kingdom of God comes back and smashes all human kingdoms, political and ecclesiastical, till they are blown away like the dust by the fierce winds of God's righteous castigatory judgments?

Nebuchadnezzar's insanity of seven years measures the whole period of human government, which is the interregnum in the Theocracy intervening from the fall of Jerusalem, B. C. 587, till the coming of Jesus on the throne of His millennial glory. In prophecy a day stands for a year, therefore human rule on the earth will just last seven years, i. e., a year for every day in those seven years.

We have three chronological systems by which we measure time, the lunar, the planetary, and the solar. The lunar chronology measures time by the revolutions of the moon around the sun; the planetary by the revolutions of the planets around the sun; the solar chronology by the revolutions of the earth around the sun. According to the lunar chronology (which gives us 354 days in the year), we have 354 times 7 equals 2478. The time which has elapsed since the Theocracy was superseded by human rule 587 plus 1911 equals 2498 minus 2578 equals 20. You see it just gives you twenty years until human rule will run out and Divine rule come back. The calendar chronology, 360 times 7 equals 2520 minus 2498 only leaves 22 years. Solar chronology is measured by the revolutions of the earth around the sun and has 365 times 7 equals 2555 minus 2498 equals 57. Therefore you see that according to lunar chronology, 354 times 7 equals 2498 minus 2478 equals 20; according to the calendar chronology, 360 times 7 equals 2520 minus the time that's already elapsed, 2498, is 22. The solar chronology, 365 (in a year) times 7 equals 2555 (the number of years) minus 2498 (the time that elapsed) equals 57. Hence you see the lunar chronology expires the Gentile times in twenty years more; the calendar chronology will expire the Gentile times in twenty-two years; while the solar chronology will expire the Gentile time in fifty-seven years. Daniel 12th chapter gives the Gentile tribulation 1335 minus 1290 equals 45, hence you see Daniel gives the tribulation in forty-five years. Since the tribulation belongs to the Gentile times, we must count it in, therefore, according to the lunar chronology, the rapture of the saints (which will take place just before the tribulation sets in), is 45 plus 20 equals 65 years, or the rapture of the saints is overdue sixty-five years. According to the calendar chronology, the rapture of the saints is overdue twenty-three years; 45 minus 22 equals 23. According to the solar chronology, the rapture of the saints will be due 57 minus 45 equals 12, or in twelve years.

Of course we do not know which one of these chronologies is correct; not that God's clock ever gets out of order; this is not the case, the heavenly bodies constituting the celestial universe never do fail in their periodical revolutions. Millions of years roll away and they never deviate from the orbit God has given them. The reason why no one knows the day of His coming is because our calculations are not infallible. All the facts of the chronologies concur in the conclusion that we are living in the time of the end, and that the Lord is very near. Therefore the true policy is to be always ready and constantly on the outlook; as we know neither the day nor the hour in which the Lord will appear.

(p) As you see in the prophecies of Daniel, the seven years of Nebuchadnezzar's insanity constitute the measure of human government on the earth, at the expiration of which this chronological image will be knocked into smithereens and never seen again.

We have in Nebuchadnezzar's insanity not only

given us the period of human government on the earth, but the character and manner of the same. Here you see him living among the herds and flocks like a brute. Daniel in his visions sees wild beasts all the time, the lion, bear, leopard, he-goat, carniverous eagles and vultures, showing up the fact that while God's government is by justice, love and mercy; man's government is by the carnal powers, like the animal's rule; the ox that has the sharpest horn and the stoutest spinal column rules the herd. It is significant that all human government is entirely by brute force.

Man is a trinity, consisting of spirit, soul and body. The divine government appeals to the highest enduement of humanity, his immortal spirit; when that is right, everything else wheels into line. Nebuchadnezzar, as it says, made his abode with the wild donkeys and actually lived with the beasts, i. e., brutalized himself, showing up the fact that human government deals with our animal nature and rules us in that way. As he was insane, it follows that human government is not in the realm of wisdom, but of folly. There is no doubt but in his cerebral delirium he thought he was ruling the world there among the beasts. Methinks that he gives commandment to the camels, as the Babylonians; to the cattle he gives orders recognizing them as the Medes; to the horses, as the Persians; to the donkeys, as to the Elamites; to the geese, as to the Scythians, etc.

In the hallucinations of his demented mind, he actually thinks he is on the throne of the world and ruling all nations, yet he wallows in the dirt, undressed, his hair unclipped like the eagle's feathers and his nails untrimmed like the eagle's claws. As he is monarch of the world, the people watch him, bringing him food. Yet you see the inspired Word certifies that he actually brutalized himself, showing up thus sadly the attitude of human government. It is on the plane of brutality considered from a social standpoint, and that of insanity, when diagnosed from an intellectual standpoint.

Glory to God for the auspicious day-dawn in which we are permitted to live; the meteoric stars shooting athwart the spiritual horizon ominous of the grand deliverance so very nigh. We are exceedingly happy, in the providence of God, to walk on the ragged edges of the expiring Gentile dispensation. We are more fortunate than the patriarchs and prophets, who longed for His glorious appearing and died without the sight. Reader, be sure you are ready to run out and meet Him with a shout. The true attitude of saintship is that of constant readiness and joyous expectancy.

CHAPTER XXVIII.

THE JEWS.

Of course we are all the true friends of God's ancient people; we cannot afford to be otherwise. In the days of Esther and Mordecai, God sent awful judgments on the people in the world-wide Persian empire, under the reign of Ahasuerus, because they maltreated the Jews.

When I was preaching in Japan in my journey around the world I found them shouting over the great victory they had achieved in their war with big Russia. I told them they were mistaken, and they had better quit shouting and praising their Mikado for his wisdom and their soldiers for their heroism. I said to them, "We admit your Mikado is wise and your soldiers brave, but they never gave you the victory. Great Russia, more than six to your one, would have swallowed you up if the Christian's God had not helped you. Russia has awfully persecuted the Jews; flogging, killing and driving them from their homes. God wanted to give her a thrashing. If He had used Britain, Germany or America, it would not have been so humiliating; but He gave the honor to you little

Japs, thus humiliating her in the sight of all the world. If you do not desist from taking the glory to yourselves, you will so grieve the Holy Spirit that God will send awful judgments on you, to humiliate you."

Then they said, "Preacher, we will give the glory to the Christians' God for His wonderful deliverance out of the hands of great and powerful Russia."

The prophecies appertaining to the Jews are receiving their fulfillment on all sides. Oh, how rapidly they are gathering back into their own country which God gave them! Since the fall of Turkdom two years ago, when they dethroned and imprisoned the Sultan and admitted the Jews into Solomon's temple and the Mosque of Omar, whither it had been a penalty of death for them to enter the last twelve hundred years, they have bought more land in Palestine than ever before. They now have fifty colonies in that country, and if Turkey had not closed the land office against them, even while I was there, very recently (May 16, 1911), they would still be buying land with great rapidity. They closed the office against them because they had bought so much that they became alarmed lest they would buy it all and get the whole country into their hands. It is a shame for them to have to buy their own land, from people who have taken it from them by robbery; yet they are glad of the privilege, to get it that way.

Though the Turks, becoming alarmed, have closed the office against them, it will not stay closed long. God's hand is on the whole matter. He will attend to it and open the door.

In my travels throughout that country, I was constantly in view of beautiful stone houses, and almost all of them are built by the Jews. In Jerusalem they are in a large majority. The city outside of the wall is already much larger than the old town within. The houses are all nicely hewn stone from bottom to top, floors and roof all stone and slate; the most comfortable, beautiful and durable houses in the world, and built by the Jews. I visited a great colony in the suburbs of the city, claiming to be the Gaddites, i. e., to belong to the tribe of Gad.

(o) We stopped in our travels and spent a night in the Jewish hotel in Samaria upon the highlands, overlooking the sea, a beautiful new city built by the Jews, overshadowing the old site of Cæsarea down on the coast which was the Roman capital of Judæa in the days of our Savior and His apostles. Like all other cities, it perished during the awful Jewish tribulation which God permitted to come on them A. D. 66-73, because they rejected their Christ. The Jews have colonized and rebuilt it in charming beauty on the highlands in full view of the old site.

In my peregrinations, I saw a big lot of Jews on one of those beautiful fertile plains, founding a colony They are pushing the work in all parts of the country. Wherever they drop down, by their wonderful thrift, they turn the whole country into the land of corn and wine, flowing with milk and honey.

The fruits of that country are the best in all the world, every orange is sweet and juicy and the lemons twice as large as in other countries and exceedingly juicy. The oranges in this country are frequently dry and pithy. I never saw one such in Palestine. The land grows them so copiously that the trees, though standing thick and covering the whole earth, bend down till they have to prop the limbs to keep the fruit off of the ground. That country produces a vast variety of exceedingly delicious nuts, besides everywhere abounding in the sweetest grapes I ever ate.

(r) When Napoleon Bonaparte left his Elba exile and came back to Paris, the English army met him at Waterloo, under the command of Arthur Wellesley, Duke of Wellington, and so signally defeated him that he never attempted to rally again. Anselm Rothschild, who years antecedently had been entrusted with a large sum of money by the king of Hesse Castle to keep Napoleon from getting it, and under whose administration it had so accumulated that when he had returned it to the king after his flight from Napoleon, he had very liberally rewarded him for his fidelity and wisdom; happened to be in France at that time and heard the old English Duke talking and felt impressed that he was going to whip Napoleon. Consequently he constrained a fisherman to carry him across the English Channel, with great peril of the storm raging on it. Entering London, he found the prices of everything down 50 per cent., through fear of Napoleon, thinking he would conquer at Waterloo and come at once into London. Mr. Rothschild at once employed six clerks to help him buy property, and all went ahead with all their might a couple of days, till the battle was fought and news came, "The English are victorious." Then the prices took a sudden rise and went up so high that they doubled, trebled, and quadrupled on all their purchases. This gave a grand boom to the Rothschild's fortune, which has been growing ever since. Fifty years ago it was estimated at 365 millions of dollars. I investigated among the intelligent Jews who said it was doubtless now a thousand millions. Hence, as the Jews are the bankers of the world and hold the purse of the nations, they will soon buy all of that country if they have a chance. In the last two years God has given them an open door and they wonderfully used it. Though Satan has very recently closed the land office, all join us in prayer to God to reopen the door.

(s) The Turkish Government has long been owing a vast sum of money to Baron Rothschild which she will never be able to pay, as she is even now in revolution, the Sultan dethroned and prisoner for life, the government a secret Committee of union and progress, cognomened, "The Young Turks." Consequently she is only permitted to run through the jealousy of her Christian neighbors, which are envious either with other, lest in the dismemberment each may not get her share in the spoils.

The Empire has long been a smoking volcano. Two years ago (1909) she had an eruption dethroning the Sultan, who made vigorous efforts, "vi et armis," to recover his throne, but signally failed and is now (July, 1911) a prisoner in his harem for life.

The inquiry arises, Cannot Baron Rothschild close his mortgage on Palestine for that vast sum of money and take it at any time? That is a complicated matter and might prove contrary to the state policy of the age, under which nations, "ad libitum," borrow vast sums of money from one another, with good security in the way of mortgages, and let it run indefinitely, simply by keeping the interest paid up promptly, which is true in this case.

During the last two years, since the dethronement of the Sultan, and under the liberal policy of the "Young Turks," the Jews have bought so much land that the Turks became alarmed lest they would just buy it all and thus exclude them from it altogether.

(t) While I was recently in that country, there was quite a sensation among the Jews, arising from the recent adoption of the Constitution by the "Young Turks," making the government no longer an absolute monarchy, as from ages immemorial, but constitutional, somewhat like England. This Constitution recognizes Hebrew citizenship, it also makes them subject to military service. For this reason many of the Jews flit away, but all of them still hold their property and when the sensation passes by, they will in due time return and go on with their works.

A redeeming fact in connection with that requirement of military service (which is very scarey to the Jews, because since they were driven out of their own country by the Romans, A. D. 73, they have never had their nationality anywhere nor been subject to military service) consists in the fact that the Constitution adopted provides for their full and final exemption by the payment of $250.00, in which case the government gives them their free papers for life. As the

Jews are the greatest money-makers in the world, you see that ordinance requiring military service of every citizen will not amount to anything with the Hebrew children, as they will just pay out, get their free papers and go ahead.

One of the auspicious omens of the Lord's near coming is the unprecedentedly rapid gathering of Israel from all parts of the earth, back to their native land. In the American colony in Jerusalem I conversed with one of the oldest and most prominent brethren, who was a Jew, native of India, having come from that far-off land.

When I was traveling in the Orient in 1899, the war with the Boers in South Africa was "en passo," and there was ever so much talk about the status of the Hebrews in the earth. Many were saying that they would not return to Palestine because the British Government was proposing to donate to them a vast area of beautiful and rich land in the delightful temperate zone on the Congo in South Africa. When the matter culminated and the offer was made, they called a Hebrew ecumenical convention, in which the leading spirits of Abraham's family, from the whole earth, representing their eight millions of people scattered over the globe, convened to consider the liberal offer of Britain, the greatest colonizer, civilizer, educator and evangelizer of the age. Upon deliberate consideration, they decided the matter in the negative, returning their thanks to the donor, but giving as a reason for declining the generous donation, that they had a country of their own, whither they were bound, according to the infallible word of the great Jehovah, to gather His people out of all lands into the fair and delightful fields of Canaan which they, in all their colonies, make literally to fulfill the brilliant phraseology of the Hebrew prophets, "a land flowing with milk and honey and abounding in corn and wine."

Every true Christian is a friend of the Jews, not only praying for their restoration to their own country, but helping them to get back.

(u) We may not expect their conversion to Christianity till after this great gathering from the ends of the earth, as Ezekiel thirty-seventh chapter certifies that the dry bones will be reconstructed, and afterward covered with flesh, joined with ligaments, enveloped with skin, inspired with life, and finally stand on their feet a glorious army rallied under the banner of Jesus their King, and honored with the most glorious privilege this side the pearly gates, i. e., to constitute His reception committee when He shall return after the long run of the millennial centuries on the throne of His triumphant kingdom to reign forever.

Jacob prophesied (Gen. 49:10) the departure of the sceptre when Shiloh came. Herod was the last of Judah's line, who died while Jesus was a fugitive infant in Egypt. Archelaus his son succeeded him on the throne of Judæa (Matt. 2nd chap.), but he would not dare to take his father's crown till it was put on his head by the very hands of Augustus Cæsar himself. No king in all the earth at that time would dare to wear a crown unless imperial hands had placed it on his brow.

Though Archelaus went all the way to Rome, that long and perilous journey, to get the Emperor to give him his father's crown, he positively refused, and would give no reason, though you and I well know the exegesis of his new departure, taking away the kingdom of the Jews and turning Judæa into a Roman province and sending off Sophonius, to take charge of it as Roman governor (in which line Pilate was the sixth), and so there you see the last of the Jewish kingdom. It is because he was obligated to fulfill Jacob's prophecy (Gen. 9:49), as the princes of the earth have in all ages (and will so continue) had to fulfill the prophecies in the Bible, though, like Augustus Cæsar, they know it not.

As Jesus told Pilate, while standing at his bar, that He was King of the Jews by birth, consequently the Jews have never had a kingdom on the earth since He was born; because their kingdom went to Him, and He has had it ever since and will possess it forever.

"But blindness in part had happened unto Israel till the fulness of the Gentiles come in." (Rom. 11th chap.) Therefore you see the whole Gentile world will receive the Word before the Jews, as they, having been the first, are also, to be the last. Therefore we are to be loving and patient with them, while they gather in the dry bone (i. e., converted) state.

When the Lord comes to take up His Bride in the glorious rapture, He will wonderfully reveal Himself to His ancient people, dwelling amid the sacred mountains, classic vales, and flowery plains of their beloved patrimony which God promised to Abraham and his seed forever. As you know, the great tribulation will set in so soon as the Bride is taken away. During those awful visitations of God's righteous judgments against the wicked nations and fallen churches in all the earth, Zechariah last chapter tells us that it will go exceedingly hard with the Jews in Palestine, as, amid those desolating wars, two-thirds of them will be cut off, as incompetent for the glorious honor of their Lord's reception and coronation; meanwhile the surviving third, will become the happy recipients of that transcendent honor of all ages and nations, i. e., a place in the committee delegated of Heaven to receive and crown their own King, the son of David, the heir of Judah's line, to reign over them forever.

(v) N. B. It is only the elect of Israel who are gathering to the Holy Land. The non-elect are wild with money-making schemes, dispersed in all the great commercial centers of the world, and giving no concern to the wonderful fulfillment of the patristic prophecies.

There are really two elections in order to a place in the Bridehood. The first, chosen out of the world into the Kingdom of God; then out of the Kingdom into the Bridehood. Isaac was not permitted to take a wife from the idolatrous daughters of Canaan. Abraham sent away to Mesopotamia for Rebekah, a godly woman. When she arrived at the patriarchal tent in Beer-sheba, she entered into wedlock with his son. The Jews are now being elected from the whole Gentile world and gathering into Canaan. During the tribulation, the Armageddon wars will thoroughly sift them, as you see, eliminating two-thirds; while the surviving third, having passed all the fiery ordeals and every possible test of the adversary, will receive this unprecedented honor, never participated in by their progenitors, i. e., the reception of their own brother Jesus descending from Heaven in His glory, and will crown Him King of the Jews forever.

During all His earthly ministry He dared not proclaim His Christhood, lest they would crown Him King, as in that case the Romans would have killed Him, and He had to have those three full years to teach that wonderful Bible School in which He qualified His apostles for the greatest and most responsible work committed to a human body, i. e., the launching of the Gospel Church on the Day of Pentecost. Sunday before His crucifixion, when He rode the donkey colt into Jerusalem and they all shouted uproariously, "Hail King of the Jesus!" they fully expected to crown Him King during the on-coming Passover. Oh, how all their hopes were crushed, when, instead of seeing Him crowned they saw Him cruelly crucified! Yet that glorious coronation is impending, reserved for the faithful few now being gathered from the disbursement of Israel from all the earth, and having passed through all the tribulation ordeals. They will finally, amid the shouts of angels and archangels, enjoy this glorious honor of crowning their own Jesus, Heir of the blood royal, King, to sit down upon the throne of David and rule over the house of Jacob forever. (Luke 1:32.)

CHAPTER XXIX.

HOMEWARD BOUND.

My five noble comrades were W. T. Vaughan, D. D., Somerset, Ky.; Levi Wenger, of Clayton, O.; Chas. Rhiter, of Hutchinson, Kan.; Henry Volz, of Randolph, La.; and T. J. Schingler, of Donaldsonville, Ga. These precious Holiness evangelists had traveled with me the long journey through Scotland, England, France, Greece, Italy, Syria, Land of Uz, and extensively throughout the Holy Land, and were all very weary and longing for the homeward-bound run. We had run a very great deal on foot, exploring the historic sights of sacred lore, wandering through catacombs, descending into sepulchres, exploring caves immortal in sacred lore, climbing holy mountains, and many lofty towers, straining our eyes to look on sacred mountains trodden by patriarchs and prophets far away, and had ridden in carriages day after day. Meanwhile we were exposed to contagious diseases and in perils from robbers (some of the brethren actually got robbed). The most terrific trial of all was the rough and stormy seas, which do not trouble me, but made my comrades awfully sick. Oh, how they suffered on the sea amid the storms! At one time, though tossed by the tempest and incessantly sick, and though having reached our destination, we could not land, lest we be wrecked on the rocks, but had to sail round in a circle, over the same track for thirty-six hours, as the captain was afraid to cast anchor, lest the storm break us loose and the anchor be lost. Some of the brethren suffered awfully with sore feet, as we had so much walking to do in places where we could not ride.

If you ever make this journey, you will get tired of hearing people shout, "Backsheesh!" That means beggar money. Oh, there is no end to the clamor for backsheesh! If you would respond, you would never get anywhere, they detain you as long as you give and then rob you of what you did not give. Therefore we had to be very careful and discriminating, only giving backsheesh when we saw they were blind, lame, halt, or afflicted in some way so they actually deserved it. In that country they have plenty of coins, only worth one cent or a fraction of a cent. Therefore I made it a rule to keep supplied with beggar money, and when I saw a worthy subject, handed out unhesitatingly.

At first the brethren went for sights, were astounded, electrified, and carried away, seemingly indefagitable in their peregrinations. This glowing enthusiasm gradually wore off, till finally it just seemed that they were satisfied, had seen all the sights they wanted, and were all getting homesick. Our last run of forty-three hundred miles was from Naples to New York. We finally embarked on a great German Lloyd steamer,

700 feet long, 90 feet wide, and carrying on our voyage about 1500 passengers and 500 sailors.

Sixteen years ago, on that same line, I ran from Italy to New York. An awful storm struck us five hundred miles west of Gibraltar and was on us five days and nights; so dense the clouds that you could not tell day from night, noon from midnight; great mountain seas went rolling over the ship, deep enough on the decks (where we walked so much in fair weather) to swim a horse. Therefore all doors and windows were closed water tight, and we could only look out through the port-holes and see the mountain waves climbing the skies and lashing the stars, keeping sun, moon and constellations totally eclipsed day and night; meanwhile no light could ever be seen upon the deep save that reflected from the foaming billows, on all sides white as snow. It seemed that I could see God, sitting on His chariot of storm, drawn by steeds of tempest, commanding the scene which, for grandeur and sublimity, eclipsed the wildest flights of imagination.

As we were running the same route, I felt lead not only to talk about it, but to pray the Lord to keep His arm under the ship and His hand under the sea lest we have a repetition of it. But the brethren were nervous and scarey, and put the breaks on me, even in my prayer (which we held morning and evening in our state room), putting hands on me and begging me not to pray and talk about those things, but to join them all in their importunate prayers for fair weather and tranquil seas. God answered **prayer, giving us** the calmest and most lovely voyage on this long run of all the seven we made in our tour. Though much of the time rain was falling, and of course some wind, yet the ship was so heavy that she kept very still and our brethren had no sickness to amount to anything; though, among so many on board, I really saw much nausea.

It was our privilege, sailing over the great Mediterranean Sea, to be at Joppa twice, whence Jonah sailed for Tarshish. There we were detained the thirty-six hours on account of storm, because the landing was too dangerous to undertake it; meanwhile the brethren talked much about Jonah, the storm he encountered, his ejectment into the sea, the degulotition of the sea monster, God's answer to his prayer, his final deliverance and subsequent ministry.

(u) In our Palestinal peregrinations, we again passed by his nativity, home and tomb, off to the left on a conspicuous hill as we approached Cana of Galilee. In our final run from Naples to New York, we came in sight of Tarshish in Spain, pointed out to us from the ship, whither Jonah was bound. Infidels cavil over the fact that there are no whales in the Mediterranean. N. B. The Word does not say a whale. The original word there used by the Holy Spirit "cetus," simply means a sea monster. No doubt but it was a shark, as they abound in that sea. I saw a great school of them in my expedition, as they were leaping up and sinking down in sight and instantaneously out. I counted about twenty and some of them fifteen feet long and big as a horse around the body. The mouth of that fish is very large in proportion to his size. Therefore there was no trouble in the reconcilement of the inspired history with the zoological world. These sharks were following our ship to eat the offal cast overboard.

Reader, you have patiently followed me on this my fourth tour to the Bible Lands and the historic world. I need not ask you if you want to go; I know you do. Every true pilgrim, traveling to the New Jerusalem above the stars, longs to see its prototype, Jerusalem on earth. The word is a Hebrew compound and means the possession of peace. So I hope you have Jerusalem in your heart even now, and are heroically marching to the New Jerusalem for which every pilgrim is bound. I know of nothing this side the New Jerusalem so enjoyable as the visit to the Holy Land and the historic world, where Adam and Eve were created and the wonderful things about which we read in the Bible transpired. Rest assured it is a powerful auxiliary to your Bible study.

Sixteen years ago I made the journey entirely alone, yet not alone, for I never so realized the presence of Jesus by my side in all my life, as when I got away from my native land, for I never saw any person whom I had seen before. Wandering in strange lands, amid perils of robbers, epidemics, shipwrecks, etc., it seemed that Jesus came closer to me than ever before, and walking the decks of foreign ships, where I could not speak to any one because they knew not my language, oh, how He walked by my side and talked with me night and day! Amid burning deserts, alone with the

Arabs (about whom an old English sailor warned me in these terrific words, "They will cut your throat for a shilling"), it seemed I could actually see Him walking by my side. Foreign traveling, alone, is not desirable, so I advise you to have company.

(x) Traveling expenses are more costly now than ever, because the financial world is constantly going up to higher prices. This originates from the abundance of gold in the world, produced by the mines in Alaska and South Africa. I always travel with Cook's Agency, which is all over the world. Approaching your landing at a foreign port, you will see in the crowd standing on the wharf, a man, white, black, red or brown, "Cook's agent" flashing in big letters over his breast, or on his hat, or both. When you land, he will immediately take you to Cook's office, where you will get your money changed, as you cannot use the American in any other country without financial loss.

"Brother Godbey, how much will it cost me to visit the Holy Land and the historic world?" (A trip of from fifteen to twenty thousand miles). When we fixed up to sail on our late voyage, I propounded this question to Cook's agent in New York. His answer was, "A thousand dollars." Ordinarily you would pay about that amount. If you do as others have done, catch me up before the Lord takes me to Heaven, you can make it with me on five hundred dollars; but all because I am acquainted with everything, having made the journey four times.

N. B. When you leave America, everybody you

meet wants all your money, and that is the reason why it costs you so much. On this tour I struck good Holiness missionaries who were anxious to save all the Lord's money they possibly could, and found them paying double their necessary expenses. Of course they changed at once and I was very glad to help them a little. I will never go again for myself, as it would be quite a superfluity. The Lord's people are the light and hope of the world, I delight in helping them whenever I can. They are few in number and much needed to save the dying millions. This journey is the best education you can get; all who make it so pronounce it. Besides, it will be exceedingly helpful to your Christian experience to walk in the footprints of Jesus in the land of His nativity, ministry and martyrdom. Therefore if you catch me before the angels take me to the Holy Land beyond the stars, I will be delighted to serve you as an escort.

"What preparation do I need to go?" you ask. Five hundred dollars are the great "sine qua non," without which you cannot make it, but with that amount you can make it with me, thus economizing several hundred dollars of the Lord's money.

In my four tours I have heard people lamenting their mistake in taking too much with them. That is a point which it seems we cannot control, although I have done my best with my comrades. (In the second tour, Brother Hill, my son-in-law, and Brother Payne, of California, accompanied me; on my third tour, the three Texas boys, John and Ed Roberts and Allie Irick, went with me round the world; and on the present tour, the five above mentioned accompanied me.) They all expressed much regret on the tour over the mistake they made in taking too much.

(y) "Do tell me just what to take, so I will know and not make the mistake." Take a little light valise, which you can carry everywhere in your hand, as in the Old World the cabmen, who want all your money, have so manipulated the street-car men that they will not let you take a valise with you in the car, therefore, if your valise is too heavy for you to walk and carry it in your hand, you have to go in a carriage, paying ten times as much as on the street-car, because the cabmen charge you as much for the valise as they do for you and everything you have. I have never had any more than I could take in my hand and walk anywhere I wanted to go; but always had to pay cabmen and carriages, thus wasting the Lord's money, because my companions had baggage so heavy that they could not carry it and as their escort I had to go with them. As to clothing, you do not need a single new garment for the trip, as they will quickly get dingy from constant rough-and-tumble wear, and look no better than your old ones. Therefore you will need only a change of old ones and no new ones. If you wear out something and need it, you can get it where you are in the Old World and get it for half of what you can get it here. So you will have nothing to do but throw away your old one and put on the new, and save your money. Of course you take a small Bible, as you will constantly need it to read about the places of sacred record which we will be exploring. Therefore there is no reason why you should have a valise so heavy that you will have to take a carriage. I have to-day the same little valise I bought for my journey sixteen years ago. It will outlast me. I carry it in one hand on foot everywhere I go, and everything with me, so I never have to pay for a carriage to haul me and charge me ten times the street-car fare. If there is no street-car, I walk, unless compelled by my traveling companions, as above specified.

(z) Therefore if you go with me, bring nothing but a little light valise to carry a small Bible and a change of old clothes, which you can take in your hand, and walk along briskly everywhere. (Of course none of you will think about taking a trunk; it is too foolish to talk about it.) In foreign travels you meet all nationalities with all costumes, consequently nobody notices anything of that kind; but everybody dresses to suit himself, and it is all right. It is understood that style goes with the majority, therefore if you want to be in the fashion, dress in rags, and if you have old ragged shoes, use no socks, then you will be in the fashion, because you will see more people in that costume during your tour than in any other.

I trow that not a few who are, in the providence of God, reading this book, will visit the Holy Land beyond the great ocean and long blue sea. But if you never do, be sure you reach the Holy Land beyond the glittering stars, "where the wicked cease from troubling and the weary are at rest." Showers of blessings on you all!

THE END.

www.ingramcontent.com/pod-product-compliance
Lightning Source LLC
Chambersburg PA
CBHW020741100426
42735CB00037B/159